THE ENIGMA OF
NUMBERS

'Very secular, very academic, quite scholarly.' Tacking warmth, however; lacking spirituality and more indepth theological knowledge. 'Very caught up in what is psychologically analytical. A superb reference for historical allusions on numbers.

Despite some of the criticisms I have, this is a masterfully ambitious project as a book.

Lance Storm

THE ENIGMA OF
NUMBERS

An abundant use of references to Marie-Louise Von Franz and also many quotes of C. Jung.

This is really a Jungian text.

Pari
Publishing

PARI PUBLISHING

Lance Storm has a Bachelor of Arts degree (University of Adelaide) majoring in psychology, an Honours degree (1998) also majoring in psychology, and a PhD in parapsychology (2002). In 1995, he received the Laurence T. Schneider Prize in Art History and Theories from the University of Adelaide. Since 1999, he has published dozens of articles in prestigious journals such as *Psychological Bulletin*, the *Journal of Parapsychology, Journal of Scientific Exploration*, and the Jungian journal *Quadrant*. He is co-recipient with Dr. Michael A. Thalbourne, of the D. Scott Rogo Award for Literature (2002). In 2003, the Parapsychology Association awarded him the Gertrude R. Schmeidler Student of the Year Award for work in parapsychology, and in 2007 the Parapsychology Foundation honored him with a Frances P. Bolton Fellowship. Besides his parapsychological career interests, his other academic interests include Jungian psychology and the psychology of motivation, emotion, perception, and personality. Storm is also interested in Jung's concept of synchronicity, and is currently preparing an anthology of articles on synchronicity dating back to 1969, which will be published in 2008. Storm's other interests include writing, reading, film studies, bushwalking and travel. As a keen traveller, he has seen much of Australia, and he has spent time in the United Kingdom, the United States, Japan, Bali, Hong Kong, Singapore, Portugal, and Ukraine.

A catalogue record for this book is available from the British Library.

ISBN: 978-88-956040-0-8

Book design and cover by Andrea Barbieri.

Printed and bound in the United States of America.

The chapter "From Three to Four" is an expanded version of Lance Storm's article "From Three
to Four: The Influence of the Number Archetype on our Epistemological Foundations," and
was published in *Quadrant* (2003, vol. 33, pp. 69-81).

The chapter "Synchronicity" is based on Lance Storm's article "Synchronicity, Causality, and
Acausality," and was published in the *Journal of Parapsychology* (1999, vol. 63, pp. 247-269).

The information on page 48 has been authored by an employee or employees of the Los Alamos
National Security, LLC (LANS), operator of the Los Alamos National Laboratory under Contract
No. DE-AC52-06NA25396 with the U.S. Department of Energy. The U.S. Government has
rights to use, reproduce, and distribute this information. The public may copy and use this
information without charge, provided that this Notice and any statement of authorship are
reproduced on all copies. Neither the Government nor LANS makes any warranty, express or
implied, or assumes any liability or responsibility for the use of this information.

Pari
Publishing

To family and friends

Special thanks to Alison W., Petra, Andrew, David, Ashley, and Barry

TABLE OF CONTENTS

INTRODUCTION

The simplest ideas are the most powerful. Perhaps one thinks of the wheel, but numbers have much more effect and potency than wheels. Numbers appear so simple that we usually take them for granted. Exceptions include when we are buying a lottery ticket, or deciding on a memorable PIN number for getting our money out of the bank.

At such times the aura that surrounds numbers comes into play. Throughout the ages numbers, like names, have been imbued with magical powers. *The Enigma of Numbers* is not a book about magic, but about how people have assigned mystical and other meanings to numbers, and why numbers permeate our lives so much.

These meanings and influences have been with us for a very long time. Lance Storm begins his account with Pythagoras and the ancient Greeks, but does not neglect the Chinese, whose *I Ching* (Book of Changes) predates Pythagoras (the arithmetic embedded in the Book of Changes led Leibniz to believe they had discovered the binary system—the basis of all modern computing, but that is another story). He also acknowledges the traditional Jewish Kabbalah, another ancient source, and the practice of *Gematria*—adding up the numbers corresponding to the letters in words.

The ideas of number do not seem to have developed quickly. First came the individual numbers. It was much later that the idea of an unending sequence of numbers arose. The very common, but very special, small numbers—numbers such as 2, 3, or 8—influence us in our daily lives. Lance Storm treats these in turn, ending, as has been the case in the western world since ancient Greek times, at ten. Each one has its own significance, which Storm explores from many sides.

And where does the significance of numbers arise? C. G. Jung, the Swiss psychiatrist, who penetrated deep into the human unconscious, traced them to what he called the 'archetypes'. Small numbers are prime examples of archetypes: they are obviously fundamental, yet hard to pin down since they manifest themselves in so many different, even contradictory, ways. Storm and the present writer believe that Jung was fundamentally correct. Storm is a psychologist who not only handles the difficult ideas surrounding archetypes, but also presents them in a highly readable form.

Most books about numbers are written by mathematicians for mathematicians. This book is different. It is not a book only for the erudite mathematician; it is a book for all people attracted by the unending enigma of number.

Most books about numerology are written by cranks. This book is different. It is written by a psychologist with a profound scientific understanding. He observes and explains what is happening when people—which means all of us—respond to the archetype of number, but he keeps his feet firmly on the ground.

The Enigma of Numbers fills several needs in the community. It unashamedly accepts that numbers have a certain numinosity, but it treats this in a scientific way. Storm is not carried overboard by the enthusiasm of some ways of interpreting numbers. He considers numbers both as parts of systems and as individual, and powerful, symbols in human psychology.

His book fills a gap in discussions of number. A glance at library shelves will usually reveal many books on number systems and the history of numbers, but usually none on the psychological and symbolic import of numbers.

All of this *The Enigma of Numbers* does in an engaging way. There is no preaching, just respectful observation, recording and analysis, founded on a compendious knowledge base. It is a very welcome addition to the literature: a book to be read through and then, then will not be left on the shelf, it will be used as a reference again and again, numberless times.

John N. Crossley
Melbourne
November, 29 2007

FOREWORD

Human beings crave meaning. Some find it in religion as the word of God; others discover it in science as the mathematical plan of the cosmos. Some create it in their art and music, where others gratefully sense it. Many detect it in human affairs, implant it in governments and nations, or construct philosophies to profess it. But without it we cannot live. Just as we need food to nourish our bodies, so too do we need meaning to nourish our souls. We are all seekers of meaning.

We read meaning in the architecture of snowflakes and clouds; in the texture of wood grain and rocks; in the pattern of water, constellations and galaxies; in the ordered structure of nature and the universe; and of course in numbers. Since the time of the ancient Greeks, and undoubtedly long before, humans have found meaning and import in numbers. Pythagoras thought numbers were the very elements of reality. Kepler believed they determined the planetary courses of the solar system. Carl Jung saw in numbers the instrument par excellence for the mind to understand order itself. And throughout history we have seen the development of Numerology, Astrology, Magic, *Gematria*, the *I Ching*, and countless other forms of number lore, by means of which seers and prophets have divined the course of future events and interpreted the meaning of personal and societal experience.

In a parallel historical development, the quantitative character of numbers became more and more important. A major shift in emphasis occurred with the Copernican Revolution, which introduced numbers and mathematics as the very language of science, thus opening the modern era of quantification of the physical world. The ability to quantify the nature of matter and physical processes through numbers is the hallmark of today's "exact" sciences, which boast of accuracies of a few parts per ten billion. Vast technological, scientific, economic and commercial institutions are now built on the foundation of numbers as quantities. One of the deepest and thorniest branches of mathematics itself is number theory, which explores the quantitative properties and relationships of numbers.

Yet despite the fabulous accomplishments of modern quantitative science and technology, the question remains of why mathematics and numbers themselves apply to the natural world. Are numbers somehow embedded in nature? Do they exist apart in their own abstract realm (as Plato suggests)? Or are numbers the invention of the human mind? It seems that exploiting the quantitative character of numbers has brought us no closer to their meaning or to finding meaning through them.

Thus, we are drawn back, like the prodigal son, to numbers as qualities, symbols, vessels of meaning. Can we ultimately find meaning through numbers? Will we ever find meaning without numbers? Numbers remain a mystery—an enigma, which is deftly explored in this book. We may never answer these questions, but Lance Storm takes us on a rich and illuminating adventure into the history and meaning of these most elusive, profound and mysterious objects of nature and the human imagination—numbers.

Roger S. Jones
Author of Physics as Metaphor *and* Physics for the Rest of Us

PREFACE

Shedding light on number from a psychological and symbolic perspective is a task not completely suited to words or reason. Since number permeates our world so abundantly and at so many levels, it clearly influences our lives in ways that go beyond language and thought. Ironically, the ubiquitous nature of number, its everyday appearance in a world of enumerated objects and numerical ideas, is so commonplace we are almost oblivious to it—we have taken it for granted—yet we mediate and put order to the world through number just the same. So too, the transcendence of number, its deeper symbolic aspect as it imbues meaning in thought and deed, causes us to mediate and put order to the world in a more subtle way.

At this transcendent level, and at the risk of anthropomorphizing number, it appears to 'behave' spontaneously and in paradoxical ways, and, by virtue of this 'behavior', it is almost impossible even to begin to find scientific laws that might regulate number, or social rules that might 'tame' number and place it completely under the dictates of human will and reason. However, to a very large extent, we have achieved outstanding success in the attempt, but we discover that we have mostly *quantified* our world, and failed for the most part in the equally paramount task of qualifying, through the 'number archetype' at its structural level in the human psyche, the multiplicity and diversity of forms and events, concrete and abstract, of the world in which we live.

This task might seem to be complicated by an awareness of the changing historical and cultural context in which we find ourselves. But number is non-local and ageless and is not bound by any context. From this aspect a 'neutral' language that might assist us in the task of qualifying number seems possible—in fact, the universal qualities inherent in number have correspondences in the psyche and in nature which one might think would allow for an immediate and untainted (uninterpreted) experience of number.

But the moment we speak of the *numinosum* is the moment we interpret its phenomenology *into* a cultural form. Essentially, however, nothing is lost or hidden in this form. The accessibility of number is greatly enhanced through language, and further, a cross-cultural approach, which focuses on meaning, shows that the fundamental 'nature' of number and the way we use it, crosses all humanly imposed boundaries. For example, we can see that counting and measurement are universally recognized activities, while every culture's construction of time and space, identity and difference, causality and acausality, and so on, recall our species-specific faculty for discriminating things in a characteristically human way.

However, in the midst of all this 'universalizing', the limits of our human sense organs and cognitive functions show us our potential for personal, interpersonal and cultural difference, so that a diversity of interpretations is inevitable. Myths, nevertheless, are always the product of both innately human predispositions and the cultural and historical milieu, so they are, more or less, decipherable regardless of the personal, interpersonal and cultural quotients.

Being human, in all the possible ways that this can be taken, above all means giving account of what we have done, now and in the past. Anthropological and psychological approaches to other cultures give us a reflective and reflexive perspective on our own culture. Carl Jung has observed that while other cultures are 'contained' in their religions, myths and symbolic life, the western way has developed in a direction that has increasingly led to greater and greater social and cultural fragmentation. Scientific positivism and the subsequent generation of a materialistic attitude have taken, or are taking their toll on most societies. In the majority of cases where only quantitative measures are given precedence, it is clear that the qualitative factors will be undermined, or even overlooked. This translates as a loss to human consciousness, and a distinctly human need to correct this imbalance is the only thing that has ever legitimized, for one thing, the establishment of a number symbolism.

It is the aim of this book to illuminate the qualitative, symbolic aspects of number. It may or may not be taken as a purely pragmatic approach, but it remains, as it is, unexpurgated, and possibly uncompromising. That risk may arise because it is a fact that language has the irritating quality of excluding so much when it is used to define its subject, and it is further limited in its use according to a particular discourse, which may be irksome to some, amusing to others, so that changing discourses in 'midstream' (as I do) may have a disorienting effect on the reader.

While preparing this text, two traps needed constant avoidance: on the one hand, over-intellectualizing the subject to the point of alienating those readers interested in a straight-forward presentation of the facts, and on the other hand, producing an incomprehensible and esoteric text, accessible only to mystics and numerologists at an aesthetic and intuitive level (this book, however, will not help predict the future!). No offense is intended to those who may identify with these types. Above all, I hope that I have succeeded in 'treading the middle path' by writing in a style that is both entertaining and informative, and hopefully, not in a style that is cloyingly repetitive—I leave that for the reader to decide.

My deepest thanks must go to C. G. Jung (posthumously) and the Jungian authors, all of whom have influenced this work, first, through the insights they have afforded me, and second, by having availed me of a wealth of knowledge which has been of immeasurable benefit in illuminating the complex issues of the deeper unconscious layers of the psyche, of nature itself, and the interconnectedness of the two, both of which are seen to be commensurate with the phenomenology of the number archetype.

Plate 1. PYTHAGORAS

Detail of The School of Athens *(1509) by Raffaello Sanzio [SOURCE: Wikimedia Commons].*

Plate 2. PLATO AND ARISTOTLE

Detail of The School of Athens *(1509) by Raffaello Sanzio [SOURCE: Wikimedia Commons].*

THE PHILOSOPHY OF NUMBER

*Mathematical concepts evolve, develop, and are incompletely
determined at any particular historical epoch.*

Philip J. Davis & Reubin Hersh

As far as the Western world is concerned, the philosophy of number (which, for our purposes, will be argued with particular reference to mathematical concepts) really begins with the ancient Greeks—in particular the Pythagoreans. Our history of the philosophy of number, therefore, shall begin with Pythagoras.

Pythagoras

The Greek philosopher, astronomer, and mathematician Pythagoras, was also a co-founder (with Thales) of Greek mathematics. He was born about the year 580 BC in Samos, and died in 500 BC in Metapontum (in modern Italy). Pythagoras established a school in Crotona in Magna Graecia where he taught the occult wisdom he had learned over a period of thirty years on the road. Though attributed to Pythagoras himself, uncertainty exists as to the actual personal contributions of his doctrine. His ideas and opinions, and those of his followers, however, are grouped as Pythagorean, since they express a common philosophy, which to the modern mind can be seen as an attempt to slot all existence into a grand unifying theory of the universe. This attempt is evident in the somewhat mystical reference of all tangible objects, ideas and qualities to a specific number. Much of his doctrine, therefore, is expressed in archaic language of an intuitive or poetic form, or in mythological metaphors, but these can often be transposed into more acceptable philosophical or scientific ideas.

Some of the basic concepts of Pythagorean number theory are taught today in our schools, while other ideas and observations are quaint or superstitious. It must be noted that much of this Pythagorean knowledge came from Persia (modern Iran), India, Crete and Egypt, as well as from Kabbalistic and Chaldean sources, so that the pool of Pythagorean knowledge not only indicates an admirable cross-cultural or multicultural attitude to knowledge acquisition, but also demonstrates a discriminate level of thinking (manifested as an eclectic selectivity of concepts or ideas) because of an unwillingness to incorporate ideas or notions from paradigms that conflicted with those of the Pythagoreans. For example, $\sqrt{2}$ being irrational (i.e., it cannot be expressed as the ratio of two numbers), was a problem to the Pythagoreans, yet other cultures had no problem with it. The Pythagorean paradigm did not, or could not be adjusted or modified, even under the weight of a more compelling, pragmatic worldview of (say) the Egyptians.

One of the major Pythagorean 'first principles' was that the universe and all it contained was of Divine origin, mathematical in nature, and dependent on number and form. These were the spiritual constituents of everything material, and were the 'templates' (in a sense) or the 'ideas' behind all that was knowable to the human mind. After Pythagoras established the existence of irrational numbers (attributed to Hippasus in 450 BC) the Pythagorean ideal came into question. Pythagoras avoided this dilemma by claiming that only whole numbers (integers) were numbers at all, while irrationals were concepts (human constructions). Irrational numbers were even considered insane. So emerged another concept: 'types' of numbers.

The confusing dichotomy raised by the idea of there being *types* of numbers requires some kind of resolution to help clarify the distinction between what is, and what is not a number. According to John McLeish, in *Number: From Ancient Civilisations to the Computer* (1992), the Pythagoreans had three definitions for number: "[1] number is 'limited multitude'; [2] it is 'a combination or heaping up of units'; [3] it is 'a flow of quantity' " (pp. 81-82). But McLeish also notes that:

> Because numbers were divine archetypes, in God's mind from the
> beginning, the study of arithmetic was, literally, a way to 'figure out'
> the divine plan.... [R]eality is not made up of things; they are but pale
> reflections of the divine thoughts. (p. 82)

Numbers, then, set limits to things (the world could be counted and
quantified with numbers), but they also had a divine aspect (a quality), which
was reflected in the world of things. These ideas and the Pythagorean belief
system in general were to influence Plato considerably.

Plato and Aristotle

Plato (427-347 BC), most renowned of Greek philosophers and founder
of the Academy in Athens, and well traveled like Pythagoras, followed the
Pythagorean doctrine by also postulating an idealistic, partly mathematical
viewpoint of nature. So much so that he effectively suggested that there
existed a realm beyond space and time, which was the only true *topos* for
contemplation of number forms, because he saw this realm as being perfect,
ideal and eternal—quite the opposite of the physical world which was
imperfect and changeable.

Everything in nature was endeavoring to reach these levels of perfection
'laid down' as *a priori* ideas and forms accessible only by reason and thought.
All that could be perceived by the senses were merely patterns quite suitable
for initiating the study and discovery of the truths underlying reality. This
glorification of reason and criticism of the external world and, therefore,
experimental science, was to continue with only some exceptions up to the
modern era.

Plato's closest philosophical rival was his contemporary Aristotle (384-
322 BC), who disagreed with him on the existence of Ideal Forms. Aristotle,
philosopher and member of Plato's Academy for twenty years until Plato's
death, was also a traveler. After some thirteen years abroad he founded the
Lyceum in Athens in 334 BC, where he taught logic, morals, politics and
rhetoric. Aristotle believed in an external world (as did Plato), but was critical

of Plato's views concerning priority of mathematics over nature.

Aristotle, while he agreed that physical events 'obeyed' specific mathematical laws, believed, however, that these laws were only statements of occurrence. Mathematics could be seen as supportive of natural events, and in this regard it was endorsed as a kind of humanly constructed 'reality', but was not to be taken as superior to physical or sensory experience. Aristotle seemed to be suggesting that mathematics was an invention of the human mind—an abstraction—that only drew parallels with nature, but he did not see mathematics as having a possible objective and axiomatic reality.

Aristotle believed that mathematics had no reality outside the mind: it was abstracted only from the physical world. No evidence exists to confirm or deny whether Aristotle saw the abstraction of mathematics as in some way being a system that perfected or crystallized experience of the empirical (which would support Plato's ideas). It is likely though that Aristotle, by relying on so-called 'infallible human intuition', would most certainly be making the same subjective assumption about mental processes as that made by Plato. The 'Cave' analogy from Plato's *Republic* was supposed to be a reminder of the subjective factor involved in human cognitive functions. Imagine that we live in a cave, and that the world we experience is comprised of mere shadows on the wall of that cave. Imagine further that we cannot turn around and see outside the cave; that we cannot know the world as a higher being sees it. We would have to admit that our knowledge of the source of those shadows would be minimal at best; a mere creation of our reason. Suppose then that one were to witness that true reality. One's vision of that 'truth' must then be related to others as an interpretation of perceived stimuli. But at two levels (how well the vision is explained through inadequate language, and how the listener will consequently 'envision' the vision), the related truth would be a considerable distortion of the actual truth. Hence, the limitation and subjectivity of both perception and reason.

Pythagoras, Plato and Aristotle and their schools, as well as the contributions of Euclid, Apollonius, Archimedes and many others, advanced the understanding of number to a phenomenal degree, and of course, provided the foundations for further advancement throughout the centuries up to modern times. The split between Platonic and Aristotelian thinking has been maintained as well, with contributions from nearly every philosopher and mathematician since then expressing their views, sometimes with only slight variations to the original arguments. Consider Immanuel Kant (1724-1804), to take a philosopher from a relatively recent epoch. Kant proposed a system of *a priori* categories, one of which was quantity that included 'unity', 'plurality', and 'totality'. We use categories to make meaning and sense of the world. Kant said that numbers are not objects but schemata or rules by which magnitudes can be represented, and that makes them concepts, thus agreeing with Aristotle. Kant did not complete his philosophy and state that the *thing in itself* beyond the subjective impression of number was real (which would follow Aristotle's line of thinking), but the idea that 'quantity' (i.e., unity, plurality, etc.) is *a priori* seems contradictory. *A priori* means "before", but *before* what—before we could think of it? That means quantity had existence prior to our existence and that means Kant would have to think of it as a form. By the time humans came on the scene, quantity, and its concomitant quality, would exist as primordial images (age-old ideas) in the psyche of the human mind/brain from some time immemorial. These ideas are discussed further in the next section.

Introvert　　　　　　　*Extravert*

Plato versus Aristotle—a Resolution

We cannot expect that Plato's realm of Ideas and Ideal Forms accurately explains the physical world. Not that Plato thought otherwise—he said himself that the world was accidental and imperfect, but then this statement must also refer to the human mind. Plato's system, therefore, is also unreliable and imperfect by way of the subjectivity of the reasoning mind. Furthermore, his idealistic philosophy seems to be one-sided in nature—introverted in fact. Idealism is a form of distancing from the phenomenology of external reality with a focus on internal or intra-psychic reality. Such a philosophy tends to have appeal to the introvert, since this type gives greater credence to the subjective factor over objective experience. This may be the source of much of the friction between Plato and Aristotle, since Aristotle's philosophy tends towards a more extroverted, materialistic approach, and it has always been a fact that introverts and extraverts, generally speaking, do not see the world in the same way.

Plato's approach to knowledge acquisition, one which also undermines experimentation, can in no way be seen as naïve and lacking in credibility: it is incomplete only. Those of an Aristotelian persuasion would merely pick up where the Platonist leaves off and 'reality-test' a new concept (where possible) in order to validate its 'truth'. And this is exactly what we see today: the theoretician on one side, in purist Platonist mode, and the experimental physicist or applied mathematician on the other side, in practical Aristotelian mode, each reciprocating the other one's efforts.

Using one of Aristotle's laws of deductive reasoning—the law of excluded middle—and a scant appeal to Cartesian dualism, it is almost as if the thinking mind insists on an either/or approach to problem solving. The Platonist sees mathematics as a body of knowledge built up from a sequence of discoveries, in the sense that mathematical 'entities' pre-exist in the world and are unearthed by human contemplation. The Aristotelian sees mathematics as a catalogue of inventions born of the human mind, in the sense that the mind is free to create any form of mathematics it desires, even concepts that bear no origin in the physical world.

Currently, in the sciences, and amongst a populace entranced by the mystique of science, there is a stronger bias towards the latter Aristotelian view, that number and mathematics are abstract inventions of the human mind. As Morris Kline describes mathematics in *Mathematics and the Search for Knowledge* (1985):

> Although it is a purely human creation, the access it has given us to some domains of nature enables us to progress far beyond all expectations.... To thoughtful scientists it has been a constant source of wonder that nature shows such a large measure of correlation with their mathematical formulas. (p. 227)

Mathematicians of this view stand outside what they would call a mystical interpretation. They believe that the elements of mathematics—not just natural numbers, but point and line, negative numbers, irrational numbers, complex numbers, infinite sets and series, formulae and so on—are all human constructions. Such constructions as these, since they have no representations in the natural world (excluding the natural numbers), are taken as proof that mathematical concepts are invented, but as John Barrow observes in *Pi in the Sky* (1993):

> Inventionism fails to provide insight into the fact that Nature is best described by our mental inventions in those areas furthest from everyday life and from those events that directly influence our evolutionary history. (p. 177)

Barrow's argument finds support in Eugene Wigner's essay 'The Unreasonable Effectiveness of Mathematics' (1960) where the question of mathematical constructions, insofar as they can describe purely abstract systems that may even be aesthetic in nature, "prove so effective when applied to the physical world":

> David Hilbert's work in abstract mathematics turned out to provide the infinite dimensional vector space needed for quantum theory. Heisenberg arranging number into patterns turned out to be matrices that had been developed by mathematicians. (F. David Peat, personal communication, January 15, 2007)

Furthermore, even though we have come to accept mathematical concepts, and use them effectively and productively, no one can say why they exist in the form they take. It can be shown how they are derived and can be argued as concepts, but it is also clear that natural numbers (or even those numbers beyond a basis in physical reality), and even mathematical concepts, have qualities, which cannot be taken as merely epiphenomenal to our intentions. Nor might these qualities be accurately described as emergent properties. Many types of numbers and mathematical concepts are laden with *a priori* and unique qualities beyond their more obvious, quantitative phenomenologies, and they demonstrate these qualities through specific properties and outcomes. In other words, the natural numbers themselves, and therefore, mathematical concepts (since their structures depend on numbers) seem to be imbued with their own unique phenomenology: qualities that are not 'derived', but are 'essential' in nature. It is as if they have qualities that are not so much invented, as discovered. (Subsequent chapters will reveal many of these qualities in number.) In fact, it is often the case that the irrational result of a mathematical process is cause for great concern and surprise. In *Accent on Form* (1954), L. L. Whyte claims that:

> the unexpectedness of a mathematical result gives us the feeling that it is not our own creation, that the world of number exists of its own right.... The appeal of mathematical form reaches deep into human character. (p. 19)

And, as Carl Jung (1960) states in his major essay 'Synchronicity: An Acausal Connecting Principle', concerning numbers:

> they are not only concepts but something more—autonomous entities, which some-how contain more than just quantities. Unlike concepts, they are based not on any psychic condition but on the quality of being themselves, on a "so-ness" that cannot be expressed by an intellectual concept. (para. 871)

These statements seem supportive of Plato's doctrine because the idealistic, metaphysical response would be that all numbers have an *a priori* existence as ideas outside space-time and are normally unconscious to us. When numbers do become conscious, their 'so-ness' or 'just-so' quality suggests that numbers as 'autonomous entities' must be discovered, not invented. One wonders, though, if numbers are discoveries only, or if perhaps, as an Aristotelian would believe, numbers are the result of human invention alone. Jung attempted to resolve this dualistic dilemma by stating:

> They [numbers] are *discovered* in as much as one did not know of their autonomous unconscious existence and *invented* in as much as their presence was inferred from analogous representational structures. (para. 871)

As it is for number, so may it be for mathematical concepts. From Jung's perspective we may call these concepts products of human experience and contemplation; human creations from the time they come into consciousness—but they are certainly not the 'creations' of human inventiveness alone. Certainly they depend on 'psychic' conditions, as Jung points out, and these conditions can often be detected, but they do not simply appear *sui generis*—there must be an original seed, or kernel, or archetype, from which these concepts can spring forth. (The use of the word psychic throughout this book generally refers to the normal processes of the psyche as Jung used the term, though in parapsychology it refers to paranormal phenomena.)

Clearly, mathematical concepts originate in the mind, but whatever we produce, no matter how abstract and independent of the observable world, they are still constituents of the psychic world of possibilities. The mind/psyche is the organizing principle of itself and it is engaged in a dynamic process that involves consciousness and the unconscious. From the latter will emerge in consciousness only an interpretation of its experience. Consciousness governs the efficacy of this dynamic because that which culminates is a rational elaboration, qualifiable according to the degree of comprehension and differentiation in the psyche. The less differentiated is the conscious function; the more likely will there be a conflation and incompatibility of ideas.

In *On Divination and Synchronicity* (1980b), Marie-Louise von Franz describes the dynamic aspect of the unconscious aspect of the psyche:

> the larger our consciousness is, and the more it develops, the more we get hold of certain aspects…of the unconscious, draw it into our subjective sphere, and then call it our own psychic activity…. [But] there is still an enormous area…which manifests as it did originally, completely autonomously. (pp. 21-22)

The rise and fall of theories, concepts and ideas is indicative of the above-mentioned dynamic that stems from our relative position in nature. We cannot be certain of the reliability of our knowledge claims (mathematics and other uses of number), but what we do know is that nature has a mercurial quality, and like Hermes, the Greek god of revelation, is illusive and unpredictable. We cannot step outside the human psyche to observe just exactly how we arrive at our 'creations', and we can never differentiate the subjective input of our mental processes from the objective input of unbounded nature. Every observation or thought process is influenced by a myriad of internal and external elements of the natural world. John Barrow (1993) makes this point about the 'nature' of that natural world, and our mental processes:

> True reality is 'coded' as it were by our perceptive and cognitive apparatus and we come thereby to know an encryption of the true nature of things. We see that it is quite possible for us to know the coding that transforms true reality into perceived reality and yet be unable to invert it and recover the picture of true reality from our perception of it. (p. 153)

Barrow describes the limitations of the brain in physiological terms and refers to our subjective perception of the external world, whereas von Franz describes the nature of inner processes in psychological terms from the perspective of a limited ego complex. In both cases the functions described yield results that are subjective and relative. Altogether, we never 'have the whole thing', but only ever possess a certain amount of knowledge of the unconscious, of nature, and of number. This makes it impossible to ever give complete credence to Platonic and Aristotelian viewpoints independently of each other.

*   *   *   *

A final blow came to the idea of mathematical objectivity in 1931 when the mathematician Kurt Gödel showed that by taking a few basic mathematical axioms, a proof of arithmetical law involving finite numbers could be established, but Gödel further established that an opposing 'truth' was also possible using the same axioms. In *Beyond Numeracy* (1991), John Allen Paulos outlined Gödel's procedure, noting that:

By distinguishing rigorously between statements within a formal system and meta-statements about the system by utilizing clever recursive definitions, and by assigning numerical codes to the statements of arithmetic, Gödel was able to construct an arithmetical statement which "says" of itself that it is unprovable and thus establish his result. (p. 96)

Gödel further showed that establishing new axioms to resolve these difficulties would only create similar anomalies. The axioms of mathematics contain an irrational factor, which make it impossible for mathematicians to make absolute statements in mathematical terms. In fact, they make postulations based on the axioms and then move toward logical deductions under the assumption that the axioms hold a certain 'absolute' validity.

Mathematics is therefore incomplete and inconsistent at a fundamental level, but having the natural integers at its root one must also accept that natural numbers, although having a definite 'presence' in nature and appearing quite rational and ordered, also contain an irrational component which extends beyond our understanding (this premise was implied earlier). The mathematician Hermann Weyl (1949), in *Philosophy of Mathematics and Natural Science*, described this component of the natural integers as "something abysmal which we cannot grasp," and stated further that:

it is surprising that a construct created by mind itself, the sequence of the integers, the simplest and most diaphanous thing for the constructive mind, assumes...[an] aspect of obscurity and deficiency when viewed from the axiomatic angle. (p. 219)

Weyl is clearly of an Aristotelian persuasion in believing that the natural number system is a human invention pure and simple, so he cannot understand how it could be so that the axioms have undone the certainty of the integer construct by revealing unexpected aspects that were certainly not intended by its inventors. But 2500 years ago the 'obscurity and deficiency' underlying all conscious contents (including our understanding of numbers) that stand as representations of the world was hinted at by Plato in his general belief that the observation of imperfect nature must yield imperfect results, and therefore, an imperfect science—only he forgot to mention the imperfect mind!

Plato admitted the presence of an unknowable dimension to things discoverable, yet seemed to be suggesting that these things could be grasped in their entirety by contemplation, by way of pure reason alone. The Platonic paradox starts with the belief that nature itself is a deception (we cannot know the world as it truly is), yet ends with the belief that the best way of unmasking this deception is through the rational contemplation of the ideas and forms that construct nature, to the necessary exclusion of the irrational aspects of things. In a sense, Plato tried to reason with the irrational. Exclusive appeal to Plato's philosophy gives an incomplete view of the world (albeit a worthy attempt as such). But we cannot reject Plato's philosophy altogether. A rebuttal of Plato's ideas, as well as those statements by Barrow, Whyte, Jung, von Franz, and Weyl, would take one in the direction towards which the Aristotelian viewpoint inclines, but we will see in later chapters that the qualities in numbers are clearly not human inventions. Those chapters set up an argument favoring the recognition of a transpersonal dimension to numerical representations and constructions. Plato assigned individual characters to numbers, which originated in the division of the Monad, the One. Such a philosophical outlook suggests the influence of the number archetype acting as an inner factor that accounts for numerical images, ideas and forms in a Platonist sense. Since the construct of the number archetype, as a pre-existent component of the psyche, is shown to have an irrational component, there is the implication that the number archetype, insofar as it has this irrational component, is more than a human construction.

In conclusion, the worldviews of Plato and Aristotle are incomplete. Though they are two entirely different perspectives on the construction of knowledge and the appearance of things, both have rather parochial approaches to the nature of the world and the role of number in that world.

Summary

Plato endeavored to understand, by way of the mental complex of reasoning, the irrational dimension of things in the world, such as numbers. While Ideal Forms, by pure reason, can only be partly accessible to the mind, it is senseless to ignore them completely. There must be a kernel of truth in Plato's assumptions because there is a specific way in which we go about constructing knowledge about the world—it is not always (if ever) a matter of observation and then applying (say) a mathematical 'goodness-of-fit' paradigm to those observations as an Aristotelian might do. In fact, Plato's ideas and forms were the forerunners to the archetypal bases underlying human knowledge. Therefore, any presumptuous and exclusive advocacy of the Aristotelian viewpoint would also result in an incomplete picture of the world.

We can never completely know all the underlying processes that might be described in the application of numbers, nor can we completely know the numbers themselves: they are like Frankensteinian monsters with lives and secrets of their own. Ultimately, they manifest as a union between the human mind (consciousness) and a mysterious partner, Nature (the unconscious) that, inhered of unlimited possibilities, cannot avoid making its own nebulous contribution to this union. Furthermore, like a child, the product of this union not only exhibits qualities of both 'parents', but also possesses its own unique identity. Partially, this identity is number in its archetypal aspect, and consequently (and more completely) its symbolic aspect. These two aspects are considered in the next two chapters.

Plate 3. MINERVA

Head of Minerva *(1896) by Elihu Vedder. The archetypal qualities of numbers are venerated in various cultures to the extent that they may achieve anthropomorphic or even godlike status. For example, Minerva (Athena) is associated with the transitional prime number 7, since, as the ancients say, she is 'unmarried' and 'virginal' [SOURCE: Wikimedia Commons].*

THE ARCHETYPE OF NUMBER

Number is the most fitting instrument our mind
can utilise for the understanding of order.

Carl Jung

No other Jungian concept (apart from the collective unconscious) has caused more misunderstanding and misinterpretation than Jung's concept of the 'archetype'. Critics usually attack Jung's theory of archetypes from its 'weakest' point—its unfalsifiability—which is not a weak point in itself, but is only apparently weak. Jung originally referred to archetypes as 'primordial images'. In that sense they are much like instincts, and can only be inferred from their effects. Most critical attacks center on the ubiquitous, and consequently, matter-of-fact representations which attach to archetypes. These are the common-place, straight-forward and concrete appearances of many archetypes (for example, *mother, father, child*, etc.), but these are not the archetypes *per se*—they are the archetypal images which are experienced in human consciousness and come to suggest the archetype in the first place. Other archetypes are more abstract in nature, such as sexuality, energy, persona, and number, but all archetypes are qualitatively different from each other so that number, for example, as manifested in consciousness, is underscored by the *archetype* of number. In this chapter, the archetype of number will be considered in detail.

The Archetypes as Modes of Apprehension

The archetype *per se* was hypothesized by Jung to be a nodal point in the psyche forming a center around which specific images constellate, thereby providing the archetype with particular qualitative aspects. The archetypes are human-wide and constitute what Jung calls the collective unconscious. The collective unconscious, as the domain of psychic activity of a universal nature characterized by the archetypes, is distinct from Jung's other postulate, the personal unconscious, which contains our own individual histories of experiences and memories, either forgotten or remembered. The contents of the personal unconscious are immediately recognizable as such, since they were, for the most part, in consciousness at one time or another. But the collective unconscious contains the archetypes, the representations of which can have ambiguous effects in consciousness, since they are characterized by their numinosity, and can arise spontaneously and may often be unrecognizable—hence, their symbolic aspect.

For the most part, the purpose of the archetype is to aid the individual in establishing order and meaning to life processes and experiences. Jung, in the *Dictionary of Analytical Psychology* (1987), therefore postulates the existence of archetypes because they give:

> co-ordinating and coherent meaning both to sensuous and to inner perceptions, which at first appear without order or connection, and in this way frees psychic energy from its bondage to sheer uncomprehended perception. At the same time, it links the energies released by the perception of stimuli to a definite meaning, which then guides action along paths corresponding to this meaning. It releases unavailable, dammed-up energy by leading the mind back to nature and canalizing sheer instinct into mental forms. (p. 116)

And again, Jung writes: "[this] energic process has run its unvarying course from time immemorial, while simultaneously allowing a perpetual repetition of it by means of an apprehension or psychic grasp of situations so that life can continue into the future" (p. 118). This description of the archetype as a mode of apprehension contrasts with Jung's definition of the instincts, which are regular "purposive modes of action" (p. 118). It can be seen that there is a complementarity between instinct and archetype, since the archetype provides a channel of expression for the instinct. Human behavior, therefore,

[handwritten annotations:]

SPIRIT ————→ INTELLECT

PLATO ————→ ARISTOTLE

UNIVERSAL ————→ PARTICULAR

archetype → Prototype - Stereotype

IDEAL - EXAMPLE - REAL PERSON

comes to exhibit a diversity of expressions through any one particular instinct by virtue of the manifold paths or proclivities that can be determined by various archetypes for any given instinct.

The archetype, then, is a necessary postulate. Archetypes facilitate the psyche in arriving at a content beyond a mere sense perception as an image which is generated in the unconscious and then reaches consciousness, and further, the archetype allows the psyche to go beyond a mere validation of this perception. Jung argues that the environment—the chief source of our perceptions—is not the *efficient* cause of the psychic structure (i.e., the environment doesn't provide the structural contents of the psyche), though its contribution is acknowledged. More to the point, from the perspective of the archetype, there must be an "autonomous quality of living matter" (p. 115)—a life-law or ground plan already structured into the psyche—which gives the psyche its particular and innate 'creative power'.

The Archetypes as Patterns of Behavior

To continue the point just made, archetypes as 'patterns of behavior' (or, more precisely, patterns of perception which elicit patterns of behavior) are *a priori* structural givens—they are inherited in the sense that they come with the topology of the brain and central nervous system. Archetypes are not, however, to be mistaken for inherited ideas, images or concepts, which can only be generated from within an ethnological context. The proclivities for these ideas, images and concepts are self-evidently possible, but are given in the first place by the fact of the archetype. Andrew Samuels summarizes the nature of the archetype in *Jung and the Post-Jungians* (1986):

1. "Archetypal structures and patterns are the crystallization of experiences over time."

2. "They constellate experience in accordance with innate schemata and act as an imprimatur [sanction, license] of subsequent experience."

3. "Images deriving from archetypal structures involve us in a search for correspondences in the environment" (p. 27)

Samuels describes the archetype as something like a skeleton upon which images, ideas, and motifs, etc., are layered as the flesh of the archetype.

Critiquing the Archetype

J. A. C. Brown, in *Freud and the Post-Freudians* (1971), has argued that no scientific discovery has ever been made of an archetype, but this is impossible—at no stage can the archetype be manifested and thereby discovered. It is much like the instinct—it is only suggested in the behavior, but cannot be found (say) in the brain structure. The archetype is a pattern, innate and undetectable by any scientific method and is only knowable from its products, its creations in consciousness.

One can only infer the archetype from its effect, just as pollen-collection in bees, or nest building in birds allows one to infer fundamental behaviors of the respective species as existential realities (the 'being' in the behaviors) made possible by the instinct. Like the archetypal images in humans, these behaviors cannot come about *sui generis*, but must have a causal link to inherent categories of expression and behavior.

In 'Jung's Theory of Archetypes: A Critique' (1996), Andrew Neher makes the same assumption as Brown. He assumes also that personal experience is enough to account for our understanding of the world, as if the mind were a *tabula rasa* ('blank slate') onto which the only knowledge knowable is that which comes through the senses. Personal experience, then, needs no intrinsic, structural predisposition in the mind/brain to allow for this understanding. The mind/brain is taken as a sponge that soaks up everything that comes in through the senses, and categorizes these sensations without the need of an *a priori* capacity to do such a thing. The capacity for such categorization, and the logical consequences of that capacity (i.e., the three summary points made by Samuels), are overlooked by Neher, hence the gap in this type of criticism. Archetype theory, however, fills that gap by presupposing an innate capacity to categorize or pigeonhole events into common themes (archetypal themes). Jung observed a universal, that is, widespread, predisposition in humans for this behavior.

In *Pseudoscience and the Paranormal* (1988), Terence Hines, like Brown and Neher, criticizes the idea of the archetype from the same perspective, but he also faults the concept of the domain of the archetypes (the collective unconscious). He sees both archetypes and the collective unconscious as unnecessary postulates, since such facts or realities as "finding food and a mate, avoiding predators and enemies, obtaining protection from terrible weather and geological phenomena, raising children, and so forth" are given as "the same basic problems" of every human culture (p. 139). Hines, therefore, feels that the archetypes and their appearance in "myths and legends of all peoples" merely appear because they share these *common features* (p. 139).

This criticism does not compromise the archetype at all—the archetype *per se*, according to Jung, is not only innate, but also ubiquitous in all peoples. Hines's focus is on the general *appearance* of behaviors from culture to culture, which he takes as empirically readable (and rightly so). But he does not consider the origins, nor the mechanism for modification, of these behaviors, and furthermore, he conflates the archetypes *per se* with these behaviors, thereby justifying, in his mind, the redundancy of the concept.

The human experiences cited above, and those stated by other critics (Geza Róheim, for example, in Brown's above-mentioned book) are representations of archetypes *in the behaviors* that are mistakenly used to define the archetypes *per se*. The archetype *per se* should not be *defined* by its form, but should be *determined* or *derived* from its form. ('Deriving' the archetype this way should not be regarded, as a 'hard and fast' rule because the sensory data gathered from the phenomenal world is only a contributing factor to the *form* of the archetype, indicating only the possibility that an archetype *per se* can or should be inferred.)

In *Individuation* (1966), Josef Goldbrunner clears up Hines's oversight by explaining the archetype as a proclivity that enables experience:

Man [*sic*] could have no experience at all if he was not born with the subjective personality to experience parents, a wife, children, birth, death, community, a profession, God.... The experiences of the millennia have deposited themselves in the pathways of the brain and thereby made us potentially ready to act again in the same way. The archetypes are the 'psychic aspect of the structure of the brain'. They penetrate our consciousness, when a potential readiness to act is awakened into activity (pp. 104-106).

For the most part Hines, by his very words, confirms the presence of something (the archetype *per se*) by admitting the *natural* occurrence of certain behaviors, but he never asks why these behaviors should be the way they are, or why experiences are perceived, responded to, or categorized the way they are.

That there is a biological reality to the archetype may be imminently verifiable, since it has already been established that specific areas of the human brain are the local source of particular behavioral and cognitive functions. Neuropsychologists are in general agreement that damage to certain areas of the brain causes loss or diminution of the functions associated with those areas, so it is reasonable to assume that archetypes, by their complementarity with instinct and behavior, are integrally enmeshed in the brain structure. It is possible, therefore, to see the archetypes as *entia* contingent (or even isomorphic) with neural clusters or neural circuitry that even extend into the brain stem and central nervous system. In the chapter 'An Emergent Theory of Consciousness' from M. H. Marks and F. E. Gordon's book *Theories in Contemporary Psychology* (1976), R. W. Sperry hints at the archetype when he states that a major function of the brain must be its capacity to "detect the overall qualities of different kinds and different species of cerebral process and respond to these as entities rather than to their individual cellular components" (p. 455).

Evidence exists to support this hypothesis, but more importantly, consciousness (and its development) and with it an ego complex—both essential components of mind/brain structure and function—can be recognized as dynamic *archetypal* factors in action. Going further, it can be seen that factors of the phenomenal world represented as symbols in the psyche, as well as dreams and fantasy contents, etc., may all take their places as *gestalts* structured neurologically in the brain. There would, therefore, be a neuro-physiological substructure to these entities (archetypes, including consciousness and ego) that lends scientific support to Jung's theory of archetypes.

But Jung's postulate of the *psychoid* archetype goes beyond neo-cortical processes, 'down' through the levels of the brain stem and central nervous system, even to depths beyond the usual processes of the psyche, which could be called 'quasi-psychic' (reflexes and instincts, for example). That there is an archetypal component attached to these psychoid processes is given in the actions of the lower organisms which do not have a brain, and function without consciousness (unconsciously and instinctively), yet behave 'intelligently' and 'meaningfully'.

The possibility of a direct isomorphism of archetypes onto brain structures is only tentatively suggested, but may be acceptable as a working hypothesis in explaining the physical processes underlying the canalization of psychic (mental) energy into our apprehensions, behaviors, and the modification of those behaviors. The concept of the archetype is shown not to be limited in scope to neo-cortical systems, but would extend to all forms of life that exhibit quasi-psychic functions.

The Archetype and the Idea

The mental forms of the archetypes are not unlike Platonic Ideas, but there are some key differences. The Idea is given as immutable and unchanging, whereas the form of the archetype is manifold. Also, the Idea is given an empirical base by the archetype in being "a philosophical expression of the psychological archetype" (Jacobi, 1974, p. 50), as noted in Jolande Jacobi's book, *Complex/Archetype/Symbol*. So, while the Idea is clear and is crystallized as an immediately recognizable entity, the archetype, by virtue of the dynamism of the archetype *per se*, may shift in form so that new representations of the archetype may emerge and submerge, coming in and out of consciousness, according to the circumstances of the individual.

Plato attempted to align or equate his Ideas with numbers (by analogy), as many others have attempted in the mystical tradition, in order to set up a hierarchy or structure that would schematize the realm of Ideas. Psychologically, however, since Ideas are experienced in the psyche of the individual, it can be seen that such attempts are aimed at putting order to the collective unconscious. This kind of structural paradigm, based on the numbering of qualitative factors (Ideas, archetypes) translates as a model for philosophical or psychological entities where each is set in place in a kind of field or grid-form, analogically speaking. There would be a fusion or overlap of entities as is suggested by the image of an inter-connecting grid, but while the Self is given in Jungian psychology as the central archetype, it is difficult to imagine which Idea or Form would, or should be attributed the role of the central ordering factor. One possible uniting factor may reside in the metaphysical concept of the *unus mundus* (Latin: 'one world')—this concept is dealt with in the chapter "Synchronicity."

The Archetype of the Self

As far as the Self *as archetype* is concerned, this archetype "designates the whole range of psychic phenomena in man [*sic*]" (para. 789) as Jung relates in *Psychological Types* (1971). In this sense the Self equates with "the unity of the personality as a whole" (para. 789), and this unity is analogous to the qualitative factors of the number One. While the Self may extend in concept, philosophically, to the number One (as Monad) and the *unus mundus*, these could only be partial extensions, leaving the Self as a fragmented representation delimited by Ideas and Forms of restricted value. The Self must be seen as beyond philosophical conjecture—it *is* immanent, but it is also transcendent because it extends into the arena of unconscious processes (which have been empirically verified) and, therefore, cannot be completely known or bounded.

Once you have a NDE or an OBE, the Self-monad and unus mundus evaporate into consciousness even beyond the archetype.

The Archetype of Number

Jung (1960) has mentioned the role of number as "an *archetype of order* which has become conscious" (para. 870). By this he means, as can be ascertained by the above description of the 'reality' of the archetype, that there is a predisposition for numbers to manifest themselves, in and through their archetypal forms, in meaningful contents which have come to be such by the canalization of psychic energy in a direction towards consciousness.

Appearances in the environment as representations in numerical form, are easily distinguished and are even understandable normally, but it is another remove altogether when faced with the number archetype in its symbolic guise, as it irrupts into consciousness from the collective unconscious. In its symbolic form, the number archetype can pose the singular problem of meaning for the individual, and for the collective.

Meaning, of a type constructed on numerical or patterned forms, manifests in a very human way (that is, it is archetypally pre-determined) in thoughts and thought processes, discourses, ideas, images and imaginative speculations, etc., which are structured according to the specific number (at an archetypal level) as it relates to the extra- and intra-psychic conditions of the given moment. During these given moments, the issue of meaning is not only activated (which is an ordering principle in itself, partly emerging from the ordering principle of number, and partly constructed within an ethnological context), but is advanced further (modified, elaborated upon) by a human need to act upon that which is currently meaningful in ways appropriate to the individual and the collective. Such action will mean changes in consciousness, and such changes may in turn reactivate archetypal processes so that the psychic system is in constant resonance and in constant metamorphosis.

As number manifests in consciousness through the archetype, then, any meaningfulness so established will exhibit a co-coordinated and structured aspect—it will be ordered according to an inborn, unconscious disposition of the psyche, so that putting order to knowledge and perceptions will mirror the number archetype. The Neoplatonist philosopher Plotinus stated:

Number exists before objects which are described by number. The variety of sense objects merely recalls to the soul the notion of number. (cited in Schimmel, 1993, p. 16)

We can read this statement as a philosophical intuition of the number archetype. In fact, as opposed to the symbols generated from the archetypes, that do not demonstrate ordering properties, numerical symbols of 'pure order' are derived from the number archetype (mythologically, for example). But even so, as Jung personally related to von Franz (1974) in her book *Number and Time*:

> one only subsequently recognizes the relation of number to mythological assertions, although the contents of number undoubtedly adhere in an *a priori* fashion to these assertions; they are only later made conscious [they are not added on, in an *ad hoc* fashion]. In this sense number is a genuine symbol, not only by virtue of its arithmetic nature, but its contents as well. (pp. 143-144)

The association of gods with numbers attests to a substratum of order in the psyche which, as Jung remarks, is directly connected with the archetypal world of the collective unconscious, and hence demonstrates a degree of veneration of archetypal manifestations in cultures that assign supernatural properties to numbers. In many cultures there is the impression that the gods and goddesses and their associated phenomena, including numbers, are enmeshed and interrelated in a type of field. It is possible to draw on research in neuro-physiology, as just discussed, and speak of this field in terms of interconnecting neural networks or clusters. John Crossley's (2007) book *Growing Ideas of Number* gives some examples.

Jung (1960) believes that number magic arose as the result of "certain numbers and combinations of numbers hav[ing] a relation to and an effect on certain archetypes, but the reverse would also be true" (para. 871). That is, the magical and numerical qualities associated with the gods and goddesses (archetypes) are the result of the psychic conflation of archetypes with numbers. The mind/brain, as one self-contained, interlinked system, may give rise to mutual contamination of forms, archetypes, numbers, ideas, and so on, with each other, which would account for the relative inanity of some associations, while in other cases, a coherent and even valid overlap of forms, archetypes, etc., would account for genuine similarities or isomorphic resonances, which amplify and integrate, in a meaningful way, those emerged associations as they irrupt into consciousness.

But what do we make of Pythagoras' equation of Justice with the number four (or eight), or Nicomachus' association of the number seven with Minerva, the Roman goddess of Wisdom? What are the reasons behind the belief that the number eight had symbolic ties with the Cube, or Cybele, the Roman earth-goddess? Psychologically, such associations are psychological projections. Minerva (Athena) is 'sensibly' associated with the number seven, since, as the ancients say, she is unmarried and virginal. Since the number seven was already known as a prime number, it being incapable of 'producing' other numbers of itself (that is, it has no other divisors except itself and one), Minerva and the number seven came to be 'like' each other. The seventh day (Sabbath), on which no orthodox Jewish person was permitted to work, or create, or produce anything (that is, must remain virginal), and the later association of the Virgin Mary with seven, further shows the tendency to venerate numbers to the extent that they may achieve anthropomorphic, or even godlike status. Here we can see how a certain number (i.e., seven) has an effect on a certain archetype (the virgin), and *vice versa*.

In the case of the number eight the Roman nature-goddess Cybele, Justice, and the Cube, attain their symbolic ties with the number eight because eight is the first Cube, or cubic number ($2 \times 2 \times 2 = 8$). Alchemists and philosophers of old associated the cube (since it has three dimensions) with solidity, and matter, and therefore, the earth. The number eight, being derived from number two (the first female number) was thrice magnified in feminine grandeur, thus becoming associated with the *Magna Mater* (the Great Mother goddess), otherwise known as Cybele, the earth goddess. Through her divine sense of truth and knowledge of the natural way of things, the number eight became associated with Justice, both divine and secular. This type of associative thinking applied to all numbers, so that numbers could be symbolically referenced to the gods and goddesses, to human qualities, and to cultural values. Again we see the reciprocal relationship between number and archetype.

Such a high regard for the number archetype has remained present in later centuries, as observed in the important position mathematics occupies in all the sciences. This veneration is not simply based on the reliability of number (when used quantitatively), but is based on a form of dependence and pro-active attitude generated in response to the infallibility of the number archetype. Psychologically, the archetype can give indication of complexes and even symptoms within a psychic system as indicated by an archetypal image, but the archetype as a symbol is more generally abstract than complexes and symptoms. Number has this abstract dimension in the symbol and von Franz explains in *Number and Time* (1974):

> If…we admit that the unconscious participates in the formation of our representations of natural numbers, then all statements about them become recognizable as realizations of only partial aspects of the number archetype [as symbols].… Numbers, furthermore, as archetypal structural constants of the collective unconscious, possess a dynamic, active aspect which is especially important to keep in mind. (p. 33)

This dynamic aspect is immediately detectable in both the symbolism of each number, and in the symbolism of numbers that comprise a continuum.

Summary

Archetypes are structural components of the psyche that determine the particular expression of instincts, and provide ways of interpreting sensory data. The archetype *per se* is inferred from the archetypal image, since there must be a causal factor behind that image, though like the instinct, no proof of the archetype *per se* as an entity is likely. Jung's postulate of the number archetype is the archetype *par excellence* that allows for the attribution of order to phenomena in the world as a partial means of interpreting those phenomena. The number archetype does this by co-coordinating both sensory data, and stimuli or irruptions from the unconscious into patterned or sequenced configurations. Through these interpretations, phenomena are either quantifiable, or they may demonstrate singular or plural *qualities*. Number has a symbolic aspect, which may take the form of single images (for example, gods and goddesses), sequences or continua, or even esoteric ideas.

In the next chapter, numbers as conveyors of meaning are considered further, whether the meaning is extrapolated from the number symbols themselves, or the numbers are used as mere pointers to meaning.

The phenomenon that best displays all of this is in the entire "math-art" of music, from the organized rigors of controlled sound from the math of instruments, to the math on the music literature, to the performance, to the math physics of sound.

All of Yang and Yin are eminently present in a symphony orchestra and an opera!

Plate 4. THE LAST SUPPER

The Last Supper (1498) by Leonardo da Vinci, depicts 12 apostles dining with Jesus Christ. The Christian tradition explains the ill-omened character of the number 13 as having originated at this 'last supper' with Judas Iscariot (Christ's betrayer)—fifth from left, elbow on table—nominated as the unlucky (thirteenth) apostle-cum-dinner-guest [SOURCE: Wikimedia Commons].

THE SYMBOLISM OF NUMBER

*You can observe the power of number exercising
itself in…all the acts and thoughts of men.*

Philolaus

The 'individuality' of each number is a challenging concept, since the axiomatic (self-evident) nature of number forces us to accept the *qualities* of their manifestations, which means we cannot claim them to be inventions exclusively—certain aspects of numbers do seem to be discovered. It is from this standpoint that numbers show us their symbolic aspects: symbols being the best possible representations or formulations of things unknown or inexpressible. The following chapter is an overview of the symbolic aspects of number.

Number Symbolism in Ancient Times

In *Mysterium Coniunctionis* (1963), Jung makes clear the nature of the symbol: *Semiotics → Signs → Symbols → metaphor → Similes → personifications*

> If symbols mean anything at all, they are tendencies which pursue a definite but not yet recognizable goal and consequently can express themselves only in analogies. In this uncertain situation one must be content to leave things as they are, and give up trying to know anything beyond the symbol. (para. 667)

It follows, epistemologically, that our always limited but increasing desire for knowledge impels us to rely on the symbol in all its forms as a mediating

[handwritten annotation at top: This would be the perfect line as an opener for a class in linguistics or semantics.]

[handwritten annotation in left margin: Die hieroglyphics or archaic numerals]

function that will never be completely exhausted of meaning, but will become more and more meaningful, or will change in meaning.

There is no doubt that the aim of a culture is to maintain its symbolic analogies as a means of canalizing psychic energy, but the desire to know 'beyond the symbol' is taken up by many esoteric practices, including *Kabbalah* (reviewed shortly), and the mantic arts (reviewed in later chapters).

There is a strong correspondence and similarity between the archetype and the symbol. The number archetype can be determined from the symbol, since the symbol is determined by the archetype, but archetype and symbol are not necessarily identical. In fact, the symbol is merely the mythical or human aspect of the archetype. As Jacobi (1974) writes:

> When the archetype manifests itself in the here and now of space and time, it can be perceived in some form by the conscious mind. Then we speak of a *symbol*. This means that every symbol is at the same time an archetype, that it is determined by a non-perceptible "archetype *per se.*" (p. 74)

The archetype *per se* exists by inference alone, whereas the symbol is self-evidently manifested.

The symbolism of number, as mentioned previously, extends back in time to the complicated philosophical system of Pythagoras and his community of followers. The two-way split of his community into the *akousmatikoi* ('those who hear') and the *mathematikoi* ('those interested in science') inevitably established the two most common ways of viewing number. Back then, and more so today, either a mystical approach could be adopted, where number is seen as having *qualities* (magic, power, etc.), or a more staid, scientific path might be followed, where number maintains its most respected characteristic: its *quantitative* aspects (counting, calculating, etc.). It should be noted that in both cases, number has ordering properties—number assists in the regularization, systematization, and schematization of disparate elements into a coherent whole.

In the case of the mystical approach, number reaches into the symbolic realm of superstition. The idea of lucky and unlucky numbers persists to the present day, yet it is clear that numbers, as conceptual *entia* cannot have such enduring or absolute qualities. From one culture to another, and even within a single culture at different periods in history, contradictory interpretations concerning the 'merits' of various numbers give indication of a constructed and applied value system that is projected onto numbers. *Triskaidekaphobia* ('fear of the number thirteen') is a case in point. The Christian tradition explains the ill-omened character of the number 13 as having originated at the Last Supper, with Judas Iscariot (Christ's betrayer) nominated as the unlucky (thirteenth) apostle-cum-dinner-guest. But the associations are older than that going back to Babylon and China. The number thirteen also has an association with Hades (Pluto), god of the underworld, which suggests ominous parallels, yet it is an auspicious number in the *Kabbalah* (an ancient Hebrew alpha-numeric system used to uncode secret information in sacred texts), and in some communities it is considered lucky to be born on the thirteenth day of the month. The ancient Mayans considered it 'positive' and 'auspicious' because it was the number of the 13 deities and the 13 heavens (Schimmel, 1993, p. 206).

These and similar contradictions surrounding other numbers suggest that the subjective experiential basis that determines the superstitious dimension of number symbolism must be considered as at least one causal factor underlying the ambiguity of some belief systems that use number to derive meaning. Many mantic systems which rely on number as a means of aligning life events and possibilities with number outcomes must be excluded from this consideration, however, since the goal of these systems is not to define number in concrete terms, but to give indication of tendencies or consequences, *in neutral terms*, as suggested by the sequential relationships characteristic of number. Mantic practices, then, are not necessarily superstitious in nature. In a later chapter "Numerology," however, the methods of arriving at these tendencies or consequences can be seen as somewhat arbitrary. On the other hand, there is empirical evidence that astrology and the *I Ching* are founded on valid principles arrived at through observation over countless centuries. Nevertheless, in all forms of divination one must also consider the validity of the interpretation, which it should be noted, is a subjective consideration common to all disciplines, methods, and practices that generate raw data.

At its height, number symbolism became the paragon of aesthetics in many cultures, as indicated in the cultural products of all societies—particularly, it seems, in cultures where art and architecture, music and craft, and so on, are taken to very high levels of complexity, as is evident in the technological and/or scientific advancement of most cultures the world over. J. E. Cirlot (1962), in *A Dictionary of Symbols*, views numbers as "idea-forces" (p. 220), which mean they have 'characters' in a Pythagorean/Platonic sense. A few of these characteristics are given in the chapter "A Brief History of Number." For example, the 'philosophical' One (the Monad) forms the starting point for all the numbers, so that the movement from unity to multiplicity originates in the monad, thereby implying a shift further and further away from the 'spiritual' point of origin into the world of matter by extension into space, either physically or conceptually. The unity principle describes the Indivisible, the Whole, the Total. It became associated with unique and solitary phenomena in nature, such as the Sun, monoliths and columns, special trees, or even more prominent, and awe-inspiring natural features of the landscape, such as mountains or remote sites. The concept of movement and the creative 'masculine' principle followed thereafter. The uneven numbers became positive and 'active', while the even numbers became negative and 'passive'. These two classes were established on empirical grounds. The number One symbolically, and in a very real sense, is a constantly resonating or oscillating entity impelled by its innate polarity: it is a so-called 'paradoxical unity'. The connection of the Number One with the number Two is as inviolate as the connection between Unity and Plurality: each defining the other according to their differences. The number two, being divisible, describes the elements of nature, which could be parted, unfolded or opened. Things which could be split, fragmented or torn asunder or set against each other implied or engendered conflict, opposition, and more generally, earthly existence and the vicissitudes of life. *Thus duality*

Generally, from ancient times, in both the East and the West, uneven numbers have always been 'masculine' while even numbers were considered 'feminine' (for example, the number one is 'masculine', and the number two is 'feminine' in most cultures). An exception to this schema is reported by Annemarie Schimmel in *The Mystery of Numbers* (1993). The pre-Columbian Maya believed that "the conjunction of woman (3) and man (4) produces a unit, 7, which is endowed with life" (p. 130). Another exception is given in the ancient druidical initiation rites where the number three also symbolized the feminine principle, again contradicting the assumption of the inherently masculine personality of the Trinity of Church dogma. In the absence of such evidence, there is a risk of schematizing number to the point of making absolute statements about numerical entities as being, in this case 'masculine', or in that case 'feminine', by way of associations gleaned from a limited number of socio-cultural/historical antecedents, when a kind of 'deconstruction' may be the better course of action in order to avoid confusion. Von Franz (1974) gives a warning concerning 'genderization':

> Different cultures possess different "sacred numbers" and the same may be considered now more as "spiritual" or "material," now more "masculine," "chthonic-lunar," or "feminine."…[A]dhering to a Pythagorean outlook [means] interpretation thus regresses onto the level of historically familiar conclusions regarding number symbolism. (pp. 31-32)

From Von Franz's perspective we can see that deeper considerations and continued investigations of number must apply to the symbolic interpretation of numbers before reliable judgments concerning their meaning can be made.

The ordering property of number, and the semiotic use of number, serve as a means by which deeper meanings and knowledge concealed in secret texts can be decoded. One such system of interpretation—the *Kabbalah*—uses number as a means of encoding and decoding sacred knowledge.

Kabbalah

Christian mysticism is known to have its roots in Pythagorean numerology, but Pythagorean thought also influenced the Hebrews, as did the Neoplatonic and Gnostic philosophies. Jewish mysticism drew upon these sources and by the twelfth century *Kabbalah* came into prominence. This section considers the meaningfulness embedded in numbers as proposed by the Kabbalists.

The history of the *Kabbalah* extends back to a mythic past, since its alleged origins can be 'traced' from the Divine Sphere, to Adam, and to Noah, and to Abraham, who apparently leaked some of the sacred information to the Egyptians, and finally to Moses. Traditionally, then, Moses may well have learned a great deal of the Kabbalistic practice from the Egyptians. The first four books of the *Pentateuch* (thereby excluding *Deuteronomy*) have concealed in their texts the *principles* of the secret doctrine. *Deuteronomy*, in fact, like the other books of the Old Testament, still conceals some meaningful Kabbalistic references.

An unbroken line of tradition culminated in the first written record of Kabbalism—the *Zohar*—by the Rabbis Eleazar and Abba, who based the work on treatises written by one Schimeon ben Jochai at the time of the destruction of the second temple. *Kabbalah* means 'to receive', and refers directly to a received doctrine of esoteric knowledge handed down by word of mouth. As Westcott (1974) writes, such knowledge included "hidden truths, religious notions, secrets of nature, ideas of Cosmogony, and facts of history in a form that was unintelligible to the uninitiated" (p. 25). The 'tradition', another meaning of *Kabbalah*, maintains three propositions, as Charles Poncé relates in his book *Kabbalah* (1973):

1. The creator God of the Bible is a limited God and…is subordinated to yet a higher, limitless and unknowable God, the *En-Sof*.
2. The universe is not the result of creation *ex nihilo*, but the result of a complex operation performed by the emanated attributes of the *En-Sof*, the *Sefiroth*.
3. The *Sefiroth* are a bridge connecting the finite universe with the infinite God. (p. 15)

These three principles are not in keeping with the beliefs of rabbinical Judaism, and Kabbalistic philosophy and practice in general are far from the traditions of Orthodox Judaic practice.

see The Book of Raziel, the Archangel of Esoteric Knowledge.

The Symbolism of Number   39

The practical component of *Kabbalah* includes the belief that God's written word contained the 'essence of His being', and since God was a *deus absconditus* ('a hidden and unknowable God') one could unearth the meaning of the essence of God by the use of three systems devised for this purpose—*Gematria, Notarikon,* and *Temura.* (The Sefirotic Tree is of course the most fundamental concept of *Kabbalah,* but this will be discussed in the chapter "Ten (The Decad).")

Gematria is the practice of converting the letters of words to numerical values (*see* Table 1). Words with the same numerical value are said to correspond with each other so that the number is representative of a group of different but related ideas or images. For example, when the Hebrew letters of the phrase 'until Shiloh comes' (in romanized Hebrew YBA ShYLH) from *Genesis* 45:10 are converted to numbers and added together they total 358 (10 ⊦ 2 ⊦ 1 ⊦ 300 + 10 + 30 + 5 = 358). The Hebrew word 'Messiah' (MShYCh) from the same passage also totals 358 (40 + 300 + 10 + 8 = 358). The Messiah is, therefore, related to the coming of Shiloh. But, a third parallel, found in *Numbers* 21:9, speaks of the 'Serpent of Moses' (NChSh), which also gives 358 (50 + 8 + 300).

Table 1. *The Hebrew Letters and their Numerical Values.*

1	A	Aleph	10	Y	Yod	100	Q	Qoph
2	B	Beth	20	K	Kaph	200	R	Resh
3	G	Gimel	30	L	Lamed	300	Sh	Shin
4	D	Daleth	40	M	Mem	400	T	Tav
5	H	Heh	50	N	Nun	500	K	Final Kaph
6	U/V	Vav	60	S	Samech	600	M	Final Mem
7	Z	Zain	70	O	Ayin	700	N	Final Nun
8	Ch	Cheth	80	P	Peh			
9	Th	Teth	90	Tz	Tzaddi			

see "The Book of Numbers" by Peter Bentley.

The conclusion reached by Christian Kabbalists was that the serpent on the cross, mentioned in the Old Testament, was a prefiguration of Christ.

By the rules of *gematria*, the letters of the three unnamed men in *Genesis* 18:2—"and lo, three men"—total 701, which is the same letter-total for Michael, Gabriel and Raphael. The rabbis actually took it to be so, that these three angels were the 'men' referred to in this *Genesis* passage.

Notarikon (Latin: *notarius* = 'shorthand writer') involves the use of first and last letters of key words to make new words. For example, in *Deuteronomy* 30:12, Moses asks the question: "Who shall go up for us to heaven?" In the original Hebrew the first letters of each word spell the Hebrew word for circumcision (*mylah*), while the last letters of each word spell the tetragrammaton YHVH (*Jehovah* = God). In other words, the answer to the question is that the circumcised shall go up to God.

Notarikon is also practiced another way. Each letter of a word can be taken as the first letter of a new word. For example, *Amen* in Hebrew provides the three letters *Aleph*, *Mem*, and *Nun* (AMN), which stand for the phrase 'the Lord and faithful King'. Christians have used *Notarikon* on the Greek word *Ichthus* ('fish') that gives the sentence *Iesous CHristos THeou Uios Soter* ('Jesus Christ, the son of God, the Savior').

Finally, *Temura* ('permutation') involves the complicated procedure of rearranging the letters of the Hebrew alphabet in various systematic ways to create new words by substituting one letter for another. One method used in *Temura* involves half the Hebrew letters being written left to right, *Aleph* to *Kaph*, and then in the next row the remaining letters are written right to left, *Lamed* to *Tav*. For example, the words Sheshak (ShShK), a town mentioned in *Jeremiah* 25:26, is decoded by letter substitution as the town of Babel (BBL) mentioned in *Jeremiah* 51:41 (*see* fig. 1).

From a numerological point of view, only *gematria* is of interest here, since it is the only system that actually uses numbers to derive meaningful correspondences in the same way as names are converted to numbers in numerology (in other words, both systems give numerical values to letters).

Figure 1. *Sheshak = Babel. (Shin is replaced by Beth, and Kaph is replaced by Lamed.)*

A   B   G   D   H   V   Z   Ch   Th   Y   K
T   Sh   R   Q   Tz   P   O   S   N   M   L

A New Testament example of *gematria* appears in *Revelation* 13:11-18, where a warning is given concerning 'the beast' which comes up out of the earth. The name of this beast has a number by which he may be identified: "it is the number of a man; and his number *is* Six hundred threescore *and* six." Such cases were taken by Christian Kabbalists as proof that *gematria* had authenticity, even though practitioners of strict mystical Judaism were already quite convinced of this fact back in Old Testament times. In other words, Kabbalists were well aware of the deliberate practice of the original chroniclers of concealing special messages in the texts.

There appears to be some evidence that *Kabbalah* is not a *post hoc* system of interpretation, and that its derivations are not mere coincidence. Psychologically, the ordering system of the *Kabbalah*, because it has survived for so many thousands of years, must be satisfying to the soul (emotionally speaking) for those who believe and practice it. To derive deeper meaning from a text is itself its own reward, and *Kabbalah* is shown to be a consistent system, which furthers its credibility. There seems to be some evidence that many—perhaps all—the names in the sacred texts were originally considered from a numerological standpoint by the original chroniclers, but without a detailed study of all the biblical works, this hypothesis remains only that—an hypothesis. Consequently, it is impossible to state for certain that all the correspondences found in the texts are intentional or coincidental.

A popular example of *gematria* that may have been deliberately encrypted in the *Pentateuch* is given by Westcott (1974, pp. 29-30). It concerns the story of Abraham and Sarah and the birth of their son Isaac when Abraham (Hebrew = 'father of multitudes') was 100 years old and Sarah (Hebrew = 'princess') was 90. Before Isaac's birth, Abraham (ABRHM

= 248) was called Abram (Hebrew = 'high father'; ABRM = 243), and Sarah (ShRH = 505) was called Sarai (Hebrew = 'contentious'[?]; ShRY = 510). Abram and Sarai's numbers jointly total 753 (243 + 510), as does Abraham and Sarah (248 + 505 = 753).

As a couple, then, before and after the 'annunciation', their number totals were the same, but Abram is seen to be deficient in the fifth letter *Heh* (which stands for the feminine principle according to tradition), while Sarai must lose the *Yod* (the tenth letter) by substituting it for *Heh* also, so that she gives up *Heh* (that is, five) to Abraham (i.e., *Heh* + *Heh* = *Yod*). In some sense, the changes in the names (and, therefore, the changes in name numbers) suggest that an exchange had taken place that was symbolic in nature. Abraham's gain of the feminine principle may have been a psychological process of *anima* integration (a manifestation of his inner feminine in conscious life). His transformation mirrors a transformation in her (i.e., *Yod* to *Heh*) from an overly feminine identity or condition (*Yod*) to a relatively more balanced one brought about by the conscious manifestation of her inner masculine (*animus*). Thus, a biological reference is implied in this exchange. Abraham uncovered the *Yod* (which stands for the *orificii membri*) so that the sterility was broken. It is known that Sarah could not bear children, but we must assume that there was a time when she had her cycle, since it is stated in *Genesis* 18:11 that "it ceased to be with Sarah after the manner of women." We are led to believe, however, that with old-age she came into a condition where she could not ovulate (was infertile), implying, as stated, some kind of hormonal imbalance (note, for example, how the birth control pill stops the menstrual cycle by introducing an excess of feminine hormone into the woman's blood stream, which creates a false state of pregnancy). By 90 years of age her cycle also ceased (no doubt as a natural consequence of old age), but a change in circumstances allowed her to bear a child.

Whether or not the birth of Isaac is a miracle depends on one's belief system. St. Augustine said that a miracle is not so much contrary to nature as contrary to what we know about nature. Natural (biological, psychological) processes may well have taken place between Abraham and Sarah of which we can only speculate. It seems that in this case there is an intentionality in the text, and the interpreter is given the task of unearthing that meaning. Perhaps examples of this kind raise more questions than they answer, but what is learned, and therefore what is of value in the ancient texts (through *Kabbalah*), is that something of the nature of human relationship dynamics and life processes is concealed, but can be revealed if one knows how. Thus, for the Kabbalist this state of affairs is ideal because, first, revelation is an ongoing process, much like scientific discovery, and second, secrets are secrets for very good reason—they are only valued in the right hands. This kind of mystery and potential for breakthroughs in the sacred text guarantees a continued interest in the *Kabbalah*.

In conclusion, the *Kabbalah* is a received doctrine of esoteric knowledge and practice, used to discover the hidden meanings in the sacred texts of Judaism. Under the influence of the Greek traditions (Pythagoras, Plato, etc.) and Christian mysticism, that which started as a mystical practice amongst ancient Hebrews grew to become the *Kabbalah* as it is known and practiced today. *Gematria*, *Notarikon*, and *Temura* are three ways of deriving esoteric knowledge from the texts, and this knowledge constitutes a covert body of wisdom that enhances the overt knowledge readily gleaned from the texts.

Although the methods used in *Kabbalah* seem arbitrary (i.e., not valid), they *are* systematized (i.e., reliable), and as long as the practitioners follow the same rules for deciphering the texts as laid down by the original chroniclers, the findings are not coincidental. This factor alone means Kabbalah has internal validity. *Kabbalah* is an ancient practice that uses number to uncover meaning, wisdom and greater understanding.

Number Symbolism: The Biological Connection

It is noted that there is an uneven number of chromosomes in the males of most species (including *Homo sapiens*), whereas there are an even number of chromosomes in the females. This fact suggests that the natural processes of the objective psyche generated a spontaneous content (appearing as an 'invention') that irrupted into consciousness to become a cultural product (i.e., gender enumeration), which only later (through 'discovery') became mirrored as a biological truth. As just pointed out, however, this fact does not seem to resonate psychologically in the same way in all cultures. Therefore, any symbolic variations, whether they may or may not contradict each other when compared cross-culturally or historically, must be due to strict adherence to the interpretations of the *partial* aspects of the meanings of numbers (recall von Franz's words above). These interpretations must be seen as descriptive constructions built upon immutable and invariable patterns specific to numbers outside those constructions. In attempting, therefore, to establish a neutral language concerning number symbolism it is not surprising that paradoxes arise. This problem will be noticed occasionally throughout this text. However, as von Franz (1974) also states:

> In order to grasp the meaning of these aspects more closely we must first return to simpler facts, namely, to the individual numbers themselves, and gather together the sum total of thought, both technical and mythological assertions, which they have called forth from humanity.... It is not what we can *do* with numbers but what *they* do to our consciousness that is essential. (p. 33)

In other words, any given culture can misinterpret the archetype, and this can be seen to be a major cause for misunderstanding and even catastrophe.

Underlying our conscious use of number is the eternal presence and potential of meaning in number as yet inexpressible and unconscious to us, but which awaits only our discovery of it, or its revelation to us. Numbers as symbols perform this revelatory function.

Number Symbolism in Modern Times

Having briefly outlined some of the more traditional, mystical and cultural aspects of number symbolism, attention is now drawn to the practical and symbolic possibilities that have arisen from the study of numbers using modern quantitative methods, which include the application of number concepts as the means by which order can be put to ambiguous material.

In 1990, the decimal expansion of π reached more than a staggering one billion digits. Initially, one would question the purpose of such an expansion given (for example) Asimov's calculation that only 35 decimal places are sufficient to measure the diameter of the universe to an accuracy of one millionth of an inch. There would seem to be no useful purpose, in any practical sense, to the calculation of π's decimal expansion up to and beyond billions of places, but Theoni Pappas, in *More Joy of Mathematics* (1994), notes that one practical value of the expansion in recent years has been to test the software and hardware capabilities of the new super-computers. She also adds that new laws and concepts can spring from such calculations, and patterns that emerge in the expansion may raise questions as to the apparent randomness of the digits of such numbers.

In *A Number For Your Thoughts* (1986), Malcolm E. Lines suggests that since the expansions of irrational and transcendental numbers continue infinitely without cycling, it can be implied that any sequence of digits we nominate can be found, and infinitely often. He even suggests that these expansions could be decoded substituting, for instance, letters for digits to produce useful information. Apart from the question of which language should be used in the decoding process (though this should be irrelevant given the *infinite* source), the only other practical restriction, which may limit a fruitful outcome, is a physical one, since the lengths of these expansions may need to be incredibly long before meaningful decoded statements can be identified. However, the current level of understanding, or the way in which we interpret the information, may inhibit the discovery of new knowledge or the efficient application of this knowledge, even when it is readily available. But this problem is no different from the problems raised in any kind of frontier work—there is always the undefined which must be made meaningful.

The crucial factor of this type of analytical work (i.e., information seeking in the infinite expansion of irrational and transcendental numbers) is that its products may be meaningful. The infinite expansion of π, for example, may well become a new symbol for the *prima materia* referred to in the chapter "Zero (The Void)"—the initial chaos of material from which all things, tangible and intangible, become manifested in some ordered way:

a prime source in coded form that may yield products that are both striking and compelling.

Concerning the irrational nature of π, an interesting fact emerged in the eighteenth century, know as the Buffon Needle Problem, named after the Comte de Buffon. This 'problem' was actually used as a means of calulating π and involved the tossing of a three-inch long needle onto floorboards three inches wide. The probability that the needle will fall and land across the joining seam of any two adjacent boards is 2/π. It is possible to estimate π by tossing the needle often enough (say, in the order of a few thousand tosses) and then dividing two by the ratio obtained (where the ratio is the number of times the needle lands on a seam divided by the number of tosses). The fact that an approximation of π can be generated stochastically suggests some kind of hidden order in the universe, where so-called chance events seem more like nonrandom and meaningful events.

The Buffon Needle Problem is shown to be a means of determining π, and although there are better, more accurate ways of deriving this transcendental number, perhaps this stochastic method suggests something as yet unrecognized about π's transcendental nature. The empirical, mathematical and statistical reality of π is clear, but beyond this we might hazard a guess that π (like all symbols) has a meaning (even in an objective sense) that constitutes part of its irrational and transcendental nature. This meaning would be embedded in its phenomenological connection with matter and the way it behaves under certain conditions if we argue that random (chance-like) elements are not involved in the derivation of π using Buffon's method, but rather, we can show somehow that the derivation is a nonrandom process. Of course, to make this assertion it would be necessary to postulate a principle that unites these derivations under a single rubric, which at the same time allows us to withdraw the accusation of mere coincidence. To arrive at such a principle may well require a new attitude from investigators, as well as new perspectives on the laws of chance and statistical outcomes. This approach may require a restructuring of our rational, quantitative thinking that should surely include the welcome admission of the balancing influence of qualitative, intuitive 'thinking'.

This approach also suggests that our entire world picture may 'gel' somewhat more coherently. If this attitude serves to crystallize our resolve more adequately by instilling a certain confidence, and comes to have a motivating effect on us as well, then we are still better off, even if naïve questions are only replaced by more sophisticated questions, with few answers forthcoming. In fact, in some cases, new questions often 'work' better than answers.

Summary

Numbers exist *a priori* in the universe as necessary organizing principles of nature. We perceive order by virtue of the consistency and predictability inherent in the phenomenology of number. This further puts order to our universe, thereby contributing to our knowledge and increasing our consciousness. Number has a symbolic aspect, the symbol being the best means by which number can be represented or formulated, since its irrational dimension is unknowable and inexpressible.

All cultures give evidence of the influence of numbers in one way or another. Whether these influences result in superstitious, mystical, magical, divinatory, or scientific knowledge claims, they are meaningful in the sense that the knowledge claims generated within a culture are purported to be of use to members of that culture. In certain situations knowledge is only meaningful in accordance with the paradigm or worldview in which that knowledge was generated. In any case, the number archetype is often pivotal in the construction of those knowledge claims.

In a sense, then, numbers, with or without written symbols, are abstractions that are only relate-worthy or useful or meaningful if they are applied to some empirical practical purpose and application.

Plate 5. VICTOR WEISSKOPF

Physicist Victor Weisskopf (1908-2002) claimed: "Quantity becomes quality in the atomic world; one electron more may lead to a complete change of properties." The qualitative aspects of matter come about quantitatively through number, and our understanding is incomplete if either aspect—quantity or quality—is ignored [SOURCE: Los Alamos National Laboratory].

DEFINING NUMBER

It is very surprising that…the series of whole natural integers…which is so simple and transparent to the constructive spirit, also contains an aspect of something abysmal [irrational] which we cannot grasp.

Hermann Weyl

What is a number? If you consult the Concise Oxford Dictionary (in fact, most dictionaries) it will tell you that a number is a word or figure or symbol telling "how many." If, for example, you look up 'twenty' in the dictionary it says: "twice ten." If you look up 'ten' it says: "one more than nine." The entry for 'nine' is "one more than eight," and so on all the way down to 'two'—which is "one more than one." And 'one' is?—"half of two," of course! Most dictionaries then proceed to give examples of number usage, such as "time of *seven* o'clock" or "score of *three* points in tennis." So it is clear that the dictionary is not the book to consult for any kind of meaning of a number beyond simple examples. Furthermore, we learned how to count in pre-school so you are expected to have known all along what 'nine' or 'three' means. So, how do we define numbers?

Formally, the natural number series (the series of numbers we use in our everyday lives) is defined in two ways in mathematics—either it is the set of numbers 1, 2, 3, and so on (these are the so-called positive integers), or they are the same set of numbers 1, 2, 3, and so on, with the inclusion of 0 (i.e., zero). This latter set is known as the non-negative integers. The former is used mostly in number theory, while the latter more-sophisticated series is confined to work in set theory, mathematical logic, and computer science.

As pointed out already, we use natural numbers to count and to put order to things. We can glimpse this point in the definition of natural numbers given by mathematician Bertrand Russell—each natural number *n* is defined as the set whose members each have *n* elements, which is to say, for example, that *n* = 15 bananas makes a set that is equinumerous to (i.e., the same in number) as a set of *n* = 15 apples. By this definition, the number of counted objects (i.e., 15 in our example) indicates a powerful measure of consistency across all sets of *n* = 15, no matter what is in the set. Note here that we deal with quantity, not quality, since the mathematician in this instance is not so much interested in types of fruit so much as items that can be generically defined in a single way, as a single thing—a set of *n* elements. In that sense, Russell's definition does have practical value. *Frankly ... big deal....*

Number and Color

Aside from a practical understanding of number, we do not know what a number may mean, and at best, we have only an intuitive understanding of number which we somehow implicitly picked up along the way, sometime between early childhood and adolescence. It is much the same problem with color. We know a red apple or green grass when we see it, but the color is always the feature of an object—never a thing in itself—and we learned all about color the same way we learned about numbers—by examples.

An interesting parallel arises between number distinction and color recognition. We acknowledge the six or seven colors of the rainbow (with indigo as optional), but this is not universal. Berlin and Kay, in *Basic Color Terms* (1969), showed that all languages have color words from as few as two (shades of black and shades of white) to as many as eleven (black, white, red, green, yellow, blue, brown, purple, pink, orange and gray). It appears that the more archaic or 'primitive' (original) the culture, the fewer the color words.

Of those colors just listed, the Bible does not mention pink or orange; Homer described the ocean as wine-red (or is this poetic licence?); Aristotle referred to the rainbow as having three colors—red, green and violet—while 'yellow' was seen as a contrasting shade between red and green. Other sources claim red and orange followed by yellow-green were the only colors discriminated in ancient Greece. Whether we can ever arrive at concrete facts which might reveal how the ancients actually came to 'colorize' their world remains to be seen. More to the point is the general fact that the ability to classify or preferably, to discriminate, seems relatively recent in human evolution, particularly in the evolution of consciousness.

It appears that the idea of number, as with color recognition, lies *in potentia* in the human mind (whether pre-literate or not) but this capacity may either remain dormant or follow a certain line of development. For example, it is held among color theorists that indigo is a color discriminated by only those of a 'higher' consciousness. This may only mean that certain individuals have been constantly and deliberately exposed to the frequency of light we call indigo a sufficient number of times that they eventually *learned* to see that color. It certainly suggests a training of the mind—a mind obviously able and ready for the task. Indeed, Crossley (2007) implies this capability from his observations of various societies with only a few number words where "the range of number words rapidly increases by adoption or adaptation of the incoming vocabulary [of a society with many such words]" (p. 82).

Rational and Irrational

What we can say about color and number we can also say about anything of which we become conscious. The sensory data of that experience associates with *a priori* knowledge stored in the unconscious and is employed to whatever purpose one sees fit, largely on pragmatic grounds (that is, by inner need). And so it shall certainly remain because the experience of number, as it is with color, is largely empirical and any speculation beyond this is mostly philosophical. By philosophical I mean that although color can be explained in terms of a specific frequency of light reflected from an object to neural receptors in the retina, or a number of items can be grouped in recognizable patterns, or simply counted if too large and represented by a symbol, there is no way in which any new knowledge about color or number can be communicated as science if it cannot be tested or measured.

Some scientists actively engaged in the process of testing and measuring recognize this situation as 'business as usual', while others might ask: "Why would you want to communicate any more than the facts; What more could you say that hasn't been explained?" But such questions (not exclusive to scientists) are products of a mind-set that seeks specific goals and sees the achievement of these goals as self-fulfilling and conclusive proof of the validity and all-embracing truth of its quest. What we are slowly learning, however, is that scientific achievements are indicators of only one truth among many truths, but we use this truth (science) because it makes practical sense to do so. From this perspective the knowledge which science furnishes has become the knowledge above all knowledge.

It is also just the case that knowledge does not consist of only the rational products of science, but that the irrational (not the non-rational, but that which is *beyond* the rational) must be accepted as valid on its own terms, so that what is physically and quantitatively true in science is no more superior to that which is psychologically and qualitatively true outside science. Why this is so is demonstrated continually in the scientific world by the findings of controversial researches that, often with the greatest of resistance, eventually become incorporated into the practical affairs of those seeking answers that fail to appear in the current epistemology. Usually this resistance, or the limits of the current body of knowledge, or both, keeps the antithetical views of the rational and the irrational separate and incommensurable. Indeed Isaac Newton must have sensed this when he kept his studies in hermetic philosophy separate from his work in mathematics, physics and astronomy not just because alchemists worked in seclusion, but because his ultimate goal of finding 'one catholik matter' via a 'universal solvent' was an attempt to unite two diverse modes of thought.

Eventually, advocates of both sides ('rational' and 'irrational') must yield to the circumstances, which may require compromise from both. For example, Carl Gustav Jung recognized the value of the paradoxical and seemingly nonsensical writings of the alchemists when he discovered the connection between the unconscious psychic processes of the adept and his experiments with matter. Although tenth-century Persian physician

Avicenna scoffed at the literal-mindedness of the 'puffers' (so named from their constant use of the bellows), and many disillusioned, but subsequently enlightened alchemists closed their laboratory doors for good to pursue the finer, more spiritual points of the art, most alchemists were never aware of the 'psychic' component in their alchemical 'transmutations'. Understandably so, since the unconscious datum in the alchemist's psyche was not recognized as 'personal' (related to the ego) and was therefore often 'seen' as a vision in the laboratory flask or vessel.

Michel Gauquelin provides another example of a proto-science demystified by statistical analysis to yield information about the specific 'relatedness' of the Moon and the inner planets—Mars, Venus, Saturn and Jupiter—with the professional lives of exceptional individuals. His work continues, suggesting a certain justified credibility—what does not submit to the scientific method will always be considered philosophy or pseudo-science by skeptics.

It is clear, therefore, that the irrational can, on occasion, submit to the rational processes of scientific method, but it would seem, for the most part, that the subject of science will remain the quantifiable phenomenology (the measurable aspects) of the physical world, while the qualifiable aspects as they pertain to number (what remains when number is stripped from the physical world which it 'counts') will remain the subject of philosophical and psychological speculation. However, as stated, the two approaches are not entirely incommensurable—indeed they are shown to be compatible, even on occasion demonstrating a lively and dynamic 'relationship' in spite of their opposing positions. In *Knowledge and Wonder* (1966), physicist Victor Weisskopf observed the reciprocal nature of quantity and quality by noting the qualitative aspects of matter that come about quantitatively through number:

> all the regularities of form and structure that we see in nature…are
> based upon the symmetries of atomic patterns…. One electron added
> or removed makes so much difference in the atomic world. The
> pattern of the last electron added determines the configuration of the

atom. This in turn determines the way the atoms fit together, whether they form a crystal, a liquid, or a gas.... Quantity becomes quality in the atomic world; one electron more may lead to a complete change of properties. (p. 27)

Quantitative and Qualitative

In the twentieth century there has been an accumulating body of evidence that the psyche (or the human mind) is a factor embodied in the reality of matter (the brain and central nervous system). Thus, it is fair to draw the conclusion that the quantitative and qualitative factors of our numerically ordered systems, and the natural, phenomenal appearance of number in the world, are generated (in the case of the former) and detected (in the case of the latter) at one and the same fundamental level: the level of the 'number archetype', where the archetype, which has its roots in a material source, has an unconscious determining influence on our interpretation of the world. It must follow that the predominance of quantitative measures over qualitative factors is a bias of Western society—particularly in the last few centuries—since it is not given *a priori* in any culture that one or the other should take precedence. Unfortunately, the time in history when number was used not only to measure and count, but also to indicate the quality or pattern of that which it measured or counted has been lost—the spirit of that time, however, has remained.

In this postmodern age it is understood that we give meaning to events in the natural world; that our mythology (our world-view) shapes our history (how we see the past and imagine the future); that external reality is a social construction. Although this 'truth' is acknowledged, it only goes so far. According to this view, assigning numerical significance to phenomena, or placing events in numbered sequences, which then constitute models or systems, will be seen as either random or purely arbitrary acts (outcomes reached by the whim of social convention), or will be seen as designed and calculated operations of no qualitatively (meaningfully) numerical significance or consequence—decisions reached by the deliberation and manipulation of socio-cultural and empirical facts.

Social factors, the current level of knowledge, and the limitations of the inventor, therefore, may all underlie the construction of a system that has a certain number of stages or steps. In many cases this may be true, but certainly not in all cases—there are always exceptions. It is often the case that the assignment of a number of stages to a certain cycle or system *of a specific number, formed from an essential, enumerable fact*, could not have been done in an *ad hoc* way, since that would suggest that further stages or steps can be subtracted from, or added to that system or structure with no effect on that system or structure (apart from the obvious quantitative changes). In the same way, it would be impossible to make structural or numerical changes to many observed phenomena without extinguishing their phenomenology, even reality, altogether. Each number has its own quality that is essentially different from all others, and this quality permeates the entire system or structure. In the words of René Adolphe Schwaller de Lubicz in *A Study of Numbers* (1986): "Quality is the number, and quantity is the value which measures and fixes the quality" (p. 46).

The 'completeness' of Jung's four-function typology, or the tessellation of the regular hexagon, just two examples, are the result of devising or recognizing structures from specific phenomenal 'facts', and are ordered by the principles of number as an archetypal reality in the former case, and empirical reality in the latter. Jung could not have settled on three or five functions, given the conceptual and empirical background upon which they were based, because a four-function typology is meaningfully significant in a way that a three- or five-function typology is not. There are other typologies: some have fewer than four factors, some have more, with each serving a specific purpose, sometimes to the exclusion of any form of compatibility with any of the other typologies. Jung noted the classical significance of the number four and built this into his system for psychological reasons. Each of the four differentiated functions is mutually exclusive of one another and is not reducible to any of the other functions.

See "Creative Evolution" by A. Goswami, p. 71.

The Myers-Briggs Type Indicator (MBTI)—an adaptation of Jung's four functions and two attitudes to an eight-type system—is a modification of both Jung's original typology, and the concepts underlying it. The MBTI has Extraversion-Introversion 'reduced' to functions (not attitudes), while a new 'bipolar index' (Judging-Perceptive) is merely a refined way of restating the Thinking-Feeling and Sensation-Intuition functions, respectively. There are now four bipolar psychological indices: Extraversion-Introversion, Judging-Perceptive, Thinking-Feeling, and Sensation-Intuition. These indices can be represented as an ogdoadic structure (see the chapter "Eight (The Ogdoad)"), and the reader will discover that, symbolically, an eightfold system or schema is usually a 'higher', more refined representation derived from a fourfold system or schema. Often, however, an ogdoadic derivative, while more complex than its original tetradic form, is not necessarily more sophisticated, just because it ostensibly provides more information. Furthermore, it is also the case that the derivative can even be burdened with imperfections.

From a different perspective, the hexagon is the only regular polygon that self-tessellates, *and* has the smallest perimeter for a given area, compared to the perimeters of (say) a square or triangle of equal area. There is thus an economy in sixfold structures, as exemplified in nature (for example, the honeycomb, and the compound eye). Such a phenomenology is intrinsic and exclusive to a certain kind of ordering property associated with the number six. In these and similar cases, the point is that specific numerical *qualities* can be commensurate with the quantitative aspects of a particular system or phenomenon.

Regarding numerical constructions from a qualitative perspective, it is not so very important that one system or model might seem more dynamic than another similar system or model, or that one system or model might appear static and rigid (even limited in use) compared to another (although these comparisons *do* show quantitative and qualitative differences). Nor is it necessarily of much concern what each system or model is supposed to describe, measure or ascertain that is at the heart of a qualitative investigation of number. It is more to do with what is being meaningfully reflected in such systems or models, which, it will be shown, require considerable deliberation.

One might put it simply as 'the sum of the whole is greater than the sum of its parts', for in many cases, there are properties in these systems or models that may be described as 'emergent', but might more correctly be defined as essential or intrinsic in nature. The same is true of numerical forms in nature.

Considerable deliberation *is* necessary when reflecting upon numerical systems and models because it is clear that some systems and models do not embody deep numerical qualities in their structures. For example, one could not in good faith proclaim that there are deep philosophical or mystical (archetypal) undercurrents flowing beneath the number structure of the '*seven* steps to better relationships', or the '*five* secrets to health and happiness' (the subject matter of so many self-help books and magazines). This kind of misappropriation of number symbolism, carries a mere pretense only of a systemic process in its structure, and in itself has no scientific legitimacy. It is not even likely that the authors were inspired or influenced in any way by the number archetype (encapsulating the archetypes of number seven or number five in our examples), where the archetype has influence on cognitive processes. One can easily see that the issues of relationships, health, and happiness are not wholly susceptible to quantitative procedures. Such issues are constantly evolving, and revelation is part of that process. New ideas emerge all the time. Such systems cannot be defined and limited to any given number of 'steps' or 'secrets' by the personal insights of only one or a few researchers.

Nevertheless, there appears to be emergent properties that imbue meaning into the frameworks of many systems, models, patterns, and structures that may seem, at first, to be determined reflexively. In fact, this meaning is as much an entity as a construction, where the assertion of meaning can come as much through discovery as through invention. It is a meaning that is not solely generated (constructed) in consciousness because it is there as an *a priori* fact, waiting only to be perceived as such. I reserve a special distinction in number symbolism between meaning and interpretation: meaning, for want of a better word, can be an empirical experience that stands outside interpretation, whereas interpretation is socially constructed. The essential factor underlying 'meaning' in reality, however, is likely to be beyond the *'a very meek and humble acquiescence to a mysterious Truth.*

scope of our abilities to know. This type of meaning refers to an awareness, or intuition, or recognition of the fact of the existence of things, animate and inanimate, that is not based on the notion that these things are structurally ordered (as, for example, the orderedness of a complex organism constituted of millions of cells or molecules), but is based on a *gestalt* (i.e., wholeness) of universal order and integration. In a rather circular sense, it becomes meaningful and purposeful for one's existence to maintain that all existence is meaningful and purposeful: an existence carried by, or founded upon an unknowable reality, which is yet able to instill in consciousness a sense of continuity and coherence. In this there is meaning. That fact alone develops not from rational judgments or conscious learning alone, but is underscored more so by irrational factors beyond expression, as given by that unknowable reality. Numbers, as only one category of symbols, can be bridges to that reality. *So Numbers would be another gateway to Theology.*

As we have come to know it, quantification (counting, measuring, and so on) comes from the conscious side of life: its approach is structured, organized and functional, and moves towards the limits of consciousness, but goes no further. Qualification (meaning, relatedness, and so on) moves within, and comes from all levels of the psyche, but its approach is also structured, organized and functional in its own way, so that number as an organizing principle, carries an identity (a quality) that colors the system, and is more than a mere enumeration.

That there is more to number than meets the eye is an age-old belief and the persistence of this belief cannot be explained as childish obsession. Number fascinates and compels, and psychologically, this suggests some form of compensation for an otherwise one-sided attitude. History has shown us the results of single-minded obsessiveness where compensation was lacking. That number does fascinate and compel speaks of its symbolic qualities.

The usage of number explains the world, even in ways we cannot yet imagine. Number is axiomatic (self-evident), it is unchanging—its determinants are inherent in nature, hidden and revealed. This is the mystery of number: a limitless frontier for exploration and a challenge for the future.

A more uncommon [icon?] when an icon than the character stepping outside of the gold-leafing (heaven) and letting the figure's foot touch the world and "Come down to earth."

Notice also how God is seen as young and in the image of Christ.

Plate 6. GOD THE GEOMETER

The compass symbolises God's Act of Creation in this thirteenth-century image. The modern sciences demonstrate their dependence on number through mathematics, calculus, statistics, and so on, although many would dispute the claim that all phenomena in the universe are structured in a conscious way— that is, by the 'hand' of a Supreme Being, a Divine Arithmetizer [SOURCE: Wikimedia Commons].

Notice, too, how the world is seen as curvilinear organisms encircled by the clearly definitive sphere.

A BRIEF HISTORY OF NUMBER

Figures bear witness, better than the babel of languages,
to the underlying unity of human culture.

Georges Ifrah

The earliest forms of number systems belong to our Paleolithic ancestors (20,000-7000 BC) and began not with number *per se*, but with one-to-one correspondence. This established the principle of counting, in the sense that making notches on (say) an animal shin-bone was quite adequate as a means of recording the number of days, or weapons, or members of a tribe, and so on. The first kind of statistical procedure (the census) was born at this time, even if number theory was not. For example, the concept of different symbols representing different amounts, which could be used together to show increase or decrease, had not yet emerged. There is also indication that these bones may have been used to record cycles of the moon, since there were noted groupings of 29 or 30, and sometimes 7 or 14 marks on the bones. These first counting exercises, then, may not only have been inventories indicating possession, but may also have been rudimentary calendars, suggesting an awareness of the passing of days, and perhaps the first intuitions of cyclical rhythm and the concept of time, and the passage of time—numerical correspondences are associated with calendars, astrology and astronomy in most early cultures.

Today, ancient counting techniques still exist. Georges Ifrah in *The Universal History of Numbers* (2000) notes that as recent as the early twentieth century "various parts of Africa, Oceania, and the Americas…have numerical techniques that allow them to carry out some 'operations', at least to some extent" (p. 10). These same societies have a "fear of enumeration" and even "find numbers repellent" (p. 554). Many societies the world over are satisfied to count 'one, two, many', and in some cases combinations of number words serve to count upwards from two. For example, 'two-one' serves for three, 'two-two' serves for four, etc. This construct is even used in the English words 'eleven' and 'twelve', which come from the Anglo-Saxon words for 'one-more [than ten]' and 'two-more [than ten]', respectively, and most people can see that 'thirteen' and 'fourteen' derive from 'three-ten' and 'four-ten'.

Many thousands of years had to pass before more complex rules for counting were to be established. After counting and tallying with notches or marks came the symbolization of number, which was "better suited to the tasks of assimilating, remembering, distinguishing, and combining numbers" (Ifrah, 2000, p. 23). According to Ifrah, mental processes allowed "operations on things to be replaced by the corresponding operation on number-symbols" (p. 23). From concrete numeration (one-to-one correspondence with pebbles or notches on bone or wood, etc.), to oral numeration ('Sun' = one, 'eyes' = two, and so on), to written numeration (i.e., symbols), the ancients reached the stage where multiples of notches could be replaced with unique pictograms or glyphs. Ancient Egypt, China, Greece and Sumeria, as well as the Amerindians of South America (Maya, Aztecs) amongst others, all used signs or symbols (letters or pictograms or glyphs) to represent numbers of things.

The Origins of Number—East and West

Usually the abstraction of numbers as symbols had connotations beyond the concrete forms of numerals, which merely denoted quantities. This is evident in the ancient Greek art of arithmetic which was a spiritual exercise kept away from the slaves, yet which still used the same symbols (ultimately the Greek alphabet) for numeration (counting). The intricate detail of the head-variants of Aztec numbers carved in stone on temple walls also indicates that numbers, by their figurations as gods, were considered much more sacred than numerals, which were only for counting.

This differentiation of sacred and profane indicates an important distinction between numbers as archetypes expressed in the abstract by symbols, and numbers as numerals expressed concretely as quantities, or signs of quantities. The archetypal basis of number, by dint of its ineffable nature, still poses a problem today because the number archetype cannot be quantified and only ever constitutes a transcendent (enigmatic and god-like) aspect, which, as in these ancient cultures, was deemed sacred: the preserve of the elite. (This issue is taken up in later chapters.)

The Greek alphabet of twenty-four letters and three archaic letters were each assigned numerical values, which became known as the Ionic or Alexandrian system, and this system was used in Europe up until the tenth century before it was replaced by Roman numerals (which were primarily alphabetical). Only in the twelfth century were the Hindu-Arabic numerals adopted in Europe. The contributions from the Hindu world (trigonometry, algebra, the decimal system using number-symbols, the symbol for zero, and a place system—units, tens, thousands, etc.), and the Arabic world (Al-Khwarizmi's algebra, quadratic equations and algorithms—a routine for solving a particular problem—and Omar Khayyam's even more sophisticated algebra) attest to the important contributions to mathematics from this part of the world and cannot go unmentioned. The Western tradition, however, also depended largely on ancient Greece because of the influences on Christian doctrine of the philosophies of Socrates, Plato, Aristotle and others. Christian philosophy, essentially becoming a hybrid of Greek philosophy and Hebrew monotheistic texts, dominated European culture right up to the current era, and with this domination the Greek tradition (classical science, philosophy, mythology, literature, etc.) was maintained as well. It is on account of these historical antecedents that the first formal approach to number theory in the western world is usually attributed to the ancient Greeks. In particular, the Pythagoreans in the sixth century BC held principles that elevated numbers to the realm of 'Real Existence'. As W. Wynn Westcott writes in *Numbers: Their Occult Power and Mystic Virtues* (1974):

as numbers are the primary constituents of Mathematical Quantities, and at the same time present many analogies to various realities, it was...inferred [by the Pythagoreans] that the elements of Numbers were the elements of Realities. (p. 14)

The Pythagoreans believed that nature was built according to mathematical principles. This was self-evident, given the harmonic order observed in music, which, by analogy, was used to describe the cosmos—'the music of the spheres'. The Pythagoreans were more concerned with the symbolic and qualitative aspects of number as opposed to the quantitative aspects. Accordingly, numbers were seen as 'corresponding' with moral and ethical qualities, as well as any other kind of abstract concept, idea or notion that lent itself to association with a particular number. For example, Westcott gives some of the Pythagorean associations made with the number one— "Confusion," "Commixion," and "Obscurity" (p. 33), and so on, while the number two was called "Fountain of Symphony," "Patience," and "Intelligible Intellect" (p. 36).

Aristotle considered these 'appropriations' strange and incoherent. In his *Metaphysics* he criticized the Pythagoreans most vehemently, their abstract approach seemingly too arbitrary for his pragmatic disposition. However, many of the contributions made by the Pythagoreans have been of inestimable worth to mathematics. Pythagoras himself is most famous for his theorem, where the square on the hypotenuse of a right-angled triangle is equal to the sum of the squares on the other two sides, or $c^2 = a^2 + b^2$, where *a* and *b* are the two shorter sides, and *c* is the hypotenuse—the longest side (*see* fig. 2). The theorem was used as a means of calculating the length of one side of a right-angled triangle (without measurement) if the other two lengths were known. Interestingly, this procedure was known in China (used in land surveying) and Ancient Egypt (for pyramid-building) hundreds of years before Pythagoras' time.

The Pythagoreans constructed numbers using *gnomons* (indicators) to show symmetry and pattern. *Gnomons* were thus indicative of the order and uniformity of the universe. Numbers as units were represented geometrically, and each additional *gnomon* increased the size, that is, area of the shape, but did not alter its proportions. The following are just some of the Pythagorean numbers.

Figure 2. *The Pythagorean Theorem:* $a^2 + b^2 = c^2$

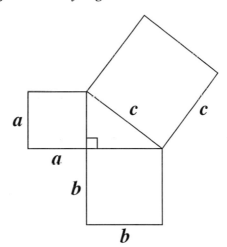

Triangular Numbers

Triangular numbers of the series 1, 3, 6, 10, 15,…, are given by the formula: $N_T = n(n + 1)/2$, (where N_T is the triangular number and n is any integer greater than, or equal to 1). Triangular numbers are produced by the successive addition of numbers (as units) in a line where each new line is formed from the next natural number in series, thus forming a triangle. That is, 1st line: one unit; 2nd line: two units; 3rd line: three units; etc. (*see* fig. 3).

Square Numbers

Each *gnomon* is comprised of successive odd numbers (as units in an L-shaped annexe) of the series 1, 3, 5, 7,…(*see* fig. 4).

Figure 3. *The first five triangular numbers, including the* Tetractys *(1 to 10).*

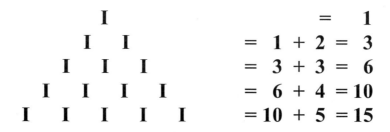

Figure 4. *The square numbers, 1, 4, 9, 16.*

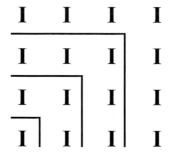

A square is formed and the resulting series, by addition of successive *gnomons*, is 1, 4, 9, 16, etc., which are the squares of the natural numbers (n^2) in series: 1^2, 2^2, 3^2, 4^2, etc.

Rectangular (Oblong) Numbers

Each *gnomon* is comprised of successive even numbers (as units in an L-shaped annexe) of the series 2, 4, 6, 8,...(*see* fig. 5). The series resulting by the addition of successive *gnomons* is 2, 6, 12, 20, etc. Taking the triangular numbers and doubling each term yields the same series.

Figure 5. *The rectangular numbers, 2, 6, 12, 20.*

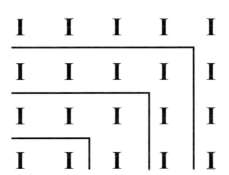

The concept of numbers deriving from polygons can be expanded to accommodate other polygons. For example, pentagonal numbers (1, 5, 12, 22, etc.), hexagonal numbers (1, 6, 15, 28, etc.), and so forth, can also be constructed.

Pythagoras also divided numbers into odd and even:

Odd Numbers

Odd numbers can only be divided into unequal parts (not halved) with one part odd and the other part even. There are three types of odd numbers:

1. *First and incomposite:* these are the *Prime Numbers*. Prime numbers have no divisors. That is, no other numbers will divide into them and leave whole numbers except themselves and unity (one). For example, 2, 3, 5, 7, 11, 13, etc. Two is the only even prime number. All prime numbers are incomposite—they are not composed of other numbers. Every whole number can be factored into prime numbers in one way. For example: 715 = 5 × 11 × 13. An even number (disregarding 2) is always the sum of two prime numbers. For example: 4 = 2 + 2; 6 = 3 + 3; 8 = 5 + 3; 10 = 7 + 3, etc. This is known as Goldbach's conjecture, but has never been proved.

2. *Second and composite:* These are composed from other numbers. For example: 9, 15, 21, 25, 27, 33, etc. As well as being divisible by unity and themselves, they are divisible by other odd numbers. By having another 'foreign' divisor they are called second, and are composite because they are composed of other numbers.

3. *Second and composite Prime:* This third type of odd number is second and composite, but is also prime (first and incomposite) with reference to another number. For example: 9 and 25; 3 divides 9, but does not divide 25. There is no common measure.

Even Numbers

Even numbers can be divided into equal parts (two halves), or two unequal but even parts, or two unequal but odd parts. For example: 10 = 5 + 5, or 6 + 4, or 7 + 3, respectively.

Evenly Even Numbers

Evenly even numbers are even numbers that divide into two equal and even parts, where each part again divides evenly and this will continue to unity. They form the series [1, 2,] 4, 8, 16, 32, etc., where each new term is double the previous term.

Evenly Odd Numbers

Evenly odd numbers divide into two odd parts and therefore cannot be halved continuously to unity. For example: 18 divides into two equal but odd parts, that is, 9. Any odd number will form an evenly odd number if doubled.

Unevenly Even Numbers

Unevenly even numbers will divide into two equal parts and these parts can be divided equally but the process ceases before unity is reached because eventually the division yields two odd numbers. For example: 28 halves to 14, which halves to 7.

Unevenly Odd Numbers

Unevenly odd numbers result as the product of two odd numbers. For example: $3 \times 3 = 9$; $3 \times 5 = 15$.

The Pythagoreans sub-divided even numbers into three other groups—Perfect numbers, Deficient numbers and Superabundant numbers.

Perfect Numbers

Perfect numbers are equal to the sum of the parts produced upon all possible divisions of that number. That is, perfect numbers generate themselves from their divisors. The number six has three divisors—one, two and three—so that $1 + 2 + 3 = 6$ (the first perfect number). The number 28 is the next perfect number: one half is 14, one quarter is 7, one seventh is 4, one fourteenth is 2 and one twenty-eighth is 1. Thus: $14 + 7 + 4 + 2 + 1 = 28$.

Perfect numbers are very few: between 1 and 10 only 6 is perfect, between 100 and 1000 only 496 is perfect, and between 1000 and 10,000 only 8128 is perfect. These perfect numbers were considered by the Pythagoreans to be akin to virtues because they were so few in number. The next in sequence—33,550,336—was only discovered in the fifteenth century. They are indeed as rare as the early Greeks suspected.

Deficient Numbers and Superabundant Numbers

Two numbers of a 'theriomorphic' (animal-form) type—Deficient numbers and Superabundant numbers—were seen by the Pythagoreans to have rather special qualities. The sums of the parts are less than the whole for deficient numbers. For example, the number 14: one half is 7, one seventh is 2, and one fourteenth is 1. Thus: $7 + 2 + 1 = 10$, which is less than 14. As opposed to the virtue of perfect numbers, deficient numbers were looked upon as monstrous because they had a lack of parts. The number 14 was deficient like *Cyclops*, having only one eye. Primes, therefore, are the most deficient having the least number of divisors of any other type of number. The sum of the parts is more than the whole for superabundant numbers. For example, the number 12: one half is 6, one third is 4, one quarter is 3, one sixth is 2, and one twelfth is 1. Thus: 6 + 4 + 3 + 2 + 1 = 16, which is more than 12. The number 12 was super-abundant like *Briareus* the hundred-handed giant, or *Argus* the hundred-eyed giant.

Hermaphroditic Numbers

Hermaphroditic numbers were formed by multiplying an odd with an even number—multiplication being considered the mathematical equivalent of sexual union. For example: 3 × 2 = 6. Odd numbers, being male, would couple with even numbers, being female, and would always produce an even number. Any even number is, therefore, hermaphroditic, since it can be the product of an odd and even number. Couplings were not excluded to the union of even and odd. Numbers which were 'alike' could also be 'multiplied' together—two odd numbers always yielded odd, two even numbers always yielded even. Since the ancient Greeks saw the number six as hermaphroditic they can be said to have taken six in its dualistic form only. In this regard, six merely refers to ambivalence and equilibrium.

Rational Numbers

All the above numbers are the major Pythagorean numbers. The following is a brief description of the major number types, from the time of Pythagoras to the present era. Pythagorean numbers are natural numbers, but by including fractions (one integer divided by another, i.e., *a/b*) the wider class of rational numbers was born. The Egyptians were already using fractions in Pythagoras' time since their arithmetic was based on dimidiation (halving). The complete 'Eye of Horus'—the *Oudja* ('whole', 'healthy') eye—represented the unit, the *hekat*, for measuring the volume of liquids, grains and fruit, while the different individual parts of the glyph indicated 'Horus-eye' fractions. The system became very complicated when it came to the addition of fractions, since numerators greater than one were not used (with exception of the frequently used 2/3 and 3/4). Detailed tables were consulted for solutions, so that, for example: 1/7 + 1/7 was dealt with as 1/4 + 1/28, instead of 2/7.

Euclid, in the third century BC, introduced the concept of 'one number measuring another', which essentially meant fractions, while before this time, the Pythagorean approach involved reducing a base unit to integral multiples. At the same time another problem surfaced which became a great challenge for Greek mathematicians and this was the discovery of irrational numbers.

Irrational Numbers

An irrational number cannot be expressed as a fraction—a ratio of two whole numbers in the form a/b. The square root of 2 (approximately 1.4142), the first discovered, is one such example, and it is this irrational number that caused the Pythagoreans a great deal of trouble. This was because rational numbers in the Pythagorean doctrine were the basis upon which all things were defined. The problem with $\sqrt{2}$ (and all irrational numbers in general) was that these numbers undermined this philosophy: existence could not be defined if the terms were undefined, and irrational numbers certainly defied all reason. In fact, the Greeks thought of irrational numbers as insane. By Pythagoras' Theorem a unit square has a diagonal of $\sqrt{2}$ units that could not be expressed in mathematically finite terms (*see* fig. 6).

However, $\sqrt{2}$, or any other irrational number, did not cause problems in the real world. For example, the Indians handled irrational numbers without difficulty. They used $\sqrt{2}$ and $\sqrt{3}$ in religious practices. The Egyptians, a very pragmatic civilization, used the *cubit* and the *remen*. The unit square (1 cubit × 1 cubit) cut a diagonal of two *remen*—there was no need for $\sqrt{2}$ (*see* fig. 7). Calculating area was simplified by the general fact that 2 *remen* equaled $\sqrt{2}$ *cubits*, or put more simply, two square *remen* equaled one square *cubit*.

Figure 6. *'Constructing' √2 from the unit triangle.*

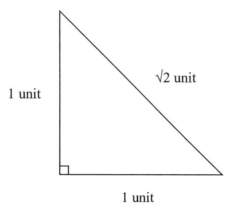

Figure 7. *The diagonal of one square cubit equals 2 remen,
so that 4 remen² = 2 cubits².*

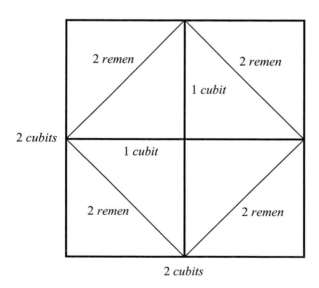

At first the Greeks could not get around the 'problem' of √2: it was incommensurable with unity, which meant that a common measure of all magnitudes was not possible. Ultimately they simply did not identify √2, or any irrational square root, with a number. Since Pythagoreans represented numbers by geometrical forms they saw no need to deal with lengths. If it was necessary to measure a line, a known length could be sub-divided, which eliminated the problem of irrationals, and fractions as well. In general terms, number and magnitude were regarded as separate issues and it remained that way even until Euclid's time, almost three centuries after Pythagoras.

Many irrational numbers were known to the ancient world, but the general rule is that the square roots of all prime numbers (√3, √5, √7, etc.) and square roots of most composite numbers (√6, √8, √10, etc.) are irrational. Any multiple or fraction of these numbers are also irrational. Irrational numbers are not confined to square roots. For example, the cube root of 5, expressed mathematically as ^{3}√5, is irrational. Irrational numbers can be fourth roots and fifth roots and so on. In fact, there are an infinite number of irrational numbers and all are represented by special symbols, since there is no easier way of expressing them. Such is the case with three special irrational numbers, Ø (*phi*), π (*pi*) and *e*.

The golden ratio, Ø (*phi*), can be constructed geometrically from the length to width ratio of a 'golden' rectangle whose sides are '*x*' and '*x* – 1'. The ratio Ø = (1/2+√5/2) is derived (approximately 1.6180) and it was known to the ancient Greeks who used it in architecture. It was also used in Renaissance times, and in the twentieth century by artist Piet Mondrian as a guide for the careful placement of his colorful quadrilinear forms. Architect Le Corbusier also used it as the template for his 'Modulor' man in his built environment— 'well-proportioned' according to the golden mean. Using this ratio, a logarithmic equation can be derived, which will generate a spiral pattern resembling many spiral forms in nature (phyllotaxis), as in the leaves and flowers of certain plants, and in the shell patterns of snails and various shell-fish.

A simple arithmetic method can also be employed to derive an approximation of Ø. Leonard Fibonacci of Pisa (who introduced Arabic numerals to the West) referred to a series of numbers in his book *Liber Abaci* in 1202, which the mathematician Edouard Lucas, in the nineteenth century, called Fibonacci numbers. The Fibonacci series is first constructed by adding two consecutive terms together (starting from zero plus one) to produce the next term in the series. The following series results:

$$0, \ 1, \ 1, \ 2, \ 3, \ 5, \ 8, \ 13, \ 21, \ 34, \ 55, \ 89,...$$

By taking two consecutive terms (the larger the better) and dividing the larger by the smaller, a close approximation of Ø results (approximately 1.6180). This series is shown to have 'representations' in nature long before Fibonacci derived it. The spiral patterns of shellfish and plant-life have been mentioned as having logarithmic parallels, but these spiral forms are also quantifiable using Fibonacci numbers. For example, pine-cones have two sets of spirals: five in a clockwise direction, eight in an anticlockwise direction; pineapples have eight clockwise and thirteen anticlockwise spirals; the center of the daisy flower has tiny florets also running in two sets of spirals, twenty-one clockwise and thirty-four anticlockwise. These examples feature five numbers which make up a sub-set of the Fibonacci series (..., 5, 8, 13, 21, 34,...). From these examples, it can be seen that nature has used adjacent pairs of Fibonacci numbers in its constructions. As Graham Flegg states in *Numbers: Their History and Meaning* (1983):

> No one who is truly versed in the art of numbers and the structures which can be built from them can fail to be aware that they have a particular kind of beauty which is all their own.... Numbers reveal the unity which underlies all of life as we experience it. (p. 5)

Since many spiral forms exist in nature (two-dimensional types— logarithmic and Archimedian, and three-dimensional types—conchoid and helical), it would not be surprising that a number of different ways of generating these spirals should be possible using mathematical principles, and it is reasonable to assume that whether nature uses mathematics or not, there may well be more than one mechanism behind the generation of spiral forms in nature. Darwin's theory of evolution has shown that many forms (species) have evolved similar features (convergence) even though their lines of descent were not the same. For example, organs for 'vision' (perception of light), such as eyes, have evolved in many dozens of unrelated species.

The mathematical sciences have greatly benefited from the Fibonacci series, as have the fields of biology, chemistry and electrical engineering. So much so, that an international organization, the Fibonacci Association, was formed in 1963 and has been publishing *The Fibonacci Quarterly* ever since.

Although Ø (as the golden ratio) is irrational, the approximations of Ø, derived using any two terms from the Fibonacci series, are rational. For example, the 11th term divided by the 10th term (89 ÷ 55) yields 1.61818 recurring. This is a cycling decimal, but irrational numbers do not cycle—the decimal forms of irrational numbers continue forever.

Although the two ways of deriving Ø are acknowledged by numerologists, it is often overlooked that Ø can be rational or irrational according to the derivation. John King, in *The Modern Numerology* (1996), makes the mistake of claiming that it is possible to derive the 'Divine Proportion' as an *irrational* number using the Fibonacci series. He is correct in stating that irrational numbers, when written in decimal notation, are infinite in length, but *if they cycle* they are *not* irrational. To avoid confusion, a new symbol should be used to replace the rationally derived approximation of Ø, but no mathematician has yet come forward with an alternative. (The general notion of an irrational quality inherent in the natural numbers—that is, rational numbers—was introduced in the chapter "The Philosophy of Number").

For the purposes of accuracy in the world of matter the application of Ø, as either a rational or irrational derivation, is inconsequential because increasingly accurate approximations of Ø become impossible to measure due to either the imperfections of all measuring devices, or simply, the lack of accuracy of these instruments. For example, Isaac Asimov has noted that the transcendental number π, to an accuracy of 35 decimal places, will suffice in measuring the expanse of the known universe to an accuracy of one millionth of an inch!

Both the geometric method (yielding Ø as an irrational number) and the arithmetic method (yielding Ø as a rational approximation derived from the Fibonacci series) suggest an inter-connectedness with nature and human rational 'inventiveness', the latter of which is ordinarily viewed as being separate from nature. That is, it is possible to look elsewhere, outside those number concepts which appear to be consciously and deliberately constructed, and discover that numerical entities, which are the same or similar to these concepts, can be generated in seemingly unrelated ways (recall Comte de Buffon's Needle Problem on page 46, as a means of deriving π using a stochastic—that is, probabilistic—method.)

From Pythagoras to the Renaissance

Pythagoras' philosophy was so popular, even in his own time that a large community of followers flourished. After his death this community split into two groups: the *mathematikoi* ('those interested in science') moved to Tarentum after a revolution on the 'Italian' peninsula (now modern Italy), and the other group, the *akousmatikoi* ('those who hear') took on the role of traveling mystics. Thereby, the interest in number, which Pythagoras started, continued in one form or another down through the ages.

Amongst the first to be influenced by Pythagorean thought were the Hebrew scholars, who entertained purely allegorical ideas about number. Christopher Butler, in *Number Symbolism* (1970), argues that the Alexandrian Jew Philo Judaeus (c. 30 BC-50 AD) "attempted a reconciliation between Hellenistic and Jewish thought" (p. 22). For instance, Philo considered the inherent properties of perfection in the number six (already recognized by Pythagoras) logically and naturally aligned with the six days of Creation in *Genesis*. The Creation was a 'Perfect' act of God *because* it took *six* days to complete.

For believers, this form of symbolic analogy supposedly gave "evidence for the miraculous interconnectedness of things" (Butler, 1970, p. 23). But Butler believes Philo was more intent upon raising Hebrew 'mythology' to the level of "Greek theology, science and ethics" (p. 24), so that a newfound and well-deserved respectability might be appropriated for the Hebrew texts. The Kabbalists were to pursue this line of numerological thinking even further (see the chapter "*The Symbolism of Number*").

What Philo did for the Old Testament, St. Augustine endeavored to do for the New Testament. Numerical significances in the Old Testament were frequently associated with New Testament events, including any number of parallels with Christ and the Church. St. Augustine even went so far as to say that the Church was pre-figured in all these "true histories and mystical allegories" (p. 27). Noah's Ark, for example, is isomorphic with the city of God (the Church), and it bears the same dimensions of 'Man' (and the 'Son of Man' = Christ), whose measures (length, width, height) are proportional to those of the Ark (300: 50: 30).

Most of the 'exegetes' during the many centuries after St. Augustine through to medieval times (fifth to fifteenth centuries) and even during the Renaissance, continued conceptualizing God the Creator as the Divine Arithmetician, relying on Biblical sources for their ideas. However, Martinius Capella (fifth century) demonstrated a more 'classical' approach, reviving and expanding the Pythagorean and Platonic philosophies. Capella identified the numerological significances of Greek and Roman gods, and more generally, aimed to unify the cosmos into a system, which was demonstrably and numerically ordered, as the Pythagoreans had also attempted.

Many centuries later, the Renaissance thinker Pietro Bongo (sixteenth century), like Capella, maintained a similar metaphysical approach to the creation. The Renaissance libraries had accumulated such a large number of works on numerological themes that Bongo was able to write his great work on number symbolism, the *Numerorum Mysteria* of 1618, with impressive scholarship. He stressed the importance of numerology in understanding number in a symbolic way, and gave reasons, for example, why there were only four elements, and only seven planets, and so on. He explained the nature of the Decalogue (ten commandments), and the Trinity, and pointed out the significance of triadic forms in nature. Bongo even gave a detailed inventory of 'good' and 'bad' numbers.

For those of a classical and/or religious disposition, then, number was applicable to human experience in a direct way. One only had to look hard enough to see its influence, and if one applied oneself even more so, as these scholars had done, endless litanies of numerological correspondences could continually be discovered by observation, with one correspondence being just as valid as any other.

It appears that the works of the exegetes like Capella and Bongo show a "tendency to allegorize in search of understanding" (p. 44), writes Butler. As Butler also states:

> This tendency carries with it great benefits in any attempt to unify disparate spheres of knowledge. But its attendant danger is that the bonds of unification will prove to be nothing but metaphor, and one may be left with a mere structure of words. (p. 44)

It is clear to the modern mind what Butler is implying in these and other statements. The exegetical approach of the Church Fathers, and theologians cum philosophers in the tradition of Pythagoras and Plato, and the metaphysical/mystical approach of polymaths, astrologers and occultists of all times, proclaimed in their texts the over-riding notion that the 'Divine Arithmetizer' had put structure and order to the Universe—specifically the universe of things—through number. Number was a means of unifying the disparate 'spheres of knowledge'. And there may be a partial truth to this proclamation, whether or not such a belief results in a 'mere structure of words.' All the modern sciences demonstrate their dependence on number through mathematics, calculus, statistics, and so on, although many would dispute the claim that all phenomena in the universe are structured in a conscious way—that is, by the 'hand' of a Supreme Being, a 'Divine Arithmetizer'. Pre-scientific scholars simply 'imposed' an ordering system of constructed categories or 'classifying devices' that depended on analogical and metaphorical thinking. Certain correspondences needed to be found to validate this process. It is as if the whole centuries-long enterprise of numerology had been nothing more than an accumulative exercise of the imagination, although one is not using the word 'imagination' in a pejorative sense—as a source of much knowledge (even scientific knowledge), imagination is highly regarded by those who have benefited from this faculty.

From a rational, scientific standpoint Butler's caveat makes sense. The ability to construct associations is a typically human characteristic, and one which very often demonstrates a high order of discrimination and valid application in its functioning (although its line of reasoning and applicability may be obscure or inappropriate, as Butler implies). Yet it would be inappropriate to assume that all number associations, because they are the result of pure imagination, have no validity just because there are no rational bases to them at all. Butler offers the possibility that numerological thinking could possibly produce legitimate hypotheses on par with those proposed in mainstream science. 'Actual observation' would enable confirmation or otherwise of the alleged numerological and numerical structures and substructures that make up the universe. It is, therefore, important to maintain a critical, qualitative approach regarding these and other observations and investigations of number symbolism. The quantitative approach is firmly in the hands of the scientists, but a marginalization or a careless dismissal of all those 'classifying devices', and their analogies and metaphors, may have serious consequences for the sciences and society. From an aesthetic point of view, for example, a purely rational approach usually undermines the meaningfulness inherent in number. As was discussed in the chapter "The Archetype of Number", the various pantheons of gods in all cultures are anthropomorphized archetypes of the collective unconscious. Since the number archetype inheres the psyche with ordering properties, it can be seen how, in previous examples, the number seven might come to be associated with Minerva, or the number eight might come to be associated with Cybele (these examples were also discussed in the chapter "The Archetype of Number").

This way of classifying number is most important in that it recognizes the transcendent dimension of number, without which only the current understanding of number as a consciously usable, unidimensional tool of everyday life would predominate, as it has in the modern world. Such a limitation is a loss to the culture, in the form of a suppressed mythopoeic imagination, and reduced contact with the deeper structures of the psyche.

Without this contact we lose touch with ourselves, and therefore cannot hope to understand human nature, and the motives of others at all. Most importantly, an aesthetic approach to number, which focuses on the qualities of numbers, relativizes our intellectual dogmatism. It does this by giving due recognition to the structure of the psyche as comprised of proclivities which push consciousness forward. Brought up to speed by the particular cultural parameters of a given *Zeitgeist*, ancient principles are transformed into relevant, but diverse forms of knowledge claims instead of so-called universally valid theories, which tend to marginalize subaltern groups and their knowledge claims.

This kind of marginalization has always been with us. The seventeenth-century alchemist Robert Fludd, for example, felt this same social pressure during the Renaissance. While Fludd investigated numbers using a mystical and introspective approach, his rival Johannes Kepler used a methodical and scientific approach, which was, nonetheless, steeped in classical Greek number mysticism. Both attempted to explain the mathematical order of the universe, and their correspondence attests to their different natures and ways of seeing the world. While Kepler was developing his Laws for the physics of planetary orbits, Fludd still had difficulty with the concept of a rotating Earth, and even repudiated the idea (a spinning world would generate vast winds of devastating effect!). Fludd focused on the central issue of the individual's realization of God in 'Man' through transmutation of the soul. However, both agreed on a number of Plato's basic tenets. They believed in mathematical ideals, the 'truth' in numbers, and the power of both to uplift the human soul. Fludd's introspective orientation consolidated a growing interest in the dynamics of the psyche and its images, thus leading to the foundation of certain schools of modern day psychology and psychiatry centuries later. Kepler's keen observations of the world enabled him to reach a critical understanding of his theories, and this approach thus became the cornerstone of the modern scientific method.

By the end of the Renaissance and the accompanying birth of the modern era, scientific principles, as we have come to know them, were well established, and with them the search for and discovery (invention?) of new types of numbers. Accordingly, even more intellectually challenging numbers followed in the coming centuries: negative numbers, transcendental numbers, complex numbers, and so on.

Negative Numbers

Negative numbers were used in ancient China (100 BC) to calculate area, and reference is made to negative numbers in third-century Greece. In sixteenth-century India, negative numbers already had restricted usage, but with the official introduction of negative numbers into Europe in the same century, the rational number system was expanded even further and the set of real numbers was established (which includes the irrational numbers). Negative numbers became necessary so as to make subtraction a possibility under all circumstances, although at the time the idea of such numbers was not accepted at first. Even in the twentieth century, mathematician Leopold Kronecker disregarded such unqualifiable concepts as negative numbers. He offered a solution to negative numbers, but it was too complex and failed to win acceptance.

Transcendental Numbers

All the above-mentioned Pythagorean numbers are algebraic numbers. That is, they can be expressed as solutions in an algebraic equation. For example, 3 − x = 0 and $x^2 + 3x + 2 = 0$ are algebraic equations. Transcendental numbers, however, are a class of numbers that cannot be expressed as solutions to algebraic equations. The numbers $\sqrt{2}$ and $\emptyset$ are, therefore, irrational only, but not transcendental. That is, $\sqrt{2}$ is derivable from the equation $x^2 − 2 = 0$, while $\emptyset$ is found as x in the equation $x^2 − x − 1 = 0$.

French mathematician Jacques Liouville first proved the existence of transcendental numbers in 1844, and they are in fact infinitely more numerous than algebraic numbers. A number a^b is always transcendental where 'a' is any algebraic number (excluding 0 or 1) and 'b' is any irrational algebraic number. The Russian mathematician Aleksandr Gelfond proved this in 1934.

The irrational number π (*pi*) (approximately 3.1416) is the ratio of a circle's circumference to its diameter. It was only referred to as π since the eighteenth century (named as such by the Swiss mathematician Leonhard Euler), but was used in architecture, geometry and geography by the Chinese (355/113, correct to 6 decimal places!), the ancient Greeks (22/7), the Babylonians (25/8), the ancient Egyptians ($4[8/9]^2 = 256/81$), the Indians ($\sqrt{10}$) and even by the Old Testament Hebrews (3)—these are listed from most accurate to the least accurate approximations of π.

Pi (π) dates back to the time of Apollonius in 225 BC, who made the first detailed calculation of the number, and today π is the most commonly used irrational and transcendental number in mathematics. It is employed in geometry (formulae for calculating all dimensions of circles, tubes, cones and spheres), astronomy (orbital dimensions), electronics, and the laws of electro-magnetism. It was not proved to be irrational until 1761 by the Swiss mathematician Johann Lambert, and it was a century later in 1882, that it was further proved to be transcendental by German mathematician Ferdinand Lindemann.

Kronecker denied the existence of π. He discounted any such proof of transcendence and argued that irrational numbers did not exist. He considered it nonsense to talk of, and reason with, mathematical things that could not be constructed by definite means. There may well be no means of 'constructing' these 'mathematical things' by reason and for the sake of reason. An answer may lie in the very names of these numbers—they are *irrational* and/or *transcendental*—they defy rationality and/or immanence. They exist as paradoxes because they cannot be the subject of unequivocal statements—they have only mathematical 'reality'. As much as it is possible to apply these numbers in their approximate, but adequate form, they 'exist' finitely, but always maintain a 'reality' which conforms to the 'rules of the infinite'—such is the abstract and irrational nature of all symbols.

The irrational number *e* is also transcendental, and after π is the next most commonly used irrational number in mathematics. It was introduced in the eighteenth century by Euler and is approximately equal to 2.7183. Charles Hermite proved its transcendence in 1873. The importance of *e* is seen in its role in the world of finance (compound interest calculations, etc.), trigonometry, geometry, and other areas of mathematics including calculus.

Complex Numbers

Like the negative numbers, the complex numbers were also difficult to accept at first. These numbers were introduced in the eighteenth and nineteenth centuries, making it possible to form powers and roots involving negative numbers (previously impossible in the linear system of real numbers). This involved the introduction of planar (two dimensional) numbers—otherwise known as imaginary numbers. There was now a solution to problems of the form $x^2 + 2 = 0$ or $e^x = -1$. An imaginary number, i (which equals $\sqrt{-1}$) is combined with a 'real' part to form a complex number. For example, $(1 + i)$ and $(\sqrt{2} + i)$ are both complex numbers. Complex numbers have proved to be important in the fields of physics (hydrodynamics), astrophysics (space-time calculations), electronics (electric currents), and aerodynamics (the shape of airfoils).

Quaternions

In 1843, William Hamilton invented quaternions in the search for three-dimensional numbers, after the two-dimensional complex numbers were introduced. His hope was to find more exotic numbers that obeyed the same rules of arithmetic as did ordinary real and complex numbers. It is now known mathematically that no such numbers exist. Quaternions are four-dimensional, and in fact, three-dimensional numbers *cannot* exist.

Like many of the above-mentioned numbers, quaternions were met with suspicion. Quaternions take the general form, $q = a + xi + yi + zk$ (a is the 'scalar' or constant, and $xi + yi + zk$ is a vector, where x, y and z are real numbers). Quaternions have four descriptive characteristics—x, y and z (which are axes values of three-dimensional space), and the scalar a, which does not describe a dimension. In the recent past, they were used in computer technology for describing rotations, but today more useful mathematical tools have displaced them. Afer quaternions, came a panoply of complex numbers, including octonions, sedenions, biquaternions, coquaternions, tessarines, and hypercomplex numbers. These numbers will not be described here as it should be clear to the reader by now how readily does human inventiveness lend itself to the construction of increasingly more intricate numbers. However, the key point, worth keeping in mind, is that these numbers are bound by the quantitative and qualitative rules of the number archetype.

Summary

The emergence of new types of numbers, and the continued stream of innovations and applications of number, especially in the last few centuries, coupled with the remarkable insights and consequences that have occurred in many cultures due to number, demonstrate the versatility of the human mind in dealing conceptually with the realities of the enumerative material world. All these developments not only involved an ordered and methodical approach, but also required an imaginative and speculative dimension of mind, so that both natural and supernatural worlds might be described, or brought into association with conscious knowledge. However, concomitant with all that is known and understood about number, rationally and mythologically, are those perhaps more disturbing, but equally challenging factors—infinite decimal expansions, transcendence, irrationality, multi-dimensionality and infinity—all of which plainly indicate that there are no limits to number. In fact, all these anomalies are aspects of the infinite, which also *represent* the frontier of the infinite: the real beginning of the history of number.

Plate 7. INFINITY

I Zwicky 18 (lower left) is a recently formed galaxy that may still be producing its first generation of stars. The <u>observable</u> universe is comprised of an estimated one hundred billion galaxies! The size of the universe may extend to trillions of light years across, or it may even be of infinite expanse. No other image best illustrates the concept of infinity than that of the vast, limitless deeps of outer space [SOURCE: National Aeronautics and Space Administration, USA].

Well, if we're alone, I'd like to know why all the rest of this is out there!

INFINITY

If there be an infinity, then it is one, and cannot change.

P. D. Ouspensky

As far back as fourth-century Greece, Aristotle (384-322 BC) considered two kinds of infinity: the *potential* and the *actual*. Potential infinity referred to 'unending process' or infinite repetition. For example, counting the natural numbers is a process that can continue indefinitely (infinitely). Though potentially possible, such processes would involve a finite number of repetitions, given that an infinite act is humanly impossible, so that infinite counting could never be realized in reality. Actual (complete) infinity is the continuation of a process interminably. Outside human experience there may be infinities, though demonstrating or showing an example of such in the real world (in nature) or the universe would be impossible.

Zeno's Paradox

The philosopher Zeno (342-270 BC) dealt with the problem of infinity by postulating the existence of conceptual *entia* such as the point, which had position, but no magnitude (i.e., it had location without extension). The point could not be increased by addition, or decreased by subtraction, and therefore did not exist in actuality. Contrarily, the magnitude of anything could be infinite (philosophically speaking) because infinite divisibility by an infinitesimal magnitude always left a divisible remainder. The infinitesimal magnitude must be of no magnitude (such as zero or the mathematical point), which ultimately meant that any magnitude had infinite length, or infinite expanse, or infinite volume.

From these and other assumptions, Zeno concluded that traversing a finite distance was impossible, because the motion could never end. The mistake in his assumption was in isomorphizing continuous motion (imagined as an infinite number of traversable mathematical points) with the number line. In fact, all the fractions of a distance that comprise the finite distance, of magnitude other than the mathematical point, must come to a finite sum. The finite distance gives the limiting sum. Put another way, the *continuity* of movement from mathematical point to mathematical point over a finite distance cannot be taken as the same thing as the traversal of increments comprising an infinite number of discrete units (fractions). The two concepts are incompatible. Zeno saw a compatibility between the two, hence the paradox. Actually, a number of paradoxes by Zeno have survived, all of which concern either the division of space (as just described), or the division of time.

The Limits of Infinity

Archimedes evoked the concept of the infinite when he measured the area under a curve. He used 'n' number of rectangles of equal width, but changing height, and summed the areas to yield an approximation of the area under the curve. The accuracy of this 'integration' process (later to become the principle of integral calculus in the seventeenth century) depended on the number of rectangles used. That is, by increasing the number of rectangles under the curve (which must become increasingly thinner), one could reduce the *difference* between the calculated estimate of the area under the curve *and* the actual area under the curve, so that a more accurate measure of the area could be made (*see* fig. 8). Archimedes intuitively recognized the limits of such 'infinite' summations (integrations). This paradox, it seems, would set up a situation where a limit of counting must manifest itself.

In *The Emergence of Number* (1987), J. N. Crossley interprets the limits of counting in three ways. There is:

(i) "the practical limit" determined by "a number without a name" (p. 22).

(ii) "the situation where there is no clear way to proceed" (p. 22).

(iii) "the case of there being no limit" (p. 22), that is, "counting indefinitely" (p. 23).

Figure 8. *Integrating the area under the curve (note the spaces under the curve still left 'unaccounted' by the rectangles).*

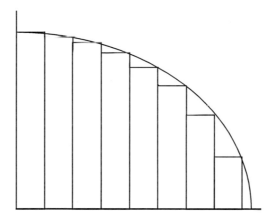

To illustrate the *first limit*—a number without a name—we can use Archimedes 'Sand Reckoner'. Archimedes reckoned the 'sphere of the universe' would hold 10^{63} grains of sand. He devised a number system based on myriads (10,000)—a myriad of myriads was 10^8. Numbers as large as A = 10 to the power (8×10^8) were described, with no way to advance beyond this number naturally, except by proceeding, as Archimedes had done, to A^2, A^3, etc.

Similar to this method is the repetition of a quantity to generate greater numbers. In English, for example, one million million stands for

1,000,000,000,000. This form of numbering (by words) cannot continue *ad libitum* because the number of Latin roots is limited.

Crossley (1987) gives one of the largest numbers ever offered (as reported by W. D. Johnstone in 1975) as being that "devised by Rudolf Ondrejka [and is equal to] 10 to the [power] 6 [American] billion" (p. 23). But 'One Skew' (after Stanley Skewes, a professor of Cape Town University, South Africa) is the largest so far, equaling 10 to the power 10 to the power 10 to the power 34. This number is calculated to be the largest number of which at least one prime number has been proved to exist that would be smaller than 'one skew'. The skew is one of the largest numbers to have ever been of some practical use in mathematics.

Lines (1986) points out that "the total number of atoms in the entire universe is 'only' about 10^{75} (p. 30), which puts these larger numbers into perspective. In September 1985, a proof by Dr. Ronald Graham of Bell Laboratories, New Jersey, "established that a certain quantity involved could not possibly exceed a number which he called G_{64}" (p. 202), where $G_0 = 3^3$ to the power 3 to the power 3 to the power 3, and $G_1 = G_0^{G_0}$, $G_2 = G_1^{G_1}$, etc., continuing on until G_{64}. Lines queries G_{64} as the largest useful number devised so far, since it is believed that the number actually being sought is the humble six, suggesting that the upper limit of G_{64} is somewhat over-determined.

Of the *second limit*, Crossley (1987) reports at least three sub-cases "where there is no clear way to proceed" (p. 22):

(a) A block may exist ("temporary or semi-permanent," p. 23). For example, counting in fives or tens using fingers and hands, or counting in tens or hundreds, etc.

(b) a vague but specific number is "arbitrarily large" (p. 23). For examples, numbers above the limit of G_{64} or the 'intensive plural', which is taken to mean a number or quantity of great size. In some cultures the word for a specific number—for example, 1000—also means 'beyond counting'. Arbitrarily large may also mean the number is 'infinite'.

(c) "unending repetition," (p. 27), where the next number is formed by 'reapplying a device' or 'repeating an action'. For example, '2-counting', that is, 1, 2, 2-1, 2-2, 2-2-1, or "repeated opening and shutting of the hands" for numbers greater than can be counted" (p. 28).

Of the *third limit*, counting may continue indefinitely (in theory, to infinity)—this is a generally accepted possibility. But indefinite repetition has two aspects: the first is "placing one thing...after another" (p. 28), that is, counting in a form such as tally keeping, and the second aspect is the recognition of the idea of infinity. In the former, this method of counting is most readily recognizable in the Hindu-Arabic decimal system as used the world over, but no adequate verbal system can match the elegance of this system, especially from a 'speech economic' point of view. We all have a clear idea that any finite number can always be increased by simply adding one. We would also intuitively expect that any series of numbers (odd, even, square, triangular, etc.) could all run indefinitely—after all, we do not expect that we could ever run out of such numbers. Recognizing infinity is a direct corollary of this fact. The limit is born of 'unending repetition'—one cannot arrive at a final sum.

Cantor's Transfinite Arithmetic

With regard to the second aspect of 'recognizing infinity' (ii) above, it can be seen that it is only a short conceptual step from going "as far as you like" (Crossley, 1987, p. 29) to counting interminably. These and other speculative notions were to become the basis for some very controversial theories about infinity as proposed by Georg Cantor in the 1870s. Cantor was much ridiculed for his theories, but he is also considered to be the mathematician that did more for infinity than any other. He showed the relevance of one-to-one correspondence in 'measuring' infinity. He also argued that there were many sets of numbers of infinite cardinality. That is, the elements of one set could be placed in one-to-one correspondence with the elements of another set in the same way that a tally-sheet can be kept to count off, one by one, a number of items or the passing days. Furthermore, these sets, which he labeled $Aleph_0$ (aleph-null), obeyed the laws of *transfinite* arithmetic. For example, $Aleph_0$ + $Aleph_0$ = $Aleph_0$, and paradoxically $Aleph_0$ × $Aleph_0$ = $Alpeh_0$. As long as the integers of these sets are even, odd or square numbers, etc., they always have an infinite cardinality of $Aleph_0$, and the whole set of integers is never greater than a part set. Ultimately the transfinite laws established by Cantor were only true to the extent that infinity is boundless in either direction, from the infinitesimal to the infinite.

Cantor's work did not stop here, for he found that there were other cardinalities. Cantor argued, by a complex proof of contradiction, that the cardinality of real numbers (rational plus irrational numbers) was greater than $Aleph_0$ because he showed that they were innumerably infinite, and he labeled them the cardinality of the continuum (C). Having a higher cardinality than the natural numbers, real numbers, and therefore the irrational numbers, constitute the 'norm' of the two types of numbers (by the trans-arithmetical equation $Aleph_0$ + C = C): there are more irrational than rational numbers!

Figure 9 indicates that the 'point set' (the number of points) on a line AB has the same cardinality as the point set of another line $A'B'$ (recall Zeno's paradox), which is also equal to C. It is probably not very surprising at this stage to learn that $Aleph_0$ × C = C, and further, C × C = C. Also, that which is true of the line segment (where the same number of points are also found in a line of infinite length) is also true for two-dimensional and three-dimensional forms, such as the square or the cube. That is, there is an infinite number of points both at the point source ('O' in fig. 9), and in a line, or plane, or volume of any size—even infinite size.

In *Physics as Metaphor* (1983), Roger Jones says this of Cantor's analysis of infinity:

> In the attempt to come to grips with the very essence of counting, the work begins, like a fugue or a set of variations, with the very deceptive theme of one-to-one correspondence. Working its magic with the harmony and melody of numbers and point sets, the theme is repeated again and again in varied and startling form, revealing new delight and meaning in the infinite. (p. 168)

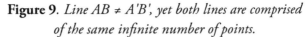

Figure 9. Line AB ≠ A'B', yet both lines are comprised of the same infinite number of points.

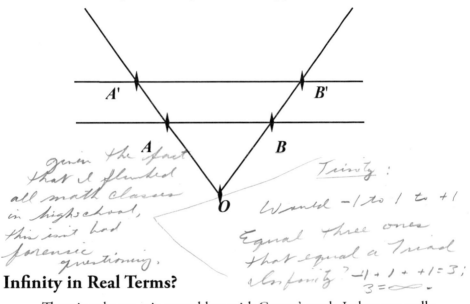

given the fact that I flunked all math classes in highschool, this isn't bad forensic questioning.

Trinity: Would -1 to 1 to +1 Equal three ones that equal a Triad Infinity? -1 + 1 + +1 = 3; 3 = ∞.

Infinity in Real Terms?

There is only one minor problem with Cantor's work. It does not really speak of infinity in a way that is anything different from Zeno's ideas of an infinity which has no magnitude in the point, yet simultaneously has infinite magnitude in the line (or in space, to go further). Infinity, however, can only ever exist as a concept or an idea, or even a theory, but it cannot be reified or hypostasized. Curiously, for mathematicians, infinity *can* have a limiting sum, or can have *no* limiting sum—it matters not. A simple example illustrating this point is the *convergent* series:

$$1/2 + 1/4 + 1/8 + 1/16 + ...,$$

which continues infinitely, each term being half the preceding term. The continued summing of these terms converges to one. That is, we get closer and closer to one by halves of the preceding term, but never reach one, no matter how many terms we wish to add to the series. Theoretically, convergent series can run to an infinite set, yet it is considered finite because it has a

1 → ½ → ¼ etc, brings us to one infinity, 1 = ∞ → ∞ = 0, which is 1 thing.

limiting sum (one), if we could take an infinite number of terms (again recalling Zeno's paradox). We have no way of physically demonstrating this convergence (e.g., by one-to-one correspondence) without reaching a stage where the operation becomes impossible at microscopic, molecular, atomic, and sub-atomic levels.

Another example, a *divergent* series such as:

$$1/2 + 1/3 + 1/4 + 1/5 + ...,$$

can also run to an infinite set, but it has no limiting sum. It is not bounded and will eventually exceed any number nominated. This latter example is quite the opposite of the former, and in fact, only the latter can be taken as making any *complete* sense because setting a limit on infinity, as in the former example, is simply not reasonable by the definition of infinity— infinity is *unlimited*. That is to say, infinity is beyond magnitude, it is beyond quantitative measures—it is, essentially, only qualitatively meaningful, and it is in this sense indeed that infinity offers the aesthetic experience that Jones espouses of a "new delight and meaning in the infinite" (p. 168).

In regard to the quantitative issue of infinity, it is important to note that in the handling of infinity *as if it were an entity*, as has been demonstrated in Cantor's analysis, and in convergent series, the illusion has set in that infinity has been 'bottled'. The infinite 'quantity', the 'cosmical number' of N, is now juggled as if it had been enumerated, which is quite beside the point altogether. Such an attitude lends itself to hubris, and a consequent blindness to the true nature of infinity. The hubris is understandable, given that an inflated mind-set comes about from identification with a 'truth' as if absolute knowledge had been acquired. The consequence is a willful stubbornness that resists enlightenment to the contrary—after all, once one has the long-sought-for truth one does not give it up easily. As Crossley has observed, there comes a point where we must give up counting and say "Many." When we can say 'many' we enter a new realm. We give up measuring the world and instead try to look at it with eyes that do not analyze, but appreciate the aesthetic of infinity in its conceptual sense as encompassing the whole universe of space and time, and most importantly, ourselves, in a *totality* which as the word suggests, unifies rather than disintegrates.

Mention has already been made regarding the practical impossibility of demonstrating the continuities suggested in finite and infinite series (actually discrete, but infinite steps). In fact, in the world of matter (particularly matter as the subject of micro-physics) it is known that only discontinuities exist at the sub-atomic level. Although we understand that a continuum is implied in motion, or in concepts such as the passage of time, Max Planck showed that there was no continuum as far as energy was concerned: energy was only available in sizeable portions (quanta).

Neils Bohr was to demonstrate further that a similar reality held true for electrons, which did not hold arbitrary positions around a nucleus, but held specific orbits and could move by 'quantum leap' from one orbit to another. Most importantly, these orbits were *a priori* realities locked into the phenomenology of the atom. An electron when changing orbit took a determined position. There was no continuum of possibilities of orbits, but discrete certainties as to the placement of electrons. What this means, as a general rule, is that infinities can exist soundly in theory as continua, but they do not seem to apply in physical reality.

Summary

Infinity is a paradoxical concept. While we can imagine the infinite, it is impossible to demonstrate its nature to a 'reasonable' mind. Cantor played with the concept mathematically, and caused a controversy in doing so. Modern physics has demonstrated the impossibility of endlessly (infinitely) splitting matter and energy. In the physical world we recognize limits, and matter demonstrates these limits in no uncertain terms. As Crossley makes clear, we also find it difficult to encapsulate infinity in our counting systems.

Conversely, mathematical transcendence and irrationality, and the possibility of endless operations of convergence (leading to, but never reaching finite sums) and divergence (leading to, but never reaching infinite sums) demonstrate not only the conceptual possibility and the paradox of infinity, but also the paradoxical symbolic process outlined in an earlier chapter "The Symbolism of Number." Here we see the interplay of the rational mind with both the 'irrational' component of the psyche and the universe, and the tension this creates.

The unfolding of the number archetype within ourselves, the activity of 'counting', may describe any number of processes that depict developments by stages, or growth, or movement, be they psychological, biological, mathematical, or mythological, etc. The following chapters from 'zero' to 'ten' give concrete examples of the above process by also including religious, alchemical, philosophical, scientific and proto-scientific ideas or discoveries which are founded structurally upon the construct of the number achetype. So saying, our journey through the number system will start with the most compelling of all integers: Zero (the Void).

So long as you're in the third dimension, you cannot use third dimensional methods, measurements and means to manipulate a tangible manifold mechanic of Infinity. You can only toy with the symbols that point to the paradoxes.

This is the prime example of man's ability to conceive but not perceive.

Plate 8. ZERO

The Uroboros (the dragon devouring its own tail) equates with the circle and zero, all of which symbolize eternal processes of coming into being (Engraving by Lucas Jennis, in the alchemical tract De Lapide Philisophico of 1605) [SOURCE: Wikimedia Commons].

ZERO (THE VOID)

Nothing can be made out of nothing.

William Shakespeare

To start anything we must start from somewhere or something.
To start with number we must start from nothing or 'no thing';
the void, symbolized by the circle: ○. *Like the circle, zero*
symbolizes no beginning and no end—it is eternal. There is
no differentiation in zero—it is not structured in a pluralistic
sense—it is not structured at all—as there is no single thing
that it can describe. Thus, the void is not to be understood
as 'darkness' or 'emptiness', or any similar pole of a pair of
opposites.

The Beginning of Zero

Zero (Italian from Arabic: *tsifer* = 'empty') was derived, with the nine numerals, in India and introduced to Arabia in the Middle Ages. The Mayans and the Babylonians had a sign to represent the absence of units of a certain order, but it was not conceived to be an integer—its operative possibilities, therefore, were not employed. Zero's twofold nature of all or nothing (depending on its position among, or next to, other integers) was only symbolically (intuitively) experienced in antiquity and classical times as a symbol of wholeness, or 'nothingness', but not used consciously for counting, measurement, etc., as was the case in the Middle-East.

The ancient Greeks also knew of zero (at least in concept), but since Aristotle claimed that zero could not be used to form ratios, he repudiated the idea of zero as a number. This absence of zero is apparent in the cumbersome alphabetical counting systems of the Greeks, the Hebrews, and the Romans.

The introduction of zero contributed much to the development of mathematics—the over-use of letters was eliminated, and a cyclical system of orderedness was established that was more in harmony with the similar cyclical processes of the natural world.

Something from Nothing

The word 'nothing' has become so over used that its deeper meaning has been lost and replaced with a colloquial definition that implies some form of vacuum, the absence of anything. This is because we imagine nothing (for example, the 'void' of *Genesis* 1:2) in a purely superficial sense, but we can better understand it as a *prima materia*—an initial precondition which holds all possibilities, all potentialities, all undifferentiated opposites in a 'state' outside human experience, beyond space and time. Psychologically, this state is the unconscious. Jung clarifies this point in *Aion* (1959a):

> Union of opposites is equivalent to unconsciousness, so far as human logic goes, for consciousness presupposes differentiation into subject and object and a relationship between them. Where there is no "other," or it does not yet exist, all possibility of consciousness ceases. (para. 301)

Jung implies that unconsciousness can be equated with nothingness, but we are to realize that through consciousness (learning to differentiate), 'nothing', the undefined, can be transformed into something with definition—the world of unknown objects.

Zero as the Void

Zero has the inherent quality of numerically representing the 'void' state just described. In mathematics, zero has 'additive identity'—the inability to obtain a new sum upon addition or subtraction of zero with another number.

Indirectly zero also takes on the symbolism of infinity—the result of dividing any number by zero is mathematically defined as infinity. It is as if zero is so infinitesimal that it sub-divides any number into an infinite number of parts because it has no magnitude. Zero is the same in concept as the mathematical point proposed by Zeno. Furthermore, zero is so all-embracing of the void that it cannot be increased by any magnitude.

You cannot increase or decrease infinity. Big Zero equals little Zero.

Zero as Negative Existence

The contrast between Zero and One, Void and Monad, is psychologically comparable to the contrast between non-existence (negative existence) and existence. These all equate with the unconscious and consciousness, respectively. In *The Kabbalah Unveiled* (1986), S. L. McGregor Mathers attempts to qualify negative existence:

> The idea of negative existence can…exist *as an idea,* but it will not bear definition, since the idea of definition is utterly incompatible with its nature. (p. 18)

After explaining that a logical and reasoned attempt at defining the ineffable would be a fruitless task (since negative existence would cease to be as it is if limits were imposed upon it by, for example, language), Mathers, not heeding her own words, then goes on to equate negative existence with God—the Absolute (also indefinable). Not mistakenly, however, Mathers 'equation' is not inappropriate, even though the factor of unconscious projection is manifested here. More accurately though, one cannot make absolute statements about transcendent issues, as Kant had stated, and which Jung endorses in *C. G. Jung Speaking* (1977) by affirming that, since we are not God, we cannot claim the truth of statements made about God (or for that matter, negative existence, or the contents of the Void, etc.) and yet:

> insofar as we are "God" we are speaking of our unconscious, being ourselves unconscious to the extent we are "God." Thus it is that all the statements we make about God are statements about the unconscious.

You may want to go back and do a little theology homework!

> It is local, it is universal, it is the One, it is the Many or the All, it is personal and impersonal because the unconscious appears to us in all these forms. One feels personally addressed by the unconscious—or one doesn't. (pp. 388-389)

Of course, Jung's statements are from a psychological perspective, but such statements emphasize the more general point that all things of which we are unconscious become the subject of ourselves. The statements we make are totally subjective (appearing objective because of their unconscious source) and these unconscious contents have projection-making factors, which imbue the unknown with qualities and definitions that are paradoxical in nature, but also paradoxically, *are still descriptive of the unknown*—at least partially.

Negative existence (equated with the *En-Sof* of *Kabbalah*), therefore, defies understanding because it is ineffable. We cannot experience anything unless we can compare and judge from our senses and perceptions and these faculties, which allow us to quantify and qualify, cannot assist us when faced with the truly unknown. Furthermore, negative existence is not only a non-object outside experience (i.e., it cannot be objectified), it also becomes the subject of our own being.

The state of unconsciousness illustrates this idea. Such a state is our own 'experience' of negative existence—it is actually a 'non-experience' like sleeping where there is no consciousness (this precludes dream states). There is experience by the physical body, but this remains unconscious since, as long as bodily sensations are not related to the ego, there is no consciousness and no concept of space and time. Effectively, we can say there is no experience during the event and no memory of the event in consciousness upon awakening. (Allowance must be made for the fact that the body and its sensory modalities may have sense experiences which are 'remembered' and can be 'recalled' using special techniques such as hypnosis.)

Such is the enigma of negative existence, as symbolized by zero, and it is a mystery now as it was in ancient times. It must be understood that this non-existence is a potentially empirical fact in the sense that any experience which we may encounter, rational or irrational, physical or psychic, relies on

Excellent definition of negative existence!

an ego, an 'I', at the center of the field of consciousness. It is from the ego that we 'know' or postulate our existence.

Historically, the endless cycle of unknowable negative existence is described mythologically by the circle and the *uroboros* (the tail-eating serpent), which psychologically represents the unconscious. Negative existence (that which cannot exist in the conscious eye of the human witness) is associated with the serpent because it symbolizes the chthonic and instinctual life of the body, which is devoid of a spiritual, conscious factor. The uroboric phenomenology of zero strongly correlates with the 'feminine' archetype of the Great Mother and the unconscious, since, as Erich Neumann (1973) relates in *The Origins and History of Consciousness*, they both have the capacity of "begetting and conceiving, devouring and giving birth" (p. 10).

Neumann hastens to add that 'masculine' and 'feminine' qualities in mythological and symbolic discourse are not "personal sex-linked characteristics" (p. xxii). Biological and sociological reductionism merely serve modern and postmodern ideologies, which then usually lead to the valorization of certain so-called masculine or feminine human traits. These in turn can lead the ego to identify with transpersonal properties. Inflation usually results, which can only be ameliorated or negated by recognizing that the "integrity of the personality is violated when it is identified with either the 'masculine' or 'feminine' side of the symbolic principle of opposites" (p. xxii). Zero, then, in a mythological sense, has an overall 'feminine' character—an association and relationship to the unconscious that came about through its irrational aspect, most cogently depicted arithmetically by its twofold nature of 'all' and 'nothing'.

Summary

Zero, when equated with negative existence, has its symbolism best demonstrated in the mathematical principle of additive identity, where zero indicates an absence of quantity. Symbolically, zero also represents the end of being (closure), or negation through conjunction. But, when equated with its infinite and 'powerful' aspect, as observed in the decimal system, where placement with other integers determines magnitude, zero becomes associated with a potentially infinite value. Zero, then, equates with the circle and the *uroboros*, which both symbolize eternal processes of coming into being.

There is always Zero (Negative Existence), but there is no beginning without the totalizing experience of unity, and so 'emerges' the number One.

$$-1 \; + \; 1 \; + \; +2 \; = \; 3 \; things$$

$$-0 \; + \; 0 \; + \; +0 \; = \qquad "$$

therefore $1 = 0$.

and . . . . ah . . . .

. . . . and, $0 = 1$ thing .

Plate 9. THE NUMBER ONE

The earliest monoliths (meaning 'one stone') were erected to revere a certain god or mark a place of worship. Memorials such as the Washington Monument (Washington, DC), as seen from the Potomac River in 1894 even look like the number One—a single, vertical stroke [SOURCE: Photograph by Alexander McAdie/US National Oceanic and Atmospheric Administration].

ONE (THE MONAD)

The Monad is the Beginning of all things.

Pythagoras

The void is taken as a paradoxical merging of 'existence' and 'nonexistence' contained in a fusion that cannot allow for discrimination. This pre-egoic state can be represented by a circle of infinite size, yet is of no actual size. This circle symbolizes a state outside space and time, and is non-dimensional, but 'all-embracing'. The center of the circle is at all points in the void. This center is 'eternal consciousness'—the point of awareness, the monad, which coexists in the void, and can be symbolized by a point in the circle: ⊙

Unity Equals Totality

All numbers can be seen as 'complete' in their own right, which is to say they represent or symbolize totality, but the movement from uneven to even to uneven, by increases of one *ad infinitum*, sets up a discrete series, which functions, paradoxically, as a continuum that is dynamic in nature and never ceases. Every uneven number contains a surplus of one, after opposites are paired, and this makes uneven numbers 'active' in the same way as primal unity 'moves' to two. Every even number is a balanced set of opposites, but the complex of conjunctions always produces a new third, which moves the series onward.

The continuum is constantly oscillating between the active and the passive, and this infinite cycle always returns to, and is exhibited in the

In this sense a (△) a pyramid moves better than a —— straight line or an L angle.

original unity. One becomes 10, becomes 100, becomes 1000, and so on to infinity—each increase by the power of ten symbolizing expansion into unity from multiplicity. Therefore:

UNITY = TOTALITY = INFINITY = UNITY

Unity (One) has many aspects—some immanent, some transcendent—and these many aspects are better illustrated by investigation and study of the phenomenology associated with the other natural numbers in their unique aspect. Each natural number has its own particular identity, thus establishing an orderedness to number that is unchangeable. In *Science and Method* (1952), Henri Poincaré claimed:

> Every whole [natural] number is detached from the others, it possesses its own individuality, so to speak; each of them forms a kind of exception. (p. 36)

Consciousness as One and Many

The term 'eternal consciousness' (used above) is taken to be an arbitrary label for a content in the void state. This monadic state may be better understood as multiple consciousnesses in the symbolic form of multiple luminosities. They are multiples because they are not yet integrated into a unified ego structure. As Jung (1960) states:

> [since] consciousness has always been described in terms derived from the behavior of light, it is…not too much to assume that…multiple luminosities correspond to tiny conscious phenomena. (para. 396)

By 'tiny conscious phenomena', Jung means "introspective intuitions" (para. 396) which may be embodied as dream motifs, visions or ideas irrupting from the unconscious. Such contents would be traced back to an archetypal source (the luminosities are the archetypal images). These experiences may be the only way we have of getting an intellectual and emotional handle on the mystery that is the Void, and though these contents can only be represented, they indicate the relative natures of consciousness and the unconscious. This relativity is paradoxical by nature because it suggests that the "contents [of the psyche] can be conscious and unconscious at the same time" (para. 397).

This paradoxical state is how the psyche presents itself empirically, and such a phenomenology requires acceptance of this paradox to maintain an harmonic dialectic between consciousness and the unconscious. Nevertheless, the 'presence', at least, of representations of 'consciousness' in the unconscious *is* indicated, and that, for our purposes, will suffice as evidence for the unconscious and the potential for the development of consciousness *from inner factors alone*. This development implies that a unification of fragmented parts—the 'disseminated luminosities'—is possible so that the 'monadic' state (the wholeness of egohood) can be brought about.

Wow

↙ But without this ... ... can we talk about it?!

Early Associations with the Principle of Unity

Since ancient times the circle with a point (although the point is optional) was used to represent God, Heaven and the Sun (as 'solar' principle). The philosophical gold of the alchemists was also represented by the solar hieroglyph: ☉

S. K. De Rola, in *Alchemy: The Secret Art* (1973), notes the symbolic connection of the circle with the macrocosm, and the axial point with the microcosm, which are combined so that the Infinite may be complete and centered. From the centered circle is derived the Greek letter *theta*, θ, which is the first letter of the word *theos* (Greek: *theos* = 'god'), thus showing how the correspondence of Sun with God was made. Circles and spheres (i.e., Sun, Heaven, natural cycles, etc.) were seen by the ancients as the embodiment of the concept of Oneness: an original state, a unity, a source of life and power, the beginning (place of origin) and the end (place of return).

Although the ancients thought in a strictly magical and mythological manner, these representations—circle and sphere—demonstrate the ability of the ancients to advance abstract concepts (as intuitive interpretations) gained from inner processes that were then projected onto the empirical world. The

Greek Neoplatonist philosopher Proclus, for example, was of the opinion that the first monad was 'the world itself'. Neumann (1973) points out that projections have their basis in symbolic thinking. The circular symbolism in particular indicates contents that share a 'unity' component—"wholeness," "nondifferentiation," and "the absence of opposites" (p. 11). Neumann sees a limitation in waxing philosophically over these formulations because they are ultimately paradoxical, and reduce our capacity for meaning-making. The symbol, on the other hand, "can be seen and grasped as a unity at one glance" (p. 11).

At this point, we easily detect the paradoxical similarities found in circle and sphere symbolism as they pertain to zero *and* one; 'nothing' (negative existence) *and* Unity. The one distinguishing difference between the two is the distinction made in one's consciousness that there is a difference. Oneness is the realization, the identification of something as having unity, whereas nothingness is not realized, not identified, and remains unknown like negative existence. Both draw very much on the same symbolism, but both are worlds apart in meaning. Neumann clarifies this point:

> Circles, spheres and round are all aspects of the Self-contained, which is without beginning or end; in its preworldly perfection it is prior to any process, eternal, for in its roundness, there is no before and no after, no time; and there is no above and no below, no space. (p. 8)

One inference to be made from these paradoxical statements is that the myriads of antithetical relationships that might exist (such as 'beginning' and 'end') are coexistent in unity. Humankind can only know beginnings and endings, hence the struggle to define them through creation myths, which usually include corresponding finality myths. In astrophysics, for example, the most popular theory of the origins of the universe at the moment, which Fred Hoyle jokingly called the 'Big Bang' theory, necessarily promulgated a 'Big Crunch' theory.

Another paradox arises—a Pythagorean one—because the monad has another dual quality—it is both analytic and synthetic in nature. The numerical One is the analytic One expressing quantity, while the synthetic

One qualitatively expresses the universal totality of All-in-One (embracing all other numbers). This 'All-Unity' is synonymous with von Franz's (1974) "one-continuum" (not the same as Cantor's continuum):

> Whereas numbers above the threshold of consciousness appear to be quantitative discontinuities and qualitative individual numbers, in the unconscious [before pluralistic categories emerge] they interpermeate and overlap,...participating in the one-continuum which runs through them all. From this viewpoint all numbers are simply qualitatively differentiated manifestations of the primal one. (pp. 65-66)

Von Franz equates unity with multiplicity so long as the discrete natures of numbers are not drawn into consciousness. This way of thinking is a psychological rule with very real social implications. For example, politically speaking, one can see the paradoxical application made of this twofold 'rule' by nations, which in their temporary unconsciousness of the individual, only see the importance of the multitudes united in strength and common purpose, but in painful consciousness, later venerate the individual through such symbols as the tomb of the 'unknown soldier'. Such age-old facts of life have archetypal reality, and no one can undermine the intensity of meaning and emotion that this rule evokes. Therefore, mythologically and psychologically, while there may be objects of oneness in the world (the individual, the group), the oneness concept itself springs from the psyche, which is governed by an archetypal unifying principle that allows us to perceive and project oneness into the world. From this twofold function is recognized not only a fundamental psychological reality of oneness, but also a physical reality of oneness.

Number One as the Monad

Philosophical speculations since the time of ancient Greece have centered on the Monad and its 'equation' with one. Westcott (1974) reports that Theon of Smyrna believed the monad (as a number) remained "by itself among numbers for no number can be taken from it, or separated from its unity" (p. 33). The number one cannot be multiplied or divided (that is, 'reproduced' or 'reduced') by itself ($1 \times 1 = 1$, and $1 \div 1 = 1$). In mathematics the number one is excluded as a neutral element to avoid this empirical fact. That is, primal unity—von Franz's 'one-continuum'—always retains its most definitive nature and quality (its immutability), and in a philosophical sense, this fact allots a degree of credibility to the concept of the Monad in Gnostic thought as "ingenerable, imperishable, incomprehensible [and] inconceptable" (Hippolytus). On empirical grounds, the philosophical facts of the above examples, and all others to follow, where each number demonstrates its own unique characteristics, can be taken to be as legitimate as the mathematical facts which are contingent with them.

Von Fanz's idea of the unity principle permeating all other numbers can be demonstrated mathematically in another way. The inability to obtain a new product upon multiplication or division of any number by one marks the uniqueness of unity: the original number states itself ($a \times 1 = a$, and $a \div 1 = a$). It is mathematically impossible to 'increase' or 'decrease' a number by the principle of unity when that other number is already all-encompassing and complete (unitary) in its own right.

While the centuries-long alchemical tradition carried in its premises the notion that microcosm mirrored macrocosm ('as above, so below') and both formed a whole (unity), the Monadology of Gottfried Leibniz (1646-1716) was a move towards a more reductive approach to the mind/body (psyche/matter) problem. Principally, for Leibniz, the simplest constituent of all substances, physical or non-physical, was the monad and the supreme monad was God, the Creator of Order. Monads have no influence on each other, individually or holistically, so that causality proper does not exist, yet monads 'enmesh' with one another in a 'pre-established harmony'. Accordingly, to account for all activity, the structure of the universe, and the possibility and permanence of existence (relatively speaking), Leibniz postulated a 'psychophysical parallelism' where minds are copies of Divinity, each of which can know and 'imitate' divine systems (such as the universe) in purposeful ways, while bodies perform acts purely because they are capable of motion by intention.

Jung (1960) notes that Leibniz endeavored to explain the nature of psychophysical events outside the causality principle, but adds that a pre-established harmony between all things "would have to be absolute and would manifest itself in a universal correspondence and sympathy" (para. 948) of all events, causal and acausal. This idea, however, does not square with the evidence. Most likely, monadology is the result of the projection of an unconscious content (again the unity principle of the central archetype of the Self in the case of monadic concepts) onto the outside world, from which is derived (or devised) Leibniz's philosophy. *Hmm.... Was he, then, backing himself into a corner?!!*

Number One as a Symbol of the Self

The principle of unity is embodied in the philosophies of the Gnostics, Theon of Smyrna, Proclus, and Leibniz, but it is also present in the modern disciplines. It is understandable that later philosophers, and even scientists, should try to unify any and all antithetical relationships when and where they were seen because it is so easy to identify with the principle of unity, and *T.O.E.* therefore, project it by seeing it everywhere, or expecting it to be everywhere. The force and power of the archetype of the Self as a united whole is at the basis of this identity. It can have an overwhelming effect and can take over the entire personality, manifesting as an obsessive desire for unity (say) in the world and its people. Such is the psychological state of conquerors of nations, who project their desire for unification of their own fragmented psyche onto an apparently fragmented world.

The concept of the Self specifically, as opposed to a projected, monadic form of the Self, goes back to a time prior to 500 BC when the Sanskrit *Upanishads* were written. Edward Edinger, in *The Aion Lectures* (1996), quotes at length from this text, but a few sentences are enough to give the idea of the Self as experienced by the ancients:

> At whose behest does the mind think? Who bids the body live? Who makes the tongue speak? Who is that effulgent Being that directs the eye to form and color and the ear to sound?

The Self is ear of the ear, mind of the mind, speech of the speech...and eye of the eye.... Him the eye does not see, nor the tongue express, nor the mind grasp.

He who dwells in all beings but is separate from all beings, whom no being knows, whose body all beings are, and who controls all beings from within—he, the Self, is the Inner Ruler, the Immortal. (p. 163)

Edinger adds that the Eastern mind-set was far in advance of Western thinkers in "psychological sophistication" (p. 163). The 'advance' here is acknowledged in the fact that by knowing that the Self is an inner factor, the possibility of projecting it onto unity symbols is reduced or even annulled.

Recognition of the Self is hinted at in the monotheistic religions, but for the most part Jahweh (Jehovah), God, and Christ were still seen as outside the body (in Heaven), even if it was granted that these figures were in some way present within the body and all other things. The situation or localization of Deity *only* in external (other) places occurs because the projection-making factor of a psychic content when an individual is faced with the unknown is activated unconsciously by association (similarity, contrast, contiguity and even propinquity), and the content, this time the image of the unitary Self (the total psyche, which comprises consciousness, of which the ego is a part, and the unconscious) is seen to manifest in the environment when projected onto suitable 'hooks'.

Projection takes place because natural entities *of a unitary nature* can have phenomenological 'equivalence' with the internal image of the 'undivided Self' (the principle of individuality), and the possibility and actuality of this type of projection implies that the greater proportion of the Self is still unconscious. It follows that the products of fantasy and imagination, and the creative principles of the mind and its cognitive capacities, as well as the biological parallels (all of which are products of the individual), are also 'seen' in nature.

Westcott (1974) lists over two-dozen Pythagorean appellations, which exemplify such projections and can be seen as descriptive of both physical and mythological (psychic) entities, which embody the Monadic, creative principle. These include:

> God, the first of all things, the maker of all things.... Intellect, the source of all ideas.... Matter, the last development of universality.... The Sun.... Apollo.... Pyralios, dweller in fire.... The Axis.... The point within a circle. (pp. 33-34)

As Edinger points out in *Ego and Archetype* (1986a): "consciousness (light) and energy (fire)" (p. 164) too have their source in "the principle of individuality" (p. 164). Jung (1963) draws a parallel between the psyche that needs these symbols of unity, and the focus on oneness in the Hermetic Art, whereby:

> its most conspicuous quality, namely *its unity and uniqueness*—one is the stone, one is the medicine, one the vessel, one the procedure, and one the disposition—presupposes a *dissociated consciousness*. For no one who is one himself needs oneness as a medicine. (para. 772)

Therein lies the importance of the monad from a psychological point of view. Without an integrated sense of oneness comes the inevitable catastrophe of fragmentation of the psychic structure. This psychological reality leads us to consider further the monad as the ego/Self dichotomy.

The Psychological Monad as the Ego/Self Dichotomy

Another characteristic of the Monad, as Plato speaks of it, is its transcendence, which places it beyond the givens of conscious life (that is, space, time, and causality), yet the Monad functions from within those same categories. Edinger's book is helpful in providing a means of rationalizing the transcendental, paradoxical nature of the Monad. Edinger's model of the 'Ego/Self axis' is the psychological parallel of the Monad—its partial aspects (namely ego and Self as derived from Jung's work) refer to the interactional and homeostatic function of ego and Self as the major dynamic force in psychic life. The ego/Self axis provides a rationale for the paradoxical nature of the psyche because, being both conscious and unconscious, it follows that other antithetical relationships are evoked and enjoined in the dialectic between consciousness and the unconscious.

Our constructed world is made up of our own polarizations as we have generated them through experience and learning. Each individual sees a dichotomy here, an ambiguity there, and seeks to resolve the dissonance that these observations may evoke. The ego has a responsibility to the Self by recognizing the superiority and authority of the Self in the psychic hierarchy, while the Self functions from its own non-conscious, unificatory standpoint, and through this function the Self is realized through the ego.

The Self is 'passive' (it waits, it plans, it deliberates), it is 'active' (it 'favors', it 'rewards', it 'strikes', it 'annihilates'). It is partly governed by social determinants, but mostly acts in accordance with life principles that determine a culture's moral and ethical values in the first place. If these descriptors of the Self seem applicable to the Old Testament Jehovah, it is not by any coincidence. Jung (1958) had already drawn that parallel in his highly acclaimed essay *Answer to Job:*

> It is only through the psyche that we can establish that God acts upon us, but we are unable to distinguish whether these actions emanate from God or from the unconscious. We cannot tell whether God and the unconscious are two different entities. Both are borderline concepts for transcendental contents. But empirically it can be established, with a sufficient degree of probability, that there is in the unconscious an archetype of wholeness.... [S]trictly speaking, the God-image does not coincide with the unconscious as such, but with...[this] special content of it, namely the archetype of the Self. (para. 757)

But it must also be stated that as a process not unlike evolution in its accumulative capacity to 'move' simple forms 'towards' more complex forms, consciousness too, as it evolves, comes to embrace a greater more complex range and diversity of knowable Forms, ideas and contents. The New Testament God, a God who shows a greater capacity for reason and morality than He did as Jehovah, became known to humankind, because humankind

*... Image and Likeness ....
but from to whom?
whom*

from time to time 'wakes up' and becomes more conscious of the world and the consequences of acting in that world. At all times, down through the ages, God forever looks and acts like that very same image in which He created 'Man', and *vice versa*.

Other factors of the Self include, from the ego's perspective, illumination or deception, appraisal as worthy or worthless, and generally (and most importantly), modification of a one-sided consciousness for which the ego must be fully responsible. The one crucial goal of individuality, therefore, can be seen as the realization of a two-part psychic system—ego and Self— each striving in their own way for unity (the Monad). All contradictions, all antithetical relationships, are resolved in the Monad as ego and Self take up opposing positions, thus setting up the dynamic just described.

The Monad ultimately translates as the God-head of Monotheism. As stated, we can barely describe the ineffable, if at all, but in the attempt we invariably describe ourselves, not in any conscious way, as this would be readily apparent, but by drawing upon the body of unconscious knowledge of the psychic totality those statements that irrupt into consciousness as clustered associations or complexes of ideas, which are essentially descriptive of the Self being monadic in nature. Although, as Jung points out, the Self bears a remarkable similarity to the God-head (the God-image in the soul) and *vice versa*, they are not the same thing. But, since they have the same phenomenology it is impossible to discriminate the difference.

Theological and metaphysical points of view may stand in contradiction with this psychological interpretation of monotheism with its basis in the unity principle, but it can be seen that the emphasis on, and the approach to the oneness of God, for those who practice monotheism, is identical in nature to the path taken by those committed to the quest for the soul. Put another way, both quests represent the one single quest for realization of the Self as the God-image, which constitutes the greatest striving of the individual (as monad) in, and of the world (the Many). Therefore, the Many perceived in consciousness exists as a multiplicity (a fragmentation) of the Monad that awaits integration.

How could their phenomenology be the same ??

In *Dictionary of Symbols* (1982), Tom Chetwynd considers One, the Monad (as a euphemism for the conscious individual) to be essentially dependent on 'the Many' (the unconscious), and *vice versa*. Chetwynd observes that:

> it is the aim of most mystical disciplines to experience it [one] when awake; and from then on to know the interplay between conscious and unconscious which is reality itself. Whereas sleep is a regressive fusion of the two—and not very interesting—the waking experience is integration of the unconscious unity, with the living diversity. (p. 284)

Psychologically and morally, this is no simple exercise. The Many (the world and its contents) must be recognized for what they truly are. As mentioned, a great deal of conceptualizing about the world and self is done through projection. Edinger (1986a) discusses this experience of self and world (one and many) in terms of the inner and outer experience of multiplicity, thereby implying a moral effort involved in realizing Chetwynd's integration of 'unconscious unity with the living diversity'. Edinger states:

> Seen from within [multiplicity] is a state of inner fragmentation involving a number of relatively autonomous complexes which, when touched by the ego, cause change in mood and attitude and make the individual realize that he [*sic*] is not one but many. From the external standpoint, multiplicity is manifested by the exteriorization or projection of parts of the individual psyche into the outer world. In this condition one finds his friends and his enemies, his hopes and his fears, his sources of support and his threats of failure, concretized in outer persons, objects and events. In such a state of dispersal there can be no experience of essential individuality. (p. 174)

Here is implied the moral effort involved in taking up the challenge of withdrawing one's projections, and 'collecting' back the fragmented parts from the world (which have autonomy in the world, as in the psyche) by acknowledging their true source. Edinger again:

The realization begins to draw that there is a unity behind the apparent multiplicity and that indeed it is this pre-existent unity which has motivated the whole arduous task of self-collection in the first place. (p. 174)

Psychologically, the 'unity behind the apparent multiplicity' is the ultimate realization and symbolism of One, and when effected in consciousness, it results in the unity of the psyche. This unity of psyche, of being one with the world, implies a One World experience—the nature philosopher's *unus mundus*—and although the concept of psychic wholeness implies a world not comprised of projected forms, and liberates the individual from the prison of illusory constructions, to describe the precise nature of the *unus mundus* within the compass of human experience may be virtually impossible. Nevertheless, the symbolism stands, the goal remains, and the quest for wholeness (oneness), itself the very reality, not metaphor or symbol of individuality, is exemplified and maintained in the archetype of Unity, symbolized by the number one. All this rests on the experience to which only the individual can attest, and the dynamism in the symbol, and the vitality gained from the symbol, is not only self-affirming, but is indicative of the symbol's veracity and, therefore, its validity.

Symbols of Unity in Culture and Religion

The importance of symbols, therefore, is clear, and unity symbolism in particular has been, and still is a prime value in civilizations, ancient and modern, for its capacity to enrich a culture. The earliest monoliths (Greek: MONO + *lithos* = 'one stone' or 'single stone') were erected to revere a certain god or mark a place of worship. Here was instilled a degree of feeling which evoked ideas of immortality and unchangeableness. Tombstones also serve this function. Structurally simple memorials, such as Cleopatra's Needle, Nelson's Column and the Washington Monument, even look like the number One: a single, vertical stroke. All embody the same idea. They symbolize a unity of feeling among the people united, for example, in heroic acts, which serve to establish or maintain nationhood: psychologically equivalent to personhood, identity, and individuality. Note, also, that this viewpoint undermines the naïve notion that these monuments merely embody patriarchal values through ithyphallic symbolism.

In the religion of the ancient Egyptians, the god Osiris went through the process of resurrection, and as *djed* pillar, he symbolized the reunited and everlasting transpersonality. Osiris symbolizes unity by stating that he has made himself whole and complete.

Concerning monotheism, John in *Ephesians* 4:4-6 makes a similar statement: "There is one body, and one spirit.... One Lord, one faith, one baptism, one God and Father of all."

The philosophical tree and the alchemical stone, paralleling their Biblical equivalents, are also unity symbols. The Tree of Life, and the Tree of Knowledge of Good and Evil in *Genesis* 2:9 (both symbolizing the Self), resurface throughout the Bible.

In *Genesis* 6:14, the wood of the Tree is transformed as the gopher wood for Noah's ark (the Self), which carried Noah (the ego), his family and the animals (the spiritual and instinctual components of the person) to safety. Then the wood was used to make the bridge onto which the Queen of Sheba would not step because she foresaw the use of this wood in the Cross of Golgotha, bearing Christ, the 'Son of Man' (or *Anthropos*, another symbol of the Self), the 'one Lord, one body...'

The stone, as unity symbol, has its earliest appearance in *Genesis* 28:11 when Jacob set upon a pillow of stone to rest his head in sleep. He then used this stone as a pillar to mark a place he called *Beth-el* (Hebrew: 'House of God', that is, the individual). Later in *Luke* 20:17 the rejected stone of the builders became the cornerstone of the Church (Christ).

The unity principle underlying monotheism has metaphysical extension in the Eastern religions of Hinduism, Buddhism, and Taoism. That is, a unitary phenomenology can be attached to the experience of reality when a mystical attitude is adopted in that experience. In Hinduism is the concept of *Brahman*, in which it is held that an ultimate reality underlies all things, objects and actions. The nature of *Brahman* in itself cannot be comprehended by the intellect when understood as the inner essence or 'soul' of all things, including the gods and goddesses of Hinduism. In the human being *Brahman* takes on the name of *Atman*, which Jung equates with the Self in *The Practice of Psychotherapy* (1966a): "the Indian idea of the atman, [with its] personal and cosmic modes of being, [forms] an exact parallel to the psychological idea of the self..." (para. 474).

Similarly in Buddhism, *Dharmakaya* can be equated with *Brahman* as the 'Body of Being' that describes reality as it appears to the Buddhist's religious consciousness. Fritjof Capra, in *The Tao of Physics* (1988), states that *Dharmakaya* "pervades all material things in the universe and is reflected in the human body as *bodhi*, the enlightened wisdom. It is thus spiritual and material at the same time" (p. 110).

Finally, in Taoism, the *Tao*, symbolized by the union of opposites, stands for transformation and change (the flux of things in opposition), and cyclicality in nature. All things living and not living are in the *Tao*, a universalizing concept, although intellectually, like *Brahman*, it is beyond comprehension. In meditation, for example, the *Tao* must be experienced through feeling, sensation and intuition.

In philosophy, psychology and religion can be seen the recurring, fundamental concept of unity, a monadic conception of reality that is taken as underscoring all reality, and this unificatory aspect of all existence appears to be a way of seeing the world as a direct result of an inner propensity to aspire to oneness, or develop in a direction of wholeness and completion that equates with the idea of oneness. But the idea or image of unity as a representation of the Self (not the archetype of the Self *per se*) is also built up from unitary images and concepts. Our experience of the world, then, is not simply the result of projection, but the world itself is the source of our ideational, affective and imaginal being as reflected in the unitary phenomena of the world. The ordering capacity of the Self is the instrument and mechanism of this structural process which constructs the psyche, culminating in a state of oneness that is dependent upon the world for its representations, but is capable of acting independently according to its capacity to construct, of itself, a representation or entity that has autonomy and being in the world.

Summary

The symbolism of the number One embodies the notion of integration, integrity, individuality, undividedness, unity, unification, and so on. Monadic systems and philosophies reflect these notions, but are also descriptive of the idea of a unified, personality structure. Psychologically, the 'totality' of the psyche (psychic wholeness) is seen as a goal, which corresponds theologically to the experience of the God-head, and alchemically, with the *unus mundus* concept where all opposites are merged. Multiplicity and fragmentation represent the antithetical and antagonistic alternatives to oneness, while unity and self-collection embody the symbolic principle of the number One in its 'higher' aspect.

There is always One (Primal Unity), but there is no conscious experience of the universe without the polarity of opposites, which permit distinction, and so 'emerges' the number Two.

One of the problems I see with "mind–brain–behaviour" studies is that a lot of psychologists and psychiatrists talk themselves out of a viable theology.

Religion and Science are not at odds so much in modern times, nor spirituality. It is psychology and religion where the real crack takes place. And both are being challenged and tackled by science and gnosticism.

Plate 10. THE NUMBER TWO

The yin/yang symbol (the T'ai-Chi T'u or 'Diagram of the Supreme Ultimate'—see fig. 10) symbolizes two opposing forces in constant opposition that create a resonating, interactional system. The two great arms of the Whirlpool Galaxy recall the T'ai-Chi T'u—for every action there is an equal but opposite reaction—a law that is true both in the universe and in the psyche [SOURCE: National Aeronautics and Space Administration, USA].

TWO (THE DYAD)

The parts and plurality belong to the sphere of the finite.

Euclid

> *The process of dualization is the process of eternal consciousness the Primal Unity—unfolding into two from which comes the formation of antitheses. This process of 'becoming' is an inevitable consequence inherent in a state where opposites co-exist in union, since separation also exists. In other words, separation is built into the process of dualization, just as conjunction is built into the process, and each mirrors the other simultaneously— cosmos and chaos. Thus, the number two symbolizes 'creation', the birth of consciousness.*

[handwritten margin note: On the birth of comparison and contrast, the first law of Aristotle's epistemology?]

[handwritten left margin note: The birth of delirium!]

The Birth of Consciousness

Consciousness, like the world and the discourses we construct to interpret that world, functions from the standpoint of duality. Only when the one 'becomes' two (when there is creation) does the world, indeed the universe, exist. Psychologically, this implies the birth of the ego. The ego can only exist because discrimination, evaluation, distinction, contrast, variation, balance, judgment and so on, are born out of the need for opposites. Neumann (1973) echoes this point:

> Only in the light of consciousness can man [*sic*] know. And this act of cognition, of conscious discrimination, sunders the world into opposites, for experience of the world is only possible through opposites. (p. 104)

where?
when?

Originally there were no abstract spatial components.... Gradually, with the growth of consciousness, things and places were organized into an abstract system and differentiated from one another; but originally...[e]verything participated in everything else, lived in the same undivided and overlapping state in the world of the unconscious as in the world of dreams. (p. 108)

See Heraclitus

As consciousness expanded so did the constructed world, physically and culturally. Going back to ancient times, with the building of the first societies and cities, there was a dependence on the awareness of space—the acknowledgement of sky and earth, above and below. Spatial symbolism went hand in hand with temporal symbolism, through the antithetical principle of light and darkness.

Awareness of the passage of days, marked by the sun and the moon, broadened our consciousness so that societies could be organized into genealogies, and experience of world events could be ordered chronologically. As Neumann also says: "The inward as well as the outward development of culture begins with the coming of light [consciousness]" (p. 109), and moving out from a fusion with the world the empirical self, the ego, established its independence in a world, which for the first time, it could say it truly knew.

The Interval between the Multitude and the Monad

The first principle of existence is the origin of the universe, and similarly, the origin of the stars. It is worth noting that mythologically the unity symbol must divide to become two in order for the world to be. The same process occurs at the atomic level with the main constituents of all stars, hydrogen and helium. The Hydrogen atom (atomic number = 1) is converted, through fusion, into Helium (atomic number = 2). In *Egyptian Mysteries* (1981), Lucie Lamy notes that "matter itself expresses the mystery of becoming in terms of number: One into Two, the mystery which is at the very basis of all 'revelatory teaching' " (p. 13). Likewise in *Genesis* 1:4, the movement from One to Two is recorded as the separation of light from darkness.

From a mathematical perspective, the number two is not only

ambiguous, but also unique, being the only natural number that yields a sum equal to its product, which is co-equal to four when its operand is also two (2 + 2 = 4, and 2 × 2 = 4). Number two is thus midway between One and all numbers greater than two. Mathematically, there is no distinction between addition and multiplication for the number two (unlike number one and all other numbers). Philosophically, this lack of distinction parallels Proclus' statement, "the dyad is the medium between Unity and number" (Westcott, 1974, p. 36). That is, psychologically, the discriminative function, which the number two symbolizes, is naturally and necessarily born at the junction between nascent consciousness and the ego (one), and full awareness of infinite diversity (three and greater).

The number two, therefore, has a 'threshold' phenomenology that is paradoxical in nature because we see that discrimination is not fully active (mathematically speaking). By the symbolism inherent in the number two, addition and multiplication should be differentiated, but as Westcott (1974) writes: "[Two is] the interval between Multitude and the Monad, because it is not yet perfect multitude, but is parturient with it" (p. 36). Therefore, symbolically, the number two cannot discriminate itself toward multitude since it is not of the multitude. Rather than seek discrimination, however, the opposite—reconciliation—is achieved, and this is in keeping with the dual nature of the 'mathematical' two, where 2 + 2 and 2 × 2 = 4.

The Principle of Duality

From unity comes duality—an endless series of opposites—Heaven and Earth, above and below, light and darkness, black and white, day and night, dry and wet, hot and cold, spirit and matter, expiration and inspiration, dilation and contraction, right and left, front and back, conscious and unconscious, male and female, 'father' and 'mother', 'masculine' and 'feminine', entropy and negentropy, positive and negative, remembering and forgetting, unity and multiplicity, life and death, and so on. In *Pan and the Nightmare* (1979), James Hillman describes the life process as the "basic polarity of organic rhythm" (p. xxiv):

> One and the same archetypal idea about the rhythm of natural life occurs in those pairs called at different times and by different theorists: accessum/recessum, attraction/repulsion, Lust/Unlust, diastole/systole, introversion/extraversion, compulsion/inhibition, fusion/separation, all-or-none, etc." (p. xxiv)

In each is present a 'hint' of the other—no opposite is entirely inert and polar. This is an 'epistemological necessity' argues James Hillman in *The Dream and the Underworld* (1979):

> Oppositionalism distinguishes by drawing to extremes. These extremes must touch, because they need each other for the distinction to become apparent…. Only those pairs having something material, essential in common can be sensibly opposed. (pp. 83-84)

The two opposites need each other to exist or there can be no polarity, no existence at all. An etymological example illustrates the extreme point of this rapprochement between opposites. The two words 'black' and 'white' have the same origins. Carl Sagan in *The Dragons of Eden* (1978) writes:

> Black comes from the Anglo-Saxon "*blaece*," and white from the Anglo-Saxon "*blac*," which is still active in its cognates "blanch," "blank," "bleak," and the French "blanc." Both black and white have as their distinguishing properties the absence of color. (p. 176)

It is also true that matter has 'spirit', and 'spirit' is in matter. The spirit/matter antithesis can be amplified through symbolism, although the symbolism used here is for the most part pertinent to Western culture and the psyche influenced by Western principles (*see* Table 2).

Table 2. *The Traditional Taxonomy: Spirit and Matter, and Associated Antitheses (using Jungian principles).*

SPIRIT	MATTER
The 'masculine'—the 'Father', Logos, Sun	The 'feminine'—the 'Mother', Eros, Moon
Active creative process of binding order	Passive creative process of Nature
Intellectual Realm, Thought	Physiological Realm, Feeling
Meaning and philosophy of Life	Natural, instinctive life of the body
Teachings of old, traditional wisdom	Life-giving factor, vegetative functions
Institutions, Concepts, Mind, Reason	Place of Origin, Substance, Matter, Emotion
Dogma (philosophical, ecclesiastical, scientific)	Living power of the psyche
Fantasy, the Abstract, the Rational	Behavior, the Concrete, the Irrational
The world of the conscious mind and its values	The world of the unconscious and its images
Consciousness/Conscious Dominants	The Unconscious/ Unconscious Dominants
Collective Consciousness	Collective Unconscious

The Spirit/Matter Dichotomy

The two terms 'spirit' and 'matter' are taken here as representations of the oppositionalism existent in antithetical relationships, and at all times in this text spirit/matter is not only used in a metaphoric or symbolic way, but is used with the acknowledgement that the final word on the 'true' nature of both is still under dispute. It is within the scope of the human capacities of reason and thought on one hand, and feeling and affect on the other, to attempt to construct definitions of the 'true' nature of matter and spirit. But neither the physicist (concerning matter) nor the theologian (concerning spirit), each depending on their own particular discourse, can say beyond a shadow of a doubt, what either really is, although many use the terms as if they did know. The layperson is convinced of his or her understanding of matter (the physicist, less so), yet spirit seems to be a contentious issue on all sides. Opinions run to extremes, from disbelief to belief; from doubt to certainty; from suspicion to total acceptance. How is it that spirit, as metaphor for superior knowledge, insight and intuition, the unknown factor behind certain types of behavior, the unformed which is forming, etc., came to be dissolved of its essential nature? How did it come to be an anachronism in the centuries up to and including the present twenty-first century? Is the term 'spirit' too nebulous? Under what circumstances was it explained away? What is spirit exactly?

Legal councils talk about the 'spirit' of the Law being more important than the 'letter' of the Law. Horse trainers know that a horse's spirit must be broken at the very start of its training regimen. The religious regard the human spirit as being at least as important as the human soul. Many argue that spirit and matter are not only interdependent, but are different aspects of the same thing. There is the idea that talk of the spirit, and theological and religious discourse in general, are products of language function that serve a particular purpose in describing, for example, a numinous or ineffable experience. It seems, however, that any attempt to verbalize an experience should not be undervalued merely because the naïve mind may be constructing a discourse around physical or psychological phenomena. Certainly, words are not the thing, but words *do* seem to lead us somewhere. But maybe the spiritual experience is just an invented concept that describes incomprehensible, intracerebral processes that are purely neuro-chemico-physiological events in the brain.

What about matter? The nuclear (quantum) physicist will tell us that matter becomes intangible at the subatomic level, having no extension in space—it is more like spirit than matter at this level—and comes to lose its physical substance, and its characteristic meso-physical properties. Rather than claiming that spiritual qualities (intuitions, insights, etc.) or the psyche (the soul), or the mind (consciousness, ego awareness) are epiphenomena of brain function, we might claim that matter is a phenomenon of spirit. It might appear, then, that the discourse of the idealist may, at a fundamental level, be closer to the 'truth' because it is more accurate in identifying the 'truth' about matter in its most reduced state. However, going back to the original statement above (spirit and matter as different aspects of the same thing), it may be more appropriate to question the absolute claims of both the materialist *and* the idealist because, from the discursive point of view just raised, words like 'spirit' and 'matter' are only labels for viewpoints. From a pragmatic standpoint, we might best take material phenomena and spiritual phenomena at face value and appreciate both from their distinctly different phenomenologies, rather than reducing one to the phenomenology of the other. This approach —alternativism—can be seen as a compromise between materialism and idealism.

Well, ok, but you cannot deny consciousness in both.

Ultimately, the prejudice against the word spirit, therefore, is born of a modernist materialistic mind-set, and rightly speaking, has no absolute claim in its assumptions. In fact, if one thing is certain (beyond 'death and taxes') it is the truth of the human spirit when it discloses itself as author of all human deeds, from the most virtuous to the most depraved. Alternatively we recognize the interpretation that specific neural structures of the material brain may be pre-disposed towards certain outcomes that may be described as the human spirit in action. Either way, the spirit, like number, is an ordering principle in itself that manifests in the psyche as purposeful (ordered), creative activity.

Don't rationalize it too much, son, or it might go away!

The reality of the spirit is now both irrefutably and unavoidably accepted as a personal, psychological issue by the medical and psychological professions (at least officially) with the inclusion of religious or spiritual problems in First's *Diagnostic and Statistical Manual of Mental Disorders—Fourth Edition* (1994). Now it is accepted (outside a religious framework) that clinical attention may be needed to cope with "distressing experiences that involve loss or questioning of faith,…or questioning of spiritual values" (p. 685). After decades of denial "the 'spiritual problem' of modern man [*sic*]", as Jung wrote of it as early as the late 1920s, has to some degree been acknowledged.

The Mind/Brain Problem

To continue the above argument, von Franz reminds us in *Alchemy* (1980a) that our concepts are "created as means of expression" (p. 152). She gives, as an example, the field of physics, where "concepts are vaguely interwoven" (p. 152) because we do not have a clear picture of reality. Terms are constructed as labels for certain distinct phenomena. Von Franz's reminder also applies to the mind/brain problem (as it does to the spirit/matter dichotomy). It has been stated that the two, mind and brain, like spirit and matter, may also be different aspects of the same thing (though what that thing may be is anybody's guess). On the one hand, the concept of mind has developed over thousands of years from classical philosophy, religion, and theology, and in modern times our understanding of the mind has been greatly enhanced with theories pertaining to the unconscious, such as Sigmund Freud's subconscious and Jung's unconscious. On the other hand, interest in the brain as the center of the personality has been with us for only a short while (a matter of a few centuries), and positivistic/empirical research into brain function is even more recent.

These two approaches have provided the basis for well-developed models that explain the 'reality' of both mind and brain. Certain phenomena will be best described by one model, or the other, or both, according to the purpose served. Models, then, are constructions that are projected onto the phenomena that comprise the particular reality under consideration. Even our ideas about mind and brain function are projections onto the very phenomena that we consider are the source of these projections by which we seek to explain both the phenomena and the projections in the first place.

Von Franz (1974) speaks of there being a possible 'tangible connection' between psyche and matter through number, which would also imply a possible mind/brain connection through number—the number archetype (and we might speak here of archetypes in general). This idea can be regarded as a discursive means of uniting two previously irreconcilable discourses about two transcendental spheres of reality. Any connection that might be made between psyche and matter, mind and brain, by using number as a kind of glue, would be considered a *conceptualization* by the materialist (at worst, it would be just another illusion), while for the idealist such a link would confirm the Platonic Idea and the many Forms—the 'primordial images' (at worst, it would be a realist compromise).... *pretty "heady" stuff*.....

But more importantly, since communication of ideas depends on language, von Franz is recognizing the possibility of a 'neutral' language, which does not serve established ideologies, and at the same time could be universally accessible and acceptable. This claim may sound overly ambitious; certainly it would be suggesting the introduction of yet another discourse (with all its advantages and disadvantages). Yet it may be a way of getting around the mind/brain problem, and the psyche/matter dichotomy.

The Relativity of Opposites

In classical philosophy, psyche 'needs' matter (physical body) to give it form (hence, materialized or manifested soul): matter *embodies* psyche. Matter in turn 'needs' psyche (spirit/soul) to express its existence, through motion, and to be a living being (hence, animate body): psyche *moves* matter. Jung (1977) draws attention to the deeper implication of this reciprocal relationship:

> when you observe the stream of images within, you observe an aspect of
> the world, of the world within. Because the psyche, if you understand

it as a phenomenon occurring in living bodies, is a quality of matter, just as our body consists of matter. We discover that this matter has another aspect, namely a psychic aspect. It is simply the world seen from within. It is just as though you were seeing into another aspect of matter. (p. 303)

The same parallels can be drawn with all opposites. Just as in the *T'ai Chi T'u* (the Chinese symbol of yin/yang) we see that part of the one is in the other (*see* fig. 10). Yin and yang represent opposing principles, but their reciprocal relationship, with each part including a part of the other, implies a system of difference too. The *T'ai-Chi T'u* does not symbolize a system of irreconcilable opposites, but is a resonating and interactional system that embodies resolution through mutual distinction and bondedness, identity and unison, growth and stability.

Figure 10. *T'ai-Chi T'u ('Diagram of the Supreme Ultimate'): The yin/yang symbol of opposites.*

In sixth-century China this dualistic philosophy emerged as a model to explain the world observed in nature. A natural order was perceived to exist that consisted of two principles that were directly opposed, but capable of uniting in attraction. According to E. J. Holmyard, in *Alchemy* (1957), yin stood for the Moon, the 'feminine', water, and things passive in nature, while yang stood for the Sun, the 'masculine', fire, and things active in nature.

Capra (1988) noted a cyclical pattern underpinning the *Tao*, which is structurally represented by the oppositional nature of yin and yang. Originally yin and yang meant the shady and sunny sides of the mountain, respectively, which may be generalized to the 'dark' and 'light' aspects of all phenomena. The *T'ai-Chi T'u* is a symmetrical arrangement of the dark yin and the bright yang, but the symmetry is not static. It is a rotational symmetry suggesting (very forcefully) a continuous cyclical movement. As fourth-century philosopher *Kuei Ku Tsu* once said: "The *yang* returns cyclically to its beginning, the *yin* attains its maximum and gives place to the *yang*" (Capra, 1988, p. 120). As the one rotates (clockwise in the diagram) it reaches its peak and the seed of the opposite is activated resulting in an *enantiadromia* (Heraclitus' term for a thing turning into its opposite).

This dualistic schema (see also the chapter "*I Ching*") became an appropriate philosophy of life in ancient China for the farmer who was constantly aware of the rising and setting Sun, the changing Moon, and the cyclicality of seasons. The physician too observed the finer aspects of oppositionalism in medicine and medical treatment of the human body with the homeostatic functioning of its organs and the harmonic flow of *ch'i* (life energy).

In *The Mysterium Lectures* (1995), Edinger illustrates the relative and reciprocal nature of opposites from an etymological perspective. In Gnostic thought the Moon (traditionally embodying the 'feminine' principle) is said to possess a noetic aspect. The word noetic derives from the Greek word *Nous* that equates with mind, reason and order, and originates as a spiritual entity, all of which would traditionally come under the rubric of 'masculine' phenomenology. But the Greek word *mene*, meaning moon, has ambiguous associations. The root *mene* was adopted by Latin scholars and used in the Latin word for month, *mensis*, which is the root for our English words 'menses' and 'menstrual'. Edinger notes further that:

The same root [mene] appears in the Latin word *mens*, meaning mind, with its genitive, *mentis*; and *mentis* is the root for our word mental. The same root is in the word *mensura* which means measure. So moon, monthly, mind and measure all belong to the same symbolism. (p. 112)

All these words have either 'feminine' or 'masculine' associations. In ancient Chinese philosophy the Sun was identified with the 'feminine' principle (contradicting Holmyard above) and in the German language, by some 'linguistic accident' (as Jung calls it) the Sun is also 'feminine'.

Contrary to western tradition, the Gnostics personified Wisdom (another traditionally 'masculine' quality) as *Sophia* (a female figure), but in the ancient Middle-East the Semite Moon God *Sin* was actually the *masculine* God of Wisdom. So too, the Egyptian god *Thoth,* who compares with Hermes and Mercury, was associated with the moon, although all three gods ruled over the male-dominated fields of science, invention, the arts and technology. Often Moon deities were depicted with horns (a symbol of 'masculine' consciousness, spiritual power and virility), so it can be seen that there is no clear claim for unanimity, as far as the Sun/Moon gender issue is concerned. These contradictory viewpoints are clarified by Edinger (1995) in one simple statement, "the principle of consciousness is the same for both men and women" (p. 113). This treatment is a most politically correct response to traditional thinking which posits consciousness as a solar, 'masculine' principle, while the lunar principle usually refers to the unconscious and female cyclical factors only. It is interesting to note how the diversity of culture-specific realities and etymological ambiguity may check the absolute claims of statements that genderize neutral concepts.

The Principle of Duality in Philosophy and Science

While human behavior and physiology were not drawn into gender politics until very recently, the human subject as the site for a total dichotomization of his/her very being is not at all a recent development in our culture. The dualistic philosophy of René Descartes as early as the seventeenth century is one such example. He proposed two kinds of substance, and two kinds of property: the substance of matter (body), which had *physical* properties, and the substance of mind (soul, spirit), which had *nonphysical* properties. The mind had influence on the body through 'animal spirits'—his way of explaining how something nonphysical could have influence on physical matter.

While the Church authorities were happy with a philosophy that recognized the immortal soul, some philosophers were dissatisfied with the notion that causal properties were inherent in nonphysical entities, and more to the point, there was even a serious lack of evidence for the existence of nonphysical substance in the first place. Accordingly, Descartes' *substance* dualism was challenged by so-called *property* dualism. As the term suggests, it was theorized by property dualists that the brain, although *physical*, also had the *nonphysical property* of mind or soul, but this was an *emergent* property of the complex, organized human brain, and upon death these properties must die, just as the decaying, disorganized brain must cease to exist. As a property dualist, one could either believe that the mind and brain had causal influences on each other (interactionism) or they did not (epiphenomenalism). Debate continues as to whether a purely materialistic approach can explain all human mental events, or whether some form of modified dualism must be developed to account for those problems which dualists feel have not been addressed by the materialists. *Consciousness' a word you keep leaving out !*

The materialist, who has come to rely on the positivistic, empirical methods of science, is also opposed by the more 'idealistic' thinking philosophers and social critics. Writing in the early part of the twentieth century, P. D. Ouspensky, in *Tertium Organum* (1964), considered the positivistic approach to be one that arrests thought. The sciences, having established certain methods of 'free investigation' into observable phenomena, imposed a materialism which condemns as inaccessible and, therefore, irrelevant that which it cannot measure by the senses or with its instruments:

> With astonishing rapidity those principles which only yesterday expressed the highest radicalism in the region of thought have become

the basis of opportunism in the region of ideas and serve as blind alleys, stopping the progress of though…. But thought which is free, cannot be bound by any limits…. [T]he true and real progress of thought is only in the broadest striving toward knowledge, that does not recognise the possibility of arrestment in any *found* forms of knowledge at all. (pp. 305-306)

Ouspensky wrote these words in 1920, but seven years earlier in 1913 Schwaller de Lubicz (1986) pre-empted Ouspensky's feeling on the subject:

It is interesting to note how the world, especially the scientific world, likes to believe in things stripped of all meaning, while other more meaningful and logical explanations are rejected as fantasies or hallucinations…. Science leads all progress, fecundates every activity, nourishes all humanity: and the same science dilates upon subjects that are absolutely of the first importance…. With what, then, do we reproach science? With its conservatism. There is its error! The materialist conception of our age impedes all progress. The many discoveries continually being made…are no proof of the value of our age's science but—since generally speaking these discoveries are the result of factors other than those given by science—a proof that it divigates and digresses upon a constantly moving and changing wave. (pp. 9-10)

Since those early decades of the twentieth century the criticisms of science and materialism have come forth steadily and unrepentantly. Jung has always criticized the one-sided certainty of science, and in 1946 he wrote:

the much needed broadening of the mind by science has only replaced medieval one-sidedness—namely, that age old unconsciousness which once predominated and has gradually become defunctive—by a new one-sidedness, the overvaluation of "scientifically" attested views. These each and all relate to knowledge of the external object in a chronically one-sided way, so that nowadays the backwardness of psychic development in general and self-knowledge in particular has become one of the most pressing contemporary problems. (Jung, 1960, para. 426)

It can be seen that it is not the scientific method that is the problem, as much as the uncompromising allegiance to the principles of science and the *modus operandi* (i.e., the ulterior motives) of the practitioners of science. The former describes the process of science, while the latter has been called scientism by Max Charlesworth in *Science, Non-Science and Pseudo-Science* (1980):

> Scientism gives a central place to scientific values such as objectivity, neutrality, rationality, so that other values—the subjective, the personal, the emotional, the intuitive, the imaginative—are correspondingly downgraded. However, there is no necessary connection between science and this ideological view of science and we can acknowledge the place and value of science without subscribing to scientism.... [I]t is possible to recognise that science is one of the most astonishing inventions of the human mind without claiming that it is the only, or even the most important, invention of *Homo sapiens*. From this point of view we can agree with criticism of the scientific ideology which has attached itself parasitically to science over the last two hundred and fifty years, while disagreeing completely with...rejection of science and the scientific method as such. (p. 46)

Postmodern social criticism of science over the last few decades now speaks of the 'constructed' nature of human knowledge claims as arrived at by science and the scientific method. Institutions (and individuals alike) have their purposes and agendas served through language as an appropriately structured version or discourse about the human world, but the main premise of any criticism of scientism is to relativize the assumed certainty of the scientific approach, its practitioners, and their knowledge claims. The same holds true for postmodern thought—it is no more than a recognition that there is a counter-position to science and scientism. Thus, the dualistic phenomenon of taking sides needs to be relativised. When that is at least considered, one might then be in a position of recognizing that advantages and disadvantages, successes and failures, must inevitably dog any system constructed by fallible minds that not only posit two opposing viewpoints, but discard one for the sake of the other.

Biological and Psychological Variants on the Duality Principle

The reciprocal nature of duality, as described in the yin/yang philosophy, also translates to the biological realm. For example, Freud observed that pure masculinity and femininity did not exist, psychologically or biologically. Jung's theory of the *anima* (in men) and the *animus* (in women) gives concrete recognition to the fact of a contrasexual component in human beings, these natures being primarily compensatory to otherwise extremely polarized consciousnesses in men and women, with correspondingly excessive attitudes and behaviors.

Differences in attitudes and behaviors in males and females (regardless of whether it is possible or not, or even politically correct, to label them as gender specific) are also influenced by hormonal activity. It is a biological fact that while the testes produce mostly androgen (male hormone) and the ovaries produce mostly estrogen (female hormone), both androgen and estrogen are produced by both sexes. However, although hormonal activity is responsible for secondary sex characteristics (breast and hip enlargement in females, and beard growth and voice changes in males) it is not clear to what degree hormonal activity affects behavior. More to the point is recognition of the fact that biological and psychological realities may combine to demonstrate the indiscrete natures of 'male' and 'female'; 'masculine' and 'feminine'.

'Psychologically', the principles of 'masculine' and 'feminine', and their oppositional natures, are embodied in the sex and gender roles of father and mother, which then become internalized in the psychic structure of the individual. It can be said, conceptually and symbolically, that the 'Father' rules the head and the 'Mother' rules the body (*see* Table 2 above). The body can also be divided into a secondary system, right side and left side (mythologically associated with 'Father' and 'Mother').

In neuro-anatomical terms, the traditional qualities of 'male' and 'female' are present in the two hemispheres of the brain: the left hemisphere is 'masculine' and the right hemisphere is 'feminine'. These facts create an interesting paradox, which is easily resolved. Before the fact of the contra-

Be careful when you call someone "an angel." Angels don't have gender. They're above it! Angels are pictorialized as male or female, but that is a human projection.

Two (The Dyad)   141

lateral arrangement of the brain was discovered—the left hemisphere governing many functions on the right side of the body, and the right hemisphere governing many functions on the left side—the Left side ('feminine')/Right side ('masculine') distinction was a phenomenally derived knowledge claim based purely on the appearance of things. The inferences of this 'psychological' system are symbolic only, since they do not correspond with the neuro-scientific evidence of brain physiology. Nor are 'Father' and 'Mother' representative of the biological parents—they are specifically archetypal images. However, these and other such literal authority figures provide the images and influences that embody the idea of these two domains. As such, 'Father' and 'Mother' ('masculine' and 'feminine') are the archetypal and transpersonal personifications of these two realms, as represented in dreams, visions, fantasy life, spontaneous notions and even symptoms.

There is, therefore, a duality of a specific form capable of both friction (of opposing elements) and harmony (in the union of opposites)—the former causing a mind/body (or right/left) split within the individual's psychic system (and capable of reaching the organic level) resulting in anything from a mild moral dilemma to a 'full-blown' neurotic disorder, but in the latter, the result is the 'pearl of great price'—the recognized treasure (inner harmony, strength and wisdom) of reconnection with one's soul, and the inner peace and balance that this reconnection ensures. In addition, there emerges a new-found creativity and higher consciousness, so that the personality is expanded into a newer, more profound personage, as exemplified in such representative figures as the artist, sage, scientist, inventor, discoverer, etc.

The Bi-Modal Brain as a Dual System

Apart from behavior, gender and sexuality, other binary functions and motifs are demonstrated in the human form (and also in other species). The human form is essentially symmetrical—outwardly, with its two arms, two legs, two ears, two eyes, etc., and internally, with its two kidneys, two lungs, hemispherical brain, and so on. The complexity of the human brain, and human physiology in general, combined with the fact that, for the most part, the entire organism functions best as a dual system, suggests that there is a natural or evolutionary preference for complex organisms to take symmetrical, binary forms. The initiation of the organism's life processes is demonstrated at the cellular level with the splitting of a single cell into two, which multiplies into a plurality of cells, the dualistic process constantly repeating and culminating in its final form.

The dualistic nature and structure of the body has been observed throughout history in all cultures. Apart from the suspicion of the left side of the body and the sinister (Latin: *sinister* = 'left') associations of left-handedness with the Devil, and the performance of gauche acts (French: *gauche* = 'left'), the dual nature of the brain, with its two hemispheres and their associated functions, has also been dichotomized. There is a danger in over-schematizing the bi-modal, hemispherical brain. David Galin, in 'Two Modes of Consciousness and the Two Halves of the Brain' (1977), warns of 'dichotomania'—a term coined by Marcel Kinsbourne. This phenomenon parallels the 'naïve localizationism' of the phrenologists in the eighteenth century. Bumps on the head were taken to refer to, or indicate certain psychological characteristics.

David Galin notes that it is inaccurate to say that rational skills, such as arithmetic, are confined to the right hemisphere. In fact, although major components of this skill *are* localized, the contributing factor of the other hemisphere is crucial in bringing about complete mastery and execution of the task. The spatial mode of the right hemisphere is important for visualization and concrete manipulation of symbols and 'counters' (fingers, etc.), or nonlinear reasoning, involving multi-dimensional, mathematical representations. So too, with dance, for example, it is self-evident that while spatial sensitivity is needed in dance, the rational, judgmental skills associated with the left hemisphere are necessary to monitor and secure a successful performance.

Even before the bi-modal nature of the brain (and therefore mind) was discovered, the 'active' mode of the left hemisphere associated with normal consciousness (which controls the right side of the body) has always been the favored disposition of many cultures because such an approach (active and extraverted) is seen as enhancing the survival of a culture by way of its adaptive functional capacity, while the 'receptive' mode of the right hemisphere (which controls the left side of the body), associated with 'altered states' of consciousness, is regarded with mistrust, or is considered mysterious and has even been posited as the source of deviant behavior.

In fact, a receptive mode of consciousness is life-enhancing too, and studies have shown that the two modes have a complementary relationship. Galin explains that language, logic, analytic and sequential determinations are controlled and executed by the left hemisphere, while the right hemisphere governs spatial sense, pattern recognition (faces, melodies), simultaneous and holistic determinations. In the normal brain the corpus callosum mediates and maintains complementarity between the hemispheres, with special tasks assigned to the appropriate hemisphere.

The bi-modal brain allows the human being the capacity to specialize and become the highly organized species that it is; yet the occasional conflict of interest, which invariably arises in a dual system, can hinder normal processes. For example, just noting the details of an environment (a left hemisphere task) will compromise the perception of the organized whole (a right hemisphere task). These two functions cannot be performed at the same time, hence the need for a bi-modal brain, which segregates the two specialized functions. We could have evolved into a species that only performed in sequential, analytical mode, but a lack of spatial, holistic faculties would have jeopardized our survival. The complex nature of the world requires, at least, a dualistic approach to interpretation of experience and phenomena, where sometimes a global perception or experience of the object is necessary, sometimes a specific, studied or step-by-step understanding is necessary. Therefore, the bi-modal brain 'cooperates' with itself (avoids dissonance) when each hemisphere is employed according to its mode, as circumstance demands, with each providing informational complementarity, which, when taken as a whole in consciousness, gives a broader representation of the world than either hemisphere could give on its own. For complex species, the bi-modal brain, and all the other binary faculties and processes point to compensatory and complementary modes of functioning. More generally, the essential nature and adaptive advantages of twofolded biological forms is indicated.

Individuation as a Dualistic Process

Neumann (1973) psychologically interprets the mythical parallels of the *uroboros* and the transpersonal 'First Parents' as symbolic representations of opposites that precede ego-consciousness. As the ego develops, the necessity to break free from uroboric 'captivity' (a natural human process) becomes more and more urgent, and is the one crucial component in the bid for independence and individuality.

Neumann sees any form of over-weening adherence to this initial state of the child as unprogressive, resulting in a neurotic character disorder symbolized by castration (castration refers to the severance of creative forces). Liberation involves the mythical 'slaying of the dragon' until a consequent rescue of the soul figure (previously unconscious and embodying the missing component of the personality) results, which is associated with the proverbial 'treasure hard to attain'—the 'soul's treasure.'

The actual 'slaying of the dragon' refers to the psychological overthrow of world-, body-, or unconscious-dominants that retard ego development. The ego assumes a heroic position in this operation that involves a reflective and reflexive, analytical, and then synthetic (holistic) attitude towards these external and internal forces.

OPPOSITE PAGE: Figure 11. *The Uroboros, Great Mother and Great Father all have dual natures. The Hero emerges from the Uroboros as child of the First Parents. There are two types of Hero. The first type (1 & 2) performs many tasks and meets failure ('castration'), succeeds later by winning the 'treasure' through the slaying of the 'Dragon', then performs other feats, but suffers an early death. The second type (3 & 4) faces the 'Dragon' first, then 'castration', returns to the Uroboros, is reborn, and finally conquers death.*

UROBOROS
Tail-eating Serpent, Primal Snake, Man & Woman (Hemaphrodite/Androgyne),
Above & Below, Life Cycle, Self-Begetter, Alpha and Omega,
Yin and Yang, Leviathan

GREAT MOTHER
Eros, Mother Goddess, Womb, Love and Affection, Life & Nature, Relationship, Grace, Humanity and its values (Table 2)

GREAT FATHER
Logos, Father God, Institutions, Ethics & Morals, Law & Order, Religion, Politics, Civilisation and its values (Table 2)

TERRIBLE MOTHER (Evil Queen, Step-Mother, etc.)	VIRGIN/GODDESS (Mother, Spiritual Guide)	FATHER/GOD (Man or Divinity)	TERRIBLE FATHER (Evil King, Brother, Uncle, etc.)
1. **Medhbh:** Uses magic against **Cuchulainn**	1. **Scathach:** Makes **Cuchulainn** invincible	1. **Sualtam (Saultach):** Earthly father of **Cuchulainn** (**Lugh:** Father-God of **Cuchulainn**)	1. **Conchobar:** Sends **Cuchulainn** to **Curoi** to be killed
2. **Medea:** Kills **Jason**'s wife and children	? **Hera:** Protects and guides **Jason**	2. **Aeson:** King of Iolcus, **Jason**'s father	2. **Pelias:** Usurps **Jason**'s throne
3. **Set (Isis*):** Seals **Osiris** in a chest/Struggles with **Horus**	3. **Nut:** Sky goddess-Mother of **Osiris** (**Isis:** Mother of **Horus**)	3. **Geb:** Earth god-Father of **Osiris** (**Osiris:** Father of **Horus**)	3. **Set:** Dismembers **Osiris**/Gouges out **Horus**'s eye
4. **Satan (Mary*):** Tempts **Jesus** three times	4. **Mary:** Mother & care-giver to **Jesus**	4. **Joseph:** Earthly father of **Jesus** (**Jehovah:** Father-God of **Jesus**)	4. **Herod:** Tries to slay the **Christ** child
* Negative aspects of Terrible Mother assumed in **Set/Satan** so that purified forms of **Isis/Mary** remain as the "Good Mother"			

HERO
1. **Cuchulainn**
2. **Jason**
3. **Osiris/Horus**
4. **Jesus/Christ**

DEATH (PERMANENT RETURN TO THE *UROBOROS*)
1. **Cuchulainn:** Beheaded by **Lugaid**, **Curoi**'s son
2. **Jason:** Crushed by timber of the **Argo**

1 & 2

3 & 4

'DRAGON'
1. **Cuchulainn:** defeats **Curoi** the Giant
2. **Jason:** defeats the **Hydra** (7-headed serpent)
3. **Osiris:** Dismembered by **Set** (**Horus:** Struggles with **Set**)
4. **Jesus:** Tempted by **Satan**

1 & 2

1 & 2

1 & 2

'CASTRATION'
1. **Cuchulainn:** Thrust into icy water
2. **Jason:** Crew disseminated at **Acheron**
3. **Osiris:** Penis devoured by the oxyrhynchus (Nile fish) (**Horus**'s eye gouged out by **Set**)
4. **Jesus:** Crucified

3 & 4

TREASURE
1. **Cuchulainn:** Wins Champion's Portion
2. **Jason:** Annexes the Golden Fleece
3. **Osiris:** Resurrects (**Horus:** Made Pharaoh-God)
4. **Jesus Christ:** Resurrects

3 & 4

3 & 4

REBIRTH (TEMPORARY RETURN TO THE *UROBOROS*)
3. **Osiris:** Immortalised by **Re** (**Horus** emasculates **Set**)
4. **Jesus:** Ascends & Transforms

Hmmm.... very interesting.

Attitude as a Dichotomy

In his theory of psychological types, Jung contributed to dualistic modes of thought and categorization by positing, on empirical grounds, two psychological attitudes—introversion and extraversion—that are the relative outlooks of the introvert and the extravert, respectively. The introvert is inwardly-oriented, being more influenced by subjective, personal factors and inner psychic processes, while the extravert is outwardly-oriented, being more influenced by objective, worldly factors and personal interaction.

Each attitude is a general orientation, but circumstances may involve the individual in the activation (consciously or otherwise) of the complementary attitude, which serves to modify the individual's outlook—often necessarily. Attitude typology is a counterpart (with function typology) of Jung's theory of psychological types (see the chapter "Four (The Tetrad)").

The Conflict of Opposites (Part I)—The Scales of Justice

Pythagoras spoke of duality as the law of this planet. His famous law of opposites includes reference to even and odd, good and evil, light and darkness—the blending of which produced harmony and balance. And just as the twenty-four hour day is twelve hours of daylight and twelve hours of darkness, Heraclitus observed the regulative function of opposites and conceived the universe as being a conflict of opposites, but also a striving for balance and justice.

Such conflict and striving for balance and justice is well represented in the endeavors of parties in litigation (as exemplified by defense and prosecution) where resolution of a legal quandary is sought through the tenets of law. Here the image of the scales of justice tipping one way and then the other is a perfect symbol of the striving for balance that, having been achieved, is justice served. Each party is aware of the oppositionalism so structured in the courtroom, but the balanced decision—the verdict—will depend on the overall effect of both testimonies on the judge and the jury,

see philosophy of law.
(The judge in the middle.)

with 'blind justice' standing over the whole proceedings.

So too, any human relationship can be extremely complex and taxing with each hoping for a satisfactory solution to a conflict. Although rather simplified, one of three outcomes is usually the solution of such oppositionalism:

1. the two individuals separate (thereby each shelves the problem) or;

2. the individuals resolve the problem (by striking a 'happy medium') and remain together or;

3. the problem is not resolved, but nor do they separate, which usually means the problem will resurface, necessarily creating an opportunity for resolution, as per (1) or (2) above, or the interminable stasis of (3).

The conflict of opposites is unavoidable and is exemplified in the moral dilemma of 'good versus evil'. Westcott (1974) notes that:

> the Pythagoreans [spoke] of the "two" as the "first idea of the indefinite dyad," and attribute[d] the number 2 to that which is indefinite, unknown and inordinate in the world. (p. 17)

Westcott also states: "Duality introduces us to the fatal alternative to Unity or Good, namely EVIL" (p. 38). Echoing this sentiment, Gerhard Dorn (sixteenth-century hermetic philosopher and student of Paracelsus) insisted on the 'elimination of the devilish binarius' in alchemical work (see the chapter "Ten (The Decad)"). Dorn's worldview needs special consideration and this is discussed next.

The Conflict of Opposites (Part II)—Dorn's Dilemma

Gerhard Dorn was an exceptional physician and pharmacologist, with an unsurpassed knowledge of his art, to the point that he served many nobles, and even dedicated his written works to them. His problem with the number two, however, reflected the problem of his time. That is, the problem which the patriarchy (as the Church) had with the 'feminine', as abstracted symbolically in the number two—the "beginning of all confusion, dissension, and strife" (von Franz, 1974, p. 90).

The idea of eliminating the number two for Dorn originated in *Genesis* 1:6-7 when God divided the waters on the second day, whereupon the number two (symbolizing the principle of distinction) became an existential reality in human consciousness. The second day is the only numbered day of the seven days of creation which was not considered 'good' by God (since it is both 'good' *and* 'evil', in keeping with the symbolism of number two).

As will become clear, the "flesh is weak" reference from *Matthew* 26:41 is also relevant to Dorn's plight, since it suggests superiority of the spiritual attitude, with a corresponding devaluation of the instincts of the body, and the material world in general. This spirit/matter duality was of course a contentious issue for the Church based on its general belief that the populace was almost always inclined towards creating schism between opposites rather than harmony. Hence, such notions as the Fall and original sin.

For Dorn, the dilemma of choice was certainly another most annoying feature of the *binarius*. Dorn's suspicion of the *binarius* stemmed from his unconscious knowledge (consciously inadmissible) that chaos and suffering *are* real, and must be accepted alongside the other realities of cosmos (order) and happiness. When we become aware of a pluralistic world, we are then able to assign value judgments to these realities. Prior to this awareness is the paradisical state of unity (the pre-conscious state of the child). Dorn himself expressed an almost regressive desire for this 'original state', which may have been conflated with the striving for unity. Thereby, Dorn's *naïveté* emerges, since he failed to see reality *as* it is, and failed to accept it for *what* it is.

Even in advancing an ideal of Oneness, he was yet impelled to speak in dualistic terms by raising the principle of twoness in the first place, which he then rejected (at least the 'darker' aspect as a component of God's own Shadow). That is, he identified God with good (and unity) and the Devil with evil (and twoness)—a reality which is essentially human-made (hence, part of the problem), but is also God-given, since God (as Dorn would have known), divided the waters in the beginning, thereby creating 'two' and giving 'Man' the propensity for constructing the whole dualistic dilemma (dividing the waters is taken as symbolic of the birth of discrimination or dualistic thinking).

Dorn's medieval discourse shows an unquestionable Christian bias much akin to that of the Church Fathers. That is, part of the general philosophy of the Church was the belief that evil resides in the body of 'Man', and that a strict adherence to the principle of the Trinity was essential, as was a resistance to 'quaternary' thinking, expressed as the failure or refusal to recognize Mary (the embodiment of the 'feminine') as equal with the personalities of the God-head. Dorn even called the devil the 'quadricornutus binarius', ('four-horned two') and called the quaternity the 'quadricornutus serpens' ('four-horned serpent'), since he saw the number four as deriving from two. To recognize the 'fourth' is a moral dilemma because it means differentiating the conflated components of the corporeal, the earth principle, matter, and the 'feminine' (as Mary), and even evil, from each other. Hence the adherence to the Trinity because it neatly relegated this problem to the unconscious.

But, actually, Dorn did eventually reach that stage where he was able to qualify the 'feminine' as equal with the 'masculine'. Von Franz, in *Alchemical Active Imagination* (1979), notes that the 'feminine' was recognized by Dorn as an 'equivalent principle', with the "same dignity as the spiritual father creator-god" (p. 32). Dorn, thereby, went a step further than the Church by differentiating matter (the 'feminine', etc.) and evil as distinct entities, but then he proceeded to deal with the problem of evil and the body in like manner with the Church. Dorn still blamed the body for its evil, its baseness, and its predisposition for sin, and was not sufficiently advanced psychologically to realize that the body's 'problem' was actually a problem with the archetype of the Shadow, which Dorn projected onto the body.

This way of dealing with the problem underscores the whole dualistic problem of the Church, and, canonically, goes as far back as to such New Testament examples as Christ's statement that the 'flesh' was weak (*Matthew* 26:41), as mentioned above. The weakness of the 'flesh' (body) was taken literally and uncompromisingly by the Church, and not understood at another level, where the body might be seen as following its own 'wisdom' and 'intelligence', and should not be held entirely accountable to the constructed moral laws of any canon.

Dorn never completely escaped this dualistic dilemma, being still very much a good Christian of his time, for all his heretical interest in alchemy and hermetic philosophy. Dorn's problem was a moral and ethical one that is very much a problem in our postmodern world that ultimately rests with the individual as a challenge to his or her own moral courage. The answer lies in the psyche. Only in the age of psychology has this understanding come through clearly, but still today, it is not uncommon for people to refuse to admit the psychological component behind the 'problem' of their bodies.

The Conflict of Opposites (Part III)—'Duplicitous Duplicity'

Special note should be made concerning the 'diabolical' nature of the number two as present in the English language. The English translators of Jung's *Psychology and Religion: West and East* (1958), taking up Jung's theme of the 'diabolical' number two, point out such words as "duplicity, double-dealer, double-cross [and] two-faced" (para. 180, n5) as being words upon which the traditional suspicion of the number two have left their mark. The Greek word *diabolos*, from which derives the English word Devil, literally means 'two sayer' or 'slanderer', hence number two's association with the Devil, Satan, Lucifer, and Evil, etc.

There are linguistic parallels and associations between the number two and evil in most languages the world over. These parallels are perhaps understandable given the common difficulty inherent in the task of decision-making, which usually requires an 'either/or' response. Any choice once made necessarily precludes the alternative(s) that may have been made, and the postmodern philosophy of Michel Foucault has indicated once again, in the language of our time, this age-old conundrum of the consequences of choice. In Foucault's *Discipline and Punish: The Birth of the Prison* (1977), and as an over-riding theme in many of his works, every historic era is seen as being dominated by a particular discourse that comes to embody the knowledge claims, truths, and norms of a society. By their very nature, these discourses, through hegemony and consensus, exclude discourses that embody other knowledge claims, truths and norms. Because societies function this way, subaltern groups are discursively constructed and marginalized so that the resulting intolerance of these groups requires the institution of disciplinary mechanisms in order to 'legitimize' the dominant discourse by normalizing (punishing) those 'excluded' individuals.

Foucault's philosophy is at least dualistic, in this regard, because it sees 'history' pluralistically, and as Robert Appignanesi and Chris Garrett point out in *Postmodernism* (1995), we see a world where a "multiple, overlapping, and interactive series of legitimate [versus] excluded histories" (p. 83) has taken place. The social friction which this situation has caused underscores the 'diabolic nature' that is symbolic of the number two.

Number Two in Art

In *Dynamics of the Self* (1989), Gerhard Adler is of the opinion that humans construct antithetical relationships when the subjective factor is given a free (unconscious) hand without conscious deliberation, and he illustrates his point by using the artwork, artistic interpretation, and the idea of 'negative space' as metaphor:

> This concept signifies that an object [the artwork] is not only definable by its contours but just as much definable by the space surrounding it. In other words, the "outline" of an object is also the "inline" of the space around it. (p. 98)

Just as real is the relationship between the human being as subject, and the cosmos as object—between the two is the *limen* of being—"inner psychic forces" in the former, and manifestations of "outer energies around us" (p. 98), in the latter.

Moving from this idea, an advance is made, by implication, toward the realization that innovations going back to Renaissance times followed this same subjective path. Adler sees the Renaissance discovery of perspective in artistic representation as going "hand in hand with the discovery of rational scientific methods" (p. 98; one might also add Cartesian dualism which came later), and born of these developments, an artificial separation of subject and object ensued. Increased consciousness in one direction resulted—increased creativity, clearer, more comprehensive and comprehensible representations of reality—but with these breakthroughs a loss of connectedness between individuals resulted, as well as a loss of "unity of subject and object" (p. 98) with nature.

Contrarily, the artworks of Cimabue and Giotto express unity. To the modern eye there at first appears to be a flatness or lack of depth in their paintings. But they begin to open up as depth is implied by the positioning of figures, one in front of the other, coupled with a naïve use of empirical (unscientific) perspective, as used to evoke a spatial sense through feeling rather than through architectonic accuracy.

Artistically speaking, then, and not just anatomically, biologically, psychologically and philosophically, we can find ourselves immersed in the dichotomy of the number two. As a consequence, the social repercussions of twoness are constantly with us. The psychological and philosophical solution to the dualistic dilemma is to see opposites as different aspects of the same thing. By focusing on this point one has an opportunity to imagine the nature of this balanced 'sameness' and experience the feeling it evokes, rather than naïvely holding the expectation of a rational solution. The former offers the individual an experience; the latter, if it were possible, would be 'spoon-feeding' and deny one the opportunity of witnessing for oneself the inner reality of psychic processes.

Summary

Conceptually, symbolically, and realistically, the number two represents the splitting or polarization of monadic forms into dualistic forms, which are related, but antithetical in nature. Not only are the opposites related, but also the presence of each opposite is in the other, since they emerged from the same source. The opposites, therefore, draw their characteristics from a monadic source that is paradoxical in nature, since it contains the opposites in one. Thus it is possible to discriminate and draw distinctions in consciousness about the world because the monadic paradox is annulled.

However, the consequence of separation brings with it both the benefit of differentiation, but also the threat of dissociation. All dualistic models carry this burden. Since things can be considered from at least two perspectives (a thing is either good or bad, acceptable or unacceptable), it is ultimately the individual, in consideration of the absolute moral obligation of responsibility to the integrity of the self (which must include the influence of a particular socio-cultural context), who must make a decision based on the relativization of consequences.

There is always Two (Discrimination), but there is no resolution of Being without the synthesizing experience of the balanced opposites, and so 'emerges' the number Three.

It is arguable that Dyadism is coming to an end! (?) In favour of T.O.E.

"Two" is what creates the ego karma of Buddhist delusion. . . . .

Plate 11. THE NUMBER THREE

Representations of three-dimensional space, or architectural space, are two-dimensional illusions that dramatically indicate how we visually interpret our world. The perspective in Santivo by Baroque architect Francesco Borromini capitalizes on a 'triadic' cognitive function in human beings that creates allusions to solidity, stability and extension in space [SOURCE: Wikimedia Commons].

THREE (THE TRIAD)

For there are three that bear record in heaven, the Father,
the Word and the Holy Ghost: and these three are one.

1 John 5:7

See
Hegel

The opposites, thesis and antithesis, conjoin to produce a
synthesis, which has the qualities of both the opposites. The
number three symbolizes resolved conflict, or compromise
between irreconcilable opposites. It follows that opposites are
brought to a synthesis in time, of which the whole is constituted
as the completed work—the third—by the unified nature of the
opposites in the number three. The number three symbolizes one
nature joined with its opposite to yield the three in relationship,
derived of the two and sharing their qualities. The number three
embodies an absolute dynamism that serves as the activating
principle that holds the three in one.

Uniting the Opposites

The number three symbolizes more than an amalgam of two opposing
principles since, although it contains the elements of both in its symbolism,
it has emergent properties, and as such, maintains its own uniqueness. Jung
(1958) has this to say about the number three:

> every tension of opposites culminates in a release, out of which comes
> the "third." In the third, the tension is resolved and the lost unity is
> restored…. Three is an unfolding of the One to a condition where it

> can be known—unity become recognizable; had it not been resolved
> into the polarity of the One and the Other, it would have remained
> fixed in a condition devoid of every quality. (para. 180)

Any knowledge claim one may feel free to make will involve the faculty of
discrimination. Only by differentiating the parts of the whole, or differentiating
the whole (One) from the world (Other) is there recognition of the *relationship*
between the two (the third). The relationship makes 'movement' possible, and
is the 'movement' (as events, translations, transformations, creations, and so
on) at physical and intellectual levels, by way of a 'threefold' characteristic, that
emerges as a result of the resolution of directionless, dualistic resonances.

Edinger, in *The Creation of Consciousness* (1984), gives a description of the
psychological equivalent of a created property (an increase in consciousness),
which is the reconciliation of oppositional, psychic functioning:

> The union of opposites in the vessel of the ego is the essential feature
> in the creation of consciousness. Consciousness is the third thing
> that emerges out of the conflict of twoness. Out of the ego as subject
> versus the ego as passive victim; out of the ego as praiseworthy
> and good versus the ego as damnable and bad; out of a conflict of
> mutually exclusive duties—out of all such paralyzing conflicts can
> emerge the third, transcendent condition which is a new quantum of
> consciousness. (p. 21)

Consciousness and the unconscious constitute a dual system, as does ego
and Self. Both systems have their own internal resonance, and the result is a
'quantum of consciousness', an increase in awareness. Consciousness is the
'field' within which the ego experiences the world. Paradoxically, consciousness
is the polar opposite of unconsciousness—it is part of a dual system, but
an *increase* in consciousness is a reconciliation between the original state of
consciousness and its opposite, the unconscious.

The Three-Dimensional Viewpoint

When we observe the physical world through our senses we experience threeness. The three dimensions of length, width and height give form to the universe on a material level. Our three-dimensional world, then, is one manifestation of the fundamental characteristic of three. While we consciously experience our existence in a space-time continuum, it is in threeness that we experience space, and in threeness that we experience time.

Kepler thought space must have three dimensions, and only three, because he felt it had a direct connection with the Trinity. Kepler argued that living beings experienced the world in three-dimensional space, just as the Creator God was threefold in nature (Father, Son and Holy Spirit), and therefore, God created space to reflect His triune personality. Supposedly, then, the Christian trinitarian concept of God is isomorphic with three-dimensional space. Accordingly, the 'discovery' of perspectival representations of reality in art and architecture during the Renaissance, which came about as a result of the geometrical extension of the subject into a three-axes coordinate system as described by Cartesian geometry, has a religious basis to its origins.

But three-dimensional space did not originate in Kepler's time, although the religious connections in earlier three-dimensional concepts of space were still present. For example, Lamy (1981) describes the 'House of Life' in Salt Papyrus 825 (detailing the rituals for conserving life in ancient Egypt) as being consciously constructed from a knowledge of three-dimensional space. The canopic chest of Tut-ankh-Amun, and the 'Room of Gold' are also constructed this way. All three 'spaces' have a ground plan with Isis in the West; Selket in the South; Nephthys in the East; and Neith in the North.

Within this fourfold ground plan, a vertical axis is suggested by "a figure standing in a cube" (Lamy, 1981, p. 95). The North-South axis aligns in one plane, signified by a standing man facing North (one foot positioned in front, the other behind); the East-West axis is raised and aligned according to the outstretched arms (the second plane), and the vertical trunk of the man gives the third axis (and third plane): thus, a cubic representation (*see* fig. 12).

Figure 12. *Three-dimensional space as envisaged by the ancient Egyptians.*

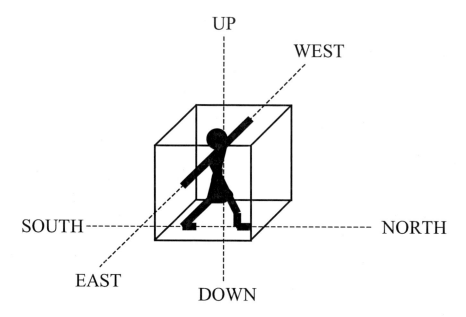

The fact that Egyptian artworks, tomb and wall illustrations are always represented in two dimensions (purely an aesthetic standard) does not detract from the fact that Egyptians were conscious of a three-dimensional worldview. Space-making appears to be an innate faculty of the psyche, empirically determined by conscious experience. (It will be seen that this idea is supported by biological factors.)

However, all spaces are constructed in our minds, and as such, the external world and the 'inner' world align for the most part, enabling human beings the possibility of mediating the matter and space of the corporeal body, and the 'inner' space of the mind, most evident in dreams and other altered states of consciousness, such as fantasy. Jacobi (1974) describes these and other states as 'planes' of experience:

> Life proceeds on different planes—material, spiritual, biological, psychological, etc.—which may reflect each other in analogies. Above

all, psychospiritual, immaterial being and happening can be embodied in images and symbols drawn from the perceptible, sensuous world. (p. 91)

In *Psychology and Alchemy* (1968b), Jung confirms that:

> the principle of the unconscious is the autonomy of the psyche itself, reflecting in the play of its images not the world but *itself*, even though it utilizes the illustrative possibilities offered by the sensible world in order to make its images clear…. The sensory datum…is autonomously selected and exploited by the psyche, with the result that the rationality of the cosmos is constantly being violated in the most distressing manner. (para. 186)

Often, in the latter case, there may be surprising paradoxes, since it is clear that the realm of mind does not need to obey the fundamental laws of physics, or the real world restrictions of matter.

The dimension of time is also experienced in triadic form as past, present and future. The space-time continuum is therefore composed of six partial aspects (length, width, height, past, present, future) that constitute a hexadic form (see the chapter "Six (The Hexad)"). For the physicist these six aspects are ancient human constructs based on the existential reality, or more accurately, the phenomenology of conscious experience.

To show how the idea of three-dimensional space is merely a construction born of human experience, the Earth's path around the Sun, for example, is a curved orbit, but in terms of astrophysics our planet follows a path that is the shortest distance between two points (a geodesic) in four-dimensional space-time according to the distribution of mass and energy in that space-time field. This is in accord with Einstein's theory of relativity, which marginalized Newton's theory of gravity and has even explained some previously unsolved problems in astronomy (i.e., orbital anomalies) and physics (i.e., the speed of light), which Newtonian physics could not explain.

The masses of bodies (planets, stars, and so on) cause a folding in space, which we perceive as curved, but is actually straight in four-dimensional space-time. Time too is affected by mass. That is, things slow down in time (the seconds tick more slowly) the closer they get to a mass. The arena of space and time has become relativized in science even though our immediate human condition and everyday conduct puts us squarely in a world that appears constant—spatially and temporally.

To demonstrate how the idea of three-dimensional time is also a construction of human experience, our actions, which seem to be given by co-ordinates in three-dimensional space, are actions that seem to take place with the unfolding of time, from its origin or creation in the past, its continuity in the present, and its resolution in the future. However, the so-called present is actually that sharp null-point of experience that almost escapes detection. Each time an observation is made it is already in the past, and every anticipation (nascent, then unfolding) is a non-existent event until it passes into the past. This ambiguous present (or indeed the lack of it) constitutes a major factor in the Hopi Indian cosmology. Time is considered to have two aspects, as von Franz explains in *Time: Rhythm and Repose* (1978):

> that which is manifest and thus more 'objective' and that which is beginning to manifest and is more 'subjective'. Concrete objects are manifest and in this way already belong to the past; inner images, representations, expectations and feelings are 'subjective', on their way to manifestation, and thus bend more towards the future…. There is no continuing flow of time for the Hopi, but a multiplicity of subtly distinguished events. (p. 5)

While the Hopi idea of exclusively experiencing events in the past *and* imagining in the future is not beyond the Western imagination, the Hopi model nevertheless indicates the diversity of interpretations of human perceptions and cognitions that can arise as a result of ethnological difference. However, the idea of a 'real' present (albeit loosely defined in terms of time-frame) is not precluded from any human experience, regardless of culture. It is purely a question of causes. The threefold system of time (past, present, future) has become necessary in many cultures, East and West, because of the resolvable dynamic implied in this triadic system. Past events can be recalled, future events can be anticipated, and both can be integrated and mediated in the 'now'. It is only in the now that creation becomes manifested, regardless of the future plan (plans are only possibilities). The present is a construct that gives a sense of recognition to the process of human deliberation in thought and action.

The Hopi model, *per se*, being essentially dualistic (focusing on objective and subjective experiences; past and future), does not give reality to ongoing creation—to the Hopi, the concept of 'doing' does not have the meaning it has in the West. The Westerner, on the other hand, barely sees the ongoing event as merely a constant transformation of the imminent into the manifested—the potential into the actual. It becomes clear that the present is only present if it is constructed to be present.

This exclusion of the 'now' may seem irrational to many, but it is in keeping with the nature of the Hopi Indian in particular, and implies the reality of multiple viewpoints and cultural diversity in general. What must not be forgotten is the role of the number archetype in these systems. Each number (two or three, etc.) has a unique and dynamic aspect, which instills the construction with its own particular reality. It seems that what is often lacking is awareness of this fact. To see the ethnological, and therefore, subjective character of a system only is to be oblivious to both the objective reality of number as potentials for meaning, and the symbolism born of this potentiality. This is the difference that makes the difference.

The Three States—Solid, Liquid, and Gas

Elements have a unique number of subatomic particles—protons, neutrons, and electrons. Conventionally, matter naturally exists in one of three states—solid, liquid, or gas—according to the respective counts of protons, neutrons, and electrons. These three normal states of matter have unique characteristics (*see* fig. 13).

In the case of solids, the molecules are tightly bound by so-called molecular forces. Solids hold their shape, and their volume is fixed according to a specific shape determined before solidification.

Figure 13. *The three states—(a) Solid (shape is held; volume is fixed), (b) Liquid (shape determined by container; volume is fixed; surface is free); and (c) Gas (shape determined by container; volume determined by container).*

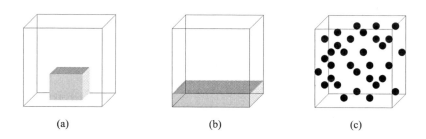

(a)   (b)   (c)

In the case of liquids, the molecular forces are comparatively weak compared to the solid, so the shape of a liquid is determined by the container. Liquids will take on a spherical shape in a gravity-free environment, but a liquid always has a fixed volume—even in a gravity-free environment.

In the case of gases, the molecular forces are the weakest of all three states. When a gas is introduced into a container, it will fill the space available, therefore taking on the shape and volume of the container. These states are relative, and by a sufficient application of energy (i.e., heating), solids will melt and take on liquid or even gaseous properties. Likewise, liquids and gases can be solidified by way of extraction of energy (i.e., freezing).

A fourth state—plasma—is postulated in physics. It is the most unusual of the four states. Under extreme conditions—as is the case in the nuclear furnace of the Sun—atoms break down and electrons jump out of their usual orbits leaving the atom with a positive charge—a so-called ion. This mixed state of atoms, ions, and free-floating electrons is called 'plasma' which is essentially a pseudo-state, but a state nonetheless with unique properties of its own. For example, plasma behaves like a fluid and a gas—it can flow—and react to, and generate electromagnetic forces. The technology that has emerged from this discovery has caused a shift from the old paradigm of cathode ray tube technology used in the conventional television screen to an innovative new paradigm of the plasma television, first introduced in the

1970s—light is created by phosphors that are excited by a plasma discharge between two flat panels of glass. The gas discharge is comprised of an inert mixture of noble gases.

This fourth state, plasma, which has emerged from three states (solid, liquid, and gas), expresses a curious age-old idea that the fourth is found amongst the three, though it may be difficult to find (see the next chapter "From Three to Four").

Number Three in Religion and Mythology

The importance of the number three is expressed in the religions of the ancient world, including those of the Middle East and India. Three offers a solution to two—a middle way based on the harmonized or balanced opposites – Christ between two thieves (one saved, one condemned); the Trinity of Father-Son-Holy Spirit; Mithra between two Dadophores (torch-bearers: one with torch held high, the other with torch lowered); Vishnu the preserver between Brahma the creator and Shiva the destroyer. All these are threefold images that present a dynamic, a movement in time, space and consciousness: a realization of unity in trinity, with each key figure (Christ, Holy Spirit, Mithra, Vishnu) being the decisive counterpart of their respective triad.

This threefold religious viewpoint is reflected in the metaphysical representation of the emanation of the Son from the Father, as given in the gnostic writings of Basilides in the second century. He proposed a 'threefold Sonship', which could be represented as 'three trichotomies', as schematized by Jung (1959a, para. 118). Each trichotomy represents emanations of the non-existent (unmanifested) God:

I	II	III
First Sonship	*Christ of the Ogdoad*	*Spirit*
Second Sonship	*Christ of the Hebdomad*	*Soul*
Third Sonship	*Jesus the Son of Mary*	*Body*

This schema is a gnostic configuration of the human existential triad that preempted the alchemical representation of the spirit-soul-body triad mentioned above. Jung (1959a) describes the three Sonships in Basilidean terms:

> The first "Son," whose nature was the finest and most subtle, remained up above with the Father. The second son, having a grosser...nature, descended a bit lower, but received some such wing as that which Plato... equips the soul.... The third son, as his nature needed purifying,... fell deeper into "formlessness." This third "sonship" is obviously the grossest and heaviest because of its impurity. (para. 118)

Edinger explains that these three sonships mirror the three states of egohood. In *The Aion Lectures* (1996) he describes one part of the ego (the first sonship) as never separating from the unconscious wholeness of the Self, a second part (the second sonship) achieves an 'intermediate position'—an ego that mediates consciousness and the unconscious, and is therefore truly conscious. A third part of the ego (the third sonship) is embedded in matter as it were, needing liberation by the Self (as Christ) with assistance by the ego, which is an aspect of the Self.

There is a kind of numinosity given to matter by Basilides, which anticipated the high regard the alchemists had for it, even from earlier times, but which reached its peak, even after the demise of the alchemists, with the subsequent 'deification' of matter as the subject and *sine qua non* of the modern sciences. Basilides had seen that a certain quality existed in matter—a living *anima mundi* ('world soul'), which was a reflection on humankind, being as we are constructed of matter. In this regard, Basilides contradicted the Church's views on the physical realm (the domain of evil), and, as a gnostic, Basilides was held with ill-repute by such Church authorities as Hippolytes who wrote most critically of him.

The three-stage developmental process symbolized by the number three is again evident in Basilides' schema. His theological cum metaphysical transformation of the Son psychologically indicates the development of the psyche. The Self, largely unconscious, is seen as the source of the ego, which separates out from the unconscious, but still remains psychically connected to the Self, just as neural connections are maintained and constructed continually between the ego center of the brain (nominally located in the frontal lobe by some researchers) and the whole cerebral system, and even the physiological realm of the body. (The Hebdomad: the 'ruler' of Seven, and the Ogdoad: the 'ruler' of Eight, are gnostic principles, which will be discussed in the chapter "Eight (The Ogdoad).")

A qualitatively different type of triad also exists in the mythologies and ancient religions. For example, in Norse mythology are the Three Norns of Teutonic myth: Urd the Aged One (Past), Verdandi (Present) and Shuld (Future); and the Three Fates (*Moirai*) of Greek myth who apply the decrees of individual destiny: Clotho (who spins the web or thread of events), Lachesis (who chooses the individual and measures the thread), and Atropos (who carries out the event).

In ancient Egypt, Shu (Space) separates Nut (Sky) from Geb (Earth), but there is also the Memphis triad of Ptah ('primordial fire'), Sekhmet ('the redoubtable lioness') and Nefertum ('the accomplishment of Atum'), as well as the Theban triad of Amun (the Hidden), Mut and Khonsu, and finally, the more familiar national gods Osiris, Horus and Isis (and Set, which actually converts this triad to a tetrad—the movement from three to four is explained in the next chapter).

These images also represent a triadic dynamism, but they each exist in a pre-conscious state, hence the equality of their parts, since no centralizing or unifying tendency has emerged, which would indicate the solution (the synthesis) of the dynamic of each triad. Therefore, triads take two forms: the 'higher', intellectual (spiritual) form with a unifying (centering) identity, and the 'lower', chthonic (instinctual) form with its undifferentiated partial aspects suggesting unconsciousness, but also instinctive (natural) processes.

Altogether, the above-mentioned triads of myth and religion, and those of Space (length, width and height) and Time (past, present and future), as well as soul-spirit-body (the natures of which are exemplified in alchemy by Sulphur-Mercury-Salt) are triadic in name only, each being a unity in essence. The Sulphur-Mercury-Salt triad is now discussed in more detail.

The Alchemical Three: Sulphur-Mercury-Salt

The associations of Sulphur with soul, Mercury with spirit, and Salt with body, were well-established alchemical 'facts' by the time of Paracelcus, alchemist and mystic of the sixteenth century. These facts were logically derived conclusions given the medieval mind-set. The human predisposition to establish order by making associations (correspondences) with all-and-sundry material and psychological phenomena suggests a degree of unconsciousness on the alchemist's part in their apperception of world and psyche. For example, correspondence is repeated in the relationship seen between the Macrocosm of God (Father, Son and Holy Spirit), and the microcosm of 'Man' (spirit, body and soul), where macrocosm and microcosm mirror each other. The more unknown is the object, the more likely will projection take place. Jung (1963) clarifies this unconsciousness by pointing out that:

> chemical matter was so completely unknown to them [the alchemists] that it instantly became a carrier for projections. Its darkness was so loaded with unconscious contents that a state of…unconscious identity arose between them and the chemical substance, which caused the substance to behave, at any rate in part, like an unconscious content. (para. 336)

So the parallels (associations) are clear:

Sulphur is inflammable, it is a constituent of hell—'fire and brimstone'—therefore associated with Satan and evil and the dark side of the psyche. But its fire is also that of a celestial, purifying nature (therefore associated with Christ, benevolence and the positive side of the soul and the spirit). Sulphur blackens the vessel within which it burns (it tarnishes silver and copper), but it is also a component of the most beautiful and iridescent of colors in nature.

Edinger (1995) describes sulphur in its compound forms that color the world: "Bismuth sulphide is brown; arsenic sulphide is yellow; tin sulphide is orange; mercuric sulphide is red; zinc sulphide is white; [etc]" (p. 99). These 'chemical hooks' provide obvious dualistic parallels with the human soul.

The soul has within it the corrupting nature of the dark and evil countenance of Satan's spirit, but also the transforming quality of the colorful, positive aspects of Christ. Christ's nature is symbolized by the rainbow and the *cauda pavonis* ('peacock's tail'), both of which were regarded as wholeness symbols by the alchemists because of their complete range of colors, and therefore, took on the symbolism of totality, thereby indicating the completion of the *opus* (the work). The philosophical sulphur, like the element itself, is therefore duplex in nature.

Mercury is the only metal on Earth that is liquid in its elemental state. It epitomizes all metals, having the shiny appearance characteristic of polished metal, but embodies the principle of flow and fusibility, which metals also demonstrate, since they can be melted, poured and molded into various forms. Such is the nature of the human soul, which is to say the psyche (mercuriality is the formal principle of the total personality). Mercury mediates the two worlds of solid and gas; the human spirit mediates the two psychological realms of consciousness and the unconscious. The mercurial principle (Mercurius as *prima materia*) is thereby found in all metals and minerals, and in the human being, having been formed from the Earth by God according to the *Genesis* account, and equally recognized in science as constituted of elements and their various compounds.

Ultimately, mercury as quicksilver symbolizes a transcendental idea— a 'supraordinate concept', paradoxical in nature, and since:

> in his alchemical form, Mercurius does not exist in reality, he must be an unconscious projection, and because he is an absolutely fundamental concept in alchemy he must signify the unconscious itself. (Jung, 1963, para. 117)

Jung adds that, as a 'living spirit', that is, as an active principle of life processes, Mercurius, like Sulphur, is duplex in nature—both active and passive. Mercurius is mutable, wily, secretive and deceptive, is inventive, ambiguous and ambivalent, but is also the opposite of all of these. Such is the dualistic nature of the unconscious, just as the alchemists described Mercurius, having unconsciously assumed the existence of a dualistic psychic life.

Salt of the Earth

Salt was associated with matter because of its mundanity, its non-flammability, its fixity and its ubiquity. The phenomenology of Salt is consistent with the human body because it appears in all the states of the human condition, physically and symbolically. Salt preserves (prevents corruption of flesh, it immortalizes), salt gives flavor to food (life), it purifies (kills micro-organisms), removes sins (a form of baptism), and it coagulates (makes solid, and gives form).

But salt renders water undrinkable, it destroys metals, and in its bitterness salt makes its appearance in human tears (with which it can bring closure and resolution, and even wisdom, understanding and insight). Salt, therefore, can equally be recognized and associated with negative aspects and positive aspects. All these associations of salt with matter, human material existence and life experience typify salt, the third and final part of the Sulphur-Mercurius-Salt triad, as equally duplex in nature, as are Sulphur and Mercury. These dual aspects thereby constitute a Hexad; a 2 × 3 form (see the chapter "Six (The Hexad)").

To the alchemists, the Sulphur-Mercurius-Salt triad represented the human totality of soul-spirit-body. These three 'elements' (salt is actually a compound) mirrored the functioning of psychic life and gave the alchemists something physical (tangible) with which to work—an operation they thought necessary as a consequence of projecting unconscious contents into matter. Their search for wholeness in themselves, outside themselves represented by the *lapis* (stone), or the philosophical gold was an ongoing quest, spurred on by inner homeostatic necessity—a drive like an instinct, but qualified and ordered or patterned by the archetype of the Self. The unconscious intimation of this wholeness came like the vaguest of notions from a distant memory of a pre-conscious, paradisiacal state once held, but lost, due in part to the development of consciousness and the birth of the ego.

The Other Alchemical Three: Nigredo-Albedo-Rubedo

The alchemical rebirth of the ego, the goal of the *opus*, can be followed by another three-part system, characterized by the three stages: (i) *nigredo* (the 'blackness' stage), (ii) *albedo* (the 'whiteness' stage) and (iii) *rubedo* (the 'redness' stage). All three stages could be observed in the 'matter' of the alchemist, but were also experienced psychologically (emotionally).

The first stage, *nigredo*, as von Franz (1980a) describes it, is "the terrible depression and state of dissolution" (p. 220). This stage was indicated by a heavy, 'leaden' disposition, and the burdened soul of the alchemist was identified with the arcane substance Lead. This was because lead *could* bring problems upon the alchemist's body and mind, and soul (when inhaled the poisonous fumes of smelting lead cause depression, toxic sickness and can even be fatal). Therefore, the alchemist's inner demons were easily projected onto lead, so that an alchemical recipe might carry a warning that lead contains a "demon which will kill people" (p. 21). But all the known metals were used by the alchemists, including mercury (its fumes were also poisonous), and the alchemist would fuse them or mix them with other arcane substances (elements or compounds) in the attempt to make the philosopher's stone (the *lapis*). *The Stone of salomon*

Through hard work (alchemical practice, *meditatio, contemplatio*, and so on) the next stage, *albedo*, might be reached. Depending on the metal and the treatment, a whitening might take place in the vessel. Many oxides and sulphides of metals (lead, zinc, etc.) are white and can also be poisonous. Repeated distillation and purification were meant to evaporate the metal, leaving a pure white precipitate. Psychologically, this process corresponds with facing a difficulty over and over again from its many different aspects, until it is understood and integrated, purified, and seen in its true light, and with philosophical detachment.

The heaviness gone, the depression lifted, the alchemist was purified physically (as was the substance) and psychologically by withdrawing his projections from the world. The *lapis* was well within sight. Unconscious contents would no longer be contaminated with matter, and the 'evil' of matter would no longer contaminate the body (for example, as sickness through poisoning). Psychologically, if all went well, the alchemist would see an inner development take place, his projections slowly withdrawn, allowing for a renewed emotional stability not previously experienced.

But, there was one final stage left—the *rubedo*. The alchemist may react emotionally and negatively to unconscious contents as they reach consciousness. This fiery state would have to be endured so that a sense of purpose and meaning might follow, which could be integrated into the alchemist's psyche as part of the transformation process leading to wholeness.

For the western (European) alchemist, the *rubedo* was best symbolized by the Annunciation in Christian dogma (a profound experience as if from 'above'), but the *rubedo* also appeared in dreams and fantasy products as the sunrise, a dawning of a new day. The high temperatures of the furnace would bring the metals to a molten state; they would be purged of their impurities, but would react violently in the process. Red sulphur, another arcane substance, also took on *rubedo* symbolism. It too burned with violent fury, and reacted with metals in the process (psychologically, the inexplicable and insatiable drive and desire of the alchemist was projected onto this phase of the work, because of its strong associative hooks).

If all this violent agitation of the soul (and matter) could be endured and understood without 'explosion' (emotional affect), a state of calm might follow. The successful alchemist, no longer a victim of personal insecurities and inadequate interpretations of the world through projection, could speak of a numinous experience, which brought wisdom and understanding. The transformed alchemist could speak of inner harmony and balance, and see a world without distortion.

The procedures leading up to the ideal state of emotional balance was, as the *opus* indicates, quite an ordeal. Some alchemical texts record that the process could take many repetitions, going over and over the steps, again and again, and in some cases, one process alone could take decades. It is clear that the *opus* could become a lifetime's work.

The three stages of the *opus* indicate the dynamism involved in alchemical practice from the point of view of personal and material transformation. The opposites of black (*nigredo*) and white (*albedo*) are united and culminate in the red (*rubedo*), and only with the completion and integration of all three stages could there be a totality of being, in personality and substance.

Number Three in Biology

At the relatively mundane level of biology, having just discussed the dramatic lifestyle of the typical alchemist of old, we find a less demanding system of equilibrium. Biologically, balance (and, therefore, to some extent, physical awareness in three-dimensional space), is ensured by the three membranous, semi-circular canals in the human ear. The biological reality of this threefold form provides the empirical basis for the psychological construction of a three-dimensional world-view. These three canals or ducts are so placed that each one is at right angles to the others (corresponding, in a sense, to the *x*, *y* and *z*-axes of the three-dimensional coordinate system used in geometry and mathematics).

Change in the position of the head, or change in movement cause a fluid (endolymph) in these canals to flow, which in turn cause tiny hairs (cilia) to move. The movement of the cilia triggers the nerve cells that send impulses down the eighth cranial (acoustic) nerve to the cerebellum, which controls posture and equilibrium. The process of reafference (action-related sensory activity) is in this case, a compensatory mechanism so that by constantly monitoring the environment the human subject has the ability to make the appropriate responses that ensure adequate posture and balance in the three-dimensional world. Here we have a three-dimensional system appropriate for a three-dimensional environment. More correctly, and psychologically speaking, the three-dimensional world is constructed as a direct consequence of the unconscious influence of a three-dimensional system projected onto that world.

Number Three in Geometry

Geometrically, the number three is symbolized by the triangle, Δ, the first polygon. There are three main types of triangle: equilateral (all sides equal in length), isosceles (two sides equal in length), and scalene (all three sides different in length). In architecture, the triangle is relied upon for structural support, and this quality of threeness is exemplified in suspended forms and geodesic domes.

see the new structure at the LOUVRE in Paris.

Three has come to mean rigidity and strength because the triangle has the smaller surface in proportion to its perimeter compared to the square. And there are no opposite corners (diagonals) to produce a 'hinging' effect as observed in the 'flexible' quality of four.

As regards the number four, geometrically speaking, this fourfold flexibility can be represented by the rhombus (an oblique, equilateral parallelogram), which has the appearance of a distorted square. Structurally, this lack of rigidity can be rectified by connecting any two (or all four) diagonally opposed corners (*see* fig. 14).

Figure 14. *Square ('tetragon') and rhombus: rectifying the flexible quality of these fourfold structures is possible by 'reducing' them to two threefold structures by cross-connecting at least one of the diagonals.*

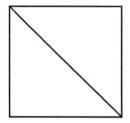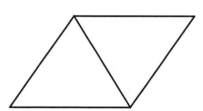

Actually, the rhombus is formed from two connected equilateral triangles. For the ancients, the rhombus came to symbolize the world above and the world below. Generally speaking, then, these two triangles symbolize two realms: the upper, Divine, invisible/intangible world, and the lower, mundane, visible/tangible world. These dual concepts came to represent other dualities, such as spirit/matter, Heaven/Earth, fire/water, etc.

To digress for a moment, physicist Wolfgang Pauli in his book *Writings on Physics and Philosophy* (1994), writes that Robert Fludd contrived the ancient notion of a fourfold universe using the rhombus model to symbolize Above and Below (*see* fig. 15).

Pauli adds:

[handwritten note:] see Ken Wilber's "Quantum Questions," pp. 169–175.

[handwritten note:] W. Pauli is considered a modern mystic!

the empyrean, the world of spirits, followed in descending order by the ether as the link with the sphere of the elements and sublunary things, and, at the bottom, by the earth, which is also the "seat of the devil." The world is the mirror image of the invisible Trinitarian God who reveals Himself in it. Just as God is symbolically represented by an equilateral triangle, there is a second reflected triangle below that represents the world. (p. 244)

A trinitarian worldview purveys Fludd's model: the Divine triangle is the Trinity above, and the Mundane triangle is the trinitarian world below. Jehovah is Father-Son-Holy Spirit, and the World of matter is built of space (length, width and height) and time (past, present, and future). The numbers one, two, three, and four all feature in this model, suggesting the Pythagorean *tetractys* to be discussed later in the chapter "Ten (The Decad)."

Figure 15. *Robert Fludd's divine and mundane triangles: Jehovah Above and the World Below: 1. Circle of the Empyrean; 2. Circle of the Ether; 3. Circle of the Elements; 4. Circle of the Earth.*

The two equilateral triangles can also be interlaced to represent the union of an opposing pair (each as a triad), in the image of the familiar hexalpha or *Mogen David* ('Shield of David'). (In the chapter "Six (The Hexad)," three examples will be given to show the symbolic possibilities underlying the hexalpha.)

*good wine
for passover!*

Summary

Threefold or triadic systems encapsulate the principle or symbolism of number three by demonstrating the process of resolution or dimensional expansion through the emergence of a third factor, as a direct result of the resonance that exists between two opposing principles. This third factor is often seen as relational. That is, number three can symbolize the relationship between opposing principles.

The number three may be most pronounced in models or structures that have a 'progressive' nature, involving movement, balance, coordination, and equivocation. The negative properties of vacillation and uncertainty are avoided in threefold systems. More broadly speaking, the system may possess an ongoing cyclical and developmental factor. However, as will become clear in the next chapter, it is often the case that such models or structures tend toward an absolute framework, since they lose the dualistic resonance that underscored their origins. Therefore, any model or structure described by the number three will have the major qualities of solidity and stability, but they will tend to be dogmatic and unyielding in nature.

There is always Three (Expansion), but there is no experience of latitude or location given by the variability and totality of the quaternity, and so 'emerges' the number Four (see the chapter "Four (The Tetrad)").

reincarnation! If 1 ♂ + 1 ♂ = 1 child, then while in the astral plane to ignore that lower vision and turn away from it, causes the monad-soul to seek the resulting factors of higher numbers. The great "secret" is to advance to 4-5-6-7-8-9-10 while here in the 3-D. That way you have no need to go back down to 0-1-2 or 3! So: MEDITATE!!!

Why bother to descend
and dwell in or at the
lesser levels of lower
numbers if you're advancing
on and into higher number?!
— Hmmm....

This whole book may be
a way that points to another
method of getting off the
wheel!

Don't stop now!
Go right on to the next page:

Plate 12. C. G. JUNG

Jung (1875-1961) believed that "without the fourth the three have no reality as we understand it; they even lack meaning." Trinitarian thinking is shown to be lacking in dimension—it is flat and intellectual, whereas quaternarian thinking establishes a relationship with reality through acceptance of all possible experiences and realities [Courtesy of the National Library of Medicine].

Like my birth date:

4/8/44

FROM THREE TO FOUR

One, two, three—but…where is the fourth.

Plato

The Problem of Three and Four

In regard to the problem of three and four, von Franz wrote (1974): "It becomes evident that a psychological problem of considerable importance is constellated between the numbers three and four" (p. 126). She noted that Jung had dealt time and time again with this problem in his writings (for examples, see Jung, 1958, 1963). In his major essay *Synchronicity*, Jung (1960) also discussed the use of numbers in divination and other systems designed to establish order in a chaotic world. He went to considerable effort in his attempt to put forward the message that numbers give a certain kind of order to processes in and of the psyche. Underlying this process was the *number archetype*—an inherited mode of apprehension in our species that dictates the way we construct the world by 'enumerating' its contents. Archetypes generally refer to patterns of behavior where the instincts, for example, are given to follow certain predisposed forms of expression predetermined by these archetypes. The number archetype, therefore, forms (with the other archetypes) a ground plan or blueprint of the psychic structure. The psyche, then, insofar as it has an underlying archetypal structure, is a preformed organ, the *sine qua non* of human functioning.

The continuity of the number archetype (i.e., its constant resonance within the psyche) indicates that an accumulative, dynamic factor may be assigned to so-called completed structures or systems that have a 'numerical' phenomenology. These structures and systems, because they are the products of the psyche, would therefore owe their origins to that pattern of behavior in the psyche that is underscored by the number archetype. For example, to the degree that we are unconscious, we may project the number archetype into the world onto suitable 'hooks'. As we observe the environment, as we construct 'explanations' or theories about phenomena in the world, we must alert ourselves to the inner subjectivity that determines to a great extent the ostensibly objective reality of those phenomena.

When we confront the products of the psyche, which we at first posited as 'existing' in the real world, we must also confront ourselves with the challenging task of recognizing just where it is that the psyche leaves off and the world truly begins. This task is, of course, more generally represented as the foremost task of gaining self-knowledge about the psyche.

What do we do when we construct numerical representations that describe the world? Are we really seeing things as they are? More precisely, what are the preconceived suppositions we refer to, consciously and unconsciously, when we count or assign numbers to those things we discover and invent? If the number archetype stands behind many of those discoveries and inventions, then by critically examining our knowledge claims from the perspective of the number archetype, we might be able to ascertain both the strengths and the weaknesses in our epistemological foundations. These actions will not only lead us back to knowledge about the psyche, but may also serve to answer the above questions.

For any given enumerated system or structure (i.e., a system or structure that has been found to contain a numerical phenomenology), it may be possible to constructively add to that phenomenology, thus forming a modified structure or system. When we start this process, however, we find that it is not only a matter of *quantitatively* 'counting in' new data, but we observe that *qualitative* changes may emerge, which affect the new structure or system. And this dual process takes place not just in accordance with the interaction of the numbered elements among themselves (resulting in an improved and more accurate model), but also in accordance with the overall symbolic variance given by the generic archetypal factors of the numbers.

This process features in the "psychological problem...constellated between the numbers three and four" (von Franz, 1974, p. 126).

The problem of three and four is realized when the limitations of a certain 'trinitarian' ideal are recognized. The realization is a spur that instigates a desire for change, ultimately manifesting as a shift away from the 'idealized' form toward some other more appropriate form. The new form will invariably be expansive, more realistic, and tetradic in nature since it is built upon the old model. Thus is evoked renewed emotional and psychological interest in the subject matter that the new model describes. Tetradic models, however, always contain a previously missing irrational element, and from an intellectual point of view, dissatisfaction might still result, although for purposes of integrity and consistency, tetradic models (quaternities) must be recognized as valid in terms of completeness, since they tend to approximate real world conditions in ways that triadic models (trinities) do not.

In this chapter examples will be given of the problem of three and four, and solutions will be proposed in the form of 'movements' from three to four. Thus it will be seen that the archetypal movement from three to four (and the number archetype specifically) has direct bearing on the nature and development of the psyche, and therefore, the structure of our epistemological foundations. This movement can best be described by illustration. The four examples described below—(1) theological/psychological, (2) philosophical, (3) psycho-physiological, and (4) ergonomic—show that knowledge and the increase in awareness of inner (psychic) and outer (world) events is an ongoing process. This process can be symbolized and exemplified by discrete numerical shifts from three to four.

Movements from Three to Four in Alchemy and Religion

In the alchemical tradition, the triad of Sulphur-Mercury-Salt was the most important of triads, and dates back to Paracelcus' time in the sixteenth century (*see* fig. 16a). It was associated with the Christian Trinity of Father-Son-Holy Spirit (*see* fig. 16b).

Figure 16. *(a) The alchemical (material) triad of Sulphur-Mercury-Salt; (b) The christian (spiritual) Trinity of Father-Son-Holy Spirit.*

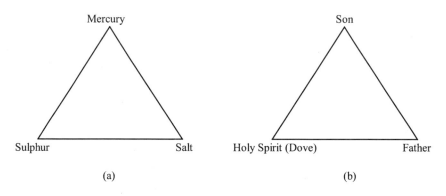

(a)   (b)

Jung (1963) considered it necessary that the *Mercurius Duplex* (embodying Christ as the philosopher's stone in the form of the 'heavenly lapis', and the Anti-Christ as the 'poisonous dragon') must, as the central figure, split into its component parts to form a quaternity. Jung pointed out that a similar process took place in the Trinity, which had long been moving toward a Quaternity until finally in 1950 the Vatican acknowledged the Assumption of Mary into Heaven (Jung, 1989, para. 237). Mary joined with the Father, the Son and the Holy Spirit, thus forming a quaternity. Two quaternities were thereby formed, as given by Jung (1963; *see* fig. 17). In this way the triad of alchemy and the Trinity of Christianity were shifted from their active states of process in motion, to passive states of completion, by virtue of the consciousness of the vital, but previously missing elements in these triads. Originally fused with the ambivalent and ambiguous Mercurius, in the case of the Sulphur-Mercurius-Salt triad, was the *lapis* and the serpent, yet conspicuously excluded by patriarchal Christian dogma in the case of the Holy Trinity was the Virgin Mary who 'resided' in the realm of matter—the very same realm of Satan and the source of sinfulness—from the time of the formation of the Church.

Figure 17. *(a) The Mercurius quaternity; (b) The Christian quaternity.*

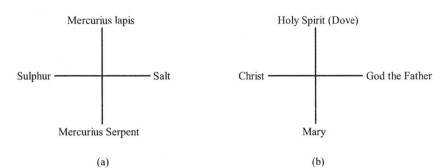

As the symbolism of these two quaternities becomes apparent they are shown to illuminate previously unconscious factors necessary for a complete picture of psyche/matter on one hand, and on the other, a long overdue representation of the feminine in the male-dominated Godhead. Each of the missing factors (now installed) exhibits material and 'feminine', but 'darker', instinctual qualities, which were marginalized and relegated to the realm of the Devil back in pre-Christian times, though more so from and during the Christian era.

While the Church does recognize the Virgin Mary, theirs is an idealized and purified form, and does not embody the reality of the 'dark feminine', psychologically present in both man and woman. The 'feminine' was conflated *and* equated with the Devil and matter, since unconscious contents usually exist in a fusion with one another, fused as they are under the rubric of the 'unknown,' and associated with each other to the degree that they are unconscious. Patriarchal values are currently considered the major repressive and oppressive forces that account for this ignorance, and only higher consciousness can differentiate these factors from their unconscious fusion. Consciousness of these factors thereby expands the task and responsibility of broadening consciousness by giving heed to those issues that were previously unconscious or ill-defined. Edinger (1995) says this about the symbolism of matter:

It's the very principle left out of Christian symbolism as it has developed over the past two thousand years. The materiality principle—the principle of egohood, the principle of the flesh, everything that pertains to the concreteness of personal, individual, fleshly, incarnated existence—all this is symbolised by the materiality principle. (p. 132)

In advance of the Church, the materialist, 'lab-bound' alchemists acknowledged the 'matter' of the Sulphur/Salt dyad, and thus recognized the 'materiality principle' and its dual nature. Matter was not exclusively the realm of evil. However, overwhelmed by Christian Trinity symbolism, they were remiss in recognizing in their worldview a 'dualistic' Christ (as *Mercurius Duplex*) that included the Antichrist. The alchemists, therefore, never quite realized in full consciousness the dual aspect of "Christ in his mystical androgyny" (para. 235) because the feminine was still partially obfuscated by masculine Trinity symbolism. Nevertheless, their *opus* signified the first stirrings towards a consciousness that acknowledged the need for a differentiation of the fused (because unconscious) dual aspects of matter.

In a similar way, the Church-dominated worldview imposed a trinity structure on the nature of the Heavenly Host, but unlike the alchemists this over-represented masculine hypostatization did not recognize the materiality principle at all, nor therefore, the feminine. Eventually, however, the Trinity gave way in the twentieth century to the Quaternity. As indicated, this change in focus served to expand consciousness. Jung's revision of the anachronistic 'alchemical triunity' and the Christian Trinity brought them both up-to-date with modern times. Both revisions required movements from three to four— movements from relative unconsciousness to relative consciousness.

However, the respective symbolisms of the two trinities do not align with each other, and the same is true of the quaternities. In the trinities, Salt is associated with body (matter), which aligns with Mary (feminine, matter). Jung has made the parallel of Mary with the Salt as the 'earth' factor (Mary's flesh brought forth the Deity), and Salt as body has already been explained (see the chapter "Three (The Triad)"). Salt (the materiality principle) is already present in the alchemical trinity (alchemy largely being a study of matter), not true - the Holy Spirit is also seen as the yin or feminine side of God.

From Three to Four   183

but the Father is missing. The Father (the spiritual principle) is present in the Trinity, but Mary is absent (the Trinity being an exclusively 'masculine', spiritual triad—that is, non-material, thereby necessarily excluding the 'feminine').

Although the alchemical trinity has an undifferentiated Christ/ Antichrist in Mercury (*Mercurius Duplex*), the Christian Trinity, having only the Son (Christ), completely lacks representation of the Antichrist (apparently still fused with the Devil, matter, and the 'feminine'). The Holy Spirit, by its nature, parallels agreeably with Sulphur (at least its positive qualities), but further problems arise. Sulphur too is duplex, as is Salt. Also, the Holy Spirit and God the Father are both idealized figures, and this would explain both the one-sided hypostatization of the two, and their neglected 'darker' factors.

There are also problems with the Christian Quaternity, and possibly the alchemical quaternity. While salt is opposed to sulphur, according to alchemical tradition (see Jung, 1963), and *lapis* and serpent are naturally opposed, we cannot say in the Christian quaternity that Holy Spirit and Mary form a *syzygy* (a pair with opposing natures), and Christ and the Father do not form an ideal *syzygy* either.

A more satisfactory arrangement is possible if the Christian Quaternity is rearranged (by having Mary and Christ trade places), so that Mary the Mother stands opposite God the Father. Sulphur and Holy Spirit could be paired, but one or the other is on the wrong axis. It would be inappropriate to parallel God the Father with the *lapis* (or the Serpent if Holy Spirit and Christ traded places first), besides which, each of these actions would mean breaking the Father/Mother *syzygy*, and it would break the symmetry of the alchemical quaternity to trade the places of Sulphur and *lapis* with each other. Furthermore, the Christian Quaternity would still be an idealization because it does not include the Antichrist, which would accommodate a parallel with the alchemical Serpent. Any rearrangement to the Christian quaternity as it currently stands is inadequate for these reasons.

In summary, there are two major problems with the Trinity/triad, and the two quaternities. First, no proper isomorphism is possible with the

I have a hard time relating sulphur, mercury and salt to the Trinity and Mary! But it's a really FUN read! —

two trinities, nor with the two quaternities, as they stand. Second, both the Christian Trinity and Quaternity, as celestial (heavenly) representations of Deity are still idealized, while both the alchemical triad and the Mercurius quaternity do not show the duplex natures of all their components. While Jung (1958) did address the second problem, neither Jung nor any other Jungian scholar has addressed the first problem, though it will be seen in the chapter "Six (The Hexad)" that Pauli argued against the quaternity, preferring the Star of David because he believed that Mary's promotion to Heaven was a one-sided process (note that even in Figure 11, Mary and Isis have no negative female counterpart and these must therefore exist as postulates of Satan's and Seth's personality structures, respectively). Roth (2004) explains the problem:

> For [Pauli], Jung's "quaternity projected into heaven" is of course some sort of Assumption [i.e., *Assumptio Mariae*]: "Disinfected matter" (the Catholic Holy Virgin Mary) is taken up in the heavens and there—together with the Holy Trinity—completes a quaternity. This quaternity is—as the one of the Christian cross—a (3 + 1) structure, meaning that three parts are equal and the fourth is the "totally different".... Furthermore, because Mary is without any sin, Evil is absent. Matter is now a "disinfected" Idea in the beyond of the heavens (in the Empyreum)...(Roth, 2004, Chapter 3, Part 4)

It is necessary, in order to account for these inconsistencies, to posit the Christian hexalpha, and an isomorphically compatible Mercurius hexalpha, which would include chthonic trinities in their structures. These will be described in the chapter "Six (The Hexad)."

Movements from Three to Four in Theology and Psychology

From a theological perspective, Paul Tillich, in *Man and Transformation* (1964) sees a threefold, dynamic pattern underpinning any theology, and posits three vital elements basic to every theology:

theos, God, or rather God insofar as He makes Himself manifest, the element of revelation. The second is *logos,* rational discourse about what God communicates when He communicates Himself. And the third is *kairos,* the proper moment in time, the time when a theologian must speak to his own age. (p. 161)

Tillich explains that if *theos* is absent (no God, no revelation), the theology is 'reduced' to a philosophy of religion. If *logos* is absent, a linguistic and rational foundation is lacking, and a nonsensical or 'ecstatic' phenomenology arises, or both. And if *kairos* is absent, the theology becomes a systematic (routine, mundane) and 'dead tradition', which does not speak to a contemporary world.

Tillich is suggesting that *theos* (God making Himself 'manifest') is recognized only from an 'experience' (revelation) that leads to belief. But from this description we are not given to assume that an emotional or meaningful attitude or relationship (*eros*) is present with the belief (or in the theology), nor will it ever eventuate. But for Tillich it must be present, which then means that he must be conflating two separate elements: *theos,* and a fourth element that would be *eros.*

This eclipse of *eros* happens again in Henderson's book *Cultural Attitudes in Psychological Perspective* (1984). Henderson interprets Tillich's schema from a Jungian perspective where *theos* (God-image) is equated with the Self. The Self is:

Perceived and experienced affectively upon its emergence from the world of archetypal images. *Logos* then becomes an intelligible account of the image. *Kairos* is the connection to be made between any individual's self-confrontation and a similar, general religious problem in contemporary life. (p. 28)

Henderson equates *theos* with the experience of the Self from an emotional perspective (i.e., 'affectively'), but this equation is problematic. Before that problem can be solved we must first deal with Henderson's four cultural attitudes—Religious, Philosophic, Social, and Aesthetic. It will be shown that these attitudes are relevant to Tillich's schema. The religious attitude, like religious emotion:

> depends on an unshakable feeling for its value, not its logic…. It requires also some knowledge, some comprehension of the meaning of what has been experienced. (p. 27)

The philosophic attitude is concerned with "getting to the truth of things" (p. 59), the facts and the ideas, etc. It rationalizes and reasons to get to the crux of the matter.

The social attitude is:

> concerned with maintaining the ethical code of the culture, whether of the established culture or any specific counter-cultural deviation from it. (p. 17)

The aesthetic attitude:

> stresses the unity of beauty and truth. [It is an attitude that] is content with naming human qualities or attributes without any attempt to pass judgment or win approval. (p. 45)

Individuals who function from the standpoint of any one of these attitudes exclusively tend to be extremely difficult to dissuade from their patterns of behavior and their respective attitudes. The ideal, well-rounded individual, on the other hand, would be seen as embodying equal proportions of these four attitudes to life, using them where appropriate.

While Henderson has made the psychological parallels between the ego/Self system and Tillich's three elements, he does not see the possibility of a parallel between Tillich's elements (as dispositions of each aspect of the personality) and his own corresponding attitudes from a perspective where experience of *theos* would speak to the religious attitude of a person, *logos* would speak to the philosophic attitude, and *kairos* would speak to the social attitude. Of course Henderson cannot make this parallel because he identified no fourth element that might be aligned with the aesthetic attitude. That is, the problem of three and four is not evoked in Henderson either. The parallel is possible, but it starts by recognizing the above-mentioned limitation in Tillich's schema—that there is a missing fourth element, *eros*. Much as Tillich has done, however, Henderson has also conflated *eros* with *theos* (more correctly, the *experience* of the Self). Henderson never uncovers the evidence for the presence of *eros* in Tillich's or his own writing. For example, he regards the emergence of the Self "from the world of archetypal images" as something to be "perceived and experienced *affectively*" (p. 28; my italics), which is to say *emotionally*, implying the establishment of a relationship (*eros*) with the Self. Henderson also talks about the religious experience as "depending on an unshakable *feeling* for its value" (p. 27; my italics).

Can *eros* (which would lead to an aesthetic attitude) emerge *sui generis* from Tillich's three theological elements as a mere epiphenomenal construction, or does *eros* represent the overlooked, irrational component typical of all triadic structures? Can Henderson equate the archetypal experience of *theos* with the Self, as he does, without first drawing out the emotional factor common to each, thereby recognizing that *eros* is an element in its own right that contributes towards the '*feeling* value' of the experience?

With the inclusion of the fourth element, *eros*, Tillich's theological elements can be equated with Henderson's cultural attitudes quite adequately (*see* Table 3). The inclusion of the fourth factor (*eros*) remedies two exclusively intellectual systems bereft of the recognition of relationship through emotion, and also provides the means by which the 'beauty and truth' of the experience can be integrated in a meaningful way. Certainly Jung speaks of meaningfulness in a way that would describe the Aesthetic attitude.

It is of interest to note, using Jung's typology, that the sensation function, as the means by which sensory data is experienced in its pure, unmitigated form, would mean only a sensory (uncritical) acknowledgement of *theos* would at first be had. Other functions come in as separate processes, thus further differentiating the aspects of the experience, or if they are fused with each other, problems may arise similar to those just discussed. Ideally, the thinking function would be brought in to conceptualize the event, followed by the feeling function, in order to establish its agreeability, and finally intuition to determine its future potential.

Table 3. *Tillich's Elements, Henderson's Cultural Attitudes, and their Manifestations.*

ELEMENT	ATTITUDE	MANIFESTATION
1. The presence of *Theos*	Religious	The experience of the Self
2. The presence of *Eros*	Aesthetic	An emotional, meaningful experience of relatedness
3. The presence of *Logos*	Philosophic	A discursive account of the Self
4. The presence of *Kairos*	Social	A response to a Zeitgeist and the social world

Note that the appearance of eros prior to logos in the sequence 1 to 4 is not necessarily binding. In fact, it is possible that logos might precede eros. However, as Tillich's and Henderson's schemas both suggest, it is more likely that eros is closely bound, or contiguous, with theos.

If, say, feeling is fused with sensation, then a judgment concerning 'relationship' with the event is made virtually immediately, and one either values or devalues the experience just as quickly. This judgment is likely to be overly hasty since the two functions are not sufficiently differentiated. Similarly, a *theos/eros* fusion would mean experiencing *theos* as an immediate revelation, in awe, rapture, or as a humbling experience, etc., (i.e., through the emotions). This lack of differentiation is notable in many religious experiences and may account for Tillich's and Henderson's failure to detect the fourth. Thus the problem of three and four is evident in Tillich's and Henderson's schemas. The fourth is always hidden in the other three, or is found somewhere else.

Von Franz (1974) observes that triadic structures are incomplete, even in their emerged syntheses. Using the human psyche as the site of the triadic structure (in archetypal form), von Franz describes Jung's step-by-step approach to the decipherment and qualitative influence of three:

> At the level of one, man [*sic*] still naïvely participates in his surroundings in a state of uncritical unconsciousness, submitting to things as they are. At the level of two, on the other hand, a dualistic world- and God-image gives rise to tension, doubt and criticism of God, life, nature and oneself. The condition of three by comparison denotes insight, the rise of consciousness, and the rediscovery of unity on a higher level; in a word, gnosis and knowledge. (pp. 124-125)

However, as Jung (1958) states: "Without the fourth the three have no reality as we understand it; they even lack meaning" (para. 280). Von Franz echoes Jung's point when she says that 'trinitarian thinking' is shown to be lacking in dimension: "it is flat, intellectual, and consequently encourages intolerant and absolute declarations" (p. 125). This intellectuality comes about because the personal quotient of the individual gives rise to a trinitized content, subjecting it to time-bound, 'situated' relativizations of personal and culture-specific discourses. Such is the erroneous approach adopted by special individuals who can claim a numinous experience (whether scientific, theological or religious) and then declare the experience as a universal truth (when they barely understand it themselves): a revelation given by God, or worse, the genius of human intellect. Attempts at mass conversion often originate as a result of this hubris.

Jung notes that the error is detected upon conscious awareness of a missing fourth element (a 'relationship to reality', that is, 'critical understanding') which has remained unconscious, undiscovered, unrecognized, but would serve the purpose of stabilizing the individual by broadening the individual's outlook, since it is consciousness in the area of relationship (to the world, for example) that is lacking. The individual is wizened to an identification with the experience (specifically archetypal), so that maturity and moral responsibility is gained, which comes with the newly emerged element. This nascent quality serves to drag the individual down from the 'airy', intellectual heights of the 'head' to the firmer, material ground of the 'body' (earth).

Descartes' co-ordinate system, which is triadic (three dimensional) in nature, provides a good example of exclusively trinitarian thinking by not allowing the influence of 'images' and the 'imagination' into its mechanism (the very factors which inspired Descartes, in the form of a dream, to devise the system in the first place). Descartes believed that all existence could be described with mathematical abstractions, thereby ignoring totally the factor of feeling in favor of a purely rationalistic approach. Von Franz (1978) observes:

> In 'neutral' language…three signifies a unity which dynamically engenders self-expanding linear irreversible processes in matter and in our consciousness (e.g., discursive thought). (p. 106)

Descartes and like-minded individuals participate in this process, but it is in the movement from three to four where the limits of trinitarian thinking are rectified. Unlike triadic structures, an irrational factor is present in non-triadic (fourfold or greater) structures or systems, even though they are a threat to certainty for some (a return to Cartesian Doubt), but for others, only a sense of feeling of the infinite possibility inherent in experience is signaled in concepts that include all alternatives of meaning and interpretations of experience. This flexibility is a key factor in fourfold structures and systems.

Movements from Three to Four in Philosophy

In ancient times, threeness or trinitarianism also figure phenomenologically in cognitive functions—particularly thinking. Plato was a 'trinitarian' thinker, yet ancient Greek philosophy shows a preference for 'quaternarian' thinking, as evidenced by the reference to the *tetractys*, which "contained the roots of eternal nature" (Empedocles). This fourfold perspective appears to be a very ancient one, but it seems that with the rise of the intellect "consciousness [had] won for itself a new and not entirely illusory freedom" (Jung, 1958, para. 245). Jung adds:

Try to tell ?
Jammor isn ?
Bernanda thin ?
Yah !

> It [the intellect] can leap over abysses on winged feet, it can free itself
> from bondage to sense-impressions, emotions, fascinating thought, and
> presentiments by soaring into abstraction.... Thus it often happens that
> people who have an amazing range of consciousness know less about
> themselves than the veriest infant, and all because "the fourth would
> not come"—it remained...in the unconscious realm. (para. 245)

In his *Timaeus*, Plato asked: 'where is the fourth?' because he did not have
it, although the text reveals it. While he tried to solve a problem concerning
the union of opposites, he attempted it in a three-dimensional (intellectual)
fashion as if pure thought would get him there. Jung argues that Plato did not
touch base with his feeling nature and, in fact, needed to make this nature a
reality in his personality to find the fourth.

We can think a thought, but this does not make it real—it remains
a thought. It must touch base with reality ('earth') by gaining substance and
connecting in a real sense ('water'): "one of the four is absent because he is
'unwell'" (para. 185) writes Jung, using Plato's words. To use the four-elements
analogy, Plato had spirit ('fire') and thoughts and ideas ('air'), but the absence
of feeling ('water') barred the way to a connection with a well-grounded
realization of his philosophy ('earth'), and, most evidently, his politics.

Jung observes that ultimately Plato's lack of feeling prevented him
from impressing his political ideas onto Dionysius the Elder. Disagreements
between the two were numerous, and Plato was ultimately sold as a slave
because of their incessant arguments—Plato was later given his freedom,
according to J. H. Terry in his book *Latin Reader* (1958). Even under Dionysius
the Younger, Plato's political theories were met with failure. Ultimately,
Plato retreated to his intellectual world of metaphysics, abandoning politics
altogether. The *Timaeus* was Plato's last work and came at a time in his life
that was virtually free of all political thought.

But the philosophical problem of three and four is alive and well in
the modern era also. Keith Campbell's *Body and Mind* (1986) is an in-depth
discussion of the mind/body problem, but it too demonstrates trinitarian
intellectualism. Campbell's 'inconsistent tetrad' resolves triadically by
omission of at least one of four propositions:

(i)   "The human body is a material thing,
(ii)   "The human mind is a spiritual thing,
(iii) "Mind and Body interact,
(iv)   "Spirit and matter do not interact" (p. 14)

Wrong. See Amit Goswami/ "Creative Evolution" [handwritten annotation]

This fourfold dilemma is constructed of two pairs of opposing principles that can be represented by a cruciform structure (*see* fig. 18).

Under the assumption that all these propositions cannot coexist simultaneously without contradiction, Campbell shows that Idealists must reject proposition (i); Behaviorist and other materialist schools of thought must reject proposition (ii); non-interactionist Dualists must reject proposition (iii); and various forms of metaphysical dualism, which accept interactionism, must reject proposition (iv). By the rejection of one, and only one of the four propositions, trinitarian structures are maintained as models for philosophical systems that can thereby accommodate 'absolute declarations' purely by denial of other views.

Figure 18. *Campbell's four propositions of the mind/body problem.*

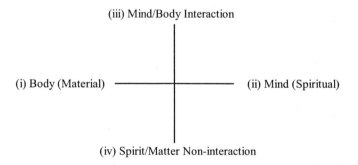

(iii) Mind/Body Interaction

(i) Body (Material) ———————— (ii) Mind (Spiritual)

(iv) Spirit/Matter Non-interaction

Trinitarian thinking, by its intellectual nature (seeking rational statements and conclusions), not only requires a decision, but also by so doing, sets up viewpoints that are intolerant of contradiction to those viewpoints. While a triadic system may be 'perfect' to an individual of one persuasion, others of a different persuasion readily detect its faults. This is because evidence or reasons exist which support all of the excluded alternative viewpoints. Deliberate denial of any one of these viewpoints only intensifies intolerance, when a calmer, more balanced attitude towards all 'real world' phenomena is just as possible, and more rewarding because it recognizes the diversity and variability of human experience, which limited threefold systems do not accommodate.

However, the problem with oppositionalist schemas (represented as dualistic or tetradic models) is that while they present all extremes of thought or possibilities of experience or reality, they do not represent exclusively any claims or opinions in only one direction. Nevertheless, a movement towards quaternarian thinking, away from trinitarian thinking, is still a necessary step in the direction of completion, in the sense that establishing a 'relationship with reality' through acceptance of all possible experiences and realities (not a denial of them) is a move in the 'right' direction toward wholeness. It should not be a task of reconciling these opposites as Campbell proposes (for intellectuals that should be impossible anyway, even though they make it 'possible'). But, for the satisfaction of the soul, which in a Platonic sense mediates mind and body, it is necessary to maintain some intellectual resonance.

Further, it is necessary to recognize that oppositionalism is a discursive concept and its elements are only the subject of situational contingencies. In another context, or circumstance, or by using another discourse, the need for a solution may be redundant because the problem may not exist. This alternativist approach is not an avenue of escape from reality, but a recognition that realist issues may be transcended because variability in one's interpretations is not only feasible, but is crucial for peace of mind.

Denial of a so-called complete reality (as paradoxical as that may sound), or refusal to accept the ambiguity of reality merely because it cannot be encompassed rationally and completely within an intellectual framework, is not implied or encouraged here. Quite the opposite. Acceptance of the incompletely known is a natural human proclivity—even an instinct. It is the basis of all relationship, for example, and life would cease to be meaningful if failure to know a thing in its entirety gave cause to a denial of relationship altogether.

Nor is the search for knowledge denied here. What is proposed is that discussion continues in directions hitherto considered ineffectual or invalid. This approach will have the effect of broadening our epistemological foundations, and the benefits of this approach will have positive ramifications extending beyond trinitarian thinking into the collective soul of humanity—even into the so-called irrational domain of the unconscious.

Movement from Three to Four in Psychophysics

Shifting the focus of the problem of three and four from abstract to concrete realms, Jung noted (1960) that:

> Just as the introduction of time as the fourth dimension in modern physics postulates an irrepresentable space-time continuum, so the idea of synchronicity with its inherent quality of meaning produces a picture of the world so irrepresentable as to be completely baffling. (para. 962)

Thereby, the missing fourth factor, of which Plato was not alone in his enquiries, and which appears to exist at many levels, in many disciplines, can be addressed in a very humble way (that is, for psychology and physics) in Jung's concept of Synchronicity, whereby a missing fourth factor (acausality) is proposed for the familiar space-time-causality triad of science (*see* fig. 19).

According to Jung (1960): "Synchronicity…means the simultaneous occurrence of a certain psychic state with one or more external events which appear as meaningful parallels to the momentary subjective state" (para. 850; see the chapter "Synchronicity" for examples of synchronicity). The fact that the events are acausal is given by the rational judgment that it is inconceivable to imagine how a causal connection could be made between certain psychic and physical events.

Jung suggests that the causality principle does not explain all phenomena, nor would a theory of an 'acausal connecting principle' (synchronicity) be sufficient on its own to explain all phenomena. Rarely observed, but possibly frequently occurring, acausal, psychophysical events may be explained by a kind of 'meaningful orderedness', which leads Jung to hypothesize the existence of a self-subsistent meaning as given by an "absolute knowledge" of these events (para. 931).

Figure 19. *The space-time-causality triad of science.*

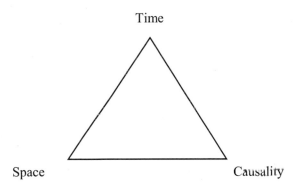

Jung states (concedes?) that the idea of synchronicity is an intellectual necessity that helps to bind together and form a theory about phenomenal events that are not causally explainable. The notion of 'absolute knowledge' is also necessary and possible (notwithstanding the accusations of subjectivism and anthropocentrism suggested by this idea) because each of the events, physical and psychic, can be known as and when their existence is made conscious, and only through consciousness can the meaning be discerned. Either one becomes aware of a psychophysical harmony, or one does not, but in both cases, the events are taken (that is, experienced) as absolute.

Meaningfulness separates synchronistic events from events that are meaningless chance groupings, because they lack the activation of the psychoid archetype (the archetype is psychoid because it can never be the subject of the psyche—the archetype itself is always 'irrepresentable' and can only be inferred from its effects in consciousness). At the basis of synchronicity is the implied harmony of psychic and physical events as they interrelate.

To account for acausal phenomena, and at the same time, allow the psychoid factor into the exclusively 'scientific' space-time-causality triad, Jung postulated the quaternity of space-time-causality-acausality (*see* fig. 20).

[handwritten marginal note, right margin:] See comparison to like particles at a distance in quantum physics.

Figure 20. *The Synchronicity Quaternity (Version I)—Jung.*

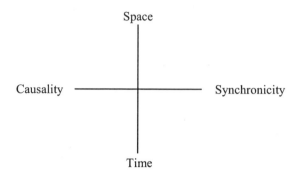

The Synchronicity Quaternity is, however, inaccurate according to Jung, and a second version is presented in the chapter "Four (The Tetrad)." Nevertheless, the principle of the move from three to four is present in this quaternity, since it represents a move away from the scientific intellectualism of a trinity to a quaternity, by including the fourth irrational factor of acausality (synchronicity).

Movements from Three to Four in Ergonomics

Cirlot (1962) notes psychologist Ludwig Paneth's feelings about the symbolism of number four:

> [the number four] as a kind of double division (two and two), no longer signifies separation (like the number two) but the orderly arrangement of what is separate. Hence, it is a symbol of order in space and, by analogy, of every other well-ordered structure. (p. 225)

The experience of fourness, therefore, relates to finding the right location in space and in the psyche at a mundane level. It relates to the feeling of comfort, stability and flexibility as observed in furniture. Although rather banal, the following 'material' example serves quite well in illustrating the difference between three and four as manifested in physical structures. Tables and chairs usually have four legs, although three legs can be used for furniture (for example, the three-legged stool). A three-legged stool is always stable, even if one leg is shorter than the other two, whereas a chair is unstable even if only one leg is shorter than the other three. These analogies indicate two physical realities:

1. Threefold structures are stable (just as trinitarian thinking is intellectually stable, although it is unshifting and lacks tolerance). The 'stool' analogy also supports the geometric concept that a minimum of three points determines a plane (viz., the triangle—the most stable of polygons).

2. Fourfold structures are flexible (just as quaternary wholeness-seeking finds an anomalous fourth aspect, which defies logic and thereby shakes the trinitarian structural edifice which gave the quaternity its basic form).

The stool and the chair, however, are actually more than just analogies, since they describe the very principles of threeness and fourness. There is an ergonomic problem with three-legged furniture that concerns stability. Since the center of gravity, and therefore, the floor area covered by the legs of a stool are the major determinants of the stool's stability, its legs must be a little longer than the legs of a chair to cover the same floor area as the chair (*see* fig. 21). In fact, stools are usually made with short legs to avoid the problem of reduced stability, as the legs get longer.

Two assumptions are made regarding this comparison of the stool with the chair:

(i) Ideally, the seats of both the stool and the chair must have *at least* approximately the same surface area (Area A_1 = Area B_1 in Figure 21), and must be at the same height above the floor (usually in the order of 45 centimeters in western countries).

(ii)   The stool's legs must extend obliquely beyond the perpendicular of the seat (that is, outwardly) so that Area A_2 = Area B_2 in Figure 21. It is thus likely that the legs of the stool will need supporting rungs for strength, to counteract the torque at the point where the legs join the seat.

Four-legged chairs do not necessarily need rungs, especially when the legs are perpendicular to the seat. More generally, threefold systems offer certainty through stability, but this stability comes at a price, requiring certain modifications if they are to be compatible with similar 'unassisted' fourfold systems.

Figure 21. *Both the stool and the chair can be as stable as each other, but the stool will need rungs to increase its strength. Ergonomically, the chair has the advantage over the stool.*

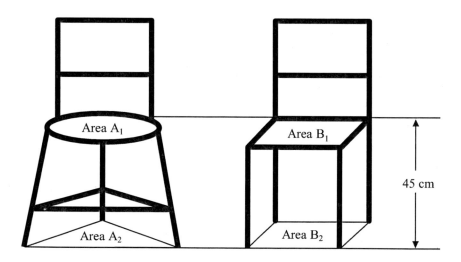

The physical characteristics of fourness can be extended to other fields. In automotive engineering, for example, the practical differences in road holding and steering between a four-wheeled automobile and a three-wheeled automobile need no elaboration. There is also the obvious architectural practicality of using the geometrical 'four' (as square and rectangle) in the standard forms of windows and doors (the geometrical 'three'— the triangle— is also occasionally used for windows and doors, but is less practical).

Another problem solved by fourness is the well-known Four Color Problem, which Francis Guthrie uncovered back in 1852 when he tried to colorize the counties of England. He found that a minimum of four colors sufficed without there being two adjoining counties sharing the same color. In other words, it cannot be done with only three colors. By showing that the number of colored inks can be kept to a minimum of four, printers were then able to keep the cost of colored atlases to a minimum, so Guthrie's solution to the Four Color Problem was a boon to the printing industry. The practical problem of verifying the solution to the Four Color Problem did not come until the age of computers when, in 1976, it was solved by Appel and Haken (1977), and Appel, Haken and Koch (1977). The minimum-of-four rule again points to the unique phenomenology of the number four in that fourness is invariably practical in a way lacking in threeness.

Another geometrical form, the rhombus is exemplary in suggesting the elastic nature of four as a 'flexed' square, which has an advantage in industry when resilience is required. Thus, the flexibility and versatility of fourfold structures cannot be undermined. They have distinct advantages over threefold structures.

Summary

Philosophically and psychologically, triadic models and systems are intrinsically specific (dogmatic) and do not indicate variability—only consolidation through intellectual progressiveness. While such progress is beneficial to the intellect, it is often determined within a one-sided absolute framework, very often the 'vehicle' of reason alone. Thus, systems, and forms, and structures that feature 'threeness' do not embody flexibility, and in fact, may demonstrate a certain form of uncompromising rigidity as in trinitarian thinking. Although threefoldness may demonstrate strength and stability, these qualities often impose certain limitations and costs.

Fourfoldness, on the other hand, reveals a different form of strength in the systems and structures it describes—a strength that lies in the fact that all possibilities are represented. Tetradic models and systems are expansive, in the sense that they represent alternatives in the form of diversification, although on occasion they may defy the rational functions (thinking and feeling), since they often culminate in paradoxical representations, even though they do represent completeness. The number four in its symbolism indicates totality, but it also indicates the paradoxical realities of nascent centrality and directionality—the ideal and goal of the differentiated psyche. The next chapter will describe these tetradic or quaternary qualities in more detail.

In this last chapter, there are many more words than there are viable, true insights. It reeks of "jargonistic, pseudo-educationese."

Ok. So 4 is better than three... have it your way. But the Egyptians wouldn't agree....

... ask James E. Tucker, M.D. ACU
why he hates going
to "wordy" psychology
workshops conferences.
many of the guests sound
like vomiting jargon
glossaries.

Plate 13. THE NUMBER FOUR

The Christian cruciform is a quaternary symbol. Such symbols have been identified with the God-image and, when meditated upon or experienced in dreams and visions, etc., allegedly bring about psychic wholeness—a sense of inner, spiritual peace, self-unity and completeness [SOURCE: © 2005, Melodi T/HAAP Media Ltd.].

FOUR (THE TETRAD)

*The one becomes two, and the two becomes three, and
from the third comes the One that is the fourth.*

Maria Prophetissa

*The number three symbolizes a spiritual dynamism that is
'restless' and 'free', but is rigid and lacking in wholeness. To
reach a state of wholeness, its dynamism must become united in
the physical world of 'matter' by admitting a fourth unexpected
element. When all the parts are recognized, the totality of the
real world is recognized. In the world of matter can be observed
the symbolism of four in ceaseless repetition in the infinitesimal
and the infinite.*

Number Four from the Infinitesimal to the Infinite

The quaternary factor is shown to recur again and again in Nature (these natural
occurrences include psychological, parapsychological, and metaphysical
phenomena). The inherent structural and geometrical aspects of the natural
world that relate to the number four avail the order-seeking psyche with
a particularly useful means of not only describing chaotic or ambiguous
phenomena more rationally through quaternary modes of expression, but
also of demonstrating the fundamental or archetypal reality of proclivities in
the psyche that appear to have a numerical sub-structure. That is, we do not
identify fourfold divisions arbitrarily, but are predisposed to recognize them
by dint of associative parallels, which are made possible by pre-structured

psychic (and possibly psychoid) tendencies. The associations are not merely projected onto the environment, since for the most part, the descriptions are factually observable, and therefore, empirical.

Fourness can first be 'observed' at the infinitesimal (atomic) level with carbon (the fundamental building block of all life as the essential element of living tissue) and its valency of four. In organic chemistry the most striking quality of carbon is the capacity of its atoms to bond and form rings and straight or branched chains (sometimes of considerable length). These forms constitute the compounds that make life possible on the planet. The carbon nucleus also rejuvenates (in the carbon-nitrogen cycle), and together with its quaternary form, bears a strong similarity to the structure of the Self, which also exhibits a fourfold structure and demonstrates rejuvenating properties (for example, transformations in consciousness). Von Franz (1978) observes the psyche/matter link as a synchronistic given—a contingency. The analogy of the Self with the atomic world:

> is not a digression since the symbolic schema itself represents the descent into matter and requires the identity of the outside with the inside…. Psyche and matter exist in one and the same world, and each partakes of the other, otherwise any reciprocal action would be impossible. (pp. 18-19)

 Anthony Stevens, in *Archetype: A Natural History of the Self* (1982), notes the four basic elements necessary for life: hydrogen, carbon, nitrogen, and oxygen:

> At the time when life on this planet began the prevalent raw materials on the earth's surface were…four in number: water, carbon dioxide, methane, and ammonia…. These simple inorganic substances were the precursors of the more complex organic molecules of sugars, fats and proteins, out of which living organisms evolved. (p. 71)

These four molecules represent a complete system, but only three are gainfully employed at any one time, as with the four nitrogenous bases of the DNA molecule (deoxyribonucleic acid). The DNA molecular chain in the cell chromosomes of all life, is a genetic code, an encryption of the biological life principle itself. The bases, adenine, cytosine, guanine, and thymine, form triplets consisting of three of these four bases, making one of twenty different amino acids, which form the proteins that are the very substance of the organism.

Advancing from the molecular world to morphology, we note the four-limbedness of creatures in the animal kingdom. It is no accident that the four-limbed perambulatory function should be so ubiquitous in nature—it is superior to two limbs in providing the animal with the surest measure of stability, grace, agility and speed.

Taste—the gustatory response—is discerned by various combinations of the four: sweet, sour, bitter and salty. It is argued that there are other 'tastes' (alkaline, metallic, etc.), but these are generally assignable to one of the four basic tastes of the tongue, since they are 'compound' forms and are reducible to at least two other tastes.

At a more conceptual level, the anatomical topographics of the human form determines an awareness of four sides—front, back, left and right. Orientation is given by the four cardinal compass points (north, south, east and west) and the four geometrical qualities of point, line, surface and solid. Ancient civilizations were influenced by the four cardinal directions to the extent that cities were planned accordingly, with gates in the city walls facing north, south, east and west. Moenjo Daro in the Indus Valley, now in ruins but one of the oldest cities in the world, dating back to the third millennium BC, shows a very early influence of the four directions on architectural thinking. Even modern cities are often planned with a fourfold structure in mind, thus taking the compass points into account.

In the 'antique' philosophy of ancient Greece is noted Aristotle's four principles of climate (Hot, Cold, Moist and Dry) from which are generated the four elements (Earth, Air, Fire and Water). It was actually Anaximenes (c. 590-525 BC) who first spoke of the four elements a few centuries earlier than Aristotle. Each element is more heavily influenced by one quality (principle) than by another. Thus, Heat governs Fire, Dryness governs Earth, Coldness governs Water, and Fluidity governs Air. The principles combine to make the elements (for example, Heat and Dryness make Fire), and the whole of nature was believed to be composed of these elements in combination with each other, in various proportions (*see* fig. 22).

Figure 22. *Aristotle's four elements and four principles.*

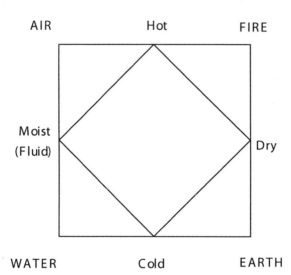

Of course, the discovery of many more elements since these ancient times has fostered an outright rejection of this fourfold schema. Most 'moderns' consider the ancients to be naïve in their belief systems, but as Jacob Bronowski noted in his television series 'The Ascent of Man', theories of any specific time in history were used to describe and explain the world and the problems of that time. In fact, von Franz (1980a) puts the four elements theory into an even clearer perspective. She argues that people of the time knew very well that four qualities and four elements did not explain reality so perfectly well:

> As soon as you think more profoundly, it does not fit, like all archetypal schemes of order which are projected, and even the very first alchemists said not to think that this [schema] was meant concretely, that it was just a way of introducing order into [their] ideas. Zosimos [third-

century Greek alchemist] for instance, says that, which means you see clearly an image of totality through the four qualities projected onto matter; even in those days it was simply a symbolic network which the human mind projected onto matter to bring order to it. (p. 152)

It is also known that the ancients were more philosophical in their attitudes, and did not investigate their 'scientific' claims experimentally. The probability of maintaining a projection of psychic contents as a long-term belief system is always high when the 'truth' of the matter is not investigated, so for those ancient philosophers, who took these simple schemata as accurate descriptions of reality, there is every likelihood that they were under the 'spell' of the 'totalizing', or wholeness-orienting archetype of fourness.

The psychological reality of four 'elements' can also be considered from another perspective. Each of the four 'elements' in the world could very likely have been introjected, so that outer qualities that resemble 'inner' qualities became descriptions of those inner qualities. But, projection is also possible (it is, in fact, difficult to know which mechanism comes first, introjection or projection). For example, once the concept of fire is grasped (at least intuitively), it becomes possible to 'see' (associate) fire with outer fire-like phenomena by projection. But, by introjection, it is also possible to believe that fire-like phenomena describe inner states. As Edinger says in *The Aion Lectures* (1996):

An unconscious content or complex can remain utterly quiescent until it is activated. As long as there is little energy change, it is earth, so to speak; it is that most solid of states. But if it is heated up, if it is activated, then it can turn into water or air or fire. (p. 183)

Applied neuro-anatomically to the brain, we can say the 'quiescent' content or complex is isomorphic with a specific neural cluster that is not in a state of activity (no particular neuron has reached its action potential, so other neurons in the cluster, as a center of a particular archetype, cannot be activated). This solid, 'earth' state is a 'ground' state, which requires energy to transform that 'earth' state to higher states.

It was also believed that, although the forms in nature may or may not have resembled the elements, the original elements retained their physical properties. This idea runs parallels with the physical properties of the elements in the Periodic Table of Elements in modern chemistry (see the chapter "Eight (The Ogdoad)").

Again, in ancient Greece, Aristotle's four causes—material cause (materials, tools, etc.), formal cause (intended scheme or plan for the material cause), efficient cause (the actions taking place) and final cause (purpose or use of the result)—offers another fourfold model that describes completely the physical (material), and mental (intentional) processes constituting the creative act. Aristotle's model is a system representing process through thought and action, and derives a sense of totality by its presence of four irreducible stages, which are the means by which the unformed may be formed. As a construction of the mind, rather than a depiction of the creative process in any absolute sense, this model, nevertheless, centralizes or targets creativity as an outcome resultant upon the necessary completion or presence of the four causes.

In classical medicine, Galen's four humors (chief fluids of the body)— phlegm, black bile, yellow bile and blood—yielded a healthy constitution, physically and psychologically, as long as they were in equilibrium. Excesses or deficiencies in these fluids would cause any of four temperaments in the individual: phlegmatic (sluggish, apathetic), melancholic (sad, gloomy), choleric (angry), or sanguine (optimistic, confident), respectively. The expression 'being in good humor', still used today, dates back to medieval times when medicines were still being prepared specifically with the objective of restoring a balance to the humors by addressing the chemical imbalances of the patient.

The 'humoral' system was further developed by Kant in the 1700s, and again by Wilhelm Wundt in 1903 into a 'classical typology'. Galen's humoral theory anticipated the discovery in modern medicine of hormones as determinants of physical and mental health. The criterion of chemical imbalance is still fundamental to the modern practices of homeopathic and allopathic medicine, including psychiatric treatment using pharmacological methods for the treatment of psychological disorders.

Galen's model speaks to the fundamental temperaments of human nature, and applies a causal mechanism through the humors to these temperaments. It was complete insofar as it was accurate in its time, so it is a model suggesting completion because it encompassed all variables relevant to their object. Although, there are vastly more than four hormones in the human body, Galen's model was an attempt to align the human being, functionally, with the principle of fourness.

While the Aristotelian elements and principles were a 'classical' means of describing the physical properties of contents in the environment, the more conventional four seasons (Summer, Autumn, Winter and Spring) are the traditional means of describing times of the year (as meteorological phenomena)—at least in the western world. In the East—or, more generally, in tropical climes—there are two major seasons—Hot and Rainy—but these can be sub-divided into four climatic conditions (Hot, Rainy, Dry and Humid).

Regarding the four seasons, Earth's orbit around the Sun is distinguished by two equinoxes and two solstices (minor and major axes, respectively), which form two pairs of opposites, totaling four. The Earth's moon is also associated with four by its four phases: crescent, waxing, full, and waning (a $7 \times 4 = 28$ day cycle). These phases not only served as an indication of the passage of days, but also, the Moon's association with four (an even, 'feminine' number), and its association with the female menstrual cycle of approximately 28 days, inextricably linked the Moon, the 'feminine', and the number four together as the embodiment of the 'feminine' principle and 'lunar' consciousness. And the representative archangel, HANIEL.

Fourness Expressed Psychologically

From our solar system we move to infinite, astronomical and metaphysical realities: in the former, the dimensions of outer space and beyond our solar system (see the chapter "The Titius-Bode Law"), and in the latter, the dimension of 'inner' space and the more conceptual (psychological) levels of mind. One facet of mind is the capacity for social interaction given by knowledge of self as related to others. Such interaction may be characterized by Joseph Luft's Johari Awareness Model. As described in 'The Johari Window and Self-Disclosure' (1971), all behavior, feelings, and motivation of an individual can be schematically assigned to one of four quadrants, which are qualitatively speaking, mutually exclusive of each other, and quantitatively account for all knowledge within the 'universe' of self and other, known or unknown by self and other, about self and other (*see* fig. 23). Thus, we have a taxonomy of four psychological components that indicate quaternary completion.

Figure 23. *The Johari Awareness Model: 'Change in any quadrant affects all quadrants'.*

	Known to self	Not known to self
Known to Others	1 OPEN	2 BLIND
Not Known to others	3 HIDDEN	4 UNKNOWN

Luft (1971) describes the contents of each quadrant as follows:

"Behavior, feelings, and motivation" referred to in:

"Quadrant 1, the open quadrant," are "known to self and to others."
"Quadrant 2, the blind quadrant," are "known to others but not to self."
"Quadrant 3, the hidden quadrant," are "known to self but not to others."
"Quadrant 4, the unknown quadrant," are "known neither to self nor to others." (pp. 210-211)

Self realization is the major aim of this model as the individual attempts to broaden the scope of self-knowledge (Quadrant 1) through introspection and shared communication with others about oneself. Blind quadrant factors suggest that tact is necessary from others as they interact with, and disclose their knowledge about the individual through feedback. The hidden quadrant is completely at the control of the individual as self-knowledge is selectively communicated to others in order to create relationships through self-disclosure, or to enhance existing relationships.

The unknown quadrant is the most unpredictable since the element of surprise is always preserved: it provides the greatest challenge, and the greatest reward to human interaction, as the fullest potential of human relationship is discovered as and when the deepest truths, previously unknown to both, are revealed (potentially to each other) intentionally or otherwise.

The Johari Awareness Model structures awareness and self-knowledge in a fourfold way, which can be seen as all-encompassing of the psychic system. Knowledge of self can either be known, or not known, and it can be known, or not known by self or by others, so that taken together, all doubt is eliminated (in the sense that all possible states of awareness are acknowledged). (A similar approach to psychological self-knowledge, that gives an idea of psychic dynamism, is given below in the Symbol Quaternity.)

The fourfold structure can be applied to any field that requires a fine focus on ambiguous data. Stuart Sutherland, in *Irrationality: The Enemy Within* (1992), gives an example of an invalid conclusion based on incomplete, or better, unstructured knowledge. A fictitious doctor, keeping a record of a symptom-related disease, found that 80 out of 100 patients contracted a disease when they presented with a certain symptom. The doctor concluded that the presence of the symptom could be used to make (predict) a successful diagnosis of the disease 80% of the time.

A fourfold presentation of all his available data would have shown him that 40 out of 50 patients (80%) also contracted the disease, even though they did not have the symptom (*see* Table 4). Consequently, the doctor's conclusion is wrong due to his failure to consider all the data. The symptom has no predictive value, because 80% of patients contract the disease whether or not they have the symptom.

Table 4. *Record of Patients' Symptoms and Disease.*

DIAGNOSIS	Disease	No Disease	Total
SYMPTOM	80	20	100
NO SYMPTOM	40	10	50

Keeping an eye on all the data by necessarily including hidden, but vital facts, gives a complete, and more accurate representation of the information available. In cases where there are two related variables, each with only two possible outcomes, all the data can be encompassed most successfully in a fourfold model. Not only can new, or absent information be incorporated into the model (so long as it is relevant data), but a characteristic sense of completion is present in fourfold structures, that can be conceptualized as an image of solidity, or can be taken as establishing some degree of certainty.

Number Four in Religion and Psychology

In religion, the mandala (Sanskrit: *mandala* = 'disc') of Buddhism, and the cruciform symbolism of Christianity (both tetradic symbols) have their origins in the psyche. Such symbols have been identified with the God-image and yield psychic stability: a sense of inner, spiritual peace, self-unity and completeness, when meditated upon or experienced in dreams, visions, etc. The two tetragrammatons (four letter names), Jehovah (*Yod, Heh, Vav, Heh*), and Jesus Christ (*INRI*, from Latin, *Iesus Nazarenus Rex Iudaeorum* = Jesus of Nazareth, King of the Jews) also demonstrate a fourfold phenomenology. Usually manifesting as symbols of religious experience, emblems of fourness often appear in visions and are said to be of divine origin.

A notable example of quaternity symbolism appears in Ezekiel's vision of 'wheels within wheels' in the first chapter of *Ezekiel* (Old Testament), which also features the ominous presence of four heads (man, lion, ox and eagle).

Psychologically, these examples are symbols of the totality of the psyche irrupting from the unconscious, usually during times of psychic disturbance. In the Jungian tradition, these symbols represent the individual's total personality, being comprised of the ego (at the center of the mandala), and the four conscious functions of Sensation, Thinking, Feeling and Intuition (found at the four corners of the mandala). Jung describes the function as being the means by which we orient ourselves in the world. In *Civilisation in Transition* (1970), Jung describes the four functions:

> [A]s soon as the unconscious enters the sphere of consciousness it has already split into the "four," that is to say it can become an object of experience only by virtue of the four basic functions of consciousness. It is *perceived* as something that exists (sensation); it is *recognized* as this and *distinguished* from that [thinking]; it is *evaluated* as pleasant or unpleasant, etc., (feeling); and finally, intuition tells us where it came from and where it is going. (para. 774)

Generally, individuals mediate the world with an ego personality governed by one of these functions (the main function), with an auxiliary function serving the complementary role of moderating behavior, or broadening the scope of experience, or interpreting that experience. The third function, which is opposite to the auxiliary function (on the same pole), may be involved, but in a lesser capacity, while the fourth function, standing as the polar opposite of the main function, is the least differentiated and, therefore, the least developed function (*see* fig. 24). Consequently, many errors in judgment, evaluation, perception, or induction (according to the function) can be attributed to the less mature function. This poor development is only to be expected, since more time is spent developing the main function at the expense of the others, especially the fourth function. However, the fourth function, the so-called 'inferior' function, often accounts for remarkable insights and peculiar, inspirational notions that have an instinctual or basic quality to them.

Figure 24. *Jung's four functions which determine the psychological type.*

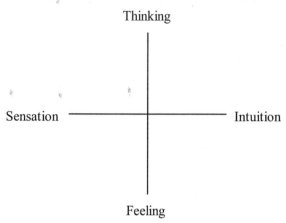

Whether an advantage or not to the ego, all the functions, especially the less differentiated ones, serve to modify and compensate the ego's onesidedness, and they also serve as a constant reminder to the ego of its degree of adaptedness to the world as it deals with the vicissitudes of life. Usually, a person does not have two functions at the same level of development if they are polar opposites, but either of the two functions on the other axis can be at a similar level of development as the main function, though this is not usual either. The functions of thinking and feeling are rational (present in these two functions is a regular mode of behavior, or a conscious method), the functions of sensation and intuition are irrational (these two functions are governed by irregular or unconscious factors).

Jung considered his fourfold typology to be intrinsically and archetypally built into the psyche, and by the fact that these four functions have a remarkable degree of autonomy and differentiation, they are represented in the myths and folklore of all cultures. For example, groupings of four people or animals who are on a quest, or have been given a problem to solve, can be readily identified as anthropomorphic or theriomorphic personifications of the four functions, as indicated by their behaviors, their characters and special features, their responses to situations, and their approach to problem-solving tasks.

In *The Archetypes and the Collective Unconscious*, Jung (1959b) states:

> "Types" are not individual cases, neither are they freely invented schemata into which all individual cases have to be fitted. "Types" are ideal instances, or pictures of the average run of experience, with which no single individual can be identified. (para. 167, n3)

The four types thus indicate dispositions in people, and Jung stressed that his typology was not to be used schematically (that is, rigorously and without compromise).

The Symbol Quaternio

The following four-stage process, illustrated by the Symbol Quaternity (*see* fig. 25), describes the transformation of the individual by way of the symbol, and also shows how the symbol itself becomes transformed at the initial point of its irruption into consciousness, through the four stages described below:

Stage 1: Transformation starts with the individual led by fate, or grace, or chance, to be the recipient of the *numinosum*—the mystical and powerful psychic experience. Phylogenetically, these experiences are available to all, but more so to those in which a tension exists in their psyche—a tension between the opposites of consciousness and the unconscious, either known or unknown by the one to whom the experience happens. The psychic tension can be seen as the product of an energic system with a dynamic nature by way of its bi-polar interchange of energy flowing between consciousness and the unconscious.

Stage 2: To give greater clarity to the *numinosum*, symbols are drawn, painted or carved, etc., to translate the 'spiritual' experience to the level of the material (the *concrete* form), to make the intangible manifest. Although the ultimate purpose and value of human beings lies in their productivity and creativity, equally important is the relief of psychic tension brought about by reduction in the potential difference of the two seemingly antagonistic domains. This relief is born out in both the productive or creative activity, and the satisfaction gained from that activity.

Stage 3: From these concrete forms are derived explanations and definitions in an attempt to speak of the ineffable. These interpretations will most likely be culturally specific. But the symbol is always a symbol and cannot be put into completely real terms because it is a bridge between two opposites of which we are only on one side, and the other side—the unconscious—is totally unknowable and only 'announces' itself through the symbol.

Stage 4: What arises from interpretation is the *abstract* form of the symbol. That is, the conscious factor having been applied to the *concrete* form yields the religious idea or dogma or other culturally specific notion. These ideas may be put into practice through rituals and ceremonies for the benefit of the collective. The success, the acceptance of the new concrete form for translation into abstract form is based on the 'rightness' of the symbol according to socio-cultural and historical specificity—the symbol speaks to the unconscious through its manifestation at the concrete and abstract levels. The ritual participant is invited to involve him or herself vicariously in the experience of the numinous power through belief and faith. This allows for outward direction (progression) of psychic energy as opposed to its damming up (regression) into the unconscious (energy necessarily seeks secondary routes if the usual, primary routes are not available). Progression of psychic energy thus allows the individual protection from the *numinosum* (which was first encountered by the original experient), since the nature of the reaction to the *numinosum* is dependent upon the emotional maturity of the individual. However, the experient is just as vulnerable to the effects of the *numinosum* even though the experience is his or her own. The cycle of four, schematized by the Symbol Quaternity, is complete.

Figure 25. *The symbol quaternity.*

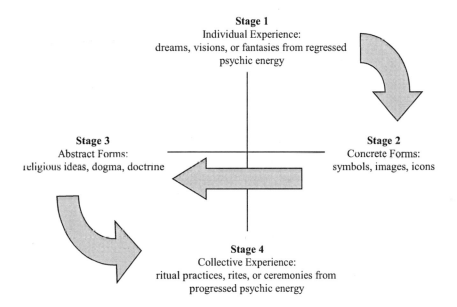

Stage 1
Individual Experience:
dreams, visions, or fantasies from regressed
psychic energy

Stage 3
Abstract Forms:
religious ideas, dogma, doctrine

Stage 2
Concrete Forms:
symbols, images, icons

Stage 4
Collective Experience:
ritual practices, rites, or ceremonies from
progressed psychic energy

The Purpose of the Symbol

The above-mentioned four-stage process, and its purpose, can be illustrated with the Jungian archetype of the Child. Jung (1959b) states: "The child motif represents the pre-conscious, childhood aspect of the collective psyche" (para. 273). This is the psychic state of the individual or society. The child symbolizes the potential for expanded consciousness. It appears when an unresolved conflict exists, or the psyche is simply in transition. The child-figure is made the culture-hero by being identified with a specific cultural item of simple or complex nature. For example, in the Japanese folk-tale, *Kaguya Hime*, an old peasant man discovers a small girl-child inside a large bamboo plant (**Stage 1**). The child is consequently identified with bamboo (**Stage 2**), one of the most important materials in ancient Japanese culture—

bamboo is a promoter of culture. The child too is absorbed into the culture, through storytelling, ritual and religion (**Stage 3**). This way, the purpose is served of maintaining the unbroken link between the present conscious mind's image of childhood, and the original condition of an unconscious and instinctive state. Psychologically, this child represents mankind's *anima* emerging from the darkness of the unconscious into a human relationship (specifically, merging with consciousness) in order to convey 'higher' knowledge from an absolute source, with the *anima* acting as a bridge to that source. The experience speaks to the community at large, consciousness is willfully enlarged through productive and creative activity, and the cultural products of the initial experience are shared by all (**Stage 4**). The original state of unconsciousness is overcome—darkness is subdued; light is created.

This constant condition of expansion of consciousness is the case in all cultures, at least until a stasis is reached where the archetype (the Child in this example) is no longer needed by a culture. However, the Child (or other archetypal representation) remains in the culture through a myth (usually a specific religious symbol) so long as the individual or collective remains unable to give reality to the 'call'. This failure is understandable given the risks associated with exposure to the unconscious—suffering can always be expected when the status quo is threatened.

If this condition continues, personal or collective growth can be restricted even further, and if psychological projection ensues, there is a strong possibility that "salvationist doctrines or practices" (Jung, 1959b, para. 287), or other substitute mythologies, may result if the child (or other archetype) 'dies' with no suitable substitute. This outcome represents an even greater danger because the extinction of a myth, as opposed to 'dreaming the myth onwards', leads to disintegration of an individual or collective and the threat of unconscious engulfment. Such cases of engulfment can be seen often, and in many societies, because a necessary increase in consciousness (generally tending to be a slow and difficult process) is hard won through sacrifice, and rather than face that challenge, the individual or collective would rather slip into denial, and hold onto the false hope that there will be no consequences for failing to act.

The Synchronicity Quaternio

Jung postulated a fourfold system which belongs to the domain of psychology and physics. Jung's Synchronicity Quaternity (Version I) was outlined in the previous chapter (*see* fig. 20). Classical physics has been upturned in this century by the relativization of space and time to become the spacetime continuum, which has 'conservation of energy' as its polar opposite. Pauli pointed out this fact to Jung, and so a more accurate quaternity was constructed, which would satisfy both the psychologist and the physicist (*see* fig. 26).

Figure 26. *The Synchronicity Quaternity (Version II)—Jung and Pauli.*

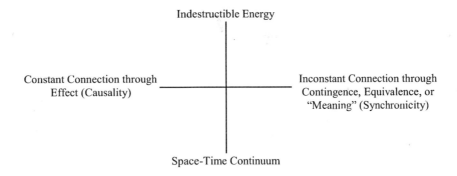

Indestructible Energy

Constant Connection through
Effect (Causality)

Inconstant Connection through
Contingence, Equivalence, or
"Meaning" (Synchronicity)

Space-Time Continuum

According to Jung, this quaternity brings modern physics and psychology into line by not compromising the postulates of either. The acausal pole (Synchronicity) accounts for all events that appear chance-like in nature and have an archetypal substratum. Though the archetypes are associated with causal events, the factor of 'transgressivity' (archetypes crossing over and manifesting in psycho-physical, acausal events) is included in the postulation. Jung (1960) writes:

> Archetypal equivalences are *contingent* to causal determination, that is to say there exist between them and the causal processes, no relations that conform to law. (para. 964)

In other words, certain necessary but scientifically unlawful circumstances (archetypal contingencies) that are present in a synchronistic event, and coincide with the causal aspects of that event, give rise to the idea of acausal orderedness (that is, synchronicity). Hence, the inconstancy, and therefore, the inability to determine or establish a causal connection between all the events. (See the chapter "Synchronicity" for a detailed discussion of these and other acausal issues.)

Four as Five?

At the stage where four different aspects of a system merge into a unified whole, but retain their 'higher' and discrete quaternary nature and intrinsic values, the quintessence ('fifth essence') moves from its nascent state to a full representation in consciousness. This is why the number five is held with the same regard in ancient Chinese philosophy as the number four in Western number symbolism. That is, the quintessence is simply the 'centered' four.

It has been argued, therefore, that the mathematically nonsensical $2 + 2 = 5$ is quite legitimate metaphysically speaking, but it is also a psychological 'truth'. This truth comes about because a metaphysical or symbolic equivalence of number four and number five ($4 \equiv 5$) means the Self-system can be equated with the principles and symbolism of both number four and number five, so that the quintessential nature (quality) of the development of the Self (5) is just as important as the degree (amount) of development of the Self (4), when the two pairs of opposites are combined. The 4 is a mathematical and a physical result indicating structure, whereas the 5 is a psychological and metaphysical result indicating meaning. (See the next chapter "Five (The Pentad)" for a deliberation on the meaningful aspects of the quintessence symbolized by number five.)

The number four shows the irreducible partial aspects of totality and completeness. It is symbolized by the square, □, and also by the circle cross-divided by a vertical and a horizontal line, ⊕. As a final curious point, the cross-divided circle is the symbol in astronomy and astrology representing our planet Earth—the fourth body from the center of the solar system after the Sun, Mercury, and Venus.

Summary

Graphically, two pairs of related opposites in four may form a target that represents the balance of the four qualities or functions (in a Jungian sense). This targeting process is a more refined and accurate version of 'twoness' because there is a vertical *and* a horizontal component, which produce a conjunction through the intersection of the two axes. The symbolism of number four, then, primarily appears in 'completed' systems comprised of two pairs of opposites seeking homeostasis that result in precisioned and fully defining, physical or mental structures. These represent total systems encompassing all viewpoints.

While irreconcilable oppositionalism may sometimes be present in these structures, the advantage is that they fairly represent all possible alternative viewpoints or realities relevant to the concepts under discussion with no exclusions (assuming they lend themselves to fourfoldedness). Conceptually, a fully embracing and flexible nature is thereby engendered in any system, concept, or structure that demonstrates fourfold symbolism.

There is always Four (Totality), but there is no experience of the natural, material essence given in corporeality, and so 'emerges' the number Five.

In music 4/4 time, 2/4 time etc, as opposed to 5/4 time, (see Dave Brubeck's "Take 5") or 7/4 time, see Richard Purvis' "Sing Unto God."

3/4 time is a waltz / 6/4, 6/8.

many Sarabands are written in 5/4 time, staggered.

Plate 14. THE NUMBER FIVE

The number five symbolizes the 'natural' corporeality of the human being. The number five relates to the five digits of the hand—a totality symbol of completion at the physical level. Broadly speaking, five-symbolism has come to relate to other natural, fivefold patterns in the physical world [SOURCE: National Aeronautics and Space Administration, USA].

See The Five Precepts
to become and remain
a Roman Catholic.

FIVE (THE PENTAD)

ain't that cute !

Five is the union of the four elements with Ether.

Diodorus

With the total integration of the four comes the 'One' that is the purest and most perfect form: the quintessence. It is comprised of four, but is not like any of the parts. It is not possible to discern either four or one from five. In this sense, too, it is the quintessence. And in the quintessence is combined the 'masculine' and the 'feminine' principles of Trinity and Duality, respectively (3 + 2 = 5), endowing the number five with the quality of union, but also, ambiguity and unruliness, based on an 'inner' oppositionalism: a secret imperfection.

Number Five in Nature

From antiquity, the number five has symbolized the 'natural', corporeality of the human being, relating as it does, to the five digits of each hand and foot, as well as the five extremities of the body—the head (or trunk) and four limbs—leading to completion at the physical level. Broadly speaking, five-symbolism has come to relate to other natural, fivefold patterns of the material world. Cirlot (1962) paraphrases Paneth:

> *Five* is a number that often occurs in animate nature, and hence its triumphant growth corresponds to the burgeoning of spring. It signifies the organic fullness of life as opposed to the rigidity of death. There is an erotic sense to it as well. (p. 225)

But Cirlot feels that this connection of number five with Eros, and Paneth's work on number symbolism in general, is restrictive because it is based on "obsessions and dreams of average people" (Cirlot, 1962, p. 224). Note also that von Franz (1974) criticizes Paneth's approach for its dependence on partial associations. As far as possible, a complete and comprehensive study of number symbolism should incorporate not just the study of dreams and personal 'myths', but "mathematical qualities of numbers, and physical number structures should also be included in such an attempt" (von Franz, 1974, p. 31).

Von Franz insists on a 'neutral' language of interpretation (something physicist Wolfgang Pauli attempted with the psyche/matter dualism). Such an endeavor may bring about an exposition of number symbolism that will be agreeable to the contemporary mind-set. As long as due recognition is given to the fact of the "psychic unconscious in the formation of the concept of number" (von Franz, 1974, p. 31), and its influence on our interpretations of the symbolism of number, a one-sided epistemology may be ameliorated by a consideration and integration of psychic contents produced as a result of the complementary and compensatory modes of the psyche. The diversity of interpretations that may result, which is evident in all fields of research, indicates these modes at work, and even with the inevitable dichotomies that may emerge, the more general goal of meaningfulness will remain paramount and undistorted.

From the Quaternity to the Quintessence

The above idea that there can be a diversity of interpretations actually has an historical reference that links us to our remote past. In ancient times the world seemed a comparatively simple place. Without the telescope or microscope, the modern laboratory, and the scientific method, the world was effectively constituted only of things that were visible to the naked eye. The invisible world was the world of gods and spirits. But a great leap forward from concrete to abstract thinking emerged in ancient Greece. Leucippus and Democritus developed their theories of atomism, which sprung from the speculative concept of a continuous divisibility of matter. The irreducible, indivisible atoms (Greek: *atomos* = 'not cut', 'undivided') were the building blocks of nature—they were beyond the senses, able to bind together without changes in properties, and remained together until a stronger force in the environment separated them. However, generally speaking, the Aristotelian world-view of the four elements had a stronger psychological hold on the 'classical' western psyche, partly due to the evidence of the senses. It seemed quite logical to the ancients that four elements made up the world. The quaternity paradigm of four seasons, four directions, etc., had overwhelming suggestive power.

In the chapter "Four (The Tetrad)" it was mentioned that quaternary structures symbolize the element of wholeness, and this wholeness or unity, is traditionally represented as the *quinta essentia* ('fifth essence'). The number five, as the quintessence, can be represented as the quincunx (:·:), the center of the four, which Jung describes as "a frame for the one, accentuated as the centre.... By unfolding into four it acquires distinct characteristics and can therefore be known" (1970, para. 774). The ancient Chinese held the quincunx with the same regard as Westerners held the quaternity because the former was essentially the centered four—the *quinta essentia*, or quintessence; a word which has survived in many modern languages to describe a thing that epitomizes and embodies the perfect, the ideal, and even the soul and heart of a thing.

The quintessence as a unity symbol is referred to in the statement of Maria Prophetissa: "the One as the Fourth." The 'One' (the 'Fourth') is the culmination of the Pythagorean *tetractys*, and it embodies the whole principle of the alchemical art of the hermetic philosophers. Paradoxically, it must be concluded that the 'One as the Fourth' is quintessential in nature. The word quintessence, as a figure of speech in many languages is a testament to the evocative power of the idea inherent in the image of 'wholeness in fiveness'.

Quaternity structures, which can be represented as two interconnecting axes—one vertical, one horizontal—form a target or cross, and they have as their center the symbolic representation of the quintessence, just as the Indians, Muslims, and Mayans recognized. In India, the center of the cross and its four extreme points have apotropaic (evil-averting) properties, while for Muslims, the human hand and its five digits were the model for good luck amulets used to avert the 'evil eye'. The image symbolized the 'Hand of Fatima', after Muhammed's youngest daughter and mother of the Imams.

Schimmel (1993) reports that the Mayans also took the number five to be symbolic of the quintessential factor found at the center of the four cardinal directions. She adds that the five colors, red, white, black, yellow, and bluish-green, constituted the Mayan deities, and the number five is still so highly venerated in this part of Meso-america that the Yucatan area still has place names which incorporate the number five.

Westcott (1974) records that the goal of the alchemists was to derive the quintessence "from the four.... Separate the pure from the impure, gently and with judgment, and so you obtain the Quintessence, the Son of the Sun" (p. 66), thereby drawing a parallel between Christ and the quintessence. Since Jung has indicated the symbolic equivalence of Christ (God-image) with the psychological Self (the total personality that stands beyond, but embraces the ego), it can be seen that the one essential driving force behind all these symbols is the unity in consciousness of the total psychic system, which has always stood as the ultimate goal. Jacobi (1974) writes:

> The five, or in other words the quaternity united in the quintessence, is not a derivative...but an independent whole that is more than the sum of its parts. It is the super-essential that transcends all the rest. (p. 171)

Von Franz (1974) also points out this fact, in relation to the Element theory of classical times:

> The *quinta essentia* is not additively joined onto the first four as a fifth element, but represents the most refined, spiritually imaginable unity of the four elements. It is either initially present in and extracted from them or produced by the circulation of these elements among one another. (pp. 120-121)

Extraction and circulation of elements to yield the quintessence was the practice of the alchemists, who also referred to the quintessence as the mediator or *pelicanus noster* ('our pelican'; an allegory of Christ). The pelican, when she preens herself, forms a circle with her neck and beak, and by analogy, was associated with a piece of laboratory equipment called the pelican. This pelican was a retort with a spout feeding back into the vessel, and was used to distill the quintessential elixir by way of a circular, repeating process. Any fourfold system demonstrates this extraction/circulation process. According to their purpose (ultimately, the process of uniting the four elements of a system into one), it can be seen that, as Jung (1970) says:

> The splitting into four has the same significance as the division of the horizon into four quarters, or the year into four seasons. That is, through the act of becoming conscious the four basic aspects of a whole judgment are rendered visible. (para. 774)

First then, must come the *differentiation* of the parts of a whole, which provides the working material for the mechanism of extraction and circulation, by way of the interactions between those parts, all with the conscious mediation and supervision of the individual. Psychologically, we can picture this differentiation as a cognitive process involving recognition of, and repeated deliberation upon the parts of the whole until integration of the parts results, in the form of a critical understanding of the inter-relationships that exist between the parts, or which may emerge from their comixture. The individual's self-analysis of a problem or situation is seen as consisting of parts or aspects which require full consideration to ensure complete understanding. Alchemically, Earth ⇒ Water, Water ⇒ Air, Air ⇒ Fire, Fire ⇒ Earth, and so on—the circularity and cyclicality indicate the repetitive nature of the process of refinement (distillation) necessary to achieve the purity of the quintessence.

Quintessentially, as stated, the number five is the point at the center formed by the intersection of the two pairs of opposites which comprise the four, just as in Chinese number theory, five is at the center of the series one through nine (four integers on both sides):

[handwritten top: a tic-tac-toe grid with X X X / ? O O / B O O] = TIC-TAC-TOE + 1

[handwritten: There are 9 squares. 4 x's + 4 o's, and 1 "final" more. 8 + 1]

1   2   3   4   [5]   6   7   8   9

[handwritten left margin: "Whatever" by Sean Dillon]

The number five occupies the central position of two major number diagrams in Chinese number philosophy: the *Ho-t'u* and the *Lo-Shu* models (*see* figs. 27 & 28). Both these models had significance in ritual, with the element of earth (corporeality) *as a spiritual principle* represented by the number five at the center. Von Franz notes that while the ancient Chinese philosophers were also influenced by the collective unconscious, as were the western philosophers, their number theory, however, was constituted differently. The Chinese depended on numerical patterns as formative elements for, and the bases of, their arts and sciences. A universal order was thereby expressed in numerical structures.

The *Ho-t'u* (*see* fig. 27) model indicates the cross, the center of which is the quintessence. It does not represent cyclicality, but stands for 'timeless equilibrium'. Von Franz (1974) uses the hovering dragonfly as a metaphor for the *Ho-t'u* as a stationary system with a highly dynamic inner condition that maintains the equilibrium of the system: "The world model of the *Ho-t'u* thus forms *the primal image of a relatively timeless state of universal orderedness*" (p. 237).

The movement from 1 to 10, meeting halfway at 5, is counted in unitary steps. This quintessential principle is the beginning and end of all events and processes, where the number five (and by proxy, zero and the number ten) is the starting point or center of the matrix from which begins the sequence, starting 1, 2, 3,…, and so on to 10 at the center, to start all over again.

Von Franz tells us that the *Lo-Shu* Model (*see* fig. 28) forms the magic number square of the first nine digits (each line, horizontally, vertically and diagonally, adds up to fifteen: the 'magic constant'). This magic square was known to the Neo-Platonists, but may date back to Pythagorean times. Magic squares and other numerical structures form matrices (Latin: *matris* = 'womb' or 'mother'), the beginning of all things. This 'matrix' is the unconscious psyche, the collective unconscious itself, from which consciousness is born.

Figure 27. *The Ho-t'u model and the four directions forming a cross. [Source: M.-L. von Franz (1974) Number and Time].*

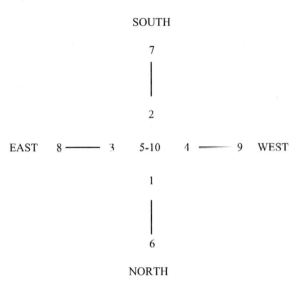

Figure 28. *The Lo-Shu model (pattern of the river Lo) forming a square. [Source: M.-L. von Franz (1974) Number and Time].*

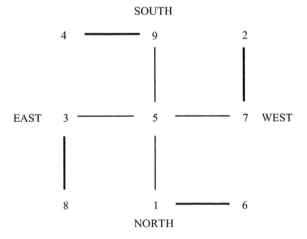

Structured as a swastika (Sanskrit: *svasti* = 'well-being'), the *Lo-Shu* model has nothing to do with the Hitlerian corruption of this symbol. Hitler's 'Broken Cross' was rotated 45°, and inverted so that it turned in an anti-clockwise direction, which symbolizes a direction toward the left (unconsciousness), while the swastika proper, as can be observed throughout Asia and Europe (for example, as the *fylfot* in Celtic countries), rotates in a clockwise direction, toward the right, symbolizing a movement towards consciousness. (The unconscious acts perpetrated by the Nazi regime indicate the destructive power that can result when a group is possessed by the collective Shadow, united under the aegis of the 'Broken Cross'.)

Taken together, the two models are constituted as such:

1. *Ho-T'u* = Earlier (Older) Heaven = Duration

2. *Lo-Shu* = Later (Younger) Heaven = Motion

These two models, *Ho-T'u* and *Lo-Shu*, are arithmetic mandalas that indicate the principles of time and movement, respectively. Von Franz notes that the *Ho-t'u* model represents *timeless* time, and the *Lo-Shu* model represents *cyclical* time. According to legend, the matrices of *Ho-t'u* and *Lo-Shu*, and similar matrices, were revealed to humanity by lowly vertebrates (tortoise, snake, etc.), which translate, psychologically, as the deeper levels of the collective unconscious. This psychological truth gives symbolic recognition to the fact that not only are numerical patterns produced intuitively in the psyche, but also that the psyche is somehow communicating an unconscious content in the form of the absolute psychic truth that matter and psyche are structured the same way on matrix forms, where cyclicality (movement) and eternity (rest) are interconnected as an ordered whole.

The Quintessence in Alchemy

Like ancient Greece, the idea of an 'elemental' world was equally strong in the oriental psyche, although here was propagated a five element system. In *Alchemy* (1957), Holmyard writes of the significance given to the number five in ancient China. Still today, in the principles of Chinese herbal medicine and traditional philosophy:

> there are five elements, namely wood, fire, earth, metal, and water; five zones of space; five 'directions', namely north, south, east, west, and center; five colors, namely yellow, blue, red, white, and black; and five stones from which man was first taught to extract copper,...[and] five metals gold, silver, lead, copper and iron. (p. 36)

Holmyard notes the connection of these elements, directions and colors with the five metals; gold, silver, lead, copper, and iron (*see* Table 5).

Table 5. *The Five Elements and Associated Qualities in Chinese Alchemy.*

ELEMENT	COLOR	DIRECTION	METAL	PLANET
Earth	Yellow	Central	Gold	Saturn
Wood	Blue	East	Lead	Jupiter
Fire	Red	South	Copper	Mars
Metal	White	West	Silver	Venus
Water	Black	North	Iron	Mercury

Jung (1963, para. 249) presents five sets of five qualities from Chinese philosophy, and reproduces a model which graphically indicates the five differentiated aspects of the whole '*chu niao*' bird (the purified spirit), as described in the Chinese alchemical treatise, the *Wei Po-yang* (*see* fig. 29). This bird has its parallels in Western alchemy with the *avis Hermetis* ('bird of Hermes'). (Unlike the Western tradition, the Chinese represented the four directions with south at the top of their diagrams.)

It is important to recognize that the central part, Earth, represents the basis or starting point of the work, the fifth element. The arrangement of the five elements, colors, seasons, and directions, describes aspects of the spirit, and the processes that the spirit goes through in order to take up its place in the 'glorified' body.

Altogether, the ubiquity and conscious dominance of number-five symbolism in China meant that the ancient Chinese held the number five with high regard. In fact, the highest goal for which a person could wish was 'quintuple happiness'.

Figure 29. *Jung's model of the five elements of Chinese alchemy, and associated qualities from the Wei Po-yang. (Note that only Red/Fire/South and Blue/Wood/ East match Holmyard's associations. A further discrepancy arises in reference to the Planet/Element relationship in Western alchemy, where Saturn/Lead, Jupiter/Tin, Mars/Iron, Venus/Copper, and Mercury/Mercury all contradict the Chinese system.) [Source: C. G. Jung (1963) Mysterium Coniunctionis].*

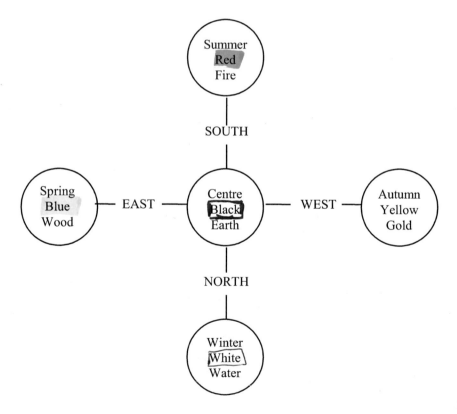

Number Five in Geometry

The number five can be represented geometrically as a pentagon (*see* fig. 30), the pentacle (the Freemason's signet mark), and the pentagram or pentangle, the five-pointed star—also known as the pentalpha, which Westcott (1974) calls the "true Solomon's seal" (p. 70). She disclaims the naming of the six-pointed star, the hexalpha, as the seal of Solomon (an apparent 'mistake' which Edinger, Heline, and many others have made).

Figure 30. *The pentagon—the diagonals of the pentagon form the five-pointed star: the pentalpha or pentagram.*

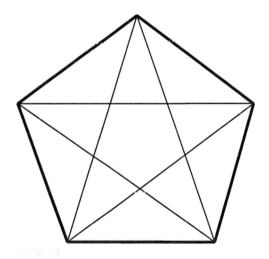

In Figure 31 it can be seen that the pentagram is constructed of five 'golden triangles' (XXY), each of which can be used to derive the golden ratio Ø (*phi*), discussed in the chapter "A Brief History of Number." Specifically, from the golden triangle, Ø = X/Y = (1/2 + √5/2) = 1.6180.

Figure 31. *The golden triangle appears five times in the pentagram, with each of the sides (Y) of the inner pentagon acting as the base of these triangles.*

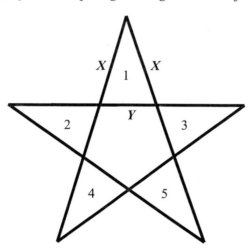

Structurally linked to the number five, then, by way of the geometrical representation of the pentagram, is an irrational and transcendental component; the constant Ø. But the number five deviates from the rational and the immanent in other ways, which point to a quintessential character that is more metaphysical than physical in nature. For example, in two dimensions, the pentagon does not tessellate (except with other polygons). F. David Peat acknowledges this problem with the number five:

> Roger Penrose discovered a new form of tiling: Penrose Tiles. The thing about tiling a plane is that with other symmetries you simply have a next neighbour rule which allows you to place one tile along side the next and this continues to infinity, you can cover the entire space. But this is not the case with Penrose tiles—that is, they are non-repeating. If you try to put down the tiles without taking into account the global nature of the space—that is, the entire pattern— then at some point there will be a gap or a tile will not fit it. So there is something very strange about five-fold symmetry. (Peat, personal communication, January 15, 2007)

Penrose tiles (the simplest being two tiles—a thin rhombus and a thick rhombus) create the problem of aperiodic (non-repeating) tiling so the beauty of translational symmetry (i.e., absolute tessellation in a plane) is lost with the number five, although there are limited symmetries within tile groups.

Nor is 5 a 'structuring number', as it is not found in crystal forms, whereas the structural representations of the numbers 2, 4, and 6 do appear in crystals. In a sense, just as the geometrical form of five (the pentagon) is a 'misfit', the number five has a mercurial, alternative symbology to its seemingly all-positive, quintessential quality.

Schimmel (1993) hints at this negative aspect of the number five by pointing out that "[f]rom early times 5 was considered a somewhat unusual, even rebellious, number" (p. 106), and since it proliferated throughout the vegetable kingdom (many plants feature fivefold leaf and petal formations), and the animal kingdom (five digits: fingers, toes, etc.), the number five "could be regarded as a 'naughty', unruly number that, like Eros, stirs up the well-ordered cosmos" (Schimmel, 1993, p. 107). It is difficult to see exactly how the number five should be considered 'unruly' in the vegetable and animal kingdoms, since it actually participates in ordering or putting structure to those kingdoms, but the conspicuous absence of the number five is certainly noted in the mineral or inorganic world, and in geometry, where it fails to tessellate. This theme of five's unruliness is continued in the next section.

Number Five as a Psychological Factor

The main geometric theme in Egyptian tombs of the 1st Dynasty was the five-rayed star, and the Pyramid Texts record that it is the destiny of every human being to become a star. We can imagine that the ancient Egyptians had the positive side of this five-rayed star in mind, when they recognized a 'stellar' fate for humanity because, as will be seen, there is a dark or negative side inappropriately associated with the five-rayed star, manifesting as human unconsciousness.

Psychologically, the pentagram (as a star) symbolizes consciousness. We are reminded of 'multiple consciousnesses' as 'multiple luminosities'

Soul, see Jung

referred to in the chapter "One (The Monad)," where Jung draws the parallel of consciousness with light. In fact, the starlight emanating from stars may generally be taken as symbolic of consciousness, but it appears that this 'starlight' of consciousness may be dimmed by the overwhelming blackness of the 'universal void' of unconsciousness.

In *The Dimensions of Paradise* (1988), John Michell describes this association of the five-pointed star with humanity (the human form), but he also mentions the star's other association with Hermes (Mercurius), the medium of Revelation and keeper of the Mysteries. Furthermore:

> [the] Christian mystics made the pentagram an emblem of Jesus, who divided five loaves to feed five thousand people and who represents the archetypal man (with five senses and five fingers to each hand). (p. 76)

Here the connection between the quintessence, Christ and Mercurius is clear. Having established the Self/Christ/Mercurius/Quintessence association, and given that the first three, Self, Christ and Mercurius are all duplex in nature, it follows that the quintessence must have a 'darker', chthonic aspect as well, otherwise the symbolism is incomplete.

It is interesting to note how very sparingly the 'dark side' of the quintessence is reported in the literature, although the 'darkness' of the other three is well documented. As it happens, the darker aspect of number-five symbolism is more apparent in the modern world. As was pointed out, the geometrical representation of the number five: the five-pointed star——shines the light of human consciousness and the empirical self (the ego). This is the same five-rayed star taken up symbolically by the United States (the white star) and former Soviet Russia (the red star), but it has become conflated with chaotic *prima materia* (the darkness of humanity as human unconsciousness), and these nations have identified with that contamination to the degree that they are still unconscious. Matter has become deified and dogmatized as materialism and rampant consumerism. In the United States, the slogans 'land of the free' and 'the pursuit of happiness' have been translated into indiscriminate endeavors for financial success, while in former Soviet Russia, deification of the State (which embodied Marxist dialectical materialism, and an unconsciously-effected materialism similar to the United States) has resulted in the same fruitless pursuits. The star has not emerged from the darkness, and does not shine as it should with all its potential brilliance.

Five symbolizes physical, material existence and the life principle, but as an uneven, 'masculine' number, and as the symbol adopted by over-masculinized nations (economically and politically speaking), materialism, consumerism, and freedom at all costs are simply the extreme patriarchal interpretations of the 'feminine', 'earth' principle, which ordinarily embodies productivity, nourishment, and the 'good life'—not exploitation, excess, and procurement for its own sake. Clearly the 'feminine' principle is also conflated in the darkness with the obscured consciousness of the star.

But the dark side of number-five symbolism does not end with materialism. It is also a case in point that the headquarters of the leaders of the United States Defense Forces is the five-sided Pentagon Building in Washington, D.C. The 'one-sided' earth-bound consciousness of those in the defense forces, perfectly represented geometrically by the pentagon, is oriented toward the maintenance of peace the only way they know how—by a readiness for war. The nation held to be the most materialistic of all nations, where capitalism reigns supreme (ostensibly under the banner of democracy and disguised as the free market economy), has adopted a most fitting symbol to represent its right to bear arms in order to protect its people, its freedom, its land, and its wealth.

No other number but the number five (represented graphically as the pentagon), explicitly or implicitly, symbolizes so well the endorsement of a forceful and physical 'last-resort' solution to problems that are most often conceptual (for example, political) in nature. War, as the inevitable consequence of an emasculated politics, brings exactly the opposite of that which it is supposed to achieve because there can be no winners in war. The description of Mercurius, who is associated with number-five symbolism, is eternally true. As the embodiment of all possible opposites, Mercurius *is* as Jung (1963) writes the "peacemaker, the mediator between warring elements and producer of unity" (para. 10), but as Jung also notes in *Alchemical Studies*

(1968a), Mercurius is "the devil…[and] an evasive trickster" (para. 284). The outcome of war always creates the illusion of victory (in a material sense) for the 'winning' side, yet brings with it the painful loss of human life, and an incredible weight on a nation's conscience, with little solace in the fact that it was all for the good of the nation and world peace.

In such cases, the five-rayed star and the pentagon have become one-sided symbols of wholeness, manifesting as greed and survivalism for those under its negative symbolism, because the necessary dynamic felt in consciousness, which would lead to true liberation and happiness, involves the spiritual counter-pole to the over-glorified (misinterpreted) materialistic principles of provision and self-love, which have degenerated into purposeless acquisition, cornucopia (over-abundance), and paranoia. More correctly, the symbols themselves have been misunderstood or even ignored—exactly the circumstance that should have been avoided. This situation was true in the 1950s and its 'hangover' effect was carried well into the 1980s as indicated in the literature of those times.

Sloan Wilson's novel *The Man in the Grey Flannel Suit* (1957) successfully encapsulates the tragic irony in the form of an American professional man, Tom Rath, who has everything except his peace of mind. Being caught up in the corporate myth of success through acquisition and power, Rath has little prospect of reconnection with his soul, but ultimately attains this through the rediscovery of his relationship with his wife. In fact, traditionally, number five has always been the number of marriage, since it was comprised of two ('feminine') and three ('masculine') united in matrimony—the 'sacred union' of two opposites. Here is embodied the principle of the missing 'feminine' in patriarchal societies, the *anima* in men, and its complementary, restorative power.

The dénouement described in Wilson's novel is not realized in Bret Easton Ellis's novel *American Psycho* (1991)—a strong indictment of the progress of Western values up until the 1980s and beyond. Ellis has his success-obsessed anti-hero Patrick Bateman fail completely at finding peace of mind precisely because his warped *eros* function and failure to integrate the feminine is far too prohibitive. Perversely so, since the graphically murderous and tortuous events played out in his mind indicate just how polluted and beyond salvation is his corrupted soul.

In the above cases the symbolism of number five has been misunderstood and ignored for the very reason that the 'feminine' is misunderstood and ignored. Symbols are meant to connect consciousness with the unconscious, 'masculine' with 'feminine'. Thereby, the dissociation of the material world is embodied in all the associations made between the number five and those factors outlined above.

The Five Stages of Projection

The Torah is the first five books of the Bible.

The pentagram is a major symbolic image in *Kabbalah* and magic practices, since it resembles the basic proportions of the human being. Although symbolic of corporeality (materialism), the pentagram as used by sixteenth-century physician and occultist Agrippa von Nettesheim was isomorphic with the 'higher' spiritual 'Man' (even including his transcendental soul and his 'irrationality'), and his five extremities, head, left arm, left leg, right leg, right arm (associated with Venus, Jupiter, Saturn, Mercury, and Mars, respectively). The Sun was 'situated' at the solar plexus, and the Moon took its place at the crux or base point.

This type of model, which incorporated the seven heavenly spheres, attests to the belief that the microcosm mirrored the macrocosm, since the attributes of the seven 'planets' were also in the body and mind of 'Man' (for example, Mars referred to aggression and initiative, Venus referred to love and sexuality). Each of these planets symbolized a stage that had to be worked through in order to reach completion (Humankind's quintessential nature).

The idea of symbolism is important here because the factor of projection is immediately raised. Jung (1970) states that "the subject gets rid of painful, incompatible contents by projecting them" (para. 783), and in *Projection and Recollection in Jungian Psychology* (1997), von Franz outlines five stages necessary for the withdrawal of a projection, from projection onto the objective world, to withdrawal of the projection back to the subject, by recognition of the projection as an unconscious content or complex.

We make incorrect assumptions about people, things and situations, etc., through projection, where these assumptions often indicate aspects of our own personality. These five stages show how we can arrive at 'quintessential centeredness' by successful accomplishment of the fifth stage. The five stages are as follows:

1. *'projection'*: The individual or society projects inner qualities onto suitable hooks in the outer world—other people, animals, inanimate objects in nature, etc., even planets and the 'heavenly sphere' have 'powers'.

2. *'differentiation'*: A higher entity (spirit, soul, or animating principle, as a god, goddess, demon, etc.) is seen as a separate factor associated or identified with, but not constituting or actually being that object itself. A person might be seen as *having* a 'demonic' disposition, but is not taken to *be* an actual demon, or (say) the planet Mars is taken as *standing for* Mars, the god of War.

3. *'moral evaluation'*: The demon in the person is either a good 'spirit' or an evil 'spirit', helpful or hindering, productive or destructive. Mars (for example) is judged to be warlike and aggressive, or protective and heroic.

4. *'questioning'*: the projection is rationalized so that withdrawal of the projection may begin. The third stage, having started an introspective outlook, allows the projection further elucidation in conscious thought so that the result is usually the conclusive determination that the whole experience was an *'illusion'*. The notion of the person as demonic is rejected as a totally unreasonable assumption (a deception), or the god Mars simply does not exist. His qualities are those belonging to the sphere of the intellect, and describe only the individual or society.

5. *'review'* of the whole process and the initial state of projection. The projection existed for a reason, and it is inappropriate to stop at stage four and dismiss the whole experience as a silly mistake. This last stage involves recognizing the source of the projection from a perspective

of responsibility and moral obligation to oneself and society. The person or society reflects upon its inner processes. In our examples, the demon is, at the very least, in the person making the projection, the 'martial' disposition is a human factor, as well as being characteristic of a society.

As von Franz (1997) states, we must answer the question of "how an overpowering, extremely real, and awesome experience could suddenly become nothing but self-deception" (p. 10). Unless one denies the existence of the psyche, a content with a psychic existence in the unconscious pushes itself upward and outward from the subject, only to be projected onto the object. The person or society must address the issue of how and why such a situation could become possible. Von Franz describes the fifth stage in action:

> a hitherto unconscious psychic content is brought repeatedly into the view of the conscious ego and recognised as belonging to its own personality. In the process this content is changed in its functioning and effects. (p. 11)

> If one wants to prevent…a renewal of the projection, the content must be recognised as *psychically real*, though not as part of the subject but rather as an *autonomous power*. (p. 13)

This fifth and final stage is clearly quintessential in nature because of the potential value it holds in its process, and the actual value that is to be gained from a successful execution of its requirements.

The Archetype of Five in Mythology

Myth and theological speculation can also be interpreted from the perspective of projection. In the case of myth, the gods of (say) Olympus, who were subsequently seen as separate from their environment, then became judged morally by the standards of ancient Greek society. With the emergence of the Sophists and Stoics, the gods were dismissed as "dead, deified, historical

The Plaintiff, the Defendant, The Judge and the Jury + 1 = The LAW = 5 the abstraction

personalities" (von Franz, 1997, p. 37), while their attributes were taken as qualities in human nature. The state of mythical identity with unfathomable, and often unreasonable, entities of a spirit world was dissolved in human consciousness so that an understanding of self could be reached through self-knowledge.

In Christianity, even as early as the founding of the Church, questions concerning the literal truth of Scripture were already being raised. An allegorical (symbolic) approach was claimed as superior to the concretistic and literal-minded perspective of the masses. Often due to the suppressive power of the Church, however, only a small number of individuals throughout the long history of Christianity have made such claims. Nevertheless, other truths of a more symbolic character became admissible to scriptural interpretation (at least in scholastic circles).

By the fourth century AD, Origen questioned the historical facts and argued for the recognition of the discursive constructions underlying scripture, which were in fact the original intentions of the chroniclers of the Old and New Testaments. Origen believed that numinous visions ('waking dreams') could be experienced, just as revelations and insights were possible in dreams during sleep, so that it was highly likely that visitations, annunciations, prophecies, etc., were the individual's experience of a 'metaphysical world', or the 'world of Platonic ideas'. The first and second stages of the withdrawal of projections were underway.

By the second millennium, moral relativization concerning the dogma of the *Summum Bonum* gave rise to a dichotomous viewpoint about the Trinity. Many theologians such as Rhabanus Maurus, Vincent de Beauvais, and Honorius of Autun are noted by von Franz (1997) for establishing (or at least fostering) the belief that:

> Fire…can mean either the hell of the passion or inspiration through the Holy Ghost; the raven is a symbol of the devil or of deeper thoughts directed toward God; the dove symbolises erotic lust (Venus!) or the Holy Ghost; the lion, which "sees what it devours," is Satan or Christ, "who wakes us with his roaring," and so on. (p. 47)

This third stage led to the fourth stage of an actual rational criticism of Christian images. The increase in a rational approach to world phenomena and the ever-increasing interest in the natural sciences, spurred a rationalist movement that was to culminate in the deification of Reason during the French Revolution. This process merely shifted the focus of projection to the concrete world of matter. Hence the new sciences of biology, chemistry and physics—disciplines which became 'filled' with inner images from the psyche.

Before the Revolution, during Charlemagne's reign, concretism was discouraged. Agobard of Lyon in the ninth century advised reason over belief in miracles, while John Scotus Erigena taught that the ascension of Christ was a "parabolic event," "not a concrete historical fact, but an event in the realm of human consciousness" (von Franz, 1997, p. 48). Psychological interpretations were gaining weight, while the projection of the god-image was being withdrawn. Even the gnostic Cathars did not take the virgin birth, nor Christ's burial, nor the resurrection, literally.

The most startling viewpoint, because of its psychological insight, came from the 'heretical' mind of Gerard di Monteforte who claimed "God as the primordially existing mind, or spirit, of Man (!) and the Son as the spirit (*animus*) of man (!) beloved by God, but the Holy Spirit as the understanding of Scripture" (von Franz, 1997, p. 49). This kind of rationalism almost led to stage five: recognizing the source of the projection. By the eighteenth century even the Church supported the previously incompatible tendencies of interpreting Scripture 'rationalistically' or maintaining the traditional dogmatism of a literal faith-inspired understanding.

Not until the twentieth century was the psychological issue of projection posed as a personal problem (originating in the psyche), and an unanswered question: "If all these assertions concerning the faith are, taken concretely, no longer credible, then where did the projection come from?" (von Franz, 1997, p. 52). The rational standpoint of stage four does not dissolve the projection, but the contents that constituted the projection are maintained in the psychic sphere "producing living effects" (p. 52) despite the person's conscious and rational outlook. Only by recognition of their '*autonomous power*' can they be integrated (owned) by the individual as a psychic reality and not as an illusion.

These same five stages can be applied to any human pursuit—even science, since the seeds for new scientific breakthroughs can be sown as a consequence of the completion of the fifth stage (assuming there is an understanding of the implications found at this stage). Thereby, the validity of old beliefs or doctrines is questioned, leading to the collapse of these scientific paradigms. For example, the *ancient* 'scientific' concept of a correspondence between the empirical dimensions of the so-called Platonic solids (i.e., Euclid's mathematically described five regular solids: tetrahedron, cube, octahedron, dodecahedron, and icosahedron) and the planetary spheres, that produced a 'music of the spheres', is seen to be a projection of an 'inner' (psychological) state which, formerly, was considered to be the actual state of the Heavens.

This rationale even brings the 'dogma' of the *modern* sciences, including the 'new physics', into question. So many contents of the unknown (psychic realities) become constituents of the new knowledge which bind the raw data into a cohesive whole. Actual observation of the world *and* psychic processes and states that are common to the generality (archetypal facts), are conflated, rendering the knowledge dubious at best.

The five stages necessary for the integration of projections, are not only seen to have psychological benefit, but also assist in the relative reduction of the subjective factor involved in knowledge production, even resulting in complete abandonment of knowledge claims when they fail to describe the phenomena they so adequately described prior to the discovery of new evidence to the contrary.

The complexity of this five-stage process indicates the difficulty of withdrawing projections on a personal, and therefore, global basis (social values reflect individual values, just as the individual mirrors his or her social world). The responsibility of gaining self-knowledge, an awesome task in itself, involves much time, patience and hard-work, but the reward of knowing oneself, symbolized as that 'quintessential' factor of soul-making, is recognized as one of the highest of all human values. And it is this value that provides the necessary incentive that helps maintain the *opus*, just as the alchemists had done in the past. Their journey, symbolized by the quintessence, and in a real sense, marked by the five stages outlined above, gives a clear image of the psychological impetus of the process as underscored by the number archetype.

Summary

The number five symbolically underscored the physical world of ancient China, but it also had significance in the Christian West, as a counterpart of Christ. The number five has a connection, through the quintessence, with the Spirit Mercurius (the personification of the unconscious), therefore admitting a measure of suspicion and controversy into the assumed purity inherent in number-five symbolism.

The quintessence is symbolic of the indispensable and vital element of all life processes. It unifies the differentiated, but dispersed and isolated parts of every fourfold system by way of its centering capacity, yielding a more refined and 'distilled' version of a previously tainted and ill-defined fusion of parts.

In every discipline and religion there is the risk of failing to address the issue of the fivefold path of owning one's projected ideas, images and forms, etc., when it is discovered that paradigms and beliefs (which are constituted of these ideas, etc.) do not hold the power they previously had, purely because new data contradicts such paradigms and beliefs. The psychological ramifications of this negligence are inversely proportional to the 'quintessential' realization of a 'true' understanding of the nature of knowledge and the psyche.

There is always Five (Corporeality), but there is no experience of the higher union of opposites that has come to represent harmony, and so 'emerges' the number Six.

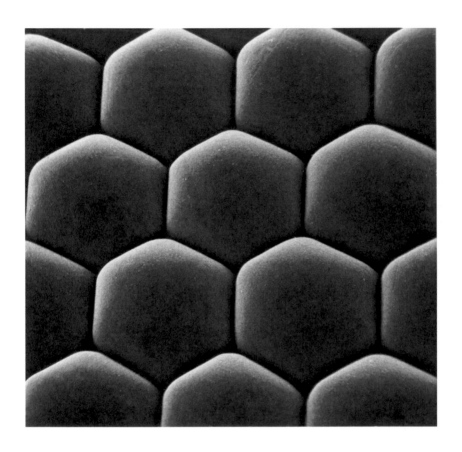

Plate 15. THE NUMBER SIX

In the natural world can be seen the orderedness and the constructive advantages inherent in sixfold structures. The six-sided or hexagonal elements that comprise the compound eye of the Antarctic Krill (Euphausia superba) show a natural economy. The hexagon allows for a greater number of single elements, which translates as greater light gathering capability for the compound eye [Copyright © 1995, Uwe Kils. Permission granted].

In music, 6th are a very beautiful and romantic combination, especially when ascending or descending on the diatonic scales.

C →
i →
E →

SIX (THE HEXAD)

*Six is the form of form…the fabricator
of the soul, also Harmony.*

Nicomachus

*The number six symbolizes conjunction, balance and harmony
because in six is seen the reconciliation of opposites. Six is perfect
in all its parts and encompasses one, two and three. Six has
two trinities, but also three pairs of opposites (twice a first
element, twice a second, and twice a third). Each element has
its own internal schism and balance, all three of which can be
represented in one sixfold system: a complex of opposites (three
pairs), all held together in One.*

Number Six as a Symbol of Harmony

The movement from three to four shows a delicate balance of active and passive
principles, respectively, both of which are irreducible and mutually exclusive
of each other. Triadic systems and models can be demonstrably lacking in
completion at two levels—they do not include their 'chthonic' (material or
'darker') counterparts, since they are usually 'celestial' and idealized in nature,
nor do they symbolize completion of a process—threefold systems are always
'*in process*'; in a state of becoming, and deceptively complete.

Equally, fourfold structures or models (quaternities), while usually
indicative of completed processes, or satisfactorily representing all
differentiated possibilities in the form of pairs of opposites, or accounting
for all possibilities of expression according to their subject, do not, upon

closer inspection, deal completely with the partial aspects of their dualistic components when represented as personifications or categories of nature, and are seen to be divisible after all.

Jung gives great credence to the movement of three to four, and acknowledges the quintessential factor embodied in the symbolism of the number five, but his references to the number six, while noteworthy, are undermined by the singular importance he places on quaternity symbolism. The number six is symbolic of a deeper harmonic order in the human psyche, which can be represented and constituted as models or concepts which are projected onto physical and metaphysical worlds, as exemplified in four major fields (worldviews) of human endeavor. These are alchemy, Christianity, philosophy, and physics (featured next). The far-reaching psychological repercussions of number symbolism, from the natural numbers one to six and beyond become apparent in these models.

Number Six in Alchemy

In hermetic philosophy and alchemy, outlined in the chapter "Three (The Triad)," the three individual elements of the Sulphur-Mercurius-Salt triad were shown to have duplex natures. Splitting these duplex forms into differentiated, polar forms yields two Mercurius triads—the *Mercurius lapis* (Mercury as stone) triad and the *Mercurius serpens* (Mercury as serpent) triad (*see* fig. 32).

Figure 32. *(a) The Mercurius lapis triad; (b) The Mercurius serpens triad.*

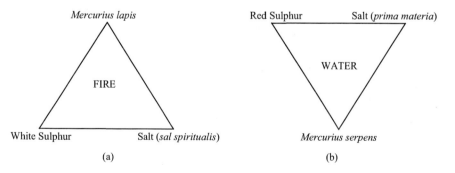

Some physical and chemical properties of sulphur, mercury and salt have been given in the chapter "Three (The Triad)", along with their associations, as made by alchemists and nature philosophers throughout history. Religious and psychological parallels can also be drawn from the phenomenologies of alchemical matter. The fascination with matter and the frustrated attempts at its transformation are explained as an unconscious, moral obligation and responsibility to individual physical and spiritual (psychological/religious) wellbeing, which may, therefore, entail a transformation of some form. In alchemical terms, this transformation required the deliverance of matter into a purified state free of corruption, but the philosophers new well enough that they themselves were involved in the *opus*. Their religious cum metaphysical writings attest to a desire for a change of personality (to use a psychological term).

The 'philosophic' (not literal) sulphur, mercury, and salt represent different aspects of the human being—the soul, the spirit, and the body, respectively, but each of these three aspects is further differentiated (split in two) and expressed as a pair. The two *Mercurius* triads shown above are interlaced to form the Mercurius hexalpha (*see* fig. 33).

Figure 33. *The Mercurius hexalpha.*

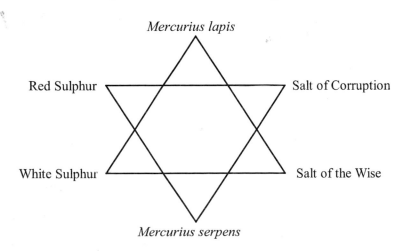

Mercurius lapis

Red Sulphur   Salt of Corruption

White Sulphur   Salt of the Wise

Mercurius serpens

Mercurius lapis and Mercurius serpens: As *lapis* (stone), Mercurius is associated with Christ and Heaven, while as *serpens*, the parallels with Satan and Hell are self-evident, as are the analogies of Mercurius with the spiritual qualities in both forms, positive and negative. The traditional role of Mercurius (Mercury/Hermes/Thoth) as mediator makes it appropriate that Mercurius should be the embodiment and creator of acts of the spirit that the 'modern' person experiences as an "elusive, deceptive, ever-changing content that possesses [one] like a demon" (Jung, 1966a, para. 384). Jung (1966a) explains this possession by Mercurius as being responsible for "impish drolleries," "inexhaustible invention," "insinuations," "intriguing ideas and schemes" (para. 384), but Mercurius must also be recognized as the author behind words and deeds of truth and beauty, and all that is divine, as well as the instigator of the urge towards reconciliation of the soul (Sulphur) with the body (Salt), and the consequent raising (sublimation) of them to the 'highest' order of aspiration.

The Red and White Sulphur: Sulphur refers to drivenness of the soul. It has motive force in that it burns, provides heat and is a source of light, and color (in compounds). But its characteristic offensive odor when it burns undermines its positive aspects. Drivenness too cannot sustain a neutral state, and must manifest in some form, such as sexual desire, ambition or power seeking, which can be polarized as either destructive (*Red Sulphur*) or productive (*White Sulphur*) in its application. Sulphur, therefore, represents the "*motive factor of consciousness*" (Jung, 1963, para. 151), but for the most part its origins are in the unconscious because the subject cannot give adequate explanation for his or her conscious motives. Usually, as an ego defense, rationalizations are taken as indicating the causal factors behind behaviors, motives, and actions, etc. The 'red' and the 'white', then, are the two opposing principles of sulphur and may be observed as compulsions needing qualification as desirable or otherwise.

Salt as sal spiritualis *and* prima materia: The associations of salt are numerous, having alignments with the body, *eros* (feeling function), purification, glass (clear, crystalline, incorruptible), wisdom, and of course, the sea. The latter association is clear, given the presence of various dissolved salts in the ocean. The dual qualities of salt have already been introduced (see the chapter "Three (The Triad)"), but the symbolism of salt in relation to water needs amplification. From the association of salt with the sea came the biblical reference of the Red Sea (symbolism of baptism) and the *aqua permanens* (permanent water) of the Church. The salt solution itself is ambiguous in nature, like the Red Sea, and "is a water of death for those that are "unconscious," but for those that are "conscious" it is a baptismal water of rebirth and transcendence" (Jung, 1963, para. 257). Salt was highly regarded as an arcane substance by the alchemists, and was even compared to the quintessence as "good and noble" and spiritually "above all things and in all creatures" (Jung, 1963, para. 241)—hence the term *sal spiritualis* (spiritual salt). Its bitterness was not over-looked and, in fact, it was this quality that supposedly "transmutes gold into pure spirit" (para. 245). But in its initial state the salt is corrupt and bitter and thereby associated with *prima materia* (primal matter), chaos, and the sea—all of which are symbolically and analogically applicable to the unconscious, the unknown and all things chthonic in nature.

In conclusion, the Mercurius hexalpha provides a visual, symbolic representation of the alchemical motifs of Sulphur, Mercurius and Salt. In this hexalpha, the opposites are united with the characteristics of each 'element' dichotomized and qualified as either spiritual (fire) or chthonic (water)— traditionally the two triangles are interlaced signifying their inseparable natures.

In human nature we might speak of predispositions and behaviors in opposition and balance, such as moral and ethical principles in contrast with carnal and instinctual drives, or psychologically, consciousness in contrast with the unconscious. These six aspects or natures comprise the completed alchemical or 'philosophic' Self in the body of matter, and the hexalphic image works like a mandala, resonating psychologically in the psyche. Empirically, the six-pointed star, as *Mogen David*, is recognized as a common motif in dreams and fantasies.

The image of wholeness is suggested by the intimation that all the psychological 'parts' of a whole person are definitively represented without exception or exclusion, there being no other partial aspects. Rational understanding is defied (the experience of the *numinosum* is purely emotional), but the amplifications concerning the parts are the inevitable attempt at expressing the ineffable through language and imagery without censor by those seeking wisdom and understanding, so that any influx of new motifs or associations that align with the parts and the whole of the model only increases the vitality of the initial experience.

Number Six in Christianity

The same effects and affects apply to the Christian hexalpha, which is derived from the Christian Trinity. The hexalphic form, such as the *Mogen David* ('Shield of David'), is comprised of two inter-laced triangles: △ indicating fire ('masculine'), and ▽ indicating water ('feminine'). This 'star' is a complex of opposites. Edinger (1986a) also describes the 'Shield' as a union of the opposites of spirit and matter:

> [the *Mogen David*] has signified the interpenetration of the trinity of spirit (upward-pointing) with the chthonic trinity of matter (downward-pointing) and hence symbolized the process of interrelation between the two. (p. 216)

The hexalpha, therefore, pre-empts the Christian Trinity, but has an advantage over this Heavenly Trinity by including the indispensable but 'dark', chthonic Trinity that has its roots in matter. Pauli objected to Jung's attempts to rectify the problem of three by converting the Trinity to a Quaternity (thus avoiding six altogether). Pauli saw Jung as merely projecting 'disinfected matter' (i.e., Mary) into Heaven (see "From Three to Four"). As an aside, Pauli (who half-heartedly attempted analysis with Marie-Louise von Franz due to the problem of his 'asymmetric' or split psyche) ultimately reverted back to his Jewish faith in his final days. No surprise that he should adopt the *Mogen David* as his preferred symbol of God. In February 1953, Pauli reproached

Jung: "As long as quaternities are 'projected into heaven' at a great distance from people…no fish will be caught, the *hieros gamos* is absent, and the psychophysical problem remains unsolved" (Roth, 2004, Chapter 3, Part 1). Here it is clear that two opposing but balanced triads of male and female clearly do a better job of illustrating the union that neither the Trinity nor the Quaternity can do on their own. *That's your opinion*….

But the blame does not sit squarely on Jung's shoulders—it must be pointed out that the desire or need for a quaternity was a request made by many Catholics the world over. According to Jung, the truly devoted followers of Christ and Mary wrote many letters to the Vatican pleading with them to place the Mother of God in Heaven where they believed she belonged. There is no real problem with the Trinity becoming a pure 'Quaternity' (which is what the Trinity is anyway—a pure, though masculine, representation of the Godhead), but of course, as argued earlier, both Trinity and Quaternity are incomplete. In this section, it will be seen that the hexalpha is a more complete structure or representation of the Light/Dark personality of the Godhead that mirrors the true (i.e., complete) nature of the Self. Indeed, as Westcott (1974) reports, the Christian Churches were already using the hexalpha "to express the union of the Divine and human natures, deemed to exist in Jesus, the Christ of the New Testament" (p. 70). The Trinity is demonstrably hexalphic upon reflection, by a merging of the components of the triadic elements, Father, Son, and Holy Spirit, with the two chthonic personalities, Serpent and Antichrist, and the neglected feminine personality of the Virgin Mary, Bride and Queen of Heaven (*see* fig. 34).

Already in medieval Christian practice the Virgin had been 'assumed' to be part of the Heavenly Host, but this dogmatic fact was not established until 1950 when the Virgin joined the Trinity in soul *and* body: the physical was now 'recognized' along with the spiritual. Most importantly, as Christians had begun to realize, the pure form of the 'feminine' as Mary was given a unique identity by being differentiated from her unreasonable associations with the Antichrist and the Serpent in the matter fusion.

Figure 34. *(a) The spiritual triad (Trinity): Father (God),
Son (Christ), and Holy Spirit (Dove); (b) The material triad:
Mother (Mary), Antichrist, and Lucifer (Serpent).*

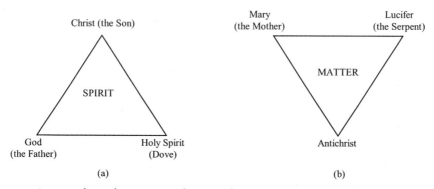

(a)   (b)

As may have become evident in the previous section, the Mercurius hexalpha represents a model of the Self that shows a *material* bias, characteristic of the alchemistic obsession with matter. However, the Christian hexalpha shows the Heavenly Host (isomorphic with the God-image in the human psyche—the Self) as a more *spiritual* representation of both God incarnate *and* the spiritual human being. The Christian hexalpha is comprised of two triads—the celestial triad and the material triad (*see* fig. 35).

Figure 35. *The Christian hexalpha.*

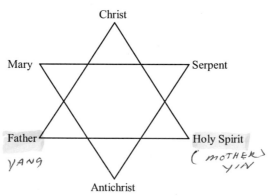

all of them are dualistic oppposites, except Father and Holy Spirit (which is the feminine side of God)...

The Christian hexalpha needs some explanation. Two trinities are present: the Trinity, with its familiar Father-Son-Holy Spirit triad of Church dogma ('Father, from whom; Son, to whom; and Holy Spirit, through whom are all things', as dogma decrees). The doctrine of the Trinity has its roots in the patriarchy. There may have been, and possibly still is a reflexive relationship between these two (Trinity and patriarchy) where the socio-cultural status of a given society (patriarchal in nature) not only gave rise to the Trinity concept, but allowed the concept the possibility of further elaboration over time, while the Trinity concept in turn influenced the culture to move in a certain direction, spiritually, religiously and socially. But the Trinity concept is not unique to the Church. As an archetypal motive factor in the psyche it reappears throughout all cultures and times, such as in the God-Pharaoh-*Ka-mutef* trinity of ancient Egypt, and other examples given in the chapter "Three (The Triad)."

While the significance of Father (God) and Son (Jesus Christ) may be apparent to most, the Holy Spirit as the 'third' that emerges from the two (Father and Son) is something of a paradox. It is the divine influence itself and mediates the other two. It is the life force and procreative power, and through it comes wisdom, increased consciousness and insight. Parallels may be drawn with the *Tao*, *Brahman*, and *Dharmakaya* as discussed in the chapter "One (The Monad)."   ?

The Holy Spirit concept originates not as a mere human fabrication, but emerges in the Trinity concept as a predisposition in the psyche. It has the archetype of the Self at its core, but is more the reification of the *process of coming into consciousness* than it is an *entity* responsible for consciousness (or any other cognitive function). It relies on the recognition of unconscious contents coming into consciousness, not just the consciousness of the external world through the senses.

The same archetypal origins apply to the trinity of matter that constitutes the other half of the hexalpha. These instinctual, material, 'shadow' elements augment the spiritual one-sidedness of the Trinity. The material, chthonic trinity of Mary-Antichrist-Serpent is not as clearly understood as the Trinity. First, the association of Mary with the other two, less divine characters

Dear author, please do your theological homework: See the indepth meaning of Pentecost!

(Serpent and Antichrist), as unpalatable as it is, is the inevitable consequence of the patriarchal values of the Church, which marginalized the feminine by associating womankind with matter (the earth), and nature, and all else which stood outside the *Summum Bonum*, as defined of God. With the advent of an increasing interest in things material (a consequence of a repressed interest in matter and an inappropriate dismissal of women's contribution and outlook) it became apparent, inside and outside the Church, that corporeal existence was as real and important as the spiritual life. Over the centuries, religion, politics, law and science became increasingly more organized. But slowly, movements away from these patriarchal values and concepts (political and scientific hierarchies, institutions, constitutions, spiritual freedom, legal systems, etc.), especially in the twentieth century, showed an ever-increasing shift of focus toward health care and welfare, environmental and ecological issues.

More recently, postmodern concerns have questioned the organized structures of religion and politics, etc., and sought to relativize the absolute claims of disciplines, belief systems and patriarchal values in general. In short, over the centuries, an integration of matriarchal values eventuated. In the previous chapter we have seen the negative side of these values in the West (excessive materialism in the form of mass consumerism) when they take hold of a culture unconsciously, and therefore cannot be regulated. But this excess has been as much the effect of heroic questing for the 'treasure in the field' as it has been the result of a one-sided over-valuation of nurturance and succor.

The repression of the 'feminine' results in the expression through the culture of the darker aspects of the 'feminine' (these are actually partially conflated with the Shadow side of the culture). Due recognition of the 'feminine' avoids the effects of this repression, and shows the true nature of the 'feminine' and the dark side of a culture as separate factors. The Christian hexalpha speaks to the neglected 'feminine', and by the integration of its symbolism, gives graphic recognition to the undermined 'feminine' in a given society, as well as a clearer insight into the nature of the Shadow (Antichrist) and instinctive/animal (Serpent) sides of humanity.

Number Six in Philosophy and Physics

In the last few centuries, space and time have come under the scrutiny of both the philosopher and the physicist. Not only were the absolute realities of space and time questioned, but also they have become relativized to each other. Kant, in his *Critique of Pure Reason* (1990), referred to space as a relative intuition in his philosophy of *critical idealism*:

> It is…from the human point of view only that we can speak of space, extended objects, etc. If we depart from the subjective condition, under which alone we can obtain external intuition,…the representation of space has no meaning whatsoever. (p. 26)

Kant spoke in like manner about time. As against Newton's idea, that space and time are absolute and infinite, Kant considered time and space to be 'sensible intuitions'—"features of our experience contributed by sensibility rather than understanding," to use T. E. Wilkerson's words in *Kant's Critique of Pure Reason* (1976). And as Einstein had shown in the twentieth century, time *is* relative (mass and velocity both affect time). Going further, modern physics has demonstrated that we cannot talk of space or time as distinct categories, but must speak in terms of spacetime events.

In terms of quaternary structures, we can see spacetime as composed of depth, height, and width, plus time, or alternatively we can see spacetime as composed of past, present, and future, plus space. Jung (1959a, para. 396) only presents the former (*see* fig. 36a), presumably the latter would be as shown in Figure 36b.

Figure 36. *(a) Jung's space-time quaternio; (b) Jung's time-space quaternio.*

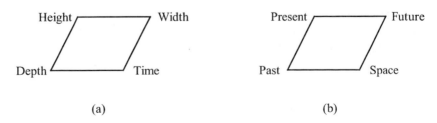

(a)   (b)

Jung (1959a) says:

> In both cases, the fourth represents an incommensurable Other....
> Thus we measure space by time and time by space.... The space-
> time [or time-space] quaternio is the archetypal *sine qua non* for any
> apprehension of the physical world—indeed, the very possibility of
> apprehending it. It is the organizing schema par excellence among the
> psychic quaternities. (paras. 397-398)

Reflecting on the way we mediate space and time reveals that we may shift
from time-consciousness to space-consciousness when making sense of the
world. And we may stay in one frame of mind, or the other for sustained
periods. Working with matter means mostly being space-conscious (*see* fig.
36a), while a withdrawal from physical activity tends to activate mostly a
time-consciousness (reading, waiting, meditating, etc.—*see* fig. 36b). It is
in this sense that consciousness is the 'world-creating' factor *par excellence*,
constantly constructing its own realities.

In the above, we see Jung's preference for the quaternity quite clearly.
But, since space and time are intrinsically interconnected with each other, and
neither functions without the other, these two quaternios are relativistically
redundant—they can be subsumed under one model. In the same way
that two triadic structures can be combined when they share compatible
phenomenologies, it is possible to combine the two triads of space and time
shown in Figure 37.

The spacetime hexalpha is comprised of two triads: the time triad and
the space triad. Time is a 'higher' spiritual or 'conceptual' entity (symbolized
by the triangle pointing upward to the sky), while space is a 'lower' material
or physical attribute (symbolized by the triangle pointing downward to the
earth). The spacetime hexalpha is holistic in nature—all six qualities describe,
dimensionally and temporally, all human existence and experience, concrete
and abstract, in matter and spirit (*see* fig. 38).

Figure 37. *(a) The time triad; (b) The space triad.*

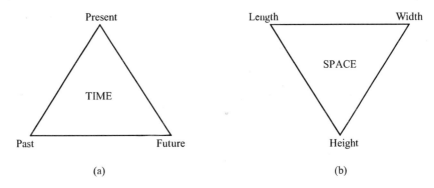

Figure 38. *The spacetime hexalpha.*

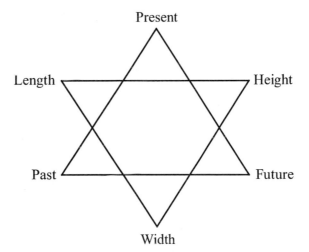

This hexalpha combines time and space and the subcomponents of each into one model, which either of the two quaternios cannot provide to the same degree of differentiation. The usefulness of this hexalpha lies in its unifying capacity, in the same way that the 'new' physics has unified space and time to explain the universe in a more accurate way according to

Einsteinian principles. The difference is that the latter is a rationally-derived, quantitative system and serves the requirements of the physical sciences. The former, however, is more aesthetically derived and qualitative in nature, being a pictorial representation of philosophical categories that serves to bridge symbolically the gap between the irrational (transcendent) phenomenology of matter/psyche and the order-seeking, wholeness-orientation of the Self, through the function of consciousness.

The hexalpha, therefore, is a symbol of a particular quality (spacetime) that functions psychologically, and from this perspective has the advantage over the corresponding scientific model, even though they each deal with the same phenomenon (spacetime). That is, an image is provided which helps to visualize the concepts of science, but more than this, since such a claim could be considered intellectually feeble on its own, evidence exists that the unconscious produces just such imagery spontaneously, and on no account is the hexalpha purely the product of only consciousness (rational deliberation), nor is it the product of idle speculation. The spacetime hexalpha (and for that matter, the Mercurius hexalpha and the Christian hexalpha) are graphic attempts to put some kind of psychological order to human (physical, spiritual), religious, and scientific realities.

Thoughtful consideration of these sixfold structures proves their value because the complex natures of these realities seem to be simplified or at least ordered to some degree. Phenomena can be shown to exhibit dualistic qualities, while their other properties might be better described using triadic structures. When these properties are shown to have partial aspects, they outgrow trinity structures, due to the limited capacity of these structures to incorporate the new or disregarded aspects associated with these phenomena, whether the phenomena can be categorized as human, physical, or metaphysical.

Hexalphic constructions contradict the traditional claims concerning perfection of the number six—at best, they are only serviceable as models. In the meantime, while the messages in these forms have some degree of social merit, the aesthetic and psychological values of the forms emerge in the meditative, and/or therapeutic benefit attained by the passive experient (since the three hexalphae are mandala forms), as given in their archetypal structure.

(See the Symbol Quaternity in the chapter "Four (The Tetrad)" for details of the mechanism of transformation of self and symbol.)

The Wholeness of Number Six in Ancient Egypt

The idea of six as representing wholeness extends back in time to ancient Egypt. Ifrah (2000) notes that the six parts of the Egyptian *hekat* do not total 64/64 = 1 (One).

$$1/2 + 1/4 + 1/8 + 1/16 + 1/32 + 1/64 = 63/64$$

The missing component, the 1/64th part, was noticeably absent in the 'mathematical' totality, and this part was said to be supplied by Thoth, who collected the pieces of Horus' mutilated eye that was torn out by Set, cut up into six pieces, and scattered throughout Egypt (*see* fig. 39). (Visually, the missing 1/64th part, a *seventh* part, cannot be detected because the eye is deceptively complete in its six parts!)

Figure 39. *The Horus eye fractions almost totaling 'One'.*

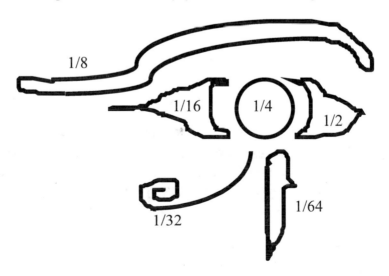

Set had previously dismembered his brother Osiris out of jealousy, and Horus, son of Osiris, was also a threat to him, since Isis raised Horus (her son) to avenge her brother/husband Osiris' death. Thoth, who is the Egyptian equivalent of Hermes/Mercurius, as he is the god of Science and the Arts, supplies the missing 1/64th part only to the one whose reckoning can determine the loss, provided the reckoner yields to the protective influence of Thoth, which is psychologically equivalent to establishing a relationship with the Self, and this leads to greater consciousness.

The symbolism of the Horus eye is specifically related to consciousness. The eye symbolizes consciousness because it is the instrument of sight from which comes knowledge—not to 'see', is to remain in 'darkness' (which is to say, remain unconscious). The eye of a god (or god-image) is the consciousness that belongs to the central archetype of the Self. The Self 'sees'; it is conscious of the actions of the ego, even though it is a consciousness outside ego consciousness. It nevertheless functions as a knowing entity, and in the Egyptian iconography any attempt by the ego (psychologically speaking) of usurping the autonomy of the Self activates the vengeful aspect of the Self, the *uraeus* or rearing cobra as seen on the forehead of many Egyptian gods.

Ifrah (2000) informs us that the restored *Oudja* Eye symbolizes the "wholeness of the body, physical health, clear vision, abundance and fertility" (p. 169). In this mythological sense, the restored Eye represents restoration of a life, the self that is now complete. That is, symbolically, the restoration of six parts in one embodies the idea of wholeness gained through life processes by representing the harmony and balance of six elements contained in one.

The ideas of sixness, wholeness, and consciousness are all interconnected, since they are reducible to the same number archetype. The *Oudja* Eye model of the Self has *all* its parts in six. In a psychological sense, however, the missing ('seventh') part, while 'completing' the totality symbol, does not add to its parts because it represents only a *gain* (a shift) in a pre-established consciousness, as represented by the seeing Eye. The Self contains a quantum of consciousness (a seventh part), which it gives to the ego.

Number Six in the Natural World

Recognition of sixfold spiritual and spirit/matter schemas and models, as well as sixfold patterns discoverable in the worlds of nature and technology, give a complete picture of the presence and unique phenomenology of the number six. In the natural world can be seen the orderedness and the constructive advantages inherent in sixfold structures. For example, the constantly repeating pattern of the six rays or sides of the snowflake remains, even in the infinite variety of shapes and sizes which are possible, because the hexagonal shape is in geometrical accordance with the properties of water. Even before the scientific explanation of the snowflake's form (based on the molecular model of the H_2O molecule and its crystallizing properties under low temperatures), Kepler believed that the snowflake took its form because its 'parts' arrange themselves in ways that are efficient and practical.

Morphologically, the number six is present in the six-leggedness of many insects and the six-sided cells of the compound eye of these insects. The bee, for example, has approximately 3000 small sections of six sides in each of its compound eyes. Associated with the bee is the beehive and its primary hexagonal structure, the honeycomb. Although the equilateral triangle and the square both tessellate, the hexagon is the one polygon of the three self-tessellating regular polygons (triangle, square, and hexagon) that has the smallest perimeter for a given area, because it is the closest to a circle in shape. (The pentagon will tessellate, but only in three-dimensional structures such as the twelve-sided dodecahedron, where each facet is a regular pentagon.) This situation gives the bee a distinct advantage, since less wax is required for the maximum storage of honey in hives, which are constructed using cells with hexagonal prisms.

As just mentioned, there is a strong connection between the hexagon and the circle. A circle's radius is the same length as any and all sides of a regular hexagon constructed to fit inside that circle (see fig. 40).

Likewise, six circles of equal size will tangent a same-size middle circle precisely, and therefore, the centers of these outer circles, when connected, will produce a hexagon (see fig. 41). The simplest means of 'closing the gaps' between the circles is to 'transform' them into hexagons, which tessellate and yield the familiar and efficient honeycomb structure just described.

Figure 40. *The radius of a circle, r, is the same length of an arc, r, used to construct a hexagon of perimeter 6r.*

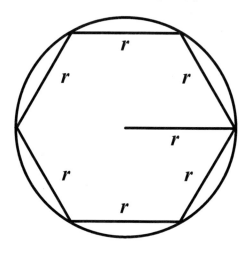

Figure 41. *(a) A central circle can be surrounded by exactly six circles of equal radii. (b) Connecting the centers of these six outer circles will form a regular hexagon. (c) 'Closing the gaps' between the circles is possible by 'transforming' the circles into hexagons.*

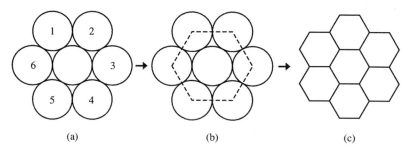

Tessellation is a key factor underscoring a major process in evolution. In *The Magic of Mathematics* (1994), Pappas observes how nature, by using specific numbers in its creations, has arrived at the forms we see in the natural world. They are 'economical' because they make optimal use of the space, time, and materials available for their production. In the human world, following nature's lead, we too use the hexagonal form because of its practical advantages.

The six lines of symmetry of the hexagon, since it provides a number of rotations without loss of symmetry, is applied in the everyday world of the trades and engineering, demonstrating unequalled technical advantages. For example, the hexagonal shape of nuts and bolts allows greater access for the spanner by offering six angles of approach instead of only four as offered by the square nut or bolt. More than six approaches (eight, ten, etc.), though of further practical advantage, would mean the surface area in contact with the spanner is reduced, thus increasing the risk of slippage and possible damage to the facets and vertices of the nut or bolt because each increase in the number of facets brings the polygon closer to the form of a circle, which has no facets. Nuts and bolts with more than six sides or facets are not very common for this reason. It should be noted too that nuts and bolts with an uneven number of sides would not accommodate standard tools (shifting or fixed spanners) because they only fit parallel facets (for reasons of security, note the five-sided stop-cock on some fire hydrants). Naturally and technically, then, six has an economy and efficiency about it. Six sides seem to be the ideal compromise between convenience and pragmatism. As Schimmel (1993) writes:

> The hexagon's role in building the world, as it was understood in ancient traditions, has become much clearer thanks to scientific observation. Indeed, [the hexagon] appears as an ideal building principle in nature. (p. 126)

The hexagon has become an ideal building principle in culture as well. Jung (1966a) quotes at length an account of the number six as given in *De mensibus* by Joannes Lydus:

The number six is most skilled in begetting,...for it is even and uneven, partaking both of the active nature on account of the uneven,...and of the hylical nature on account of the even, for which reason the ancients also named it marriage and *harmony*.... And they say that it is both male and female.... And another says that the number 6 is *soul-producing*...because it *multiplies* itself into the world sphere...and because in it the opposites are mingled. It leads to *like-mindedness*... and *friendship*, giving health to the body, harmony to songs and music, virtue to the soul, prosperity to the state, and forethought...to the universe. (para. 451, n8; my italics)

Jung has dealt at length with quaternity symbolism, which he relates to mandala forms, including the circle. As illustrated above, the circle and the hexagon have an 'affinity' for each other, having similar qualities, geometrically speaking, so that symbolically, and from observations in nature, it becomes apparent that the number six should 'naturally' embody qualities associated with the circle.

Psychologically, the circle represents the undifferentiated parts of the totality of the psyche. In its purest form, the circle symbolizes wholeness, which includes those qualities that Lydus associates with the number six. Lydus makes these associations because 'Marriage', 'harmony', 'like-mindedness', and 'friendship' are the usual products of a balanced human relationship, but the nature philosophers also observed such qualities in nature. So when Lydus speaks of the number six giving "forethought...to the universe" (Jung, 1966a, para. 451, n8) we may read that he has a view of the universe (the natural world) as being soundly structured *as if* by a 'method' that includes the quantitative and qualitative factors of number six. In the many and varied forms observable in nature which exhibit the unique 'advantages' of sixness (harmony, economy, efficiency) it is *as if* there was a kind of 'forethought' or plan behind the 'method' given in the number six (among the other natural numbers) that made these forms possible. In actual fact we can only say phenomenologically that there is a contingency between sixness (for want of a better term) and certain things in nature that appear to be made possible (created in consciousness) by the fact of this contingency.

Von Franz in Jung's _Man and His Symbols_ (1964) writes that we are "forced to think about [numbers] in a certain definite way" (p. 310):

> Even if we strip outer objects of all such qualities as color, temperature, size, etc., there still remains their "manyness" or special multiplicity, yet these same numbers are just as indisputably parts of our own mental set-up—abstract concepts that we can study without looking at outer objects. Numbers thus appear to be a tangible connection between the spheres of matter and psyche. (von Franz, 1964, p. 310)

For example, the factors of six (one, two and three) when either added or multiplied yield six:

$$1 + 2 + 3 = 6 \quad \& \quad 1 \times 2 \times 3 = 6$$

This makes six unique, since no other single integer has this quality. On this account the Pythagoreans deemed six to be a Perfect number (that is, the sum of the divisors of the number six—one, two and three—total six). As von Franz (1974) says:

> This quality determines, so to speak, the "form" or "structure" of the number six. Such characteristics are inherent to a number, independent of the objects it enumerates. They appear to be absolutely self-evident to us, which means that number's own nature forces such declarations upon us.

> We must, therefore, concede that from the psychological point of view number is an archetypal content, since the latter are known for their capacity to motivate such "necessary" amplificatory statements. (pp. 37-38)

When we experience numbers in nature, we must note that, as von Franz claims (with a slight modification), we seem to have the capacity to recognize structure and order as numerical forms or patterns. Though forms or patterns in the world must be learnt, we discover later that our recognition of them, even though they fit a certain concept (that is, are described by, or parallel the phenomenology of a particular number), does not mean the capacity (or the proclivity) to identify number in this way is learnt (although the skill can be developed). The capacity has to be there as an innate propensity or proclivity (an archetypal or brain structure) that will be activated, or better, developed or matured by constant experience of the various phenomena.

In the same way that we do not learn to use certain body organs (liver, heart, and so on) the brain, in part, has specific capacities (comes predisposed as it were) to function in specific ways. Number is an archetype that constitutes one of these capacities. The archetype is behind our 'declarations'. To paraphrase von Franz, we are motivated to make only *specific* statements ('amplifications') about numbers, while other statements are not conceivable, given the *specific* archetypal realities appropriate to those numbers.

Schimmel (1993) notes that apart from the snowflake and beehive, the hexagonal principle appears in the molecular structure of the benzene ring, C_6H_6, which the German chemist Friedrich von Stradonitz Kekulé in 1865 induced from a dream of dancing atoms that formed an *uroboros*—the tail-eating serpent. Benzene, a colorless, inflammable liquid, is used for the production of dyes, drugs, perfumes, explosives, etc., but its molecular structure puzzled chemists for a long time because no one could conceive the possibility of the molecule having a circular (hexagonal) form. One may note that Kekulé's dream, and the scientific application of its content, is a practical example of the very real connection between the circle and the hexagon, as discussed above, and is also an example of the practical value of wholeness symbolism in general.

George Miller and the Number Six

The configurational properties of the number six, as applied to the human psyche, have also been found in the field of experimental psychology. George Miller in *The Science of Mental Life* (1970) observed that consciousness is a limited capacity system that allows a maximum of six items in attention at any one time. Exposing human subjects to patterns of dots for a tenth of a second showed that up to six dots were easily recognizable, but seven or more dots could not be easily discerned. In fact, more and more mistakes were made as the number of dots increased. Blind people were also limited to recognizing six points in Braille printing, and inaccuracies developed when more than six points were used in a Braille character.

Miller does not set a limit to the sense organs as such—after all, the eyes, skin, etc., are extremely discriminatory organs. It is the nervous system, "where all the different senses converge to pass through the same bottleneck" (p. 63), that imposes the limit. In other words, in the case of number fields in the environment, our attention span may set a limit on number recognition. It then becomes a matter of our mental functioning, as given by the limits of the nervous system, as to how successful our attempts will be to reconcile the numerical facts of the physical world with the absolute limits of the psyche.

Kekulé's benzene ring, the snowflake, and the beehive, all show physical limitations that nevertheless construct economies, efficiencies and harmonies, etc. As we perceive these qualities, our own inner (mental) economy, efficiency, and harmony as determined *a priori* in our nervous system (which may mean, as given by the psychoid archetype) are aligned with the realities imposed in these cases by the number six. Number, then, is at the root of such limitations and appears as a determining factor in much that we think, devise, construct, invent, and feel, just as many of the constituents of the physical world are equally determined by numbers, which set limits on form, function, efficacy and purpose.

Summary

The symbolism associated with the number six shows the dualistic qualities similarly described for the numbers two and four, while similar triadic patterns emerge as given in the symbolism of number three. There is, however, a greater complexity in sixfold models and systems due to the sum of their parts, which can be taken as three dyads, or two triads. These structures constitute subsystems of the overall sixfold system.

Historically, the number six is identified with the qualities of harmony and balance, mostly due to its associations with complete, and therefore, functional (efficient) systems, or models, or discourses in mythology, science and proto-science, and even in nature and technology. Psychologically, the limits of human consciousness, which, therefore, muster in certain unconscious factors, are 'related' to the number six, and these limits have a determining influence on how we devise our concepts. The limits of consciousness also directly reflect on the immediacy and accuracy of our depiction of things.

There is always Six (Harmony), but there is no experience of illumination without rest and reflection, and so 'emerges' the number seven.

Unfortunately, many of
the passages in "6" show a
lack of - graduate level
theology, and a lack of   N.T.
scriptural knowledge and
Christological background. This
onestly clear under the section
on the hexalpha and
Christianity.

———— # ————

... I don't know... but I get,
the feeling this author is Jewish,
and not very pro-christian —
It's just a feeling I get —
He shows no knowledge of the study
of Trinity or Christology, only
psychological projections and paradynmes.

Plate 16. THE NUMBER SEVEN

The pottery of the Pueblos of New Mexico often features the spiral motif symbolizing inward and outward journeys of 3½ cycles each, totaling seven cycles. Completion of seven cycles, a motif that appears in cultures the world over, indicates a return to wholeness [Copyright © 2003, University of South Florida, Florida Center for Instructional Technology. Permission granted].

SEVEN (THE HEPTAD)

Seven there are; they are seven. In the subterranean deep
they are seven. Perched in the sky they are seven.

Babylonian Fragment

From the number two, representative of all antitheses, is derived
the number three, which contains form in dynamism, the essence
of existence. The number six, containing the dynamic quality of
the trinity, has an antithetical form (3 + 3, or 2 × 3). So, from
the conjunction inherent in six is derived seven, which possesses
the qualities of trinity and quaternity (three plus four). Seven
exhibits and contains the dynamic spiritual quality of three,
and the receptive material quality of four.

Seven—A Solution to the Problem of Three and Four

The number seven is the sum of three and four, so that symbolically speaking,
seven is comprised of both active and passive principles (for example, in the
form of the 'dynamism' of three, and the 'wholeness' of four). Jung (1958)
writes:

> The Quaternity is the *sine qua non* of…the inner life of the trinity.
> Thus circle and quaternity on one side and the threefold rhythm
> on the other interpenetrate so that each is contained in the other.
> (para. 125)

In response to this statement, by amplification of its symbolic content,
Edinger states (1986a) that:

a union of the quaternity with the trinity in a more complete synthesis is required…. [T]he number seven combines four and three by being their sum…. The trinity archetype seems to symbolise individuation as a process, while the quaternity symbolises its goal or complete state. (p. 193)

Numerologically, the solution to the problem of three and four is to adjoin them as a double-digit number (34 or 43) or to combine them through addition (3 + 4 = 7), or multiplication (3 × 4 = 12) (see also, the chapter "Numerology"). Medieval scholars saw this process as having religious significance by way of the four evangelists, combined in one way or the other, with the Trinity. Seven was the spiritual solution to the complete embodiment of the 'Four' and the 'Three' in 'One'.

Number Seven as a Geometrical Anomaly

Necessarily excluding the integers 0, 1, and 2, the number seven has never been easily constructed in a geometrical sense (i.e., as a polygon), as is the case with the other six integers (3, 4, 5, 6, 8, and 9). It is not possible, therefore, to easily fix an image of the number seven in the psyche unless one borrows from the phenomenology of the number six (*see* fig. 41), by presenting a solid physical representation of seven in the form of seven rods or cylinders stacked together (*see* fig. 42). Seven is the *largest* number of objects (e.g., cylinders) that can be maintained in a bundle and remain fixed (i.e., tightly bound without movement), but geometrically the shape is actually hexagonal with the seventh occupying the center. Six and seven are related in that way—six is given form not *in spite of* the seventh, but *because* of the seventh.

The psychological associations of stability, solidity, and so on, are therefore won by proxy, making these descriptors inappropriate for the number seven—certainly these associations do not come naturally. For example, the hexalpha symbols featured in the previous chapter, in no way suggest seven-fold phenomenologies. With a little imagination we can 'see' a secret harmony—a mystery—embedded in the seventh but, like the cylinders in Figure 42, we must look to the center of the sixfold structure to find it. Number seven symbolizes a transitional point or state; a middle point; a movement towards becoming. Transition is an archetypal quality that underscores other symbolic associations with number seven, such as activity and dynamism, transition and transformation, and the end of cycles.

Figure 42. *Seven cylinders stacked together indicate fixity, but its geometry is hexagonal.*

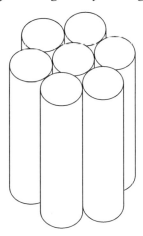

Michell (1988) also notes the difficulty in constructing a geometrical representation of the number seven, and the association made by the Pythagoreans and later scholars of the number seven with the Virgin, is amplified by this fact, since "it [the heptagon] refuses to couple with or generate any other geometrical type" (p. 78).

The regular heptagon is the first regular polygon that causes difficulty in drafting because its seven angles (θ) measure approximately 128.57143° each (to 5 significant figures), and no measuring apparatus used manually within reasonable human limits can be accurate to 1/100,000 of a unit. All the other regular polygons have their angles θ in whole numbers—triangle: 3 @ θ = 60°; square: 4 @ θ = 90°; pentagon: 5 @ θ = 108°; hexagon: 6 @ θ = 120°; octagon: 8 @ θ = 135°; nonagon: 9 @ θ = 140°; and decagon: 10 @ θ = 144°. Since any polygon can be subdivided into (N – 2) triangles, where

N is the number of angles, the angle θ, assuming a regular polygon, can be calculated using the following formula: $\theta = 180(N - 2)/N$.

Number Seven as a Temporal Determinant

Chetwynd (1982) notes the traditional association of seven with time.

> Like twelve (3×4), seven ($3 + 4$) is a basic unit of time, and time is the dimension of the spirit [space being the dimension of matter], and is the essential ingredient necessary for change or transformation. So it is the symbol of energy and movement in contrast with matter or substance, or rather, the combination of static substance, the four-square block of reality, and dynamic movement, the three-pointed triangle. (p. 287)

The association of time with number seven may have developed in human consciousness after many repeated observations of nature and the cosmos, and the transpiration of cycles. In the West, for example, the nomenclature of the seven days of the week originated in the heavens with Sun, Moon, and the then-known five major planets, or gods and goddesses associated with those planets (*see* Table 6). The names of the days of the week actually originate in India, where Sun, Moon, etc., were first identified with the seven days of the week. As will be seen, in China there was not always a strict adherence to this schema.

Von Franz (1980a) comments on the seven 'planets' and their associations with the seven metals:

> To the seven planets are attributed the seven metals, and it is quite customary in alchemy for the seven metals—tin, copper, lead, iron, and so on—to be attributed to the seven planets, but they are more than that; they are so to speak, the same as the seven planets. Iron is the same thing as Mars [in the West], and copper the same as Venus [in the West]; in the sky, therefore, one can call iron the earthly Mars, and copper the earthly Venus, etc. That was a common way of speaking about the metals in those times, so the seven stars are really the seven metals in the earth. (p. 220)

Table 6. *Western Days of the Week, their Old English and Latin Derivatives, and associated Gods/Goddesses.*

Day	Old English (OE) and Latin (L) name	God, goddess or 'planet'
Sunday	*Sunnandaeg* (OE) *dies Solis* (L)	} Day of the Sun
Monday	*Mōnandaeg* (OE) *Lunae dies* (L)	} Day of the Moon
Tuesday	*Tiwesdaeg* (OE) *Dies Martis* (L)	Day of Tīw (Germanic god of War) Day of Mars (Roman god of War)
Wednesday	*Wōdensdaeg* (OE) *Mercurii dies* (L)	Day of Odin (Norse god of Wisdom & Victory) Day of Mercury (Roman god of Commerce)
Thursday	*Thur(s)daeg* (OE) *Iovis dies* (L)	Day of Thor (Norse god of Agriculture & War) Day of Jove (Roman Sky-god, Ruler of the gods)
Friday	*Frīgedaeg* (OE) *Veneris dies* (L)	Day of Frigg (Norse Earth goddess, wife of Odin) Day of Venus (Roman goddess of Love)
Saturday	*Saetern(es)daeg* (OE) *Saturni dies* (L)	} Day of Saturn (Roman god of agriculture)

These associations indicate the unity of nature as conceived by the ancients. However, there is no binding or absolutely astronomical basis for a specific number of days in a week (in fact, ancient Rome had an eight day week). The preference for a seven-day week is likely to have arisen because of the dynamic quality in number seven as opposed to the more passive and static quality of (say) number eight, it being even. This dynamism of seven may be the underlying psychological reason why the convention of a seven-day week was adopted in Alexandria in the first century BC.

In the East, as in the West, Sunday and Monday were similarly named after the luminaries (Sun and Moon), although in Japan the five remaining days were named after the five elements (*see* Table 7).

Table 7. *Japanese Days of the Week and their Derivatives.*

DAY	JAPANESE NAME	LUMINARY OR ELEMENT
Sunday	*Nichiyōbi*	Day of the Sun
Monday	*Getsuyōbi*	Day of the Moon
Tuesday	*Kayōbi*	Day of Fire
Wednesday	*Suiyōbi*	Day of Water
Thursday	*Mokuyōbi*	Day of Wood
Friday	*Kinyōbi*	Day of Gold (metal)
Saturday	*Doyōbi*	Day of Earth

In China the weekdays are merely numbered, 'first-day', 'second-day', and so on. It is of interest to note that the five Eastern elements, used to name the five weekdays in Japan, actually align with the Western gods and goddesses, after which these five weekdays are named in the West. That is, Fire/Mars/Tuesday, Water/Mercury/Wednesday, Wood/Jupiter/Thursday, Gold (Metal)/Venus/Friday, and Earth/Saturn/Saturday.

The association of number seven with the Moon has been mentioned previously (see the chapter "Four (The Tetrad)"). Here the Moon's 7 × 4 = 28 day cycle (constituting a lunar month), indicates again the cyclical symbolism of number seven, but it is symbolic only. Originally, there were astronomical facts underlying the symbolic significance attached to this cycle, but these 'facts' are shown to be inaccurate today. The ideal twenty-eight day month is actually short by an average of 1.53 days—the more accurate lunar month being 29.53 days. However, the lunar month is incommensurate with the standardized year of 365 days (actually 365.256 days), because there would need to be just over 12 months in a year using the lunar month (approximately 12.37 months, or 12 months and just over 10 days). For symbolic and traditional reasons, the modern calendar is fixed at twelve months, each month being 30 or 31 days in length, thus ignoring the lunar cycle.

Various other compromises, differing from culture to culture, have been adopted to account for further inconsistencies, including for example, an additional 29th day in February every fourth (leap) year in the modern calendar. In orthodox Judaism, which still relies on the lunar month, an extra month of 29 days is added to the year (making it a year of thirteen months) on the 2nd, 4th, 7th, 9th, 11th, 13th, and 16th year inclusive of a sixteen year cycle. All the other months are 29 or 30 days long, in order to correspond as closely as possible to the moon cycle. (Traditionally the Sabbath day begins at nightfall when two or three stars can be sighted in the sky, indicating again the lunar influence in Judaism.)

Chetwynd (1982, p. 288) reports that the seven-day week is symbolic of the 'whole course' of a human life:

Sunday: "Marks the birth of a new separate conscious ego.

Monday: "Marks the relationship of masculine with feminine. Conscious day with unconscious night.

Tuesday: "The warring opposites are more a feature of hot-headed youth, in the first half of the week." leading up to "crisis and turning point in the middle of life.

Wednesday: "Mercury especially is the mediator who accomplishes the union of warring opposites above.

Thursday: "The full power of Manhood.

Friday: "The perfection of Womanhood.

Saturday: "Decline and disintegration into the dark realm of the unconscious. Completion."

To a limited degree these descriptions tally with the biblical account of creation as described in *Genesis* (specifically the first, second, and seventh days). The seven days of creation are:

Day One: Creation of Light, and Day and Night (*Genesis* 1: 3-5).

Day Two: Creation of Firmament or Heaven (atmosphere) to divide lower waters from the upper waters (clouds) (*Genesis* 1: 6-10).

Day Three: Creation of Earth and Seas and *Vegetabilis* (plant life) (*Genesis* 1: 11-13).

Day Four: Creation of Sun and Moon and Stars, for signs, seasons, days and years (*Genesis* 1: 14-19).

Day Five: Creation of *Animalis I*. Sea Life and Birds (*Genesis* 1: 20-23).

Day Six: Creation of *Animalis II*. Beasts, *Homo sapiens* (*Genesis* 1: 24-31).

Day Seven: God Rests. The seventh day is "delivered" and "sanctified" (*Genesis* 2: 2-3).

Certainly Chetwynd's seven days describe the natures of the relevant gods, but the biblical seven days better describe the development of the psyche in archetypal terms, including the integration of the seven archetypal factors symbolized by the seven planets or gods:

Sunday (Sun): The ego is born as the center of the field of consciousness.

Monday (Moon): The differentiation of consciousness from the unconscious. Antithetical relationships can be drawn: Heaven/Earth (above/below), Male/Female, etc.

Tuesday (Mars): A paradise or garden of the soul is constructed in the psyche as growth continues. The psyche and the vegetable body through water/fluid sustain and give energy to each other. The life principle is maintained.

Wednesday (Mercury): Relationship and communication with the Self begins. The various forms of consciousness, symbolized by heavenly 'lights', give a fourfold picture of human centeredness in time and space.

Thursday (Jupiter): Recognition, reconciliation and maturation of the deepest 'animal' (most instinctual and spiritual) natures of the soul.

Friday (Venus): Continued integration and balancing of the instincts by 'raising' or sublimating the lower nature to the human level.

Saturday (Saturn): The cycle is complete, and a period of limitation and rest ensues, until inner energies are restored for the next cycle of 'seven days'.

The 'Sun' (consciousness, ego) gives vitality and power (psychic energy), while the 'Moon' governs basic impulses and responses (unconscious forces). Further, by taking the attributes of each planet as given by Ambrosius Macrobius, we have 'Mars' as giver of a "bold spirit"; 'Mercury' as giver of the "ability to speak and interpret"; 'Jupiter' as giver of "the power to act"; 'Venus' as giver of "the impulse of passion"; and 'Saturn' as giver of "reason and understanding" (Edinger, 1996, p. 171).

Sheila Geddes, in *The Art of Astrology* (1981), adds that Mars gives "energy" and "drive"; Mercury gives "communication" and "mentality"; 'Jupiter' gives "expression" and "maturity"; 'Venus' gives "harmony" and "relationships"; and 'Saturn' gives "limitation," "responsibility" and "discipline" (pp. 21-22). Psychologically, the gods can be taken as personifications of these characteristics.

The fact that ultimately the number of planets in our solar system rose from seven to eight with the discovery of Uranus and Neptune (the ancients did not count Earth, but counted the Sun in the seven) means of course that number seven lost its symbolic parallel with the solar system. (The International Astronomical Union, in 2006, distinguished the eight proper planets from dwarf planets such as Pluto.) The ancient idea that the heavens in some way were reflected in 'Man' (the macrocosm mirrored in the microcosm) was the result of projection in large part of unconscious archetypal facts (notwithstanding the claims of some astrologers as to the properties of the planets).

From all of the above, it is clear, therefore, that the number seven has resonated in the human psyche from very ancient times at a level that has more to do with psychological rather than astronomically observable facts. As such the number seven has archetypal significance, commensurate with the number archetype.

The solar year, the lunar month, and the seven day week are all incommensurate with each other, so that our many admirable attempts over the millennia at constructing reliable, but ultimately irregular calendars, which are often inconsistent from culture to culture, only confirm the fact that time-keeping is a subjective cultural preoccupation that appears to have no bearing on the objective reality of cosmic time-keeping to which so many species seem to be reliably adjusted. After all, the biological clocks in many species are attuned to (say) the moon cycle, but by way of evolutionary processes, we may well carry a genetic imprint, a psychoid archetype, of this cycle (and other cycles). The archetype of number seven, therefore, has a rational phenomenology that is *approximately* commensurate with the various cultural permutations of the number seven as a natural number, but as unsound as this may seem, this same archetype has an 'irrational' aspect that defies our knowing, but does influence us nonetheless.

And yet, although the archetype (like the universe) may be rational and irrational (and therefore paradoxical), it is consistent in its underlying phenomenology. For example, as will become evident, symbolic elaborations upon number seven, although they vary in content and context from culture to culture, are essentially the same—they always refer to completion and cyclicality in seven stages or states (sometimes with a substructure of 3 + 4, sometimes 3½ + 3½, sometimes with a straightforward 7-step structure). These cultural products are no more than conscious attempts at reaching the deeper meaning of number seven that attaches to certain unconscious facts. We get a glimpse of this deeper meaning when we discover the overarching similarities these sevenfold constructs have with those facts.

The seven day cycle, or the seven planets, for example, may be arbitrary expressions of the number seven as an archetype that may in turn be contingent with certain physical facts which cannot be perceived directly, but can irrupt into consciousness in conceptual or symbolic form. For example, the fertilized ovum divides seven times before it becomes the blastocyst (embryonic cell), the first major stage after fertilization of the development of the human being (in fact, all mammals) at which time implantation in the uterine wall occurs. This fact is acultural and absolute to our species. Once again, it is likely that an archetypal source is responsible for the cultural products that bear resemblances to such facts, so that the resemblances may not necessarily be mere coincidences. Certainly, a basic sevenfold form is recognizable in both the cultural and the biological facts.

Number Seven in the Bible—A Symbol of Completion

From the above, it can be seen that the idea of 'completion' is inherent in number seven symbolism because a process is complete once seven stages are completed. This fact is also reiterated over and over again in myths and fairytales where the hero must complete seven tasks or seven journeys, or make some kind of sacrifice—sometimes with specific reference to body [4] and mind [3], or the space-time [4-3] continuum. After the ordeal, the hero (ego) is born (actually reborn or transformed) as a closer approximation to the Self. In the chapter "Nine (The Ennead)" it will be seen that the completion of nine stages marks a kind of completion that is qualitatively different from completion in seven stages (for example, in a 3 × 3 configuration).

The number seven has symbolized the last stage of illumination since ancient times as indicated in the Judeo-Christian Bible. Seven refers to sacrifice and learning through much effort. Seven is the number of initiation and transformation, or 'evolution in time', and as von Franz (1980a) says: "the slow process of becoming conscious" (p. 235). The Bible contains more references to number seven than any other number, and this high frequency may well have to do with the high degree of consciousness the ancients had in regard to the cyclical nature of the environment, the world and its creatures, and human development. For example:

1. The seven days of Creation in *Genesis* 1-2, led to the establishment of a seven day week by the ancient Hebrews, which was later adopted by the Romans, and by cultural immigration, the rest of Europe.

2. In *Genesis* 41:17-32 the Pharaoh dreams of seven good kine devoured by seven thin and ill-favored kine, followed by another dream of seven good ears devoured by seven empty ears. These dreams were interpreted as prophecies by Joseph, who described the cattle and harvest dream references as symbolically representing seven years of "great plenty throughout all the land of Egypt," followed by seven years of famine. These successful interpretations resulted in Joseph's appointment as a man 'discreet and wise' enough to secure Egypt's future.

3. In *Joshua* 6:3-5 is given an account of the circumambulation of Joshua's army around Jericho, seven times, over seven days, including the sounding of seven trumpets (ram's horns) by seven priests, culminating in the collapse of the Jericho city walls. In the *Bible and the Psyche*, Edinger (1986b) describes the repetition of seven as being symbolic of the resolution of an unconscious complex:

    > It [the unconscious complex] must be circumambulated—experienced from all sides—repeatedly. Circular movement around a center has the psychic effect of focusing energy on the center by constellating the Self as a field of force…. With the seventh [circuit] comes the shout [the trumpet blasts] announcing wholeness. (p. 68)

These examples are numerical references to the mystical nature attributed to seven. One further biblical example of major importance is that of the last book of the New Testament, *Revelation*, which is steeped in the symbolism of the number seven. No less than half the book (eleven of the twenty-two chapters) makes continuous reference to the number seven. Itemized unceasingly (as if to make a point) are "the 7 churches, 7 kings, 7 angels, 7 mountains, 7 crowns, 7 vials, 7 plagues, 7 thunders, 7 seals" (Michell, 1988, p. 79).

Revelation is essentially the account of a series of visions by St. John the Divine. These visions occurred on the island of Patmos, as a result of John's banishment by Domitian in 95 AD. The following year, John wrote *Revelation* in Ephesus, having been permitted to return home. The interpretation given here will be based on archetypal principles, with the incorporation of the numerical symbolism of the numbers one through seven. But, there are, or have been other interpretations:

1. The Preterist interpretation sees John's visions as describing the struggle of Christianity against the Roman Empire.

2. The Historical interpretation forecasts the Church's inception, its long history of successes and ordeals, and finally the end of the world.

3. The Futurist interpretation has the *Revelation* events placed *only* in the future, and concerns itself with the last days of the world, and Christ's second coming.

4. The Spiritualist interpretation does not hold issue with earthly concerns, but looks at the world of the spirit ('Divine Government') and its operations, and sees John's message in symbolic form.

Some interpreters take an eclectic approach and glean specific quotes from the text and interpret them in any or all of the above ways to suit their purposes.

Only chapters 6-10 and 16-17 are of interest here as far as the number-seven symbolism is concerned, although chapter 4 to the end of the book is composed entirely of symbolic material. (Chapters 1-3 concern the events of John's time, including the writing of seven letters to seven churches. Evidently the reference to number seven has some kind of synchronistic overtone in the social circumstances of John's life, and not just his inner life.) Speaking as a psychologist, Jung (1958) had this to say about John:

> The "revelation" was experienced by an early Christian who, as a
> leading light of the community, presumably had to live an exemplary
> life and demonstrate to his flock the Christian virtues of true faith,
> humility, patience, devotion, selfless love, and denial of all worldly
> desires. In the long run this can become too much, even for the most
> righteous. Irritability, bad moods, and outbursts of affect are the
> classic symptoms of chronic virtuousness. (para. 729)

One might even say that John's revelation was the culmination of a
disorganized psyche, with the unconscious compensating with images of this
disturbed state. And the revelation *was* experienced in exile away from John's
'flock', so his ascetic predisposition, and his isolation may have been factors
that contributed to the onset of his visions. Jung has said that the violence
of such visions would ordinarily suggest a form of psychosis (spontaneous
irruptions of unconscious contents into consciousness). However, John is a
different case, and Jung (1958) swiftly dispels such a diagnosis. John's visions
are "too consistent, not subjective and scurrilous enough" (para. 731) to be
those of a clinically diagnosed psychotic.

The 'vehemence' of the visions also suggests more than a compensation
for a "somewhat one-sided attitude of [a virtuous, christian] consciousness"
(Jung, 1958, para. 730). In fact, Jung is certain that the special type of
religiosity that John portrayed had an innate quality that was 'inborn', yet
nevertheless these visions were of such a degree that they could have had
severe effects on one such as John. His revelation, then, is more than just
prophecy in the form of a barrage of archetypal symbolic material fused
with Christian doctrine. It represents the brave and successful encounter of
a man faced with the *numinosum* who also had no choice in the matter. Like
the resignation to fate to which Christ had to submit, John too, was in the
(perhaps) inevitable, indeed unenviable position of enduring his experiences,
as alarming as they were.

Structurally, there are three major cycles of seven stages each (*see* Tables
8, 9 & 10). They mirror each other in cyclicality, and an extra '½ a time' is
added at the end of the first cycle (a silence for ½ an hour). This cycle of
3½ is of an indeterminate length of time, and rather than asserting a solely

temporal significance to this cycle, it may also be necessary to interpret it as having psychological significance.

The three cycles of seven represent a dynamic event that characterizes the vicissitudes of the individuating ego *and* a world going through the processes of purification by ordeal (sacrifice). In between the second and third cycle of seven is the 'Sun Woman' event, also lasting a period of 3½ (this time as 3½ years). This gives a total of 3½ + 3½ = 7, which symbolizes the end of the ordeal, and completion of the major part of the revelation (*see* fig. 43).

Figure 43. *John's Revelation: Two cycles of 3½ (the 'Inner' and 'Outer' Journeys) totaling seven.*

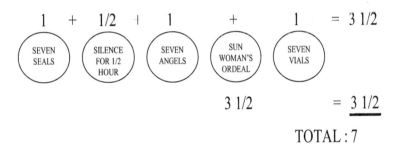

Three-and-a-half is the middle-point 'on the way' to seven. There are numerous references to 3½ in the Judeo-Christian Bible, which in most cases are expressed as periods of time of 3½ years (sometimes 3½ days) or generally, "a time, and times and half a time," as described in *Revelation* 12:14. This duration of 3½ is considered a "period of suffering" as Westcott (1974) reveals:

> The famine in the time of Elias, when Israel was persecuted by Ahab and Jezebel, lasted 3½ years. Antiochus Epiphanes persecuted the church 3½ years...[and in *Revelation*] the Bride, the Lamb's Wife, suffers 1260 days [3½ years] in the wilderness. (p. 49)

From these examples it is clear that the ancients were not only conscious of processes involving extreme effort or ardor, but also recognized time periods (cycles) or stages that had a particular symbolic relevance, which Jung would argue was given by the ordering effect of the number archetype. Thus they appeared to be responding to an archetypal concept of 'completion' (actually only 'semi-completion' as 3½), which meant in a very real sense, half the journey over (3½), and with it the worst of the ordeal. In other words, the full journey was (and is) 7 not 3½. Seven would thereby signify completion and 'future joy', as was recognized by Noah in the rainbow of seven colors after the Flood (*Genesis* 9:11-17).

As an aside, it is claimed that Newton did not objectively detect seven mutually-exclusive color bands—red, orange, yellow, green, blue, indigo, and violet—but that he merely divided the spectrum (e.g., the rainbow as we see it in the sky) into seven colors because this same division exists in music where there are seven notes with the eighth being the octave (the same as the first note; see the chapter, "The Music Of Number"). The eighth color, then, would be a 'repeat' at a higher vibration or frequency of red. Of course, in attempting to attribute musical harmony to the visual spectrum, Newton overlooked the incommensurability of the sensory modalities—the 'higher red' (as a visual 'octave') is invisible to the unaided eye, as are other spectral octaves, whereas the octaves across the range of notes played on musical instruments are audible.

Though the '7', symbolizing 'completion', is not always mentioned, it can be taken as tacit that 3½, being incomplete, would require completion in some way where there are inward circumambulations of 3½ cycles toward the center that also require 3½ outward circumambulations in order to return to the world. In fact, in many cultures, from ancient Greece to the Amerindians of North America, this type of circumambulation has been represented graphically and symbolically by a spiral of 3½ rotations.

The two-dimensional spiral of Archimedes (similar to a coil of rope) starts at a point 'outside' and spirals anti-clockwise (inwardly) 3½ rotations to the origin, the center of self-hood, while the journey back is a clockwise circumambulation back to the world. Clockwise rotations symbolize a

See Igmar Bergman's movie "The Seventh Seal"

"Seven Brides for Seven Brothers"

"The Seven year Itch" — Marilyn Monroe in   *"The 7 or Faces of Eve"*

movement toward greater consciousness, after the goal of realizing the central archetype of the Self, which takes place at the halfway point of the journey.

This same spiral symbol is used by the city-building Pueblos of New Mexico, who decorate their earthenware vessels with a similar spiral pattern that indicates the original journey of their people. As they traveled 'round and round', they finally settled in a place that was made ready for them—a promised land—which may also be taken as the goal, the individual's 'journey' made on the way to wholeness: the original home. At the halfway point—the center—reunion with the world must begin by journeying outward another 3½ cycles to complete the seven cycles or stages that lead to completion (wholeness). The two cycles of 3½ thus represent completion in the number seven.

To return to *Revelation*, John's vision starts with a door opening into heaven where he sees a throne with 'one' sitting upon it. In 'His' right *hand* is a book "sealed with seven seals" (*see* Table 8). As each seal is opened a particular 'world' event is revealed to John, which is manifested according to the quality of the seal.

Table 8. *Seven Seals of Heaven (Revelation Chapters 6-8).*

First Seal	White Horse: Conquest (6:2)
Second Seal	Red Horse: Power to Kill (6:4)
Third Seal	Black Horse: Balance/Justice (6:5-8)
Fourth Seal	Pale Horse: Death/Hell on Earth (6:8)
Fifth Seal	Souls in white slain for the Word of God (6:9-11)
Sixth Seal	Earthquake, Black Sun, Blood-Red Moon (6:12-17)
Seventh Seal	Silence for 1/2 an hour (8:1)

The first four seals cover the four horsemen of the Apocalypse. Each horse is of a different color. The first three—White, Red, Black—bring to mind the alchemical color sequence *albedo-rubedo-nigredo*, but in *Revelation* the sequence is reversed. From a relative wholeness to a fragmented state, psyche/world go from good, to bad, to worse, culminating in the fourth Pale Horse of Death (here may be a synchronistic connection, or correspondence between John's psychic disposition and the state of the world).

The death motif is actually picked up and magnified in the slain souls imagery revealed under the fifth seal (multiple egoic 'deaths'), while the opening of the sixth seal reveals more upheaval and destruction before the time of 'rest' when the seventh seal is opened (silence, indicating 'rest', for ½ an hour), which usually characterizes the symbolism of number seven.

The second cycle of seven begins when John sees seven angels, each of whom sounds a trumpet that further initiates events of an awesome nature (mostly cataclysmic) (*see* Table 9).

Table 9. *Seven Angels with Seven Trumpets (Revelation Chapters 8-11).*

First Angel	Hail/Fire/Blood on Earth (8:7)
Second Angel	Fire Mountain in Seas/Blood Sea (8:8)
Third Angel	Fallen Star (Wormwood) in 1/3 of the rivers (8:10-11)
Fourth Angel	1/3 Darkness of Sun, Moon, and Stars (8:12)
Fifth Angel	Darkness, Torment by Demon Locusts from the pit for 5 months (9:1-12)
Sixth Angel	4 Angels bound in the Euphrates, loosed to slay 1/3 part of men (9:13-21)
Seventh Angel	Earthly kingdoms become kingdoms of the Lord (11:15)

After the first six trumpets have sounded, the seventh trumpet sounds with a subsequent pronouncement from Heaven concerning a heavenly rule, as opposed to an earthly rule. Psychologically, the central archetype of the Self is now the dominant influence of psychic authority, while the ego's power is therefore seconded to this higher power. Again, the number-seven symbolism suggests fruitfulness and the end of another cycle—this time one of a spiritual yield.

As mentioned, John witnessed a period of silence for the space of ½ an hour, but for John this 'intermission' does not mark the end of a cycle of 3½ as such. In fact, the first completed cycle of 3½ is endured by the 'Sun Woman' who brings forth the man-child (*Anthropos*). In *Revelation* 12:6 she flees into the wilderness where she is fed by God for 1260 days ÷ 365 ≈ 3½ years, or a "time, and times, and half a time" (*Revelation* 12:14), which would be 1 + 2 + ½ = 3½.

The Sun Woman's ordeal corresponds with John's experience, and in a very real sense *is* his experience. There are three other events of a 3½-year (i.e., 42 months) duration running concurrently with the Sun Woman's ordeal:

1. the Holy City is trodden down 42 months (*Revelation* 11:2).

2. the Two Witnesses prophesy in sackcloth 1260 days (*Revelation* 11:3).

3. the Beast reigns 42 months after the Death-stroke was healed (*Revelation* 13:5).

All four events are variations on the same thing (transformation through ordeal). Psychologically, the end of the Sun Woman's ordeal corresponds with John reaching the center of psychic wholeness, where he discovers his inner 'sun woman', the *anima* (his soul). This experience is an epiphany for John: the opposites—ego and *anima*—are conjoined, and the *Anthropos* (the 'Son' of 'Man', the Self, the central archetype) is born in John's consciousness. John has experienced the numinosity of the Self. Essentially, the sounding of the seventh trumpet by the seventh angel, which heralds the reign of the Self (God's kingdom), is synonymous with the birth of the *Anthropos*. Symbolically, then, John (as ego) and Sun Woman (as *anima*) experience the same event from different perspectives.

The second cycle of 3½ ends with the conclusion of the third and final cycle of seven, which begins when one of four beasts (mentioned in *Revelation* 4:7; 6:3; 11:1 and 13:11) gives seven vials to seven angels. These vials deliver seven plagues upon the world (*see* Table 10).

Table 10. *Contents of the Seven Vials of the Seven Angels (Revelation Chapter 16)*.

First Vial	Sores: "grievous sore upon the men which had the mark of the beast" (16:2)
Second Vial	Sea of Blood: "every living soul died in the sea" (16:3)
Third Vial	Rivers and Fountains of Blood: "thou hast given them blood to drink" (16:4-7)
Fourth Vial	Scorching Fire of the Sun: "and men were scorched with great heat" (16:8-9)
Fifth Vial	Darkness: "they gnawed their tongues for pain" (16:10-11)
Sixth Vial	Euphrates dries up & the Armageddon event: "the battle of that great day" (16:12-16)
Seventh Vial	Voices, Thunder, Hail, etc.: "a great voice out of the temple…. It is done" (16:17-21)

The 'targets' of the contents of the first four vials match those targeted by the plagues of the first four trumpets, where Earth (the bodies of men), Sea, Rivers and Sun are all adversely affected again.

In the fifth vial is a darkness (depression), which also results in suffering, while the sixth vial presages the events leading up to Armageddon (Hebrew: 'Height of *Megiddo*, the place of troops'). A great battle is prophesied to take place at this site, which is initiated with the pouring of the seventh vial into the air. This pouring brings about a plague of hail and the words "It is done."

Henry Halley, in the *Bible Handbook* (1972), suggests that the number seven "may figure in the structure of the universe far beyond man's [*sic*] knowledge," and adds:

> [the number seven] used as often as it is, in the way it is…must have some significance over and above its numerical value. Symbolically, it is thought to stand for Completeness, a Unit, Fullness, Totality. (p. 688)

Each of these descriptors can be applied to the natural numbers discussed in previous chapters so that they do not mark the number seven as unique from the other natural numbers (for example, it is clear that there are different types of 'numerical' completeness). To be more accurate the symbolism of number seven can be seen to apply to dynamic processes that reach completion in seven stages *and only seven stages*, so that the process is inhered with a quality unique to the number seven purely because of the seven stages and for no other reason. We therefore have to look at the structure and substructures that bring a certain (unique) quality to sevenfold processes, models, or systems. As it happens, breaking down the number seven into two parts, '4 + 3', yields a dualistic dynamic in number seven. All three seven-stage cycles in *Revelation* have this dynamic.

The first cycle has the common motif of the four horses, which are animal/terrestrial symbols, followed by a three-stage human/celestial process (thesis/antithesis/synthesis), involving human 'death' contrasted with celestial 'death' (the black sun is a *nigredo* symbol), both of which find their synthesis in silence (the alchemical *meditatio*, a form of stillness, or waiting, etc.).

The second cycle has the plagues of the first four trumpets falling on Earth, Seas, Rivers and Sun, matched by the contents of the vials in the third cycle, which also fall on Earth, Seas, Rivers and Sun. These two stages, like the appearance of the four horses in the world, are terrestrial in nature (in the outer world), therefore the triadic process in each cycle should be celestial/heavenly in its general nature to compensate the system (*see* Table 11).

Table 11. *The Dualistic Dynamics of the Number Seven (as 4 + 3).*

'#4' SYMBOLISM: (KEY WORDS)	'#3' SYMBOLISM: (KEY WORDS)
Feminine	Masculine
Material	Ethereal
Physical	Conceptual
Insect, Animal	Human, Angel
Instinctual	Spiritual
Concrete	Abstract
Emotional	Intellectual
Mundane	Holy
Profane	Sacred
Terrestrial (Earthly)	Celestial (Heavenly)
Matter	Mind

There must also be a dualistic dynamism in the thesis (fifth) and antithesis (sixth) stages, which resolves in a synthesis of the two in the seventh stage. These syntheses do occur. In fact, these two triads (fifth, sixth, and seventh angels; fifth, sixth, and seventh vials) in both cases concern the thesis of reconciliation of death (darkness/*nigredo* symbolism again, as with the slain souls under the altar of the fifth seal) with the antithesis of life (water of the Euphrates), synthesized through the final word of the Lord ("It is done") and the reclamation of His kingdom. At the end of the whole ordeal, John witnesses a transformation—"a new heaven and a new world" (*Revelation* 21:1).

There is no cyclicality in the remaining text of *Revelation* (chapter 17-22). Instead of an orderly sequence of events which demonstrate a cyclical, almost planned structure, the last events ("Babylon the Great" and its fall, the doom of the beast and the false prophet, the Millennium, etc.) are more spontaneous and independent of each other, so that one devastating event after another seems to occur with no perceivable structure to this sequence. But, insofar as the significance of the number seven is concerned, it is clear that John's initial visions were communicated 'numerically' through the mechanism of the number archetype.

From a Futuristic perspective, John's revelation may refer to a possible synchronistic enmeshment of psychic events with independent world events, in the form of a series of precognitive visions. (The nature of this type of phenomenon is discussed in the chapter "Synchronicity.") Whether these events are synchronistic or not, the number archetype has put order to events of the psyche which may otherwise have manifested as an overwhelming stream of incoherent and unrelated material from the collective unconscious. This whole sequence of events demonstrates cyclicality and resolution in seven, concurrently using a '4 + 3' configuration, which indicates dynamism and opposition, and a '3½ + 3½' configuration, which merely divides the events into two main parts.

George Miller and the Number Seven

To gain some idea of the number archetype in psychological terms, with particular focus on the number seven, we again turn to George Miller—this time, to his journal article 'The Magical Number Seven, Plus or Minus Two', *Psychological Review* (1956). Miller opens his article with a confession:

> My problem is that I have been persecuted by an integer. For seven years [!] this number has followed me around, has intruded in my most private data, and assaulted me from the pages of our most public journals. (p. 81)

In the previous chapter "Six (The Hexad)" the number six was shown to relate quantitatively and qualitatively to the human attention span. Miller discovered that our nervous system seems incapable of determining arrays of more than six items without failure. The number seven, too, figures in the human psyche in a similar way. Miller found that our "absolute judgment" and "immediate memory" (p. 92) both have limited spans (seven categories, seven items, respectively) that determine a restricted capacity for receiving, processing and remembering information. Miller collated the data from a number of studies concerning the discriminative capacities of the sense organs (excluding the sense of smell) (see Table 12).

Table 12. *The Limits of the Human Sensory Modalities as Experienced in Consciousness.*

SENSORY MODALITY TESTED	RESULT
Hearing	**Pitch:** 6 tones assigned without error regardless of number of tones. **Loudness:** 5 perfectly discriminated "loudnesses" (volumes).
Taste	**Salinity:** 4 distinct concentrations of salt solution detected without error.
Sight	**Visual Position:** 10-15 different scale markers "interpolated" with total accuracy.
Touch	**Skin Response (Vibrations on Chest):** 4 intensities without error. 5 durations without error. 7 locations without error.

By taking the results from nearly two dozen different stimulus variables Miller arrived at an average *"span of absolute judgment"* (p. 90) of seven categories which were discernable by the human subject without error. As Miller claims: "There is a clear and definite limit to the accuracy with which we can identify absolutely the magnitude of a unidimensional stimulus variable" (p. 90). He concluded that we have a rather limited capacity for making unidimensional sensory judgments (one category only, for example, size, or hue), with little variance from one sense modality to the other. Further studies showed that chunking (grouping) the information would show an increase in the amount of transmitted (recalled) information, but not an increase in the number of chunks (also limited to seven).

Having established the apparent fact that "the span of absolute judgment and the span of immediate memory impose severe limitations on the amount of information that we are able to receive, process, and remember" (p. 95), and having also confirmed the long held belief that, quantitatively, this finite limit is approximately seven items, Miller then wondered (half seriously?) if these findings have anything to do with "the seven seas, the seven deadly sins, the seven daughters of Atlas in the Pleiades,…the seven notes of the musical scale, and the seven days of the week" (p. 96). In true scholarship Miller confesses that he is not sure number seven is a magic number:

> Perhaps there is something deep and profound behind all these sevens, something just calling out for us to discover it. But I suspect that it is only a pernicious, Pythagorean coincidence. (p. 96)

This type of perfunctory refrain usually helps stabilize a momentarily toppling intellectual edifice built upon the so-called certainty of scientific principles, which leads Miller to construct an imaginary rival made of 'straw'—and a 'pernicious' one at that having been intentionally constructed to topple. Notwithstanding the humor of this statement, we must still address Miller's implication. Assuming he has knowledge of Pythagorean number symbolism we must then ask how he arrived at the conclusion that 'all these sevens' are mere 'coincidence'. Actually, his claim of 'Pythagorean coincidence' serves to palm off the burden of responsibility of the scientist, when the onus is not even on the scientist alone to prove the validity of number symbolism. Miller's proposal to "withhold judgment" (p. 96) is truly his most integrated and qualified statement in this regard. But his dismissal of Pythagorean knowledge claims may inadvertently discourage others from investigating number symbolism because it debases the whole enterprise and suggests that such research would be held in poor esteem (at least by scientists) with little reward possible from such an effort.

Miller's rational approach insists on fixing a low *a priori* probability to the likelihood of Pythagorean-like statements having any basis in scientific fact. But how does one determine *scientifically* whether or not "there is something deep and profound behind" (p. 96) Fortune, or the Virgin, or the Pleiades? If these associations are purely cultural, or even archetypal (having a 'deep' neuro-physiological and psychological basis) there may be no *scientific* means of substantiating this type of number symbolism—one can only accept them on the basis that they appear in a culture. (Jung insisted that the archetype could not be proved.) Even the psychological validation of these symbols (a type of scientific determination) is interpretive, being logically derived from the presence and effects they have in a culture, or on an individual.

One can begin moving toward a solution to Miller's 'problem' with number seven by first considering such statements as those that appear in Michell's *The Dimensions of Paradise* (1988), and Westcott's *Numbers* (1974), and then tracing their derivations:

> **Michell:** The Pythagoreans said, 'it [number seven] neither generates nor is generated', meaning that it cannot be multiplied to produce another number within the first ten, nor is it the product of other [natural] numbers. For that reason the heptad was called the Virgin and was a symbol of eternal rather than created things. It was particularly related to the measurement of time, the seven ages of man, and the seven days of the week or quadrant of the lunar month. (p. 53)

> **Westcott:** Seven say the followers of Pythagoras, was so called from the Greek verb "sebo," to venerate (and from the Hebrew ShBO, seven, or satisfied, abundance), being Septos, "Holy," "divine," and "motherless," and a "Virgin."...The Pleiades, a group of seven stars in the constellation Taurus, was thought of [as having] mighty power over earthly destiny. (pp. 73-74)

The seven-Virgin association has been discussed in the chapter "The Archetype of Number," and the heptagon-Virgin association was discussed at the beginning of this chapter, as was the lunar quadrant of seven days, and the seven-day week. It can be seen that the number seven had cosmic status in the ancient world. The planets and stars governed (ruled) all things, astronomically and astrologically speaking, and the concepts of cyclicality, evolution and change became mystically and symbolically associated with the number seven. The archetype of the number seven (represented as powerful planetary or stellar configurations) was tacitly recognized through veneration by the ancients.

Many religious and alchemical texts make constant reference to cycles of seven days (the so-called lunar quadrant), or seven decades (as the 'ages of man'), etc., as patterns indicating periods of trial and ordeal, at the end of which would come a rebirth (transformation), or death and resurrection, or deliverance in some other form. Hero myths reflect these patterns, which embody trial periods of seven tasks, etc. The book of *Revelation*, with its insistent number seven theme, gives a most cogent indication of this process.

Regardless of the fact that the sciences have found no legitimate grounds for these associations, an age-old pattern (an evolved sevenfold configuration) pre-existing in the psyche gave psychological impetus to the formation of such associations. These associations may stem from psychoid factors or archetypes. Reflected in the many ancient associations with number seven and corresponding biological and psychological facts is the common theme of completion, cyclicality, and limitation. The blastocyst, for example, becomes a biological entity after seven stages are completed, and Miller's above-mentioned examples demonstrate that the number seven can be a numerical marker indicating an approximate quantitative limit to some human psycho-physiological capacities (there may be other psychoid facts yet to be discovered, which can be qualified and quantified by the number seven).

Therefore one must not make the twofold mistake of assuming that number seven symbolism (and all number symbolism) is the result of (a) some form of coincidental social construction resulting from *only* a reaction to the environment, which (b) was subsequently dispersed globally by way of a cultural migration of ideas, etc. An archetypal groundplan must be prefigured in the psyche for these associations to emerge, and certain typically human activities are contingent with this prefiguration. Miller has shown that certain cognitive limitations are determined by the human nervous system, and generally speaking, this limited capacity system cannot be overridden. It appears to be a natural condition of peoples all over the world. Such limitations are psychological facts whether we arrive at them experimentally (as did Miller), or we intuit them experientially (as did the ancients).

It is not altogether a mystical assertion, therefore, to state that unconscious knowledge of certain 'inner' facts which can be expressed numerically, may be projected into the environment by the members of any and all cultures, after which that environment takes on a socially constructed aspect (the construction cannot come first). As long as the environment provides the suitable hooks for these projections (virginity, lunar quadrants, various cycles, periods of enduring hardship, the 'ages of man', etc.), the number seven comes to have a deeper meaning that manifests in the psyche as a resonance, or even a conflation of environmental factors and projected contents.

The meaningfulness thereby constructed in the psyche may be taken as having (in part) a psycho-biological origin, due to a certain structure in the nervous system, and certain developmental processes, etc. These structures and processes have influences on the psyche, which set limits on human perceptions and corresponding reactions. Just as the world contains phenomena which have physical limitations (marked by endurance, change, etc.), or are governed by cyclicality, so too the psyche acts and behaves according to the physiological and neurological demands and limitations of the body. The psyche is governed by an inner model that limits human responses to repetitive or cyclical patterns of behavior, and activates certain pre-determined reactions and responses. The number seven has an archetypal character, generalizable to the number archetype, which reflects such a limited pattern structure in the psyche; a numerical order.

Systematic (numerical or numerological) interpretations of the world's phenomena may be a means of understanding and putting order to the world, but an empirical reality (an archetype) always forms the kernel of any constructed knowledge claim. Our perceived world is a world delimited by, and based on archetypal apprehensions. The archetype is an unknowable 'other' underpinning our knowledge claims. The range of archetypes accounts for the perceivable and conceptual differences of the world's phenomena, which are qualitatively and quantitatively reflected in our expressions and representations. There is evidence that the brain is geared to behave in this way. Evidence from the Gestalt schools of psychology as far back as the 1920s and 30s suggests that the brain identifies and reacts to its own pattern properties when these properties are activated. That is, number, as one such pattern property, or entity, or archetype, has 'determining' power.

To go further, two mathematicians Ian Stewart and Martin Golubitsky, who wrote *Fearful Symmetry: Is God a Geometer?* (1992), see the brain as an end product that has evolved to its current state in a universe governed by certain laws which affect that evolution:

> the human brain itself is a child of nature: it evolved in a universe that obeys nature's laws. It wouldn't be surprising if features of those laws are built into the functioning of the brain. Thus those patterns that the brain is able to detect may not be arbitrary: it may have evolved to detect the patterns that are 'really' present. (p. 259)

The brain (and, therefore, mind), functioning in a specific way, necessarily perceives order, pattern, and symmetry, not simply by its own natural processes, but because that order, pattern and symmetry are 'really' there in the environment; in the universe (in some cases only approximately, by our examples)—numbers are effective in describing the universe because it is from the universe that we originally got them (Stewart & Golubitsky, 1992, p. 269). It follows that the *noumenal* world of which Kant speaks, like the Platonic ideas and forms, are more than mental constructs because they extend beyond the mind/brain complex to the universe itself. The task for researchers is to distinguish the differences that invariably exist between the real and the projected patterns and structures we perceive in the universe. Ultimately, therefore, Miller's work has merely set the ball rolling for researchers to consider the number archetype more fully, more creatively, in their researches.

Number Seven as the Symbol of Human Totality

Three systems—one spiritual, one psycho-physiological, and the other alchemical—further illustrate both the symbolic and the real aspects involved in acts completed in seven steps or stages. The Indian spiritual philosophy of Kundalini Yoga and its chakra system (Sanskrit: *chakra* = 'wheel') describes seven major nodes nominally associated with various parts of the human anatomy. These are:

1. 'base' chakra (at the apex of the sacrum)
2. 'sacral' chakra (at the base of the lumbar spine)
3. 'solar plexis' chakra (on the spine below the level of the shoulders)
4. 'heart' chakra (situated between the shoulder blades)
5. 'throat' chakra (at the back of the neck)
6. 'brow' chakra (between the eye-brows)
7. 'crown' chakra (at the top of the head)

Sri Chinmoy, in *Kundalini: The Mother-Power* (1974), acknowledges other chakras in the subtle body's various joints and fingertips, and in the trunk, "but these chakras are minor and are not usually mentioned" (p. 7). In *Radionics and the Subtle Anatomy of Man* (1980), David Tansley describes the chakra as:

> focal points which receive energies for the purpose of vitalising the physical body. It is through these centers that the healing energies are directed towards the diseased areas of the body in order to bring about a state of equilibrium or health. (p. 23)

The chakra system, incorporating meditation and spiritual exercises, is a developmental model for individuals seeking maturity and wellbeing, physically and mentally. The different levels (not necessarily followed in numerical order) are stages of the process localized in the space of the human body.

Anatomically, the seven chakra coincide impressively with Wilhelm Reich's body rings as described in his muscle armor theory. Prolonged conflict and stress is not only conducive to psychological problems, but also to physical problems, specifically in the muscle tissue, altering the person's posture, rate of breathing and bodily movements. That is, psychological problems can 'situate' themselves in specific areas of the body.

In *Character Analysis* (1949), Wilhelm Reich notes that the typical 'armored' individual:

> is incapable of dissolving his armor [and] is also incapable of expressing the primitive biological emotions.... The tension of the peripheral muscle and nervous system is shown in an exaggerated sensitivity to pressure. It is impossible to touch certain parts of an armored organism without producing intense symptoms of anxiety and nervousness. (p. 366)

Therapy involving physical manipulation of the musculature within certain zones of the body (rings), indirectly addresses the psychological issues of the individual by inducing character changes and the release of trauma. Reich identifies seven major areas of the human body which constitute the source of 'intense symptoms of anxiety and nervousness':

1. the ocular ring (eyes)
2. the oral ring (mouth, jaw)
3. the cervical ring (shoulders)
4. the thoracic ring (upper back)
5. the diaphragmatic ring (above the abdomen)
6. the abdominal ring (muscles in the visceral region)
7. the pelvic ring (hips and upper leg joints)

The Chakra system and Reich's body therapy can be seen as illustrating the oneness of mind and body that may be reached in seven steps—a process involving completion after 'ordeal' as discussed in the last section.

In 1537, in his *De Rerum Natura*, Paracelsus described the fanciful transmutation of natural objects, in a series of seven steps, as a change or 'loss' of their original form to that of 'another guise'. Metal could become glass or stone, stone could become coal, even rag could become paper. These seven steps must be 'ascended' in the following order for transformation to be successful: (i) Calcination, (ii) Sublimation, (iii) Solution, (iv) Putrefaction, (v) Distillation, (vi) Coagulation, and (vii) Tincture.

Although alchemical in nature, these steps recall the processes described above, but looked at psychologically their symbolism is of a greater value than a purely concretistic interpretation could ever allow (from a scientific point of view, it is with the greatest of difficulty that one could seriously accept the possibility of the transmutation of natural objects in the way that Paracelcus proposed).

Briefly, Calcination is the intense 'heat' of a desire or affect-laden condition (for example, an emotional hardship). Sublimation is the 'rising' of a personal component to a spiritual or creative level, which can become soluble (Solution) so that its potential can be realized. Putrefaction occurs next, after which the psychic 'body' is cleansed, and the soul is extracted—a kind of 'death' takes place. Distillation means a further refinement to remove more impurities, and Coagulation means the solidification or formation of an earthly life, replacing the abstractedness of spiritual unreality with the solid base that consciousness instills. Finally, the Tincture may be attained when a maturity of personality is reached.

Most alchemists did not understand that 'inner' (mental or psychological) processes were not the same as the chemical reactions they saw taking place in the laboratory, which were replications of natural events in the real world, and put psychologically, only really served as analogies of inner processes (transformations—like rag turning into paper—are not likely to have occurred in the laboratory anyway, whether some alchemists believed it or not).

The alchemists' literal-mindedness may not be so naïve, however, since the brain as the site of our mental life, as far as our sciences tell us, functions in exactly the same way as many chemical reactions, involving the flow of neuro-transmitters (molecules and ionized elements such as potassium and calcium, etc.), electron exchange between elements, and so on. Naturally, many chemical reactions in the brain will mirror the psychological states expressed above, so that the transformations which Paracelsus described are not only symbolic, but are also neurological, and are therefore directly related to psychological processes. The 'logic' behind the statements of the alchemists says more about their intuitive capacities than the modern critic is at first prepared to credit. Often, superior insight, as given by intuition and creative inspiration, may come in numerical form or geometrical representations based on natural numbers (Kekulé's vision and Descartes' dream have already been mentioned as examples). In the case of the scientist, new knowledge claims are discovered from the projection of psychological facts, while for the ancients, the self-same projection onto the environment resulted in knowledge claims of a different order. These differences may vary in degree and kind since, given the time and culture, a myth is appropriate to a people according to the psychological processes involved in generating that myth. Only with an increased level of discrimination, however, can psychological facts be separated from physical facts. The scientific method has always been an attempt at maintaining this distinction.

So, while we consciously use numbers, the unconscious likewise 'embraces' the number concept, but more than this, the unconscious, as unlimited as it would appear to be by its phenomenology, is apparently bound by rules (as Miller has shown) which convey a strictly numerical guideline (among others) as to its functioning. This numerical guideline would be synonymous with the number archetype as a structural reality of the human nervous system. Symbolic number structures, then, are admissible as knowledge claims, but they also readily mirror, and therefore, determine the specific natures of particular *phenomena*, as they are experienced in consciousness, though they can never be taken as the absolute truth or absolute knowledge concerning the *noumena* underlying those particular *phenomena*. This is because much of the knowledge-constructing process takes place unconsciously, and we cannot know of the nature of the conflations or constructions that may take place (except by a kind of back-engineering or

Do we think 'number' while dreaming? Do we dream numbers? —

analysis of the associations which may arise in consciousness). The unconscious contents may irrupt into consciousness, or be introspectively perceived, as prefigured structures or patterns, but the nature of these forms, since they are not devised consciously, may take on a numinous aspect, and from this perspective, may require interpretation. Any interpretation will have to submit to the rigors and scrutiny of the Self-system and, if found to be inadequate, the Self will reciprocate accordingly (Jung has noted repeatedly throughout his writings the reciprocal or compensatory nature of the unconscious when interpretation is faulty).

Limited capacity systems and sensory modalities, however, should not be taken negatively as obstacles which hinder our 'true' perception of the world, but should be seen as a positive means of interpretation and mediation of the world and our experience. While these capacities should be sanctioned, for they are the source of an understanding of the universe that can become increasingly more meaningful, Miller's work should be held in mind because it establishes the fact that there are limitations to our cognitive functions—a fact of which we are all individually aware. What follows is another example of those limits.

Number Seven and 'Gregorian Whispers'

A recent example of the limited capacity system first discovered by Miller comes in the form of a demonstration by Howard Goodall in his BBC television series 'Howard Goodall's Big Bangs' (1999). Goodall called it a case of 'gregorian whispers', also referred to as 'Chinese whispers'. He asked a young chorister from Salisbury Cathedral to listen to a twelve-note melodic passage which was then passed on to a fellow chorister. This procedure was repeated another fourteen times (only one recital was given on each trial). A total of sixteen trials were run and not only did the melody change, but the length of the piece changed as well from twelve notes to seven notes, after which it remained psychologically fixed. The number of notes sung by each chorister is given in the following sequence:

12, 12, 12, 14, 12, 10, 9, 9, 8, 9, 9, 7, 7, 7, 7, 7.

Goodall's main emphasis was to show that the aural tradition was an unreliable method for passing down musical knowledge since memory was demonstrably unreliable, but a fact which he did not point out was that, slowly but surely, the limit of seven items (musical notes in this case) had not only been reached, but was arrived at by a cognitive system that depended on trimming down the 'gross' twelve-note passage to a manageable seven-note passage. While the passage changed consistently over the course of the first eleven trials, each of which was a musical passage of more than seven notes, a final seven-note passage was passed on without flaw no less than five times (nearly a third of the trials).

Although such findings support Miller's (1956) conclusions, it should be noted that Miller's results in particular are based on average outcomes, and he confirms that there are exceptional cases of, for example, 'musically sophisticated' individuals who can identify "any one of 50 or 60 different pitches" (p. 84), which pales to insignificance the average person's ability of pitch detection of a mere six. It may be possible that the same musically gifted individuals would *not* have difficulty memorizing, with melodic accuracy, much more than seven notes. Other exceptional cases of a different type may exist, but generally it appears that these skills are either innate, or acquired, or both. Generally, we either 'learn' these limitations, or are restricted by them according to our nervous system. If the former is the case, we can possibly change the way we learn in order to increase our capacity for processing information, or if the latter is the case, we must ask how the exceptional cases (for example, 'sophisticated musicians') come by a nervous system which gives them such a superior capacity over that of the average person (unless the skill is learned, which reverts us to the former case). Nevertheless, the conclusion is apparent that we must consider the typical nervous system as one restricted by an in-built factor, which, to use Jung's term, may be taken as an aspect and limiting factor of the number archetype, but it also appears that the restriction is always there, in one form or another, no matter how 'sophisticated' an individual's 'talents' may be.

Summary

The number seven signifies the end of a physical or material cycle. In late medieval alchemical philosophy, for example, the symbol of the rainbow of seven colors represented imminent completion. A cyclical quality can often be determined in systems or models of seven stages, being composed of (say) a spatial aspect (located in the human body or other physical systems) and a temporal aspect (involving the passage of time in days, years, etc.). Generally, an impression of resonance or oscillation is detected in the sevenfold model or structure.

The sevenfold nature of the model or structure has psychological repercussions that reflect a meaningful and symbolic order in the psyche that may well be isomorphic with deeper, physiological determinants in the brain and nervous system, which give rise to the concept of the number archetype.

There is always Seven (Completion), but there is no experience of the empowerment evinced in the more highly differentiated dualism of the Ogdoad, and so 'emerges' the number Eight.

Please look up the Christian Seven Sacraments or historical hallmarks of the major "pinpoint periods" like punctuation to the cultural anthropological major events in mankind's life: Birth, initiation, marriage, closure, etc

(only a non-Christian would have left these 7 out....)

Plate 17. THE NUMBER EIGHT

The Wheel of Konark, in the Sun Temple at Konark in Orissa, India, is symbolic of oppositionalism, balance, and efficiency. Eightfold systems are often expanded versions of quaternity systems and they are similarly flexible in nature [SOURCE: Jyotirmaya/ Wikimedia Commons].

EIGHT (THE OGDOAD)

The number eight, as a multiple of four (being a double quaternity: 2 × 4), has the similar qualities to that of the number four. The dynamic which takes place, as seven moves to eight, is the same dynamic evinced in the movement of three to four, being one of a movement toward stability and wholeness—a movement away from the active quality of the number seven. As a double system, each of the two quaternities (4 + 4) is opposite in nature. Action and reaction, cause and effect, light and shadow are demonstrated in this higher tension and each opposite comprises the four partial aspects that constitute the qualities of each quaternity.

The Gnostic Ogdoad

The double quaternity, the Ogdoad, was considered by the Gnostics to be an ideal symbol of the world creating Demiurge because it embodied matter and spirit, but more generally, 'upper' and 'lower' (Heaven and Earth). This dualism follows the pattern of previous dualities initiated in One, duplicated in Two, resolved in Four, further differentiated and raised in power through Six, and finally reaching completion in Eight (the Ogdoad).

The Ogdoad was also identified with Wisdom, as personified in the Gnostic Sophia (Greek: *sophia* = 'wisdom'). This raises a conundrum as to which number—eight or nine—Wisdom should be appropriated since

See 8-Fold Path in Buddhism

number nine also has traditional associations with wisdom. However, it eventuates that there are two types of wisdom. The Gnostic usage of wisdom from the unconscious (intuition, inspiration), personified as a feminine deity Sophia, is rightly associated with the Ogdoad on symbolic grounds, whereas the wisdom which is associated with the number nine is a purely cognitive, conscious type of wisdom (logic, ratiocination). 'Ogdoadic' wisdom, psychologically speaking, emerges as a result of a direct ego relationship with the unconscious, while 'Enneadic' wisdom is learned, culturally acquired wisdom derived in consciousness more akin to intelligence.

The 'Timeless' and the 'Time-bound' in the Ogdoad

The Ogdoad has been traditionally constituted as a double mandala, symbolizing a universe which embodies the 'timeless' and the 'time-bound'. Von Franz (1974) notes that the concept of the *unus mundus* popularized by the hermetic philosophers and alchemists, referred to a *topos* that transcended 'normal' conscious experience, and was thereby dependent upon symbols for its graphic expression. The *unus mundus* was more 'timeless' in its manifestation and experience since it 'unified existence'. Because of their oppositional natures the 'timeless' and 'time-bound' are 'incommensurable' categories, but not irreconcilable. Ancient divinatory systems were usually practiced by highly intuitive individuals who were less 'time-bound' than the average person and were able to shift their consciousness to a 'twilight' consciousness (a form of semi-consciousness) where it was taken that a 'timeless' framework supplied absolute knowledge in the form of inevitable outcomes qualified and governed by the circumstances of a given time moment. The natural number sequence appears to be a way of setting these events to order.

Mantic arts, such as the *I Ching*, Tarot, and other divinatory systems, employ this assumption in their methodologies. Von Franz relativizes this assumption by pointing out that we cannot say for certain whether or not the 'predicted' events objectively correspond with the natural numbers, but she also notes that the collective unconscious does demonstrate one kind of orderedness based on numerical considerations:

Since, generally speaking, contents of the collective unconscious which have not yet reached the threshold of consciousness tend to engender parapsychological syndromes [for example, synchronicity], especially when they are constellated contents (in an "excited state," as physicists would say), these contents appear in conjunction with the preconscious aspects of the number archetype. On these foundations rests the concept of divination by means of numerical combinations. (von Franz, 1974, p. 302)

Ultimately, however, the relationship of number to time remains largely unexplained, but, from the perspective of the Ogdoad, it appears that a dualistic resonance is suggested in its symbolism of the 'timeless' and 'time-bound'.

Geometrical Representations of Number Eight

The octagon, ◯ , can be used to symbolize the number eight geometrically, but the symbol of infinity, the lemniscate (the double sigmoid line), ∞ , turned on its side is more common because it not only resembles the shape of the number eight, but also describes the continual interchange between polar opposites, a balance of opposing forces, and a never-ending line, that crosses itself when traced. This crossing is supposed to symbolise death carrying over into a new life beyond death, thus representing life, death, and rebirth. The symbol was therefore carried over into Christianity.

The number eight, being the first cubic number ($2^3 = 2 \times 2 \times 2 = 8$), is also symbolized by the cube that has eight vertices (*see* fig. 44a), thus producing a relatively stable solid figure. The geometrical representation of eight in the cube is the three-dimensional 'equivalent' of the square, thus bringing to mind the number four. Both the square and the cube are amongst the two most fundamental forms in nature (*see* fig. 44). It can be seen from Figure 44b that the two overlaid squares (one rotated 45°) are a means of constructing the octagon.

Figure 44. *(a) The cube; (b) The octagon (derived from two squares).*

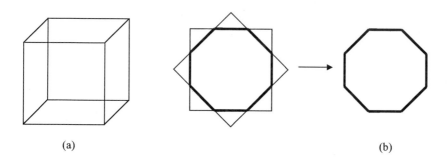

(a)   (b)

In the science of crystallography, one of six possible polyhedra (building blocks of crystals) is constructed using the *isometric* or *cubic* system. In *The Magic of Numbers* (1994), Pappas notes that:

> each unit is composed of congruent cubes. The faces of this polyhedron are congruent squares. Any three concurrent edges are at right angles to each other. Examples are pyrite, alum, garnet, galena. (p. 218)

Crystal formation is so precise, and the crystals themselves are so symmetrical, that the study of crystals as structural forms is enhanced by using the mathematical principles of geometry, arithmetic, etc., all of which are underscored by the natural numbers.

Like the regular polygons (particularly from the pentagon upwards), which can be used to form stellar representations of the natural numbers, the eight-pointed star, the *stella octangula*, can be formed by joining the vertices of an octagon (*see* fig. 45).

This star was identified with the ancient Phoenician goddess of love and fertility, Ishtar, who was also related to Venus, and later adopted by the early Christians. Evidence that the eight-sided star is incorporated into Christianity manifests in the image of St. Priscilla, found in the catacombs in Rome, and baptismal fonts, which are always eight-sided. The *stella octangula* not only became a symbol of good luck for Christians, but also for Jews (especially the Essenes, a sect of Judaism).

Her home was used by St. Peter as his headquarters in Rome.

Figure 45. *From the octagon (left) is formed the
stella octangula (right) rotated 22.5°*

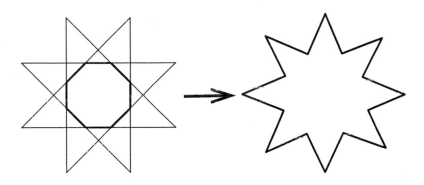

Representations of Number Eight in Religion

'Stellar' representations and any geometrical (mandala) forms of numbers have religious and psychological significance. Michell (1988) comments on the appearance of such forms in the construction of sacred sites, such as temples, churches, and other holy places:

> Sacred geometry is the essence of the geometer's art. Its use is for making descriptions of the universe by combining together in one geometric composition the basic figures which represent the different orders of number and underlie the manifestations of nature…[But] the universe can never be represented perfectly and literally…. The geometer's aim, therefore, is to imitate the universe symbolically, depicting its central paradox by bringing together shapes of different geometric orders, uniting them as simply and accurately as possible and thus creating a cosmic image. (p. 65)

The effect that these ordered, geometric patterns and structures have on the psyche is powerful, and such an influence down through the ages, across all cultures, speaks of the people-uniting and psychologically unifying power of the number archetype that predisposes the psyche towards order-seeking.

The walled enclosure or temple precinct is the special subject of 'treatment' by the auspicious number eight, being a simple variation on the circular plan, or common square, and in some cases, a variation on the 'quadripartite' city plan, which was essentially the squared circle. The octagonal shape was a compromise toward that end, namely an attempt to meet the square-plan and circle-plan halfway by literally 'cutting the corners'. Schimmel (1993) notes that this "transition from the square to the circle... [was] important in the construction of domes" (p. 156), and architecturally speaking, it is easy to see how the octagon 'mediates' this move from square to circle. Cirlot (1962) points out:

> the octonary, related to two squares or the octagon, is the intermediate form between the square (or the terrestrial order) and the circle (the eternal order), and is, in consequence, a symbol of regeneration. (p. 223)

Since the number seven was taken as symbolic of completed processes (in, for example, a cyclical sense), the number eight indicated the first step or stage in the next cycle, and so became associated with a second beginning on a higher level. Many religions, therefore, set certain events on the eighth day, eighth month, or eighth year, to indicate regeneration, resurrection, purification, etc. Examples of number-eight symbolism occur in Judaism, where the eighth day is the day of circumcision for the newborn male child, and in Christianity, where the eighth day of the Passion is the day of the resurrection of Christ, while the Elamite calendar had a so-called 'Venus' year of eight months. It has been mentioned above how all the natural numbers inevitably indicate completion in some sense or other. There are, however, qualitative differences for each of these types of completion. For example, completion in three stages describes intellectual systems that are systematically absolute, but usually lacking in dimension. Quintessential completion refers to an amalgam of four balanced aspects in two pairs of polar opposites, each of which is mutually exclusive and all embracive of the phenomena they describe.

There are symbolic similarities between number four and number eight, but the problem of three and four (triad and tetrad), discussed previously, arises again in the problem of seven and eight (heptad and ogdoad). There is an 'awkward' shift from seven to eight, much like that of three to four, and it is marked by a characteristic jump from the seventh element to an unrelated eighth element. For example, the Old Testament, through its detailed chronology, beginning with Adam and ending in an unbroken lineage with Moses (plus Christ), shows a series of eight 'true prophets'. These are Adam, Enoch, Noah, Abraham, Isaac, Jacob, Moses, and Christ (first-century Church Father Clement of Rome was one of many who identified Christ as the eighth of the eight prophets). The first seven constituted the Hebdomad, which became an Ogdoad with the addition of Christ. The fact that Christ (from the House of Judah, who was a son of Jacob) is not a descendant of Moses (from the House of Levi, also a son of Jacob) means Christ (the eighth) is not 'like' the other seven—just as the fourth is not like the other three. Jung (1963) notes that:

> the seven form an uninterrupted series, the step to the eight involves hesitation or uncertainty…. It is very remarkable that we meet it again in the Taoist series of eight immortals: the seven are great sages or saints who dwell in heaven or on the earth, but the eighth is a *girl* who sweeps up the fallen flowers at the southern gate of heaven. (para. 574)

The eighth figure in an ogdoadic grouping is often a single female among seven males in fairy tales: "Grimm's tale of the seven ravens: there the seven brothers have one sister" (para. 574), and the story of *Snow White and the Seven Dwarfs* is familiar to most. The main image here is one of a psychological division of wholeness into an ogdoadic form (as in the tetrad), but the eighth 'rounds out' the exclusive masculinity of the seven by bringing in a feminine aspect. The feminine nature of Christ was explained by seventeenth-century German mystic Jacob Boehme as referring to the virginity of his mind.

Again Jung (1963) highlights the move from seven to eight:

> The archetype of the seven appears again in the division of the week and the naming of its days, and in the musical octave, where the last note is always the beginning of a new cycle. This may be a cogent reason why the eighth is feminine: it is the mother of a new series. (para. 579)

Christ is also the 'octave' of the ogdoad of prophets—that is, he is the same as Adam, but different, because Adam takes on two roles: he is the 'old' unredeemed Adam (who sinned in Eden), and he is the *Adam Kadmon* of the Kabbalistic tradition (the first, original 'Man'). But the new Adam is Christ (the second Adam according to Gregory the Great), therefore making the eighth a higher version of the first.

In Gnosticism, a similar image of seven archons (forming the Hebdomad) is combined with the "eighth which is Sophia, the feminine element" (Edinger, 1995, p. 242), thus producing the Ogdoad. Sophia, who is identified with wisdom (of a 'feminine' quality given its unconscious source), also corresponds to the alchemical 'mother'. In this regard she gives birth to a new content of consciousness (psychologically speaking), which is to say, she gives birth to a 'philosophical' son (the *filius philosophorum*), a son of wisdom and knowledge.

Sophia has been equated with Isis and the Virgin Mary, suggesting that the son is *the* Son (Osiris/Christ) who stands for the eighth as well, thus creating a paradox. Essentially, however, they are one and the same, since Christ, as the Self, incorporates Sophia in its wholeness. More correctly, Sophia is Christ's soul, but also the unmanifested divinity of Christ before he incarnated as 'Man' (*Anthropos*).

Number Eight as a Double Quaternity

Jung (1963) gives an alchemical double quaternity which "stands for a totality, for something that is at once heavenly and earthly, spiritual or corporeal, and is found in the...unconscious" (para. 8). Here again is the macrocosm as microcosm—the original *Anthropos* differentiated by its parts: as above, so below (*see* fig. 46).

Quoting from the *Tractatus Micrerus* Jung relates this alchemical 'combination' as it appears in the *prima materia*:

> In it [the *prima materia*] are images of heaven and earth, of summer, autumn, winter, and spring, male and female. If thou callest this spiritual, what thou doest is probable; if corporeal, thou sayest the truth; if heavenly, thou liest not; if earthly thou hast well spoken. (para. 7)

Figure 46. *The alchemical ogdoad combining 'Upper' and 'Lower' (Jung).*

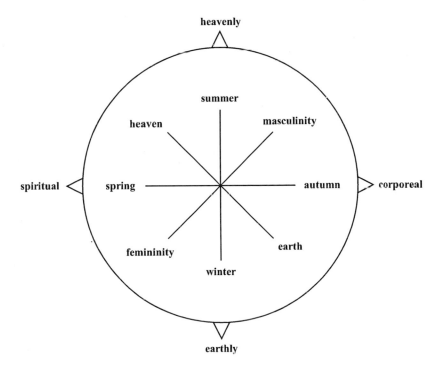

This model bears a resemblance to a combined four-element, four-quality, Aristotelian ogdoad, the two quaternities of which were discussed in the chapter "Four (The Tetrad)" (*see* fig. 47).

Figure 47. *The four qualities, the four elements, the Sun and the Moon (Jung).*

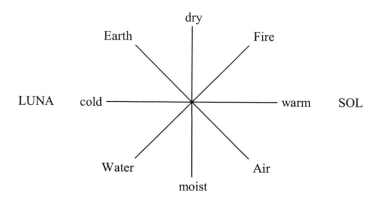

Sol (solar quality of consciousness) is associated with warmth, air, dryness, heat, etc.—qualities with which one identifies, as opposed to moisture, coldness, earth, wetness, etc., which are associated with Luna (the lunar principle of the dark shadow side of life and human nature). In the following quote Jung (1963) notes:

> The masculine, solar nature in the right half of the quaternio knows neither coldness, nor a shadow, nor heaviness, melancholy, etc., because, so long as all goes well, it identifies as closely as possible with consciousness, and that as a rule is the idea which one has of oneself. In this idea the shadow is usually missing: first because nobody likes to admit to any inferiority, and second because logic forbids something white to be called black.... For reasons of prestige we pass over the shadow in complete silence....
>
> Things are different with Luna: every month she is darkened and extinguished; she cannot hide this from anybody, not even from herself. She knows that this same Luna is now dark and now bright—but who has ever heard of a dark sun?...
>
> Despite all attempts at denial and obfuscation there is an unconscious factor, a black sun, which is responsible for the surprisingly common phenomenon of masculine split-mindedness, when the right hand musn't know what the left is doing. (para. 330-332)

Thereby, Jung has indicated the dual nature of the human psyche in men and women, and aligned it with the alchemical discourse that sees the whole of nature and the cosmos (and chaos) mirrored in the psychology and physiology of the human subject. In a man, consciousness can be seen as 'masculine' in nature, while the unconscious is 'feminine' (through his *anima*), and in a woman, the principles are reversed (with the *animus* as her unconscious counterpart). Paradoxically, consciousness *always* has a solar quality in men and women, while the unconscious is characterized by a lunar quality. Of course, it is *always* a question of relativism, not absolutism, when it comes to qualifying the natures of consciousness and the unconscious in gender terms.

Number Eight in Jung's Typology

Many fourfold systems can be expanded to eightfold systems. For example, the four cardinal directions can be increased to eight by the addition of north-east, south-east, south-west, and north-west (*see* fig. 48). Also, the four functions in Jung's typology, which characterize ego orientation, are further differentiated by two attitudes, introversion and extraversion, thus establishing eight fundamental types: the introverted thinking, feeling, sensation, and intuitive types, and the extraverted thinking, feeling, sensation, and intuitive types.

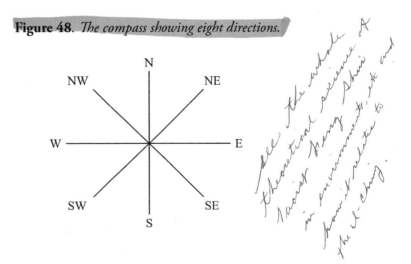

Figure 48. *The compass showing eight directions.*

These two examples (the compass and Jung's typology) show the practical advantages that are made possible through a greater differentiation of quaternary systems into octonary systems. To go even further, the Myers-Briggs Type Indicator (MBTI), developed by I. B. Myers in 1962 as a practical implementation of Jung's theory, is an ogdoadic system based on Jung's four types. There are four indices in the MBTI by which an individual's personality may be determined:

(i)   EI (Extraversion/Introversion: two directions of perception and judgment—either 'upon the environment' or the 'world of ideas').

(ii) SN (Sensing/Intuition: two kinds of perception).

(iii) TF (Thinking/Feeling: two kinds of judgment).

(iv) JP (Judgment/Perception: preference for either (iii) or (ii) above).

The bipolarity of each index gives a total of eight personality preferences. The attitudes and functions in (i) to (iii) above have been described in the chapter "Four (The Tetrad)," while Judgment and Perception are self-evident.

The MBTI has been widely used in the fields of organizational psychology, education, and vocational counseling, but there is some indication that it needs to be 'substantially modified', as was found by Aristide Saggino and Paul Kline in an article 'The Location of the Myers-Briggs Type Indicator in Personality Factor Space' (1996). They found the personality factors Extraversion, Tough-Mindedness, and Anxiety were generally sufficient in themselves in describing personality without the need for the MBTI. Specifically, the JP and the SN indices essentially measured the same thing (apparently Tough-Mindedness!). TF actually measured a person's anxiety, and surprisingly, it measured their level of extraversion almost as well, even though EI should isolate extraversion/introversion exclusively (EI did, however, measure extraversion/introversion, and very accurately). Finally, SN measured what appeared to be intelligence, though only to a slight degree of accuracy.

While the MBTI is regarded as 'invalid' by Saggino and Kline, being a poor substitute for Jung's typology, they do feel that it has been proved useful in various fields of psychology. The MBTI is a quaternary system that uses four bipolar indices, each of which represent an either/or choice of a particular personality function, but the attitudes extraversion and introversion are taken as functions—not Jung's original intention. Thus a total of eight predispositions are measured, of which only a few are preferred by the individual, thus forming a personality. The MBTI can also be taken as an octonary system, but the four indices that comprise the ogdoad do not seem to be accurate, although Saggino and Kline's study cannot be taken as conclusive at this early stage.

Only with further research into Jung's four functions and two attitudes, which may require refinements in the definitions of these factors, can a more accurate system be developed that truly measures the personality traits so described. Nevertheless, it may be that some of the eight components of the MBTI are redundant, so that perhaps the simplicity of Jung's original fourfold system may also be its strength.

Number Eight in Mathematics

Schimmel (1993) points out an interesting mathematical discovery made by the ancient Greeks. Any odd number above one, when squared, is a multiple of eight, plus one. For example: $9^2 = 81 = (10 \times 8) + 1$, according to the formula $u^2 = (n \times 8) + 1$, where u is the odd number above one, and n is the multiple. Also, any two odd numbers above one, when squared and subtracted from each other, show a difference divisible by eight. For example: $11^2 - 9^2 = 121 - 81 = 40$. The difference of 40 is divisible by 8. That is, $40 \div 8 = 5$.

These mathematical oddities (and other natural numbers also have their own oddities, as demonstrated in previous chapters) speak to that 'abysmal' quality in numbers that so perturbed Hermann Weyl. His misunderstanding is born of the assumption that the conscious mind invented the natural integers, leading him to believe that all there was to be known about natural numbers was only that which had been axiomatically applied to them, consciously and deliberately. The curious 'behavior' exhibited by the integers hints at that irrational "something…which we cannot grasp" (Weyl, 1949, cited in von Franz, 1980b, p. 17). Von Franz (1974) reminds us that had Weyl further "perceived that behind [the conscious mind's]…creative capacity another preconscious dynamism of the unconscious is at work, he would not have been so surprised" (pp. 29-30). Von Franz, paraphrasing Jung, suggests that the "unconscious participates in the formation of our representations of natural numbers…[so that] all statements about them become recognizable as realizations of only partial aspects of the number archetype" (p. 33).

We can see that by using number, the many geometrical forms (star patterns, polygons, etc.), structures, models, systems, and so forth, which we have 'devised', actually owe their representativeness (insofar as they are configured numerically) to the number archetype—that acausal, irrational aspect of the psyche that accounts for the numerical orderedness of these forms, structures, models, etc. This capacity of mind is seen to align with similar 'numerical' or structural facts that are perceived externally.

Number Eight in Chemistry

In the field of chemistry, we again meet the problem of seven and eight in the Periodic Table of Elements as originally schematized by Russian chemist Dmitri Mendeleyev in 1871. By arranging the elements according to their atomic numbers, Mendeleyev showed how they displayed a periodicity in their chemical properties. So certain was Mendeleyev of his discovery that gaps were left in the Periodic Table for elements which were not then known, but were expected to be discovered, and indeed were discovered later. Thus, by the turn of the twentieth century those gaps were filled, and as of 1995 some 119 elements make up the Table, including the first 92, the vast majority of which can be isolated from the earth, followed by the 'transuranic' (those after uranium) all of which are man-made, but very unstable (plutonium was the first man-made element produced in 1947).

In the Periodic Table there are eight columns known as Groups, and the elements in a specific Group have similar chemical properties (*see* Table

13). For example, in Group Eight are the noble gases, which take part in very few chemical reactions and are thereby named the inert gases. Of particular importance is the fact that not only do group elements show trends in their properties down the column (although there is a movement away from the group trend), but also the Group number itself is the same as the number of electrons in the outer layer of the element in that Group.

Table 13. *The Periodic Table of Elements showing the Eight Groups of 'Cycling' Elements.*

I	II	III	IV	V	VI	VII	VIII
1 Hydrogen							2 Helium
3 Lithium	4 Beryllium	5 Boron	6 Carbon	7 Nitrogen	8 Oxygen	9 Fluorine	10 Neon
11 Sodium	12 Magnesium	13 Aluminium	14 Silicon	15 Phosphorus	16 Sulphur	17 Chlorine	18 Argon
19 Pottasium	20 Calcium	31 Gallium	32 Germanium	33 Arsenic	34 Selenium	35 Bromine	36 Krypton
37 Rubidium	38 Strontium	49 Indium	50 Tin	51 Antinomy	52 Tellurium	53 Iodine	54 Xenon
55 Caesium	56 Barium	81 Thallium	82 Lead	83 Bismuth	84 Polonium	85 Astatine	86 Radon
87 Francium	88 Radium						

Note: The Transition Elements, 21-30, 39-48, 57-70, 71-80, 89-102, 103+, are not included in this Table, but are constituents of groups in their own right, as far as chemical properties are concerned. The periodicity of the eight groups remains consistent, although moving down the group, the specific properties of each group dissipate to some degree

The tendency in chemical reactions is for group elements to gain electrons so as to make up eight electrons in their outer shell. An atom of a Group One element with only one electron in its outer shell (a 'monovalent' element) will 'adhere' through chemical reaction to (say) an atom of a Group Seven element in order to make up eight electrons. For example, the compound sodium chloride (NaCl) has one atom each of the two elements, sodium and chlorine, making up that compound (Sodium is in Group One, and Chlorine is in Group Seven).

While carbon with four outer electrons can combine with oxygen to make (say) carbon monoxide (CO), carbon dioxide (CO_2), and even the elusive carbon trioxide (CO_3; detected in interstellar ices), bonding with four oxygen atoms is not possible because the oxygen atom is too large for the carbon atom to accommodate four of them. Nevertheless, carbon can combine with up to four hydrogen atoms, which are smaller than oxygen atoms. Methane (CH_4), for example, has a maximum of eight shared electrons.

Of particular importance is the cyclicality that is demonstrated by the elements in these eight groups of the Periodic Table—they demonstrate complete and fairly consistent sub-systems—and the step from seven to eight is also important, where mythologically, the eighth was shown to be unlike any of the seven that preceded it. Working through the Periodic Table (*see* Table 13), an alkali metal in Group One, followed by five elements to the right, leads to a halogen in Group Seven, and then a noble gas in Group Eight, after which the cycle begins again, one through eight.

There is not so much a 'problem' of seven and eight in the Periodic Table as it is a 'shift' in properties of the elements, which may be taken as somewhat of a chemical anomaly. Any one noble gas is 'unlike' the other seven elements that precede it, because it will not take part in chemical reactions (as the others do) due to its inert property. This property, however, is not absolute, since those 'inert' gases that fall below krypton inclusive in Group Eight will react with other elements such as fluorine. These rare exceptions, in a sense, 'prove the rule', since their rarity stands outside the general pattern that is observed for Group Eight elements. From this perspective, the symbolic aspect of 'the eighth' is not seriously undermined. In fact, it is interesting to note that the quality of inertness of the noble gases is like that of a quality of mind (which Jacob Boehme calls 'purity'), both of which may be equated with the virginal and immutable quality of the 'feminine' and 'receptive' element personified in the "*girl*...at the southern gate of heaven" (Jung, 1963, para. 574) of Taoist legend, as mentioned above.

now we're getting somewhere!

Number Eight in Ancient China—the *I Ching*

'Receptiveness' is the major quality associated with the *eighth* trigram in a series of eight trigrams used in the ancient Chinese mantic art of the *I Ching*. The trigrams (*pa kua*) were each given a basic characteristic such as 'The Receptive', 'The Creative', and 'The Arousing', etc., because the images associated with them were taken from the world of nature and social experience (*see* fig. 49). Therefore, natural phenomena, such as water, thunder, and earth, etc., appear in the symbolism of the trigrams.

Figure 49. *The eight trigrams (pa kua) of the I Ching.*

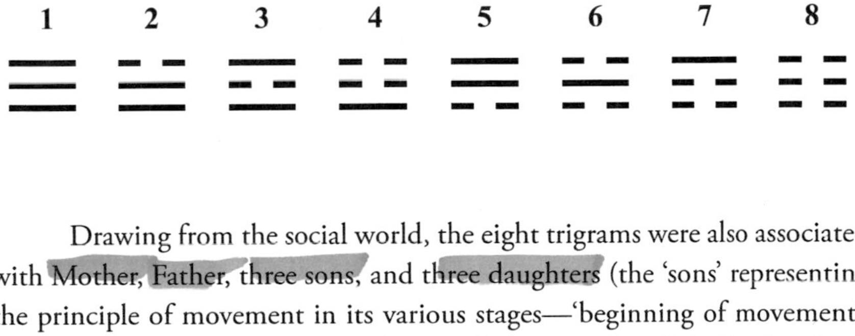

Drawing from the social world, the eight trigrams were also associated with Mother, Father, three sons, and three daughters (the 'sons' representing the principle of movement in its various stages—'beginning of movement', 'danger in movement', and 'completion of movement'—while the daughters represent devotion in its various stages—'gentle penetration', 'clarity and adaptability', and 'joyous tranquility'; *see* Table 14). The Father and Mother, of course, represent Creativity and Receptivity, respectively (*see* Table 2 in the chapter "Two (The Dyad)" for other dualistic associations with Mother and Father).

Table 14. *Meanings and Associations of the Eight Trigrams.*

Ch'ien	☰	heaven	Creative, male, active	Father
K'un	☷	earth	Receptive, female, passive	Mother
Chen	☳	thunder	Movement, perilous	1st son
K'an	☵	water	a pit, danger	2nd son
Ken	☶	mountain	Arresting, progressive	3rd son
Sun	☴	wood, wind	Gentle, penetration	1st daughter
Li	☲	fire	Brightness, beauty	2nd daughter
Tui	☱	marsh, lake	Pleased satisfaction	3rd daughter

The cardinal points of the compass and the four seasons were also collated with the eight trigrams (*see* fig. 50). The whole of existence could be determined from these eight trigrams—changes in environment (seasons), location in space (direction), the constructed social world, and the natural world—all depicted in eight fundamental trigrams formed of broken and/or unbroken lines (that is, by the application of a binary system). (See the chapter "*I Ching*" for the derivation of the eight trigrams, and the subsequent 64 hexagrams, which are used in the divinatory process of the *I Ching*.)

As a form of divination the *I Ching* with its 64 hexagrams (all the possible dual combinations of the trigrams, where one or two trigrams are at the core of each hexagram's interpretation), give a forecast of likely events or outcomes, based on past and present life situations, through a casting of yarrow sticks or three coins. The trigrams can be interpreted situationally from their literal meanings, and their environmental and human associations, while the 64 hexagrams expand the art to an extremely precise and sophisticated form of divination.

Figure 50. *The eight trigrams collated with the four seasons and the four directions.*

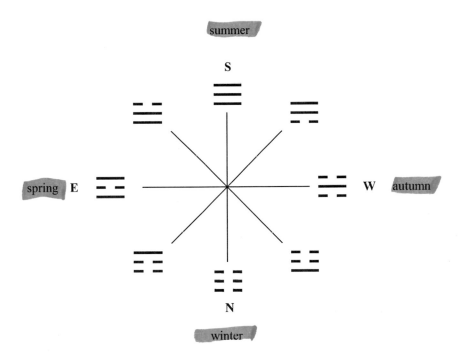

Fundamentally, one of the most precisioned and immediate of all the mantic arts, and psychologically, one of the most compelling, tracing back to over 5000 years ago to China's remote past, the eight *pa kua* of the *I Ching* represent the symbolic aspects of number eight in a number of arcane and subtle ways. In circular form, they represent completion and cyclicality (much like the Periodic Table of Elements). As an interpretive tool, they embody age-old, archetypal characteristics of human nature and life situations that mirror the nature and function of the environment, and resolve in similar ways. As a philosophical system, they represent the maturity and wisdom that only timeless empirical experience and repeated observation can provide. The *I Ching* itself as a total system embodies these 'powerful' aspects of the number eight.

Summary

The number eight carries in its symbolism and its practical reality, aspects and conditions similar to that of the number four. In many cases its symbolism can be taken as an expanded, more sophisticated form of number-four symbolism, and with that fact comes the realization that as a 'doubled-four' (2 × 4), dualistic patterns emerge in ogdoadic structures and models. These patterns demonstrate both oppositionalism and balance, but include a greater complexity of representations and ideas, yet the overall patterns remain flexible and efficient.

The end of a cycle and the beginning of another, often more sophisticated, cycle is demonstrated mythologically, physically, metaphysically, and chemically in eightfold systems, while the symmetry, solidity and stability in these physical structures and representations earns the number eight (by its associations, and from a conceptual standpoint) a degree of certainty, elegance, and aesthetic charm, which might translate symbolically as spiritual power, regeneration, and transformation.

There is always Eight (Regenerative Power), but there is no experience of the knowledge that brings wisdom, and so 'emerges' the number Nine.

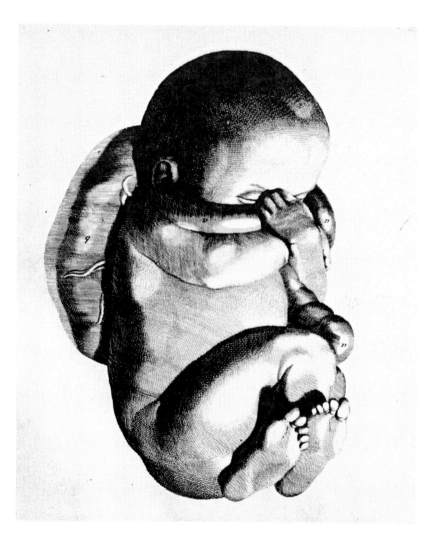

Plate 18. THE NUMBER NINE

The nine months of pregnancy form a particularly strong base for the number nine symbolism found in many cultures. Number nine represents perfection and 'final limit'. [Courtesy of the National Library of Medicine. Permission granted].

NINE (THE ENNEAD)

Thrice to thine, and thrice to mine, and thrice again, to make up nine. Peace! the charm's wound up (The Three Witches, MacBeth).

William Shakespeare

The number nine is comprised of three triads (3 + 3 + 3 or 3 × 3). Though magnified and differentiated threefold, they yield a triadic symbolism, just as the double triad in the hexad imbues number six with a dyadic symbolism. Three levels of being—corporeal, intellectual, and spiritual—are represented in the symbolism of number nine, and number nine marks the end of the single integer series before returning to unity in 10.

Number Nine—A Complete Number, but not Perfect

The number nine traditionally symbolizes completion, and to a limited degree only, perfection. In the present chapter it will be seen that many associations with perfection come from the fact that the number nine signifies the end or completion of a cycle at a metaphysical level (the level of 'spirit', psychological function, and so on), just as nine is also the last and highest single digit. However, King (1996) notes that the number nine referred to "imperfection and incompleteness" in ancient Greece (p. 75), but the number-nine cycle does not represent incompleteness according to the ancient Egyptians. Their sacred 'Ennead' (discussed shortly) was considered complete just as any other number can indicate a system or structure that is complete. The many examples in the previous chapters show that completeness is a quality of a number-structured system to the degree that it is efficacious.

On the other hand, the ancient Greeks regarded the number six as the perfect number due to its many qualities not shared by other numbers, but we have seen that movement beyond six to ever-higher numbers relegates six to a subordinate position. The number series itself, then, relativizes all numbers to a position that does not necessarily impart status to any given number in that series.

In a later chapter—"Ten (The Decad)"—the number ten will be referred to as *the* number of perfection, but only by dint of its totality (i.e., unity) and wholeness symbolism. Number nine, because it is one short of the perfection of ten, symbolises completeness *only*, but not perfection. It falls short of number ten, and it is perhaps not surprising that the prevailing traditional opinion on the number nine, and all the fadic numbers (single integers) except number one, is that it not generally be considered perfect. But, again, it would be a mistake to assume that 'imperfection' implies 'incompleteness'—the Egyptians did not make that mistake, and the preceding chapters confirm that the Egyptian viewpoint is the right one. We must recall that number symbolism itself requires constant analysis and evaluation so that a critical understanding might be reached that is both reasonable to the intellect and satisfying to the soul. Acknowledging both the 'rational' and the 'irrational' factors that may emerge in the investigation of number can help one reach this critical understanding. We can see that completion is possible in a system, but perfection need not be concomitant with it.

Geometrical Representations of Number Nine

The number nine can be represented geometrically by a nine-sided regular polygon by using three overlapping equilateral triangles, which are 40° out of phase with each other (thus forming the nonalpha). The nonagon results when the nine vertices are connected (each inside angle $\theta = 140°$) (*see* fig. 51). Inscribing the inner vertices can also form a nonagon.

Figure 51. *(a) Three equilateral triangles 40° out of phase with each other yield a nine-pointed star—the nonalpha (also known as the star of the muses); (b) The nonagon is formed by joining the nine vertices of the nonalpha, or by inscribing the inner 'virtual' nonagon.*

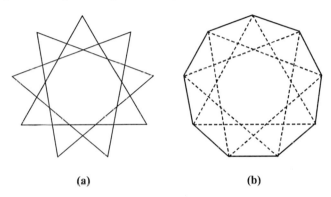

(a)   (b)

Number Nine as a Paleolithic Archetype of Order

The configuration of 3 × 3 as ⠿ is a markedly familiar representation of the number nine, and has been found as an arrangement of round cavities in the Jean Angelier cave in Noisy-sur-Ecole in France, and other sites. It was carved in the rock surface and is believed to be a way of ordering time and space. Numbers, geometrical figures, and systematic (repetitive) carvings or scratchings put order to the world and are present in all cultures, even those dating back to stone-age times. Von Franz (1974) speaks of these symbols as indicating 'ordered, rhythmical activity', and are therefore orientation models like the *Ho-t'u* linear cross and *Lo-shu* matrix described in the chapter "Five (The Pentad)."

As orientation models they work psychologically because they exhibit a structure that has inevitable effects in consciousness, given that they are nonrandom re-creations from a psyche predisposed to such activity. The energy of the psyche is more likely to be canalized in profitable ways rather than wasted through aggressive acts or psychological displacements, so that geometrical forms are bound to emerge as artworks or other such cultural products more often than random meaningless forms. In the case of number-nine symbolism (as the 3 × 3 matrix) a specific thought process and internal structure model is activated in consciousness—having produced the image, thoughts about it must follow. The result is the completed work.

The Nineties—The Decade of the Brain

Numerologically, many events that transpire in a given decade of any century are noted for their correspondences (symbolically speaking) with a particular ten-year cycle. In other words, many major events of a given decade may demonstrate symbolic associations with the number of the decade, either as a result of the suggestive effect of the number archetype, or as a peculiar form of synchronicity (see the chapter "Synchronicity.") The idea of a numerological influence on the affairs of humanity is more fully discussed in the chapter "Numerology". The evolution of consciousness proceeds hand-in-hand with the passing of the years, which are measured using numbers, and while dating systems are socio-historical constructions that have no absolute validity, the archetypal values of the numbers themselves do resonate psychologically, manifestly influencing our behavior as inspired creative acts, or even cultural contagions. Any review of historical events may indicate selection bias due to personal judgment. Some major events, such as the various wars (civil or worldwide), are ongoing across various decades so any numerological effect is understandably muted. No review can be exhaustive, so for illustrative purposes only, the table below features a schematized history of twentieth-century events that coincide numerologically with their corresponding decade names (*see* Table 15).

OPPOSITE PAGE: Table 15. *The Dominating Historical Events of the Decades of the Twentieth Century.*

DECADE NAME	NUMBER: THEME	MAJOR EVENTS
Tens	One: Unity	• Ernest Rutherford discovers the structure of an atom (unit of matter) • Roald Amundsen reaches the South Pole (world axis—unity symbol)
Twenties	Two: Discrimination	• Women granted the right to vote in USA (awareness of opposite sex) • League of Nations established (awareness of cultural rights of nations)
Thirties	Three: Expansion	• Auguste Piccard reaches stratosphere (extension of the 3rd dimension) • Prohibition ends in USA & AA founded (mind expansion through false 'spirit')
Forties	Four: Totality	• United Nations founded (birth of the political idea of a world totality) • "Big Bang" Theory formulated (conceptualization of the universe as a totality)
Fifties	Five: Corporeality	• First organ transplant (movement towards artificial prolongation of life) • DNA discovered (a deeper understanding of body function & life processes)
Sixties	Six: Harmony	• Civil Rights Act passed in USA (move towards peace between racial groups) • Peace Corps founded (the growth of an anti-war consciousness)
Seventies	Seven: Completion	• USA pulls out of Vietnam (end of war) • VCRs introduced (device that fosters a restful 'stay-at-home' attitude)
Eighties	Eight: Regeneration	• Gorbachev calls for Glasnost (openness) and Perestroika (restructuring) • Berlin Wall falls (beginning of rebirth and renewal of fundamental freedoms)
Nineties	Nine: Wisdom	• Era of the Internet; use of Internet grows exponentially (new knowledge source) • Apartheid Laws repealed (acknowledgment of human rights)

For this reason ???!
that help me

The number nine symbolizes the mental (cognitive) functions—thinking, knowing, understanding, wisdom, intelligence, etc. It is associated with the head, the mind, and the intellect (in China, number nine is associated with the hat that covers the head!). As it happens, former president of the United States George Bush, Snr. pronounced the nineties (9 × 10) the decade of the brain. As if by incantation, but more out of synchronistic compulsion, the whole world leapt out of its seventies cultural malaise (a restful 'stay-at-home' mentality) and eighties egoism ('power-seeking') into a celebration of the brain, the mind, and the intellect. It was as if a promise had been made that resonated across the globe like a cultural tidal wave. Like the thirties and the sixties—two decades of innocence and single-minded directedness, yet tainted with suffering (depression, war, etc.)—the nineties saw a harkening back to those rebellious and changeable earlier decades, but it seemed that the intellect this time had prime place in that whole iconoclastic age that was the twentieth century.

In the nineties, Richard J. Herrnstein and Charles Murray launched their controversial book *The Bell Curve* (1994)—a pessimistic look at IQ testing (specifically), and psychometric testing (generally), as well as racial differences in intelligence. They also looked at the social implications of their findings, and even gave recommendations that might rectify some of the problems they found, such as the low levels of intelligence in some populations.

By the late-nineties, Ulric Neisser, together with a number of other experts on intelligence had launched their book *The Rising Curve* (1998)—a response to *The Bell Curve*. *The Rising Curve* raised a number of issues covered in *The Bell Curve*, such as the gap in IQ of approximately 15 IQ points between African-Americans (Blacks) and Caucasian-Americans (Whites), with Whites having the higher IQ of the two populations. Since the IQ level of Blacks in the 1990s was the same for Whites in the 1940s, the gap was attributed to environmental factors (education, welfare and social conditions). In fact, current evidence shows that the gap had been shrinking since the 1940s.

The Flynn Effect (after James Flynn), which describes rises in IQ scores throughout the world of approximately 15 IQ points per generation (every

30 years) since the late-nineteenth century, is also discussed quite profusely throughout the book by a number of scholars, sometimes with animated enthusiasm. Environmental and genetic factors are given as causes for this rise. Cultural influences, education, urbanization, changes in socio-economic status, improvements in nutrition, etc., are all offered as causes for the rise in IQ. However, Flynn (1987) insisted that the rise in IQ does not mean intelligence is rising. He argued that IQ is merely a correlate that has "a weak causal link to intelligence" (p. 190). His is the view of the minority, while the majority feels that intelligence is rising. The debate continues. From the perspective of the number nine, it seems as if this numerical symbol has stirred up an interest in mental functioning of a depth not previously experienced in western society.

Body, Mind, and Spirit

Other phenomena reached their peak in the nineties, such as the fashion statements of body-piercing, ornamental scarring of the flesh, shaved heads (mainly men), and tattooing, etc. These obsessions with body image collectively represented a massive retaliation by society against the single-minded obsession with the brain and intelligence, resulting in a physical obsession with the head and body. Body-piercing in particular became a frenetic, new wave expression of the body-conscious individual that radically contrasted with revolutions in neuro-anatomy, brain physiology, and mind-focused communication and information access through the Internet. The fashionable mode of conversation became, and currently still is the 'chat-line', conducted screen-to-screen rather than face-to-face, while 'small-talk' became even smaller and more difficult in places that, ironically, were meant for social gatherings, but were instead shamanistic, dance-oriented noise-fests. The body was indeed having a revolution of its own.

This corporeal retaliation against the one-sided intellectualism of the nineties was a 'turnaround' event encapsulated in a statement made by Jung many years earlier in *Two Essays on Analytical Psychology* (1966b):

> Old Heraclitus who was indeed a very great sage, discovered the most marvelous of all psychological laws: the regulative function of opposites. He called it *enantiodromia*, a running contrariwise.... Thus the rational attitude of culture necessarily runs into its opposite, namely the irrational devastation of culture. We should never identify ourselves with reason, for man [*sic*] is not, and never will be a creature of reason alone, a fact to be noted by all pedantic culture-mongers. The irrational cannot be and must not be extirpated. (para. 111)

According to the principle of three, one would expect a *coincidentia oppositorum* ('coincidence of opposites') to have emerged during the nineties as a result of the union of the incommensurable opposites of body and mind—a necessary and inevitable spiritual counter position that would resolve the oppositionalism of that time. As it happened, the rise of spiritual (new religious) movements, cults, and sects of near epidemic proportions in the nineties were evidence of this union. There were any number of these movements, and as is so often the case, there was a 'dark' side to this counter position. Of particular impact was the Nazi nerve gas poisoning in the Tokyo subway perpetrated by the 'Aum Supreme Truth' sect led by Shoko Asahara in Japan in 1993, and two years later in 1995, the mass-immolation in Waco, Texas of David Koresh and his 90 followers. It seems that the majority of these movements end in catastrophe, partly triggered by mass psychoses and chiliastic or millenarian perturbations typical of the age.

Obsessive pseudo-religious movements of this type have always been with us, and are not exclusive to the nineties. Such examples abound throughout the late twentieth century. The murderous race war campaign propagated by Charles Manson and his 'family' in the sixties, and in the seventies, the Jonestown mass-suicide of more than 900 people instigated by Reverend Jim Jones, are exemplary cases, which set the trend for the nineties. And indeed, the nineties saw a rise in fanaticism, mass-suicide and murder, under the banner of religious freedom and liberation from the hypocrisies of this world, never before seen in the twentieth century. Cults and sects like the Order of the Solar Temple (74 suicides since 1994), Heaven's Gate (40 suicides in 1997), and the Indonesian Witch Hunters (more than 150 murders since 1998), just to name a few, sprang up all over the world. Societies of the nineties were so spiritually deprived that individuals sacrificed their independence and freewill completely to these movements, and the trend continued into the twenty-first century.

However, there were other, possibly more productive alternatives to the destructive fanaticism of these movements in keeping with a healthier spiritual alternative to the body/intellect focus of the nineties. A number of cultural phenomena emerged at that time, such as a renewed interest in parapsychology, though modified as a pop-style form (with the inappropriate inclusion of crypto-zoology, ufology, and thanatology), a new-age revival of the ancient belief in angels (complementary to the UFO-related phenomenon of extra-terrestrial visitation), and the new 'spiritual' domain of cyberspace, as a 'virtual' reality. These and any number of other similar phenomena, reached their peak of interest in the nineties and it remains to be seen which of these will be integrated into the culture of the new millennium and which will fade away as mere fads of the time.

Thus a 3 × 3 pattern—a threefold cultural triplicity—emerged and consolidated itself in the nineties, with an accompanying socio-cultural impact of far greater magnitude than was seen in any other decade. We not only had an obsession with the *corporeal* (body image, associated with the triad of matter, empirical/secular experience, and physical space), but there was also a keen interest in the *intellectual* (social and academic concern with IQ, associated with the triad of trinitarian thinking—see the chapters "Three (The Triad)" and "From Three To Four"), and a concomitant interest in the *spiritual* (contact with the deeper layers of the psyche, associated with the triad of the mythopoeic imagination, mystical/religious experience, and psychic 'space'). A 3 × 3 structure is also evident in the creation mythology of ancient Egypt reviewed next.

The Ennead in Ancient Egypt

There were four main religious centers in ancient Egypt (Heliopolis, Memphis, Thebes, and Hermopolis) from which a complete and interconnected creation myth emerged. Each center carried the myth onwards so that it developed and resolved from a first 'primal' act at Heliopolis to the final act of 'manifestation' at Thebes. Lamy (1981) describes the mythological generation, or 'creative enumeration' of the nine divine entities (attributes) of the ancient Egyptian pantheon at Heliopolis that emanated from the One—Atum. These are now described.

Heliopolis: First there is Chaos (Nun) out of which is formed Cosmos as personified by Atum, whose name means 'All and Nothing'. Atum is the Creator, 'the unique Power' or Demiurge who distinguishes himself from the Nun. The creative act is also represented by Atum in the form of a 'primordial hill' surging up from out of the cosmic waters, and one may note the similarity of this motif with that of *Genesis* 1:9-10, where the 'dry land' is formed by the 'gathering together' of the waters. Thus is born the law of opposites, and (psychologically speaking) the faculty of distinction, both of which are principles of number two.

Atum 'spits out' Shu, 'the principle of air and space', the quality of which is symbolized by a feather worn on his head. Shu is also a spiritual principle. Next Atum 'expectorates' the second Principle (of Fire), the lion-headed Tefnut, who is also the principle of concupiscence, desire and instinct. Atum creates the first triad, but this triad is not made manifest at this early stage, and exists only in a metaphysical or spiritual sense (*see* fig. 52).

Figure 52. *The Heliopolis triad.*

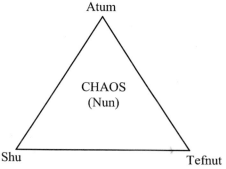

There are other versions of the creative process used by Atum. One version has it that Atum projected his own heart (the heart being the 'living' organ, symbolizing therefore the source of life) into the form of himself and his eight counterparts, Shu, Tefnut, and six other 'entities'—Geb the earth, and Nut the sky, followed by a group of four: Osiris, Isis, Seth, and Nephthys. The Unity of this 'Great Ennead' is stressed, and it is written: "none of these entities is separate from him, Atum" (Pyramid Texts, 1655).

Another version has the source of the Ennead in Atum's life essence, his 'spermatic', invisible fire, or his seed, which can be taken as symbolic of his generative power. After giving birth to himself, he then brought forth the twins Shu and Tefnut. Lamy stresses the metaphysical nature of this creative event, but she also makes an interesting association of the enneadic, spermatic process with the tail of the spermatozoon, which consists of a head with nine threads:

> It is a carrier of a centriole composed of nine (or multiples of nine) tubes, and these tubes direct the whole [creative] process of the division of the living cell, a division which is in fact a multiplication. It is the action of the sperm that causes the female ovum to contract immediately after penetration and to form an englobing membrane, thereby prohibiting the access of any other sperm. The centrosome then divides and the centrioles are carried to the two poles of the ovum. There is contact between the two pronuclei, male and female: an impalpable instant, immediately followed by the division of the cell into two new cells, which will also in turn divide. (Lamy, 1981, p. 9)

Pharaonic mathematics also describes this halving process: One transforms to Two, which transform to Four, which transforms to Eight, which becomes One (as the Ennead). Here is the 'secret' of cell division manifested as a primordial image or archetype, which took mythic form in consciousness.

Biological research in the twentieth century, along with the invention of the electron microscope, have led to the confirmation by visible evidence of the enneadic cell structure within the spermatozoon, but in ancient times this unconscious content, having irrupted into consciousness in symbolic form, was that of the creative process of life itself, not as a cell division (multiplication), but as an archetypal division into multiple (nine) forms constituting the One. Chetwynd (1982) argues the same point from a philosophical perspective, and feels that the ancient Egyptians anticipated "Platonic ideas in their conviction that the mind can penetrate beyond appearances to reality" (p. 135). Generally, ancient cultures lived closer to the unconscious than modern cultures so their cultural products were not contaminated by conscious prejudices.

Memphis: After the first stage of creation, which took place at Heliopolis, the second stage began at Memphis. Other archetypal elements come to the fore. The Memphis triad is the second triad, but is the 'first causal triad' of Ptah (primordial fire, creator of the universe), Sekhmet ('the powerful' and redoubtable lioness, wife of Ptah), and Nefertum ('accomplishment of Atum', son of Ptah and Sekhmet), and it brings about the materialization of the Ennead (*see* fig. 53).

Lamy describes this stage as 'Creation by the Word'. Divine principles and qualities now enter into "all the species of things—mineral, plant, or animal—and manifest through them" (Lamy, 1981, p. 10).

Figure 53. *The Memphis triad.*

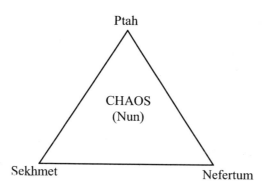

Thebes: The third triad (*see* fig. 54) is the Theban triad of Amun (the patron deity of Thebes who comes from the Ogdoad described in the next section), Mut ('mother', wife of Amun), and Khonsu (god of the Moon, son of Amun and Mut).

Figure 54. *The Theban triad.*

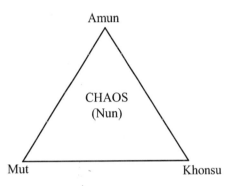

The Theban triad had consecrated to it a group of temples at Karnak called Apet-Sut, meaning 'the places of gestation'. Put more eloquently by Lamy (but rather obscurely), Apet-Sut means the 'enumerator of the places'. Gestation is identified with counting and, though a wonder to Lamy who notes also that "many features [of the Theban triad] perplex the modern scholar" (p. 11), this association should be clear. The process of cell division is a counting process involving the growth of millions of cells, which ultimately become a living form—Apet actually "designates" a pregnant hippopotamus, a most obvious symbol of gestation. It follows that this creation myth not only has literal meaning, but also is of symbolic importance. In the religious life of the ancient Egyptians the whole process of creation took place (or at least started) in the realm of the gods where the manifestation of Ra took place. He was born as the child of the lotus (Self), and was incarnated as the Pharaoh (ego).

The Theban triad points to something other than the bringing forth of that which has gestated (i.e., a flesh-and-blood child)—namely, mental process, or more specifically, the birth of consciousness. The child as archetype, as we have seen in the chapter "Four (the Tetrad)" is the newborn consciousness and promise of creative activity. This third triad is a continuation of the life process started in the Memphis triad. The human form grows and matures, and consciousness is the ultimate product of that growth process. Gestation is not merely a symbol of counting, but it stands for enumeration in its many guises (i.e., to record, to account, etc.), and is one aspect only of the function of mind. The process underlying the Theban triad is a literal and symbolic depiction of the birth of mind, intellect, and consciousness. This interpretation becomes clearer when we understand what happens in Hermopolis ("Hermes' city"), the city of the intellect.

Hermopolis: At Hermopolis—the city of Hermes, the god of writing, numbers, and the intellect—there is (perhaps not surprisingly) a twist and digression in the myth in that there is no triad. This exception means there may be a missing fourth triad, perhaps disguised as an ogdoad, since Lamy describes an ogdoad of four couples in Hermopolis. If so, the fourth is clearly not like the other three (as always), which begs Plato's question: "Where is the fourth?" because it cannot be found. But the rule tells us it must be concealed.

The ogdoad consists of four couples—serpents and frogs (i.e., archetypal contents)—distinguished in the Nun, or primordial swamp (i.e., the unconscious). The eight are:

> Naun and Naunet, meaning both 'the initial waters' and 'inertia'; Heh and Hehet, meaning 'spatial infinity'; Kek and Keket, 'the darkness'; and Amun and Amunet, "That which is hidden'. This later couple is sometimes replaced by Niau and Niaut, 'the void'. (p. 10)

The Hermopolis ogdoad can be depicted graphically (*see* fig. 55).

These eight condense into a single form, but are known as the 'fathers' and 'mothers' of Ra—not the Sun, but the solar principle (i.e., consciousness; "Ra penetrates the solar globe and causes it to shine" Lamy, p. 11). Ra is known as Atum-Ra in Heliopolis, Ra-Hor-Akhty in Memphis, and Amun-Ra in Thebes. The missing fourth triad can only be the solar principle of Ra in his three regional forms (i.e., Atum-Ra, Ra-Hor-Akhty, and Amun-Ra) and, in that sense he unites the other three cities under a single principle.

Figure 55. *The Hermopolis ogdoad comprised of four Fathers of Ra (top of diagram), and four Mothers of Ra (bottom of diagram).*

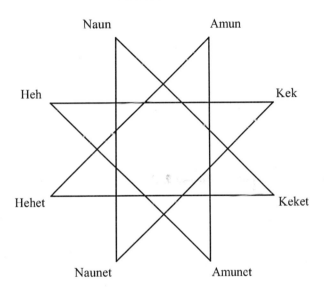

FATHERS OF RA

Naun   Amun

Heh   Kek

Hehet   Keket

Naunet   Amunet

MOTHERS OF RA

In the Egyptian myth of the Ennead is presented a 3 × 3 structure numbering nine elements in total—the threefold creative principles in each of three triads: (i) Atum-Shu-Tefnut (metaphysical, unmanifested), (ii) Ptah-Sekhmet-Nefertum (materialization of the physical), and (iii) Amun-Mut-Khonsu (the birth of consciousness). These 3 × 3 structures—the spiritual, the corporeal, the mental—describe the figure of the Ennead. In modern times we identify these three as: (i) *spiritual* (the creative process of formlessness leading to form), (ii) the *corporeal* (the life process), and (iii) the *mental* (psychological development).

The ancient Egyptians describe the formation of each of these three as a triadic process, which borrows from processes in nature. Today, we relegate these processes to genetics and learning, which in themselves are of far greater complexity than the Egyptians could have realized. However, a purely literal interpretation of the Ennead is never going to square with modern arguments from genetics and learning theory, and it would be remiss of any analysis of a myth not to speak of the symbolic factors involved as they pertain psychologically to the inner processes of the psyche and its archetypal contents. Symbolically, most of these processes have already been described, and the following section expands on those ideas.

The Psychological Ennead

Chetwynd has developed a circular rather than triadic way of representing the Ennead taken from Heliopolitan mythology. Its construction is basically psychological in nature (*see* fig. 56).

Atum is at the center (Origins), surrounded by the Eight, which came forth from Atum according to the Heliopolitan myth. Chetwynd suggests that two domains exist (conscious and unconscious), which are again subdivided making four parts with another two domains thus formed (masculine and feminine). The overall image comes to represent a model of the psyche incorporating a Jungian Self structure. Archetypally and psychologically this model is in fact a representation of the Self-as-Atum at the center, with its four functions (Osiris, Isis, Seth, and Nephthys) depicted radially.

Chetwynd's Ennead depicts "stages by which the One Power generates an indefinite variety of objects and beings" (p. 137). Insofar as Heliopolis did not have the Ptah-Sekhmet-Nefertum triad of Memphis or the Amun-Mut-Khonsu triad of Thebes, the crossover is still isometric with the Atum-Shu-Tefnut triad. These three are aligned at the center. Shu and Tefnut engender Geb and Nut, respectively, according to the Bremner-Rhind Papyrus 27 text. Geb and Nut in turn engender Osiris, Isis, Seth, and Nephthys, but "none of these entities is separate from him, Atum" (Pyramid Texts, 1655). We can only speculate as to whether Chetwynd's model has any valid psychological applications to the same degree as those Jungian variants described earlier (see "Four (The Tetrad)" and "Eight (The Ogdoad)")."

Figure 56. *The Ennead of ancient Egyptian mythology, arranged by order of birth and nature. [Source: T. Chetwynd (1982) Dictionary of Symbols].*

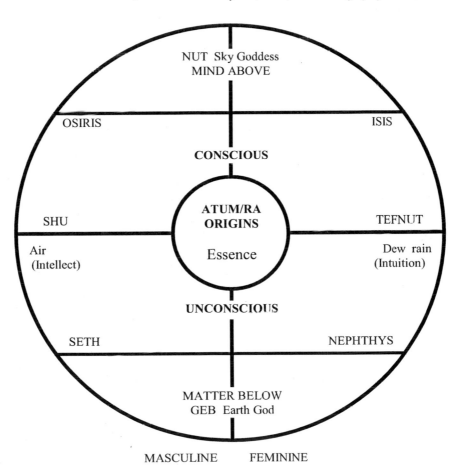

The Magic Number Nine

The ancient Hebrews saw the number nine as a symbol of truth because it 'found out' all other numbers and made them equal to nine through 'mystic addition' (that is, 'reduction'). In the same way in ancient Greece, according to Pythagoras, the number nine was said to 'limit all numbers'. Such a limitation is apparent in a certain kind of 'number magic'. Put psychologically, certain arithmetical characteristics of the number nine can be seen as pseudo-axiomatic representations of the number archetype underlying the number nine, again indicating the deeper qualities of each number which must be seen as invariable and unique, as are the quantitative aspects of each number (this fact must be considered from within the context of the base-10 counting system explained below). The following examples demonstrate these qualities of number nine:

1. The difference between two numbers, where the second is a rearrangement of the digits that comprise the first, is a number exactly divisible by nine. For example: **73,654 − 46,537 = 27,117; and 27,117 ÷ 9 = 3013.**

2. Any number multiplied by nine will 'reduce' to nine. For example: **416 × 9 = 3744.** Taking the integers in the product individually and adding them: **3 + 7 + 4 + 4 = 18**, and again, **1 + 8 = 9.**

3. Any number x, when added to nine will 'reduce' to that same number x. For example: Taking **x = 6;   6 + 9 = 15 ⇒ 1 + 5 = 6.**

4. Numbers whose digits 'reduce' to a number divisible by nine are themselves divisible by nine. For example: **6 + 5 + 7 = 18 ⇒ 1 + 8 = 9.** Therefore, **657 is divisible by 9 (657 ÷ 9 = 73)** (This property is also true of the number three. That is, a number is divisible by three if its digits reduce to a number that is also divisible by three. For the number six, the original number must be even, and then, if the digits reduce to a number divisible by six, the original number is also divisible by six. There are also divisibility rules for the digits 5 and 8.)

5. An interesting connection exists between all polygons and the number nine, through the sums of their angles, when these sums are 'reduced'. For example, the circle and the square both have 360°, and 360 'reduces' to nine, (3 + 6 + 0 = 9). The triangle has three angles totaling 180°, and 180 also 'reduces' to nine (1 + 8 + 0 = 9). This same result occurs for all the polygons since all polygons can be sub-divided into triangles, thus making their total number of degrees a multiple of 180°, which are therefore 'reducible' to nine.

Numerologist Corinne Heline makes a few points regarding the number nine that are worth mentioning here. In *Sacred Science of Numbers* (1991) she also refers to the self-reproducing, or retrograde capacity of number nine, to which the Egyptian Creation myth alludes:

> nine is the emblem of matter which, while changing and in constant flux, yet retains its identity and resists complete destruction. This is manifest in the strange phenomenon of 9 remaining 9 in its power no matter by what number it is multiplied. It eternally reproduces itself. (p. 74) *So what ? . . . . .*

The Ennead and Pharaonic mathematics demonstrate this self-regeneration.

It should be mentioned that this retrograde movement to nine is, in mathematical terms, a phenomenon entirely attributable to the base-10 system of counting. The highest single integer is 9 in the base-10 system. In (say) base-9 the highest single integer is 8 (in base-9, one represents 9 things as 10). All numbers are 'bound' (in the arithmetico-numerological sense) by the number that is one less than the number of the base used in the counting system (for example, in base-9 all numbers are 'bound' by 8). Nevertheless, the configuration of ፧ ፧ ፧ items is the same in any base, whether one counts them as 'nine' items using base-10, or counts 'ten' items using base-9, or even counts 'eleven' items using base-8, etc. The archetypal quality of 'boundedness' in the number nine (or other numbers according to the base) is still applicable because it is lawful and constellated in the functioning of the psyche as a recognizable arithmetical rule.

At this point, we must consider the difference between 'properties' of numbers and 'representations' of numbers. The property of a number, whether that number is prime, or perfect, or deficient, or whatever, is *absolute*—it remains the same in any base. However, a given representation of a number is only true in a given base, but not true in another base. The so-called 'property' of nine, given as bounding all numbers, is only a relative 'property'. Its boundedness is a decimal 'representation' as a result of the base-10 system, and is not, therefore, a property. The above rule also holds for bases greater than 10. In base-n, where n is greater than 10, the largest single digit is $n - 1$, and $n - 1$ bounds all numbers if one counts in base-n. Again, the boundedness of $n - 1$ is a representation only, and not a property of $n - 1$. Number nine, therefore, cannot bound all numbers in bases greater than 10 because it is not the largest single digit in these bases. Essentially, however, the mathematical curiosities demonstrated above do not lose their representational validity, so that the Ennead still contains nine personalities even if, for example, nine is called '10' in base-9. These personalities are immutable in their configuration and purpose.

The 'Number Nine' Body

Ancient Chinese philosophy saw the whole universe of the space-time continuum as being numerically structured or organized, and this fact was embodied in the person, since each of the human parts were given numerical significance—macrocosm and microcosm forming one universal order (*see* Table 16). This model of a numerically ordered human form compares with the 'Kundalini' body and its seven chakra (see "Seven (The Heptad)"), and the 'Kabbalistic' body comprised of ten 'sefiroth' (to be described in "Ten (The Decad)").

Neumann (1973) sees the establishment of 'body schemes' emerging as a result of projection of the image of the archetypal 'original man' onto the body as the symbol of the species *Homo sapiens* merged with the world into a oneness of being. Neumann understands these models as arising in cultures still in the "dawn world of consciousness" (p. 24) where there is no clear differentiation between the actual functions of body parts and their symbolic references to 'higher' (cognitive) functions.

Table 16. *Regions of the Human Body and Associated Numbers as Represented in Ancient China.*

#1	#2	#3	#4	#5	#6	#7	#8	#9
Foundation	Left Shoulder	Right Side	Right Shoulder	Center	Left Leg	Left Side	Right Leg	Hat

By extension, this explanation not only accounts for the fallacious association and coordination of mind qualities (emotions, cognitions) with body regions, but also with the world (for example, the 'breast' and 'heart' correspond with feeling, the 'belly' corresponds with the 'instinctual world', the 'diaphragm' corresponds with 'earth surface'). However, there can be a legitimate, literal equation of mind with body, where both do not just affect each other in a reciprocal manner, but *are* one and the same thing, arising from one and the same source: the human as a *being*. It is currently assumed that the psyche is 'situated' in the brain, but this is actually a projection. Although we cannot say for certain that the psyche is in the brain, for epistemological reasons it is difficult to say that it is not, because such a statement implies another location in the body (or outside the body!).

Earlier cultures had no problem with locating the soul in (say) the belly or heart, but there appears to be a movement upwards of the 'psychic center' (the soul) through the human body as the epistemology of a given culture changes. Hence, the chakra system posits transcendence and increased consciousness as each chakra is 'opened', from 'base' to 'crown'.

The separation of mind and body was the result of Descartes' partly canonic discourse that placed the mind (soul) under the jurisdiction of the Church (Heaven), while the body (autonomic functions, instincts, etc.) remained in the domain of the world (Earth, underworld, etc.). Such a dualistic schema has been maintained up to the current era, and while it serves a discursive purpose in certain linguistic and social contexts, it does not allow for easy recognition of the fact that the *complete* human being, holistically speaking, functions as a unitary system.

It is a mistake to assume that a 'primitive' consciousness, because it does not know any better, situates the conceptual functions of mind, emotion, spirit, etc., inside various regions of the body. These functions are, at the same time, both the discursive result of body sensations, *and* the very real influences on the mind of states in the body, in the form of experiences generated in the brain of introspective reactions, volitions, human will, and unconscious irruptions. As Neumann (1973) writes:

> Deeper-seated complexes and archetypes have their roots far down in the body's physiology and, on irrupting into consciousness, violently affect the whole of the personality, as is painfully evident in the extreme case of psychosis. (p. 288)

The holistic approach only becomes inappropriate when, as Neumann points out, separated body components, which no longer fall under the jurisdiction of the 'complete' (integrated) human being, are still considered to embody the potency, the soul, or life essence of the original whole. This notion gives rise to the superstitious belief that hair, urine, saliva, etc., maintain the essence of the original personality. Such a belief gives rise to magical interpretations and practices (involving body remnants) that have no basis in reality other than a psychological one.

In medicine, the etiology of psychosomatic illnesses has demonstrated the oneness of mind and body. The '#5' bodies (as the *Ho-t'u* linear cross, and the *Lo-shu* matrix), the '#7' Kundalini body, the '#9' body (*see* Table 16), and the #10 body (see the next chapter) suggest legitimate schematic mappings (isomorphisms) of human conscious and unconscious functions onto the body. It is not entirely wrong to say that consciousness, going 'up' or 'down' through the body, shifts to where the physiological 'action' is.

Metaphysical Representations of Number Nine

In Christian mysticism there is no parallel to the Egyptian Ennead, but there is a host of metaphysical entities that comprise the nine orders of angels, introduced by Pope Gregory in 381 AD in Homoly 34. They are Seraphim, Cherabim, Thrones, Dominions, Virtues, Powers, Principalities, Archangels, and Angels. These orders are 'celestial Hierarchies', to use Heline's (1991) term, "that form the evolutionary ladder which extends from God to man [*sic*]" (p. 75). While the contents of fantasies and other products are generally accepted phenomena, it is their source that is in dispute. Usually the tendency is to project unconscious contents into the environment (the heavens above, the forests, the earth, etc.) rather than 'own' them, hence the superstitious notions that fantastic creatures (elves, goblins, monstrous beasts, etc.) or even inanimate objects (mandala forms, wondrous cities, and possibly even flying saucers, etc.) actually do exist out there. The nine orders of angels can also be interpreted psychologically as fantasy products, which is not to say that the causal principles underlying them serve no purpose. That is, these nine orders of supernatural beings, starting with angels and elevating through the ranks to the uppermost rank of the Seraphim, represent hierarchical brain functions, or functions of the psyche, which regulate and stabilize the psychic system. The function of the order of angels, therefore, would be homeostatic. That which is claimed in religious terms to be given by the grace of God through a metaphysical ordering system, is in psychological terms, the same as that which is given by the normal functioning of the Self—that is, homeostasis as insight, inner peace, balance, etc. The same reasoning must apply to the Kabbalistic nine orders of Devils in *Sheol* (Hell), and the ancient Mexican netherworld of nine layers (each with their own devils). It would be unreasonable to assume that there were no negative 'forces' working in the psyche. The very fact of the numerous mental disorders is evidence for that, but the devils themselves are representations of dissociated mental states.

In China, the popular nine-storeyed pagoda represents levels of heaven or cosmic regions, and seventeenth-century alchemist Athanasius Kircher also envisioned a cosmic order with his hierarchy of the nine Muses in the form of the 'harmony of the spheres', ranging from heaven downwards to Earth (*see* Table 17). All of the above hierarchical taxonomies either represent 'higher' levels of consciousness, or 'deeper' levels of thought, depending on how one thinks about these things.

Table 17. *The Nine Muses and Their Rulers.*

THE MUSE	THE RULER
Urania (astronomy)	The Fixed Stars
Polyhymnia (sacred song)	Saturn
Euterpe (music)	Jupiter
Erato (love lyrics)	Mars
Melpomene (tragedy)	Sun
Terpsichore (choral song, dance)	Venus
Calliope (epic poetry)	Mercury
Clio (history)	Moon
Thalia (comedy)	Earth

Number Nine in Mythology and Folklore

Schimmel (1993) notes the absence of the number nine in any 'prominent place' in the Semitic and Judeo-Christian world, but the Indo-Germanic and central Asian cultures, as well as the more northerly civilizations, featured number nine quite frequently. The nine-storeyed pagoda in China, the ancient city of Beijing with eight streets leading to a center (nine), and the nine steps leading to the Heavenly City devised by Raymond Lully (the Christian mystic) demonstrate civic or architectural ideas that give manifestation to the principle of nine.

In India, Germany, and Iran, giants and heroes were nine cubits tall, and in many folktales they had ninefold strength, or had to perform nine major tasks. In Finland, nine was associated with illness (nine ailments as evil brothers or sisters), and in Estonian tales is featured a queen of the North and her nine bad sons. Schimmel (1993) considers that these evil countenances personify each of the "nine long dark months of the polar winter" (pp. 176-177). However, generally, each season is three months long in lower latitudes, but the dark side of nine still appears in cultures found in these latitudes (for example, as mentioned above, the nine devils of *Sheol* from the Hebrews of ancient Israel, and the nine layers of the underworld in Mexican mythology).

Number nine, as the number of completion, 'final limit', the 'end product', and even physical and intellectual 'prowess', has found symbolic or metaphoric expression in the German language. Schimmel (1993) reports such words as:

> *Neunmännerwerk*, "the work of 9 men," used for something unusually great and impressive, or *neunhändig*, "9-handed," for describing someone very skilled. Similarly, *neunäugig*, "9-eyed," means very shrewd and cunning, and a super-intelligent person is known as *neunmalklug*, "ninefold clever. (p. 175)

Number nine has a similar phenomenology to number three, having been historically related to the Trinity, but it is the Trinity in triplicate. Three 'worlds' are said to be incorporated in nine: the spiritual, the corporeal, the intellectual (this relation has already been shown in the Egyptian Ennead and the cultural disposition of societies in the nineties described above). The Anglo-Saxons used nine (as a multiple of 3 × 3) as a symbol of luck in healing and spell breaking. Presumably the charm worked at three levels, which would therefore cover all the dimensions of a person's being.

During times of hardship in Germany a fire (the *Notfeuer*) was kindled by 99 men, and the people (and even animals) under distress or endangerment had to run through the fire 3 × 3 times. This ritual enactment of a constructed danger, and the subsequent conquest of the ordeal, stood as a symbolic act of completion, so that an image of that completion could in some 'magic' way (e.g., through suggestion, hypnotic effect, etc.) work towards a resolution of the real distress or danger.

Number Nine—A Symbol of Birth

The 3 × 3 symbolism recalls the three trimesters of pregnancy, the end of each three-month period signaling a specific stage reached and the onset of a stage uniquely different from the previous one. By the end of the first trimester (after fertilization of the ovum, formation of the blastocyst, and beginning of the embryo stage), the second trimester begins, signaled by the pumping heart and bodily movements of the fetus, even though undetected by the mother at this early stage.

At the end of the second trimester the fetus has normal skin color and becomes viable, in that it can survive outside the mother with little risk to its life if it is born prematurely. This period is during the seventh month. The last two months are a growth stage, but normally the baby is only ready for birth after nine months. The centriole of nine tubes in the sperm, which directs the cell division process of the ovum, and the subsequent nine months of pregnancy, form particularly strong bases for the symbolism embodied in many of the cultural products mentioned above.

Summary

Like the mathematical anomalies pertaining to the number nine, where the arithmetical rule finds that other numbers are 'bound' or 'limited' by number nine, it is verified that a limiting capacity is phenomenal to the number nine archetype, which not only guides the act to completion, but confirms it as absolute in the form of a claim to knowledge and wisdom, even though, like 'boundedness', the claim is actually a 'representation' of reality.

Each time a mythological or symbolic cycle of nine is depicted in a culture we can surmise that at the root of this symbolism is, *at the very least*, a kind of sympathetic magic or 'enchantment'. Put psychologically, a ritualized 'completion process' in nine stages is enacted symbolically so that the processes that govern the real-world cycle from beginning to end may take place with the aid of a fully cooperating psyche-as-will acting on the program or enterprise about to be undertaken. Thus the psyche itself is already attuned to the 'pattern' of the desired outcome. *More than this*, the number nine archetype is inherently at play in these circumstances, in which the behaviors of an individual or a society are given specific focus by the archetype of nine.

Unlike any other number, because the number nine can take the form of 3 × 3 stages, the behavior will be canalized and coordinated by a 3 × 3 groundplan or matrix in the psyche, so that the behavior may take the form of three equally portioned sub-divisions, where each sub-division itself embodies the dynamism of three. The dynamism of the archetype is unmistakable, like the human birth cycle, both of which mirror each other. Nature takes its course, growth and development are unhaltering and consistent—the birth cycle is a model of progress *par excellence*, underscored by the number nine archetype that directs human behavior in characteristic fashion.

In metaphysical terms, there is no end to the cycle of nine, which gives a paradoxical twist to number-nine symbolism when compared to physical (for example, biological) systems that do come to an end. This cyclical factor arose in the mythologies because the archetypal structure of the psyche is constantly at work, governing the ongoing processes of mental and cognitive development and learning, which underpin all behavior.

There is always Nine (Wisdom), but all previous experiences must unite in the final experience of a return to unity, and so 'emerges' the number Ten.

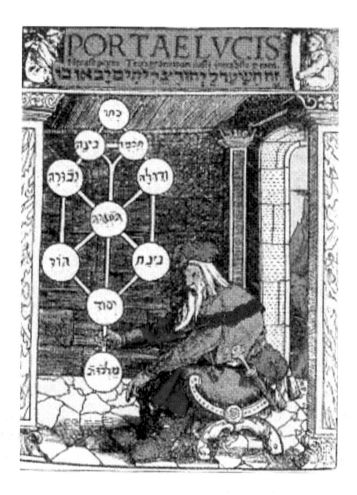

Plate 19. THE NUMBER TEN

In the mystical Hebrew tradition of the Kabbalah, the so-called Sefirotic Tree—the Tree of Life—represents the psychological structure of the total personality. It is comprised of ten emanations (sefiroth), each acting as a conduit that channels 'Divine' power to transform the individual, thus symbolizing unity at a higher level [SOURCE: Wikimedia Commons].

TEN (THE DECAD)

The number ten is an all-embracing number; outside of it none other exists, for what is beyond ten returns again to unity.

The Kabbalah

Although the number nine represents a completed metaphysical cycle concurrent with completed mental and physical cycles, the cycle of nine can be seen as 'ending' and 'beginning' again at a higher level with the number ten. That is: 9 + 1 = 1 magnified tenfold. Ten 'raises' all things to unity.

Number Ten as Perfection

The Pythagoreans viewed the number ten as having similar qualities as number one, and thus associated it with Heaven, the Sun, the Deity, and even Eternity. Number ten was thereby associated with the monad and its phenomenology and symbolism. According to Schimmel (1993), the number ten was also regarded as the "all-embracing, all-limiting 'mother'" (p. 180). Like the number one, the number ten was traditionally seen as a perfect number because it is symbolic of wholeness or the completed work. Like a cyclical process, akin to the *Uroboros* (the tail-eating serpent), the numbers advance, one through nine, so that the cycle ends where it began at a higher stage of unity. The continual cycle can best be expressed as a helix constantly moving through the same stages, with each 'ending' being simultaneously a 'beginning', at newer and increasingly higher levels.

Pythagoras and the *Tetractys*

Pythagoras considered that there were ten fundamental opposites, which formed the foundation of the world by their union and consequent harmony (*see* Table 18). It is clear, by the arbitrary nature of these opposites, that Pythagoras probably selected ten pairs and only ten pairs purely to venerate the number ten, since it is unlikely that he believed there could not be other pairs (such as up and down, life and death, etc.). As mentioned previously, it takes a good degree of discernment to argue the case persuasively for the qualitative aspects of numbers. Without discrimination, the evidence will either be compelling or unconvincing for no reason other than chance.

Table 18. *Pythagoras' Ten Fundamental Opposites.*

1	2	3	4	5	6	7	8	9	10
Odd	male	good	Wet	right	rest	hot	light	straight	Limited
Even	female	evil	Dry	left	motion	cold	dark	curved	Unlimited

Nevertheless, the Pythagoreans were enchanted by some numerological configurations, and with probable good cause. They derived the number ten from the sum of the first four digits: $1 + 2 + 3 + 4 = 10$, thus forming the Pythagorean *tetractys*. The *tetractys* was at the core of Pythagorean wisdom, and it could be represented as pebbles in the form of a perfect (equilateral) triangle (*see* fig. 57).

The *tetractys* was a sacred symbol and was held in the highest regard by the Pythagoreans. Its simple form is deceptively cryptic and only the initiated were allowed into a full knowledge of its deeper meaning. As will be seen in subsequent sections, the *tetractys* has appeared in many different forms in many different cultures down through the millennia. These variations around the *tetractys* theme are discussed next.

Figure 57. *The Pythagorean tetractys*

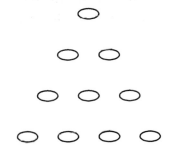

The Axiom of Mary

In medieval alchemy and hermetic philosophy the *Axioma Mariae* (Axiom of Mary), like the *tetractys*, "consists of 4, 3, 2, 1; the sum of these numbers is 10, which stands for unity on a higher level" (Jung, 1966a, para. 525), symbolizing the transformation process (psychological and physical renewal and general development of the human being). This process symbolizes the psychological realization of the goal of making the philosophical 'gold', not to be confused with common gold. This gold is a solar substance, and upon psychological reflection, represents the purest and most radiant form of consciousness imaginable. Since the number ten was associated with the Sun and gold, it also symbolized the solar principle of consciousness, as did the number one (the Monad)—a kind of re-stating of the 10 ≡ 1 conception, where ten 'raises' all things to unity.

In the hermetic philosopher's unscientific, but highly imaginative terminology, ultimate or absolute consciousness—also endowed with an incorruptible and immutable quality, and therefore, also known as the philosopher's stone (*lapis philosophorum*)—was definable by analogy, but only grasped intuitively as a psychological goal. Although taken as symbols, the 'gold' and the 'stone' were barely understood as symbolizing nascent qualities within themselves. The accompanying psychological changes in an individual of increased consciousness necessarily include enhanced wisdom, greater self-knowledge, psychic stability and wholeness, and a balanced outlook and sense of inner peace. To this end the hermetic philosophers saw the need to further the Christian archetype by including:

(i)   the dark side of the feminine (the ignored 'shadow' of the idealized Virgin Mary).

(ii)   matter in the scheme of things (not as the realm of evil).

(iii) the law of psychic opposites in Christ, and in God, and in the 'masculine'/'feminine' dynamic.

The philosophers argued that Christianity could also be expanded by personal inquiry, not just by faith alone.

The *tetractys*, then, is an ancient schema or model underlying a newfound procedure for this expansion. Jung (1966a) describes the 'fourfold nature' of the transformation process:

> It begins with the four separate elements, the state of chaos, and ascends by degrees to the three manifestations of Mercurius in the inorganic, organic, and spiritual worlds; and, after attaining the form of Sol and Luna [psychic opposites symbolised by personified 'masculine' and 'feminine' qualities],...culminates in the one and indivisible...nature of the...*lapis philosophorum*. (para. 404)

The *lapis* is analogous to the Monad and Jung (1963) emphasizes this point:

> The "four" are the four elements and the monad is the original unity which reappears in the "denarius" (the number 10), the goal of the opus; it is the unity of the person projected into the stone. (para. 294)

Jung notes the significance of the denarius as the Son of God, as many of the alchemists believed it to represent, while Dorn, who is remembered for his dislike of the binarius, held the denarius in a more favorable light.

Dorn equated the denarius with the philosophical Salt (Wisdom), and the *filius philosophorum* (the philosophical 'son'), and, therefore, he recognized the secret of the denarius as the Christ-figure, the culmination of the work. Note that the Christ-figure also compares with the *Anthropos* described in the chapters "One (The Monad)" and "Five (The Pentad)."

The Four Levels of the *Axioma*

Although the hermetic philosophers would not have seen the *Axioma Mariae* in the following way (that is, as a psychological process), the procedure outlined below describes in modern psychological terminology the same process removed from its symbolic context. This interpretation is essentially Jungian, and it stems from the western esoteric tradition. The four levels (4 + 3 + 2 + 1 = 10) describe the individual in his/her entirety—consciously (in 'four'), physiologically (in 'three'), psychologically (in 'two'), and individually (in 'one'). Each level is not only independent of the other levels, but each may also function and develop concomitantly with each of the other levels, with each either ameliorating or retarding the functioning of the other levels. The procedure begins in the fourfold state of fragmentation and moves towards wholeness in unity:

Level Four: The four elements of Earth, Air, Fire and Water are in chaos and constantly seeking balance. The four elements correspond to the psychological functions of Jung's typology: Sensation, Thinking, Feeling and Intuition (see the chapter "Four (The Tetrad)"). Jung (1977) describes these four functions:

> Sensation tells you that there *is* something. Thinking tells you *what* it is. Feeling tells you whether it is agreeable or not, to be accepted or rejected. And intuition...is a perception by intermediate links...via the unconscious. (pp. 306-307)

The functions are orientations consciously deployed by the ego, and each is compensated by an unconscious counter-position to the one adopted by the ego at any given time. Conscious life favors the development of usually one of these functions, which leaves the other three functions less differentiated. The task is to devote time to the development of these neglected functions in order to yield a more well-rounded personality. To the degree that these functions are undifferentiated, they behave with characteristic inferiority, manifesting as lack of aplomb or inappropriate behavior. Often, though, the inferior function will have an instinctual or natural quality that is marked by forthright but apt observation, quaint but relevant insight, and a pragmatism belying, or not ordinarily determined by, the usual conscious outlook.

Level Three: For the nature philosophers, Mercurius (equated with the illusive Hermes, god of revelation, transformation and transition) became the appropriate personification of this next stage by being associated with the threefold form of the 'tree of life' of *Genesis* 2:9, and the Trinity of Christian dogma. This led to the manifestation of Mercurius as a trinity: *mineralis* (mineral), *vegetabilis* (living), and *animalis* (animated with a soul).

Mercurius is also the personification of unconscious wisdom, or more specifically, the mediator of consciousness with the unconscious through wisdom personified. The ego, in its relative position to the Self, gains wisdom of the totality of the Self through personifications of unconscious factors and states as they are communicated symbolically to the ego. Of a polymorphous nature, in this case, Mercurius exists as a trinity (*triplex nomine*) because he depicts the three 'unseen' mercurial and largely unconscious processes that take place in the body of the human being. These three are:

(i)   The body is inorganic (material—comprised of elements, compounds and molecules constantly being dissolved and utilized to sustain the system—hence, *mineralis*)

(ii)   the body is organic (comprised of fluids, blood, lymph and hormones, and so on, flowing throughout the body's coronary vascular, lymph and endocrine systems, etc.—hence, *vegetabilis*)

(iii) the body is animated (possessed of a 'soul', not only living as a tree or a beast, but having autonomy and will—hence, *animalis*).

These three aspects depict or describe the totality of the human being, and are intimately linked and therefore 'involve' each other in the process of seeking equilibrium.

Level Two: The two opposites in conjunction—*coniunctio Solis et Lunae* (Sun and Moon conjunction)—personify the second stage. The Sun and Moon represent consciousness and the unconscious, respectively. This stage of conjunction involves assimilation and integration of those opposites that may cause an imbalance in the functioning of the entire physical and psychological structure.

Paradoxically, Mercurius by its ambiguous nature also consists of "all conceivable opposites" (Jung, 1968a, para. 284). Mercurius is both material and spiritual:

> He is the process by which the lower and material is transformed into the higher and spiritual, and vice versa...[and] he is the devil, a redeeming psychopomp, an evasive trickster, and God's reflection in physical nature. (para. 284)

The implications of this second, dualistic stage are brought to bear when, as is always the case with choices, the individual is beset with the unknown consequences of his or her actions. Jung (1968a) warns:

> Mercurius, that two-faced god, comes as the *lumen naturae* [light of nature]...only to those whose reason strives towards the higher light.... For those who are unmindful of this light, the *lumen naturae* turns into a perilous *ignis fatuus* [fire of fate]. (para. 303)

One is reminded of this dichotomy in the chapter "Five (The Pentad)," in regard to a brand of materialism peculiar to the United States (now well propagated throughout the world) that has come about as a consequence of a consciousness dimmed by an overwhelming lack of reason disguised as rational-mindedness. This psychological *faux pas*, dating back to the Age of Reason, has culminated in a systematic devaluation of the aesthetic, the emotional, and the natural. These are the qualities that lie at the very core of a happiness so relentlessly pursued by so many, yet as elusive as 'that two-faced god' himself.

Level One: Finally, the immortal *lapis philosophorum*, the philosopher's stone, follows. This is a symbol of the higher Self, the psychic totality, fully realized and conscious. It is the highly prized goal because of the indescribable feeling of oneness and unity felt upon its attainment. Completion of the procedure would not only embody wholeness in the individual personally, but would evoke a sense of union with all things—being at one with, and in the universe (the alchemical *unus mundus*). Edinger (1995) reminds us that the *unus mundus*:

> represents a union of the ego with the Self and with the world…. At this level, time and eternity are united…. [It] is perfectly evident that this is a borderline state that one can only glimpse from afar; once you are totally in it you are out of the ego world as we know it. (p. 281)

This psychological interpretation of the *Axioma* makes sense of the symbolism that underscores the *tetractys*. The alchemists cum philosophers took the symbolism literally (the four elements, Mercurius, *Sol* and *Luna*, and so on) because they were reacting to the imagery of fantasy products and dreams from the unconscious and interpreting them as external entities or experiences in some other world. Whether we regard this approach as naïve or not, the unconscious products were nevertheless given the respect that is their due. Having taken them literally, the philosophers then took them seriously, and therefore responded to them in productive ways. As a system of self-development, then, the *Axioma*, insofar as it was taken seriously, was the best means possible by which the philosopher, given the nature of his or her experience, could grapple with the irrational, the mystical, and the unknown, that is the unconscious.

Alternative Structures of the *Tetractys*

Edinger also sees the possibility of a psychological interpretation of the *tetractys*—specifically a psychological development much like that just described using Jungian and alchemical terminology. Edinger's version of the *Axioma* moves in the following way:

$$ONE \Rightarrow TWO \Rightarrow THREE \Rightarrow FOUR, \text{ and then, } FOUR \Rightarrow THREE \Rightarrow$$
$$TWO \Rightarrow ONE$$

The process starts at STAGE 1, on the top left of Figure 58. The original wholeness is represented by the 'pebble' at the peak of the *tetractys*. The "original Self divides into two [step a], corresponding to the theme of the separation of the World Parents" (Edinger, 1995, p. 279; see the chapter "Two (The Dyad)," particularly Figure 11).

Figure 58. *"The process of psychological development" [Source: E. Edinger (1995) The Mysterium Lectures (p. 279)].*

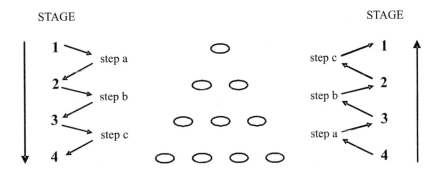

At STAGE 2 the ego develops, since the ego can distinguish itself from the world—it is separate from the world, and increased consciousness becomes an issue of great importance.

Step b is full separation from the Mother (Nature), leading to "autonomous, independent thinking" (p. 280) at STAGE 3.

Separation from the Father (Spirit) must also take place (step c), and STAGE 4 is characteristic of "a state where original unity has been differentiated into fourfold multiplicity and the individual is living fully in the world" (p. 280).

The halfway point is reached, having 'descended' into the world, but problems begin to arise. Jung (1963) describes this condition as one of fragmentation:

> the four elements represent...dissolution into the constituents of the world.... Conversely, the combination of the elements...is an achievement of the art and a product of conscious endeavour. The result of the synthesis was consequently conceived by the adept as self-knowledge. (para. 657)

Therefore, the process must continue, this time as an 'ascension', beginning at STAGE 4 (on the right side of Figure 58). According to Edinger, a "reductive analysis" (p. 280) of the shadow qualities must be undertaken—there is a separation of the ego from the unconscious (particularly from its unconsciousness, which involves a "critical attitude toward affects and desirousness," p. 281, and other negative qualities). Step a symbolizes this process as a conjunction of soul and spirit.

Success at this stage moves the individual to STAGE 3, where a *unio mentalis* ('mental union') takes place—the "world and body get separated off; body, soul and spirit remain a unity" (p. 282).

STAGE 2 marks the union of the soul and spirit with the body, which takes place at step b. The ego has accepted its condition through personal insight, but is able to apply these insights in a real sense, by giving corporeality to them. In other words, the insights do not just exist as mental states, but have applications in real world situations.

After step c, where the body-soul-spirit has merged with the world, a "universal unity prevails" (p. 281) at STAGE 1. The individual lives in the *unus mundus* ('one world'), where the ego has merged with the Self and the world, but as Edinger says:

> the creation or realization of the unus mundus—is a transcendent, symbolic condition that defies any comprehensive or adequate description. It refers to a superlative experience of unity in which subject and object, inner and outer, are transcended in the experience of a unitary reality beyond our grasp. (p. 296)

These two models (Jung's and Edinger's) refer to the same general process—the initial state of unity goes through a process of fragmentation, but returns to unity after integration of the 'multiplicities' of experience in the world and in the psyche.

The *Axioma* and the DNA Chain

As a point of interest, the *Axioma* configuration is found in the DNA molecular chain (see the chapter "Four (The Tetrad)"). In the same way that the *Axioma* runs a sequence four to three to two to one, the DNA chain—the coded molecule in the cell chromosome that contains and transmits genetic information (the secret of life)—also runs four to three to two to one:

(4) The four nitrogenous bases: adenine, cytosine, guanine and thymine.

(3) The triplets, consisting of three of the available four bases, making one of twenty different amino acids, which form the proteins.

(2) The double helix structure, which frames the chain of bases.

(1) The molecule itself as a unity—a total system of self contained determinants that dictate at the molecular level the generation of all living organisms.

Is the numerical similarity of these two structures, which are greatly separated temporally and conceptually, the result of mere coincidence?

The *Axioma* emerged some 400 years ago as a completely intuitive proto-science (though it may have its origins in ancient Greece as the *tetractys*). Although there would be no convincing scientific basis for the *Axioma*— though arguably the psychology for it is sound—we are on safer ground with the biological evidence for the DNA molecule as being structured numerically on a 4-3-2-1 pattern. But both appear to depend on archetypal structural rules delimited by the number archetype. From the perspective of depth psychology, the *Axioma* can be taken as a 'projection' of archetypal unconscious knowledge (in the form of a psychic image) due to the lack of evidence to the contrary. The unconscious material, experienced symbolically and taken literally, was not tainted by the 'inadequate' interpretive methods of the nature philosophers so it existed in pure archetypal form and remained as a psychological truth. Hence the *Axioma*, while shrouded in symbolism and analogy, has an empirically valid, psychological basis to its structure (the archetypal image). But not only is this true of the *Axioma*, it is also true of the other similar forms that we can identify. These images, being archetypal in nature, are consistent in form, lending pattern and structure to our world of ideas and knowledge claims. Like the *Axioma*, the DNA chain can also be identified or *aligned* with wholeness (unity) in the form of the *tetractys*: it is a totality symbol that unites its composite elements into one singular form.

Commenting on the four bases of the DNA chain, von Franz (1974) points out that 64 different triplets are possible (i.e., $4^3 = 4 \times 4 \times 4$), and she compares this numerical coincidence with the 64 hexagrams of the *I Ching*. An exchange of genetic 'information' to the ribosomes of the cells occurs through the messenger RNA (ribonucleic acid), which also uses triplets. Just as genetic codes are constituted in matter by the complex molecular patterns of the DNA and RNA chains, the *I Ching* is a mantic system that reveals previously unconscious information based on a double constellation of triple lines: "numerical combinations [which] are introspective representations of fundamental processes in our psychophysical nature" (von Franz, 1974, p. 105).

These two 'systems' (DNA/RNA and *I Ching*) complement each other because DNA and RNA can be seen as information systems that provide a mechanism, but not a causal explanation for life having a multiplicity of forms. Random and nonrandom selection is the evolutionist's explanation for bio-diversity. The *I Ching*, also an information system, shows acausal correspondences, but not the mechanism that might give reasons as to why life processes and events show particular qualities that are reflected as analogies in nature and are discernable as possibilities at a given time moment. The Eastern philosopher considers the mechanism for correspondences in nature to be due to human consciousness. Both systems rely on the ordering principles of number to make possible their functioning.

Von Franz comments on the regulative function of number as it appears in DNA, RNA and the *I Ching*:

> This astonishing correspondence seems, more than any other evidence, to substantiate Jung's hypothesis that number regulates both psyche and matter. The same numerical model, a pattern underlying the basic processes of human memory and transmission (and thereby also the substratum of our entire conscious processes), has been discovered, first in China through an introspective examination of the unconscious psyche, and then in the West through genetic research into the living cell. (p. 106)

Again, it appears that an archetypal substructure must exist in the human psyche that 'allows' the possibility of identifying the equivalences that exist between these three phenomena, the *Axioma Mariae*, the DNA/RNA chains, and the *I Ching*.

The *Tetractys* in the Kabbalah

While the *tetractys* can be used as a model or schematic for psychological development, the Sefirotic Tree described in the mystical Hebrew tradition of the *Kabbalah* is a model of the psychological structure (as components) of the 'total personality'—the *psyche*—or more traditionally, *Adam Kadmon*. Edinger notes the similarity between the *tetractys* and the Sefirotic Tree and believes that the sequence—4-3-2-1 or 1-2-3-4—is the same (*see* fig. 59).

Figure 59. *The tetractys and the Sefirotic Tree showing the same sequence: 1-2-3-4. [Source: E. Edinger (1995) The Mysterium Lectures (p. 282)].*

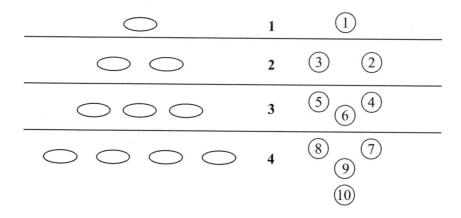

The idea of a tree as a model for human psychological processes and development must be seen as a projection of a psychological fact. As a metaphor, the tree represents inner (psychological) processes. The psyche starts as a seed in the unborn infant, it breaks through the 'earth' into 'daylight', the 'Sun' has its 'solar' influence, as does the 'water', the 'atmosphere', and the nutrients of the 'earth'. Left unimpeded, growth continues until maturity, but development never ceases as long as life itself continues. But the tree is also symbolic and extends beyond metaphor. The human psyche is effectively a tree in its functioning at every level of 'treeness'. Ultimately, as far as inner images are concerned, the psyche uses the tree to express deeper meanings that are not accommodated by any metaphor. Eventually the metaphor of a tree becomes exhausted of meaning, whereas the psyche ultimately extends beyond the known into the very depths of the unconscious itself.

The Sefirotic Tree has ten emanations or *sefiroth* (Hebrew: *sephirah* = 'number'), which are the ten aspects of the Godhead (*see* fig. 60). The ten *sefiroth* are *Kether* ('Crown'), *Hochmah* ('Wisdom'), *Binah* ('Understanding'), *Hesod* ('Love'), *Geburah* ('Power'), *Tifereth* ('Beauty'), *Netsach* ('Victory'), *Hod* ('Glory'), *Yesod* ('Foundation'), and *Malchuth* ('Kingdom'). Since moral and ethical values are assigned to the *sefiroth*—qualities "peculiar to the human condition" (Poncé, 1973, p. 100)—Charles Poncé, in *Kabbalah* (1973), also considers the *sefiroth* from a theoretical standpoint. Their symbolic nature is also emphasized, since they refer to the "transcendent realm" (p. 93), which may be interpreted as the psyche and its processes (particularly those of the unconscious).

Figure 60. *The sefirotic tree showing the ten sefiroth (Emanations of the En-Sof).*

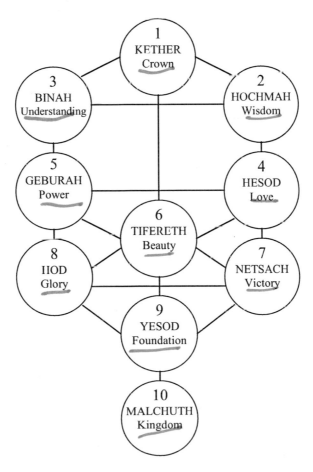

The *sefiroth* are represented collectively as an upside-down tree with its roots in Heaven, and its branches in the Earth. In that regard the *Anthropos* is likened to a tree in other discourses as well, such as that of the alchemists who wrote of the Philosophical Tree, and the Hindus, who wrote of the 'cosmic tree', both of which, like the alchemical tree, have roots growing upwards and branches growing downwards. One may also recall the tree of the knowledge of good and evil in *Genesis*, since it too embodies psychological principles such as the 'opposites'.

Central to the *sefiroth* is the source of the *sefiroth* themselves, the *En-Sof* (Hebrew: *Ayn* = 'without'; *Soph* = 'end', 'infinity'), which is the life essence, the 'being' in the *sefiroth*. The *En-Sof* is beyond existence ('beyond comprehension' and 'beyond classification') and only exists in the sense that it causes the *sefiroth* to function (they are the 'expressions' of the *En-Sof*), but beyond that it cannot be determined in what sense *En-Sof* exists.

Poncé describes the *En-Sof* as the force in the 'sap' that gives the Tree its life and existence. It is not difficult to see the *En-Sof* as paralleling the Holy Spirit in Christianity. It too is inconceivable in form and presence (usually represented as a dove), but mediates between Father and Son. Jung draws parallels between the Holy Spirit, the alchemical Mercurius and the processes of the unconscious—the enacting principle that enables communication between the unconscious and consciousness.

Poncé (1973) also sees the psychological aspects of the *sefiroth*.

> The Kabbalistic view that the manifestation and emanation of Godhead moves from an initial state of nothingness through *Kether* to the final state of *Malkuth*, the *sefirah* symbolic of the created world, is fundamentally a psychological statement about the development of consciousness or ego from whatever stands before the *psyche*—the Self, the *Atman*, the *En-Sof* or the divine prime mover under any other appellation. (p. 132)

The *sefiroth*, then, are emanations of the *En-Sof*, and they have 'luminescence'. Since they bring forth light, and they illuminate, the *sefiroth* can be seen as archetypes that are capable of coming into consciousness. Poncé explains that each *sefirah* acts as a conduit, channeling the divine power of the *En-Sof* and transforming it according to the particular quality of each *sefirah* (*see* Table 19). The *sefiroth* constitute the totality of the *En-Sof* that emanates, rather than creates itself manifestly through the *sefiroth*.

Table 19. *The Ten Sefiroth and their Meanings.*

SEFIRAH	DESCRIPTION
Kether—The Crown	"The Crown of Knowledge"
Hochmah—Wisdom	"The Wisdom of the Knower"
Binah—Understanding	"The Supernal Mother" who bears Wisdom
Hesod—Mercy or Love	"The productive and life-giving power"
Geburah—Judgment or Power	"The power of God, Justice and Control"
Tifereth—Beauty	"Mediates between Mercy and Judgment"
Netsach—Victory or Endurance	"Endurance of the Sun and Moon"
Hod—Majesty or Glory	"Glory of God in His creation"
Yesod—Foundation	"The sexual organ of the Divine Hermaphrodite"
Malchuth—Kingdom	"The exiled feminine"

The Kabbalists were quick to defend the tenfold multiplicity of the Godhead and stressed that it did not undermine Judaism's monotheistic practices. The ten *sefiroth* are manifestations of the divine unity—they are not gods. Von Franz (1974) also notes the unitary aspect of the *sefiroth*:

It is common knowledge that in the cabala the ten primal numbers, the *sephiroth*, are considered to be emanations of divine immaterial origin in the sense that the "original one" remains far removed from all things and only manifests its various aspects in each single *sephira*.... They are "spheres" and "totalities" of the unknowable primal one. (p. 83n)

Though little is known about the practical approach taken in the contemplation of the Sefirotic Tree, Zwi Werblowsky's essay 'Jewish Mysticism' in *The Jewish World* (1986) says this about the Kabbalists:

[After hours of intense meditation] they would imagine the light of the Divine Presence above their heads as though it was flowing all around them and they were in the midst of this light...and whilst in that [state of meditation] they were all trembling as a natural effect [spiritually] rejoicing in trembling, as it is written [Ps. 11:11], 'Serve the Lord with fear, and rejoice with trembling'. (p. 221)

Relationships between certain *sefiroth* suggest the archetypal substructure of the personality (the total psyche). The sixth and tenth *sefiroth* (*Tifereth* and *Malchuth*), for example, were most important to the Kabbalists. *Tifereth* is a masculine figure associated with Sun, King, and Bridegroom, while *Malchuth* is a feminine figure associated with Moon, Queen, and Bride. Their relationship is described by Werblowsky as a "holy union, *hieros gamos* [marriage], between two aspects of the Divine, the essence of the unity of God" (p. 222). Jung connects this *coniunctio* symbolism with the psychological process of realization of the *anima* in consciousness (this process is the same process described as *Level Two* of the *Axioma Mariae* above—the *coniunctio Solis et Lunae*). Contemplation (similar to the alchemistic *contemplatio* or *meditatio*) of all these relationships is the key to the understanding of 'Man', the Godhead, and the ultimate experience of the *En-Sof*.

The *Tetractys* in Physics

Just as all the above models as they appear in religion, alchemy, biology, and psychology, are typified by the one underlying principle of the *tetractys* form, it is also found that the schema describes a regular pattern inherent in certain subatomic particles as discovered in modern physics, which shows that the *tetractys* has value at levels other than biological, psychological, and metaphysical.

In the 1930s there were three kinds of subatomic particles—electrons, protons, and neutrons. These were considered the fundamental building blocks of all matter. By the 1960s there were vastly more than three particles, mostly found through experimentation with particle accelerators, and from the analysis of cosmic rays. Like the basic three, they had their own unique qualities—electric charge, spin, lifetime, etc. Many were related to the proton, but were often much heavier in mass due to higher levels of energy, which when released would reduce them to protons. It followed that something else made up the proton. The proton was not a fundamental irreducible particle.

In the 1960s, physicist Murray Gell-Mann postulated the existence of even smaller particles (quarks) that made up these heavier particles. He also observed the phenomenon that some particles could live longer than others, and he called this quality 'strangeness'. Quarks were real according to Gell-Mann, and the 'strange' quark was eventually accepted in the 1960s, at which time two new quarks joined the family. They were given the names 'up' and 'down', and these two, plus the strange quark, were necessary postulates so that combinations of the three could make all the protons and all the relatives of protons.

Relatives of the proton—those protons with very great mass energy (called 'souped-up' protons)—are of particular relevance to the symbolism of number ten because their degrees of strangeness, upness, and downness can be schematized as a *tetractys* (*see* fig. 61).

As Calder makes clear in *The Key to the Universe* (1977):

> 'Upness', 'downness', and 'strangeness' all represented real and distinguishable qualities of matter, comparable in cosmic status with

electric charge. Whether in experiments on Earth or in fierce reactions
in the heart of the Sun, nature kept careful accounts of them. Each
of the funnily named qualities implied a new law of nature. And each
of the various particles composed from the quarks all behaved a little
differently from one another, because of their different rations of the
various qualities of matter [charge, spin, etc.] (p. 74)

Figure 61. *The ten 'souped-up' relatives of the proton (u = 'up'; d = 'down';
s = 'strange'). [Source: N. Calder (1977) The Key to the Universe]*

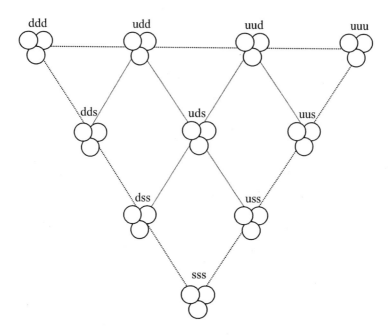

From a different perspective, the same *tetractys*—the 'baryon decuplet'
(*see* fig. 62)—shows the hadrons (strongly interacting heavy particles) formed
from the different quark combinations as shown in Figure 61. For example,
the omega-minus particle discovered in 1964 (shown at the bottom of Figure
62) is the triple-strange (sss) particle shown at the bottom of Figure 61.

Figure 62. *The baryon decuplet and its four particles: Delta (Δ), Sigma (Σ), Cascade (Ξ), and Omega (Ω). [Source: F. Capra (1988) The Tao of Physics]*

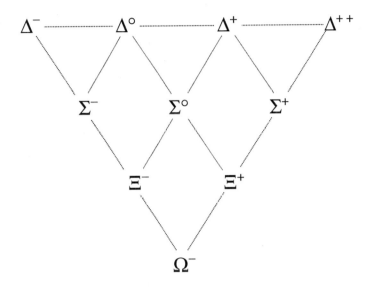

In subsequent decades evidence for other, even heavier quarks had accumulated, and these were named 'charm', 'truth', and 'beauty'. All the six quarks mentioned have anti-quark relatives (the concept of particles and antiparticles, matter and antimatter, is well accepted since the creation and annihilation of particles has been observed millions of times in the laboratory).

In the way quarks fit neatly into the *tetractys* form, it can be seen that the subatomic world follows simple structural rules, and by the 4-3-2-1 pattern, it is shown how simple arithmetic and geometric laws gave physicists the means by which they could postulate an elegant theoretical sub-structure underlying the building blocks of matter.

Summary

Psychologically, the *tetractys* (as *Axioma Mariae*) and the Sefirotic Tree are schematic of the structure and development of the psyche—the mental, cognitive, emotional, moral and ethical aspects of human functioning. These factors are embodied in the *Anthropos* figure—the archetype of the human being as an eternal image of the totality of the psyche.

Physiologically, the Sefirotic Tree also represents the human body, and in this respect it bears similarities with the '#9 body' of Chinese philosophy, except that there is no alignment of these two schemas due to the quantitative and qualitative differences between them. Each has a different order and purpose. Unlike the ninefold configuration, the tenfold schema follows a 4-3-2-1 pattern (or its reverse), each stage referring to a specific component of that schema. The DNA structure is another example of this pattern.

In Physics, the *tetractys* lends itself as a schema for putting order to the infinitesimal world of ten 'souped-up' protons (baryons), each of which is theorized as being constituted of three quarks variously clustered in groups, thus forming ten baryons quantitatively and qualitatively different from each other. If particles of the subatomic world lend themselves to the *tetractys* schematic, as does the DNA molecule, as does psychological development, then we might argue that the single underlying factor shared by all these phenomena (all of which were derived or discovered independently of each other) is also the very metaphysical 'glue' that binds these phenomena together—the tenfold principle of unity. Each schema embodies the principle of perfection in that the system is a whole, and therefore, a unity.

Matter and psyche, those two seemingly irreconcilable opposites, can therefore be described by the archetype of Unity in magnitude—the number ten. Matter has pattern and structure, so too the psyche. Each is the subject and object of the other—each depends on the other.

There is always Ten (Beginning and End), and Ten is the return to Unity. The cycle is complete.

You forgot to mention the Rosary, and how all the main mysteries and decades are based on tens.

Plate 20. JOHANNES KEPLER

In his book Harmonices Mundi *[The Harmony of the Worlds] of 1619, Kepler (1571-1630) wrote of a harmony and congruence in geometrical forms and physical phenomena. He discovered harmonies in planetary motion—a musica universalis ('music of the spheres'). These were actual but silent harmonies, and they conformed to musical laws [SOURCE: Wikimedia Commons].*

THE MUSIC OF NUMBER

If…the soul does not notice that it calculates, it yet
senses the effect of its unconscious reckoning, be this
as joy over harmony or as oppression over discord.

Gottfried Leibniz

One important message running like a red thread throughout this text is the dual aspect of number, its quantitative *and* its qualitative phenomenology. At a fundamental level, mathematics depends on the quantitative aspects of number, and these aspects arise because of the measurable 'flow' of number as a seemingly ordered continuum (actually a discrete or punctuated sequence). Mathematicians, thereby, are availed of a reliable tool, as is evident in a sub-branch of mathematics—the field of arithmetic. Arithmetical addition demonstrates most effectively the measurability of number as a counting process —a rhythmic operation similar to the processes involved in musical performance.

Music is based on division and sub-division of arbitrary time values, counted out in the musical notes and rests of the bar-line, which are sub-divisions of the stave. The musician who reads the music is also unconsciously 'counting' the notes and rests, which is quantifiable as a time dependent event because it is measurable as a flow of time. To draw the analogy between music and number completely, one must include the *qualitative* aspects of music, which include melody, harmony, modulation, dynamics (*crescendo* and *diminuendo*) and accent, etc. These factors are arithmetically derived as well.

↓ except for rubato. 'Rubato' means
to rob. Art Tatum was a genius
of this. Mozart couldn't stand it!

The Rhythm of Music—'Counting the Beat'

The word arithmetic comes from two ancient Greek words, *arithmos* ('number') and *techné* ('art'): arithmetic is the 'art of number'. Further, *arithmos* has the same root as another Greek word, *rhythmos* (from which the English word 'rhythm' derives), and this root is *rheó* (to flow). Fundamentally, therefore, (from the linguistic evidence) arithmetic and rhythm are linked to time and music—all are inextricably connected with the process of flow or movement through a continuum, but one that is discrete by nature, as given by the natural number series. By dint of a 'counting' process taking place psychically (consciously, unconsciously or semi-consciously), and physically (in humankind, and other species, and nature) during all forms of motion (flow), rhythm takes place *in* nature, is directly connected *to* nature, and indirectly *defines* nature, from a specifically numerical, and even musical standpoint.

The energy involved in this flow is the same energy involved in all living and non-living processes, which is also expressed in numerical form. In the dimension of matter, this energy is objectively quantifiable, and, given the nature and variety of its expression, is qualifiable in the human psyche through feeling, emotion, and evaluation, and these factors are crucial components of music appreciation. It can then be seen that the relationship between music and number is not simply a quantitative issue, but must also include the implied qualitative dimensions that are found in both music and number.

The Harmony of Number

The idea of quantitative and qualitative aspects underlying the roots of music, number, and nature harkens back to ancient times when associations were made between music and the heavens—the Pythagorean 'music of the spheres'—whereby the whole of nature and the Heavens above were both considered to be mathematically ordered in the form of an *harmonia mundi* ('world harmony') united in *musica coelestis* ('heavenly music'). This idea was to be quantifiably negated by Kepler who showed that the empirical dimensions of the planetary spheres did not correspond with this Pythagorean ideal, as maintained even as late as the seventeenth century by alchemists and hermetic philosophers. Pythagoras maintained that the Platonic solids would comfortably fit within these planetary spheres, but the spheres were not spherical as such (i.e., the orbits were not circular, but elliptical). What Kepler did show, however, was that musical ratios (i.e., intervals) can be formed based on the angular velocities of the planets at their nearest (perihelion) and furthest points (aphelion) to the Sun, and these are valid today—even for the planets discovered since Kepler's time. In fact, in the book *The Signature of the Spheres* (2004), Hartmut Warm has calculated a highly significant correspondence between the planets' velocities and musical intervals using astronomical and mathematical algorithms. And in 2006, Greg Fox composed his *Carmen of the Spheres*, based on sub-divisions of the orbital periods of the planets (Fox's music favourably compares to the more subdued tones of the electronic musical soundscapes scored by Louis and Bebe Barron for the 1956 film *Forbidden Planet*). In the chapter "Astrology," it will be seen that there is further evidence for a kind of harmony of the spheres, as demonstrated by astrologer John Addey.

Schimmel (1993) notes some early influences of number on music that took a religious or symbolic form:

> Renaissance composers turned to the sacred and mysterious numbers to use them in the technique of the canon, in the number of voices to be employed, and in the continuo [Bass part with figures below the notes to indicate harmonies to be played above it] and later, in the seventeenth and early eighteenth century...Bach, whose later works have been called 'largely musical mathematic' because he exhausted the different possibilities to utilise meaningful numbers to their limits. (pp. 24-25)

Bach was known to be a student of Pythagorean thought, which supposedly influenced his most mysterious of compositions, *The Art of Fugue*. It was supposedly started in 1742, and demonstrates a sophisticated musical style known as counterpoint—the simultaneous performance of distinct melodies within a musical piece that harmonize with each other. Originally the parts were not expressly written for specific instruments, which led to the belief that the work was for 'private study' and the 'inner ear', though others claim it was meant to be performed, and their have been arrangements written for, and performed by wind ensembles, string quartets, keyboards (e.g., harpsichord, piano, organ), and even full orchestra. Hans-Eberhard Dentler has supposedly resolved the mystery, and has performed the work as it was originally intended. It is the Pythagorean ideas underscoring the mystery that Dentler recognizes as being pivotal to a sound understanding of what Bach intended for *The Art of Fugue*. These elements are evident in its structure, as given by Peat (personal communication, January 15, 2007):

> **The Basic Enigma**: Enigma was the essence of Greek teaching. Indeed the 2, 3, 4 pattern of the Riddle of the Sphinx underlies the work; **Contrapunctus** [Counterpoint]: Bach refers to his fugal pieces (not the canons) with this curious term which evokes the notion of opposites as in Aristotle's "punctus contra punctum" [note against note]. Note that the term 'contrapuncta' was used by Kepler in his chapter on Universal Harmony; **Mirror Principle**: The speculum is central to Pythagoras—Bach's mirror counterpoint is strikingly visual in the fair copy; *Tetractys*: The perfect triangle created by arranging the numbers 1, 2, 3, and 4 is central to Pythagorean thought and is present in the pattern of voices of the Art of Fugue; **Four**: The number underlies the whole piece as its principle of order; **Unity**: The work is created out of a single theme and is in a single tonality; **Music of the Spheres**: This is reflected in the first seven contrapunctus. The Earth itself is represented by a Canon in the Octave; and **Fugue**: Of course Fugue is central to many of Bach's works but one should not forget that it also means the flight of the soul towards God.

But long before the Renaissance, the Pythagoreans had already established some basic precepts of music theory still valid today. Pythagoras, on the theme of his musical cosmos, discovered that two notes were consonant (i.e., harmonious, or musically agreeable) if small whole numbers were used to express their frequencies as a ratio (see Martin & Connor, 1968). Notes in unison (1:1 ratio) were the most consonant, followed by the octave (2:1) and the fifth (3:2) (*see* Table 20).

Table 20. *Two Note Intervals and their Ratios.*

Interval	Unison	Octave	Fifth	Fourth	Major 3rd	Major 6th
Frequency Ratio	1:1	2:1	2:3	3:4	4:5	3:5

[Source: S. L. Martin & A. K. Connor (1968) Basic Physics 1]

Following Table 20 across, through the ratios from unison to the major sixth, these ratios become increasingly more dissonant (discordant). Mathematically, only unison and octave are consonant, while all other intervals (distance in pitch between two notes) are dissonant to varying degrees. In traditional music theory though, unison and octave, major and minor thirds, perfect fourth, perfect fifth, and major and minor sixths are consonant, and other intervals are dissonant, such as the second and diminished fifth.

Table 21 lists the names of the notes.

Table 21. *Scale Degrees of the Octave.*

Note # in the Scale	1st C	2nd D	3rd E	4th F	5th G	6th A	7th B	8th C
Degree (i.e., Note Name)	Tonic	Super-Tonic	Mediant	Sub-Dominant	Dominant	Sub-mediant	Leading Note	Upper Tonic

Table 22 shows how the various notes listed in Table 21 may combine in pairs to form the intervals in the key of the C Major scale. In Table 22 can also be seen how those intervals, as harmonic relationships between the two notes, can be pleasant (consonant) or dissonant (unpleasant) to the human ear.

Table 22. *Intervals of the C Major Scale and their Consonance or Dissonance.*

Interval	Interval Notes	Notes in the C Scale	Consonant (C) or Dissonant (D)
Unison	Tonic:Tonic	C:C	C
Octave	Tonic:Octave	C:C'	C
Major 3rd	Tonic:Mediant	C:E	C
minor 3rd	Tonic: Flat Mediant	C:E♭	C
Perfect 4th	Tonic: Sub-Dominant	C:F	C
Perfect 5th	Tonic:Dominant	C:G	C
Major 6th	Tonic:Sub-Mediant	C:A	C
minor 6th	Tonic: Flat Sub-Mediant	C:A♭	C
Maj/min 2nd	Tonic:Super-tonic	C:D, C:D♭	D
Maj/min 7th	Tonic:Leading Note	C:B, C:B♭	D

Note: Discord results when any of the notes above the tonic are augmented (sharpened) or diminished (flattened). [Source: I. Crofton (ed.) (1986) Concise Dictionary of Music]

Jazz relies heavily on
mixing major and minor notes
and the "diminished 5th" = C + F#
                              a   C + G♭
         "augmented 5th" =

Reconstructing Harmony through Number

For the most part the Pythagoreans were pleased with their discoveries, but the problem with dissonance was not reasonably resolved until Hermann von Helmholtz showed that it was attributable to the 'beats' that were produced by two non-harmonious notes. Discord in vibrating strings came about when beating was generated between the partials or overtones (effectively, the unwanted tones). These unwanted tones are heard along with the simple tones, which constitute the so-called harmony.

Another problem in the early stages of music development concerned the Western or European musical scale. This scale consists of an unequally sub-divided octave of seven notes (the last note—the octave or eighth note—being the same note as the first note or tonic, but twice the frequency). These eight notes are called the major diatonic scale and they are formed from the overtones of the tonic. The whole number series, 24, 27, 30, 32, 36, 40, 45, 48, gives the eight relative frequencies of a diatonic scale.

The specific scale sought, for example, the C Major scale, can be formed starting from any frequency desired, but the international pitch standard of A = 440 c/s (cycles per second) is standard. In the C Major scale, this note 'A' corresponds to the relative number of 40 in the above series. The other notes are simply ratios of 440 and are derived from the series just given. For example, C = 24/40 × 440 = 264 c/s; D = 27/40 × 440 = 297 c/s, and so on.

Once the principles of scale formation were established (including the sharps and the flats), a practical problem arose. It was found that frequency ratios varied from scale to scale. While a scale could be formed by the aforementioned process, some notes in one scale, when directly translated to other scales, were of the wrong pitch. In other words, true intonation (the pitch of the note) was not a problem theoretically, but for the sake of modulation (key or chord changes), or to increase the number of available notes for melodic purposes, instruments had to have certain notes mis-tuned.

'Mis-tuning' became general practice around the time of J. S. Bach in the eighteenth century, and all instruments since then are tuned according to the more practical 'equal temperament' (as opposed to 'just temperament', which results in the problems just outlined when the natural overtone series is used to derive other scales). Sensitive ears can in fact hear these mis-tunings, which have a discordant sound, but most people are accustomed to equal temperament.

Taking the international pitch standard of the A note at 440 c/s, the following C Major scale and its frequencies result in the equally tempered scale shown in Table 23, which contrast with the same major diatonic scale of C Major. Note that only the two 'E' notes and the two 'A' notes are in unison, while the remaining six paired notes are discordant. The differences between these two scales in effect establishes the difference between that which is deemed mathematically 'perfect' in musical theory, on one hand, and on the other, that which the human ear is prepared to accept as harmonious for pragmatic (practical) reasons.

Table 23. *Comparison of equally-tempered notes with the major diatonic notes of the C Major scale.*

NOTE	C	D	E	F	G	A	B	C'
Equally-tempered scale	261	294	330	349	392	440	494	522
Major diatonic scale	264	297	330	352	396	440	495	528

Thus Pythagoras' theory concerning the 'music of the spheres' as an objective reality had to be modified for practical reasons. In fact, when the overtone series is extended to even higher frequencies it is found that quarter tones and eighth tones, etc., are produced which can sound discordant at first until, as is often the case with evolving musical forms, these new sounds become acceptable to the listener through conditioning (note for example how the so-called dissonant 7th and diminished 7th notes used quite regularly in American Blues and Blues-derived 'pop' forms of twentieth-century music, have become quite acceptable to the human ear).

Ultimately then, the complexity of music and music appreciation can be determined at two very human levels:

1. the acceptance of the practical but 'imperfect', equally-tempered scales, which make sense of musical notation (particularly modulation), and also make performance possible.

2. the esthetic evaluation we have come to develop in our own personal way, given our particular cultural and cross-cultural preferences.

In *Physics as Metaphor* (1983) Jones comments on the human factor:

> the essential point is that music exists in the ear and in the mind, and not in vibrating bodies or in the sound waves they emit. The true nature of a musical experience cannot be described as a sequence of objective pitches.... Pitch is part of musical experience, and not of acoustics. The listener...is the final arbiter of musical quality and meaning. (p. 155)

He may be the "final arbiter" but he's not the final judge! the judge of the degree of difficulty or aesthetic complexity!

Constructing Tempo and Time Signature through Number

(marginal note:) similar in principle this.

Another important factor in musical performance, once pitch problems are acceptably resolved, is the issue of tempo. In his classical physics, Aristotle equated number with time (tempo), and one can appreciate how intrinsic tempo is to musical performance once it is realized that the tempo of a musical piece refers to the pace at which the music is performed. Although tempo is now given numerically, originally, as with pitch, rates of performance were also arbitrarily determined and needed standardizing. From the end of the seventeenth century, the Italian terms *largo*, *adagio*, *andante*, *allegro*, etc., came to be generally accepted, and today the metronome gives these tempi in a standard form (which can still be interpreted by the performer, within limits).

I wonder what J.S. Bach would have thought about rap rock!

The time signature is loosely connected with tempo (Italian: *tempo* = 'time'), but time signature specifically refers to the note value and quantity of beats in a bar. Standard time signatures can be divided into simple time (each beat is divisible by two pulses) and compound time (each beat is divisible by three pulses), and then into duple, triple or quadruple time, etc., (which represent the number of beats in a bar: two, three or four, respectively). Combinations of the former (simple or compound) with the latter (duple, triple, quadruple, etc.) give the time signature, and this is indicated in the bar line at the beginning of the composition, after the clef and key signature (for example, 2/4, 3/4 and 4/4 are 2, 3 and 4 crotchet beats per bar, respectively, each beat divisible by 2 quavers; 6/8, 9/8 and 12/8 are 2, 3 and 4 dotted-crotchet beats per bar, respectively, each beat divisible by 3 quavers).

All the notes of varying lengths in musical time are derived from the whole note. By successive halvings, the breve (rarely used) halves into two whole notes (two semi-breves), the semi-breve halves into two quarter notes (two crotchets), the crotchet halves into two eighth notes (two quavers), and so on. There are corresponding rests that are formed the same way. For example, the whole rest corresponds in time length to that of the semi-breve, the crotchet rest corresponds with the crotchet note.

It is the rhythms that these time signatures establish that resonate with the listener. In combination with the melodies, the dynamics, the modulations, and so on, music demonstrates its capacity to move the individual in a way that is truly outstanding given the arbitrary nature in which the basic constructs of music were established in the first place.

The Number Archetype—The Essence of Music

It may be that the interpretive aspect of music, which has come to define music in a particularly human and subjective way—albeit a consensual arrangement arrived at over many centuries—is the major reason for the effect music can have on the human soul (i.e., music is meaningful because we make it so). The emotional and therapeutic benefits of music are widely recognized, so too the simple pleasure gained from music purely for entertainment and relaxation, as well as the presence of the music of a culture as a reflection of the feelings and ideas of its people in ritual and magic, in religion and myth, and generally, in human interaction.

With all these considerations, the involvement of number is not to be undermined. When accepting that, for the most part, music is a human construction, music is also based on the fundamental absolute of the number archetype. Thus, amongst all the other deep-seated psychological causes underlying musical appreciation is the number archetype. Number is intrinsic to the whole process of composition and performance, especially from the perspective of music as a chronological process—a temporal event—a flowing of individual sounds (notes), rests (silence), and rhythms (beats, pulses and syncopation), which count out or measure the continuum of our existence and put order to that existence. This process is recognized in the language, and is shown to hearken back to ancient times when all the factors of music—harmony, melody, rhythm, time, counting, and flow—were seen as derivative of each other, and defined each other as constituents of a world which was seen as unified and not fragmented.

The following musical examples show the importance of number in music, and they indicate by their effects, this unifying element manifested in human experience as musical and emotional energies flow where they will, in and out of human consciousness. (I have limited myself to well-known classical and 'pop' works, and use the composers of these works more than once on some occasions, since they may already be familiar to the reader, or if not, are readily accessible. These examples are not necessarily chosen for their musical sophistication, but are meant to illustrate the use of number in clear, numerical terms.)

The Music of One

In music, One means unison. The sound of notes in unison is heard as the most consonant of harmonic forms. Octave notes are equally consonant, although not the same pitch, but the note-name is the same. For example, the upper-tonic and lower-tonic are an octave above and below the tonic, respectively.

In a mundane sense, unity exists in any given musical composition. The musical work (*opus*) of the composer is imbued with the full range of emotions, character and personality of that composer. So too, the performance by a musician of a piece of music is a unitary event, which carries the essence of the musician, as energy in flow imparted to the instrument. Performance is energy liberated physically, but with control, discipline and mastery, intelligence, sensitivity and emotion, in one singular act.

Monophony is melody without accompaniment—the simplest form of music, recalling the solo voice, and the sound of the pipe or flute, all of which are equally reminiscent of a bird in song or other monophonic sounds in nature. In fact, any solo performance of a wind instrument, brass instrument, or string instrument (as long as only a single string is played) produces monophony. The traditional musical forms of India and Japan feature monophony to a marked degree, where single notes are played on such instruments as the sitar and sarod (in India) and the Japanese koto and shakuhachi (flute).

Monophony has a meditative quality, often emphasized by the pauses (rests) between the notes. Other qualities may then be attributed to the performance, according to the performer and the listener, such as stillness, and timelessness, while, paradoxically, others may discern motion and time-dependent qualities in the music. A soulfulness, then, is evoked by the music, culminating in oppositional relationships, complementarities, and paradoxes of experience. The overriding character of the monad has just such a pluralistic phenomenology that, nevertheless, embodies a unifying and integrating character, as mirrored in music generally.

Psychologically, music can initialize and bring into sharper focus one's orientation towards wholeness in the human subject. Music touches the feeling-toned contents of the unconscious, enlivens them, and brings them into consciousness, with the potential of re-uniting the fragmented parts of personal experience into a cohesive, well-structured and ordered totality.

*many 1920's + 30's orchestras
featured two pianos: Osman and
arden; Hong King + Leon aarms.
Lorrante + Teischer*

The Music of Number   397

See Plural Piano / Felix Mendelssohn

The Music of Two

Harmony not only indicates numerical intervals between notes to achieve consonance or dissonance, but also indicates consciousness of duality. Ritual and traditional chanting, usually without accompaniment (for example, Gregorian and Ambrosian chant), rely on monophonic melodies, and depend on a minimum of two voices (duet) for the purposes of harmony. The duet is also a composition for two singers or players, not necessarily with accompaniment. The piano duet is a special term referring to a one-instrument performance by two players. The musical term 'duo' can be used interchangeably with 'duet', but usually a duo refers to instrumental music. These early forms of harmony (two-note intervals) are the basis for more complex harmonic arrangements.

One distinctive feature of harmony as a dualistic pattern is the suggestion that as the music 'moves' from one state to another, emotional 'movement' is also possible. A movement, for example, from tension to relaxation is suggested by 'movement' from dissonant to consonant chords (relative discord to relative concord). The constitution of dissonance (low to high) varies over time, but the basic musical forms and emotional effects are always present. Harmonic movement as a dualistic effect can anticipate emotional responses in the listener, provided the harmonic form resonates with the feeling-tones of the listener.

These same effects can be achieved through modulation (key or chord changes) where tonal variation and the effects of these variations are of prime concern. The crucial point here is that a discernable 'system of difference' is established by way of the modulation. The preceding chord immediately qualifies the new chord. A particularly cogent example of modulation is the closing passages of Ravel's *Bolero* (1928), marked by the leap from C major to E major. The insistent drum rhythm of this Spanish dance measures the pace from beginning to end, as the piece builds up to an orchestral crescendo.

Simple duple time signatures (2/2, 2/4, 2/8) measure 2 beats per bar, and are something akin to the first type of rhythm we can imagine. They signify the basic oscillation and antithetical relationships described in the chapter "Two (The Dyad)." The guitar piece *Etude No. 6* in E minor (1929) by Brazilian composer Heitor Villa-Lobos is a fine example of a 2/4 composition with its *poco allegro* (rather lively) tempo and striding, almost marching pace. Also, Russian composer Alexandre Borodin's *In the Steppes of Central Asia* (1882) suggests very well a rolling movement with a heartbeat pace in duple time.

Twofold rhythm suggests the pulse or beat of the heart (atrial systole and diastole), expiration and respiration (ventilation of the lungs), and bipedal perambulation (the step-by-step alternating rhythm of walking, etc.). The very nature of this type of music easily recalls these rhythmic analogies, and the greatest strength of the twofold rhythm is recognized when a balance of energies is attained, or some level of feeling or emotion is evoked in response to such a rhythm.

The Music of Three

Chord theory, based on at least two, but usually three notes sounded simultaneously, and the triadic arrangement of notes, arose naturally (i.e., by trial and error) in the Middle Ages with no conscious intention of rearranging the resultant triads. Aesthetic judgments were made purely by experimentation, or by the appeal of the sound, in accordance with some basic ideas about consonance and dissonance, from which formal harmonic rules were established.

The basic unit of harmony is the chord, and the first type of chord in triadic form is the primary triad. This chord consists of the tonic, the 3rd, and the 5th note in the scale (*see* Tables 20 & 21). The subdominant triad consists of the 4th note of a scale, as a root note from which the chord grows, and the 3rd and the 5th notes above this root note. The dominant triad starts with the 5th note of a scale and adds the 3rd and the 5th above this note.

Primary triads can go through inversions (first and second inversions) where the notes of the chord in root position are rearranged so that an upper note becomes the lowest. In the C Major scale, for example, the root position is C-E-G; the first inversion is E-G-C, and the second inversion is G-C-E.

Other triads can be formed from the 2nd (supertonic) and 6th (submediant) notes of the scale. In this way, the harmonic vocabulary of music was constructed with different ideas as to what constituted consonance and dissonance prevailing throughout the centuries up to modern times. Avante-garde concert music and popular music forms of the twentieth century represent harmonic innovations that have been particularly challenging for the novice listener.

In Christian Europe the triad was associated with the Trinity and was given due reverence. Whereas the triad of three notes is harmonious and pleasant to the ear, the so-called 'tritone' in contrast was considered discordant and unpleasant. The tritone is a musical interval that spans three whole tones. Technically known as the 'augmented fourth' or 'diminished fifth', it was known from medieval times as the *Diabolus in musica* ('Devil in the music') and was forbidden in church music because of its unpleasant and unresolved sound. The tritone became acceptable from Baroque period to the present era, and is featured throughout Benjamin Britten's *War Requiem* and Bernhard Hermann's film score for *The Day the Earth Stood Still*, as well as in the heavy rock music genre typified by the music of Jimi Hendrix and Black Sabbath.

The trio (group of three performers) can either be a piano trio (piano, violin, cello), or a string trio (violin, viola, cello). Compositional forms of minuet (a moderate French dance in 3/4 time), and scherzo (meaning 'joke' because of its light, whimsical character in quick triple time) have a middle section called the trio because there was usually a woodwind trio of two oboes and a bassoon. A Ternary Form resulted: Minuet I (Binary), followed by Minuet II ('Trio', also Binary), and then a repeat of Minuet I. The sonata and the symphony also demonstrate the traditional preference amongst composers for tripartite forms, perhaps in response to the ideal construction of thesis-antithesis-synthesis. Schimmel (1993) writes that in "Indian Music it is the *tintal*, a rhythm based on the ternary system (although difficult for nonspecialists to analyse) that prevails" (p. 85).

The time signature of simple triple time (3/4, 'waltz' time), with its repeating threefold pulse, has an unmistakable immediacy about it, which can be joyful and evocative, or emotional and soulful to the listener, according to the tempo. The Villa-Lobos composition *Prelude No. 1* in E minor (1940) is an interesting example of a classical guitar piece which features threefold structures at two levels. First, the chords are almost exclusively in triads (which demonstrate the harmonic quality of the triad), and second, the time signature is in 3/4. However, its *andantino expressivo* tempo (slightly faster than walking pace) and instruction for an expressive interpretation, assures that the piece constantly shifts in tempo throughout its performance, from *andantino* to *poco allargando* (a little broader/slower), *a tempo* to *ritenuto* (slower), *a tempo* to *allargando*, etc., making it difficult for the listener to fully appreciate 'threeness' as a consistent, waltz-time rhythm.

Better examples of waltz-time are Tchaikovsky's familiar 'Valse des fleurs' from *The Nutcracker* (1876), or Maurice Ravel's 'Les entretiens de la belle et de la bête' ('Beauty and the Beast') from *Ma Mère l'oye* (1908). Both these pieces have a moderately paced tempo. Of a much slower tempo (*lento*) is Finnish composer Jean Sibelius's *Valse Triste* (1903), or Ravel's 'Le Jardin féerique' ('Fairy Garden'), also from *Ma Mère l'oye*.

In the popular music sphere, the Lennon-McCartney song *Lucy In The Sky With Diamonds* (1967) is an interesting composition with its contrasting 3/4 time in the verses and 4/4 time in the chorus. This song provides a good opportunity for the listener to directly compare the dynamic differences of the two most popular time signatures, 3/4 and 4/4. Many other examples of 3/4 time in The Beatles' *oeuvre* include *Baby's in Black* (1964) and *Dig a Pony* (1970). (Most of the pop music examples mentioned below are taken from The Beatles' composers, John Lennon, Paul McCartney and George Harrison, since they are well known and their material is readily available.)

In conclusion, triads have a richness and depth of sound to them, which results from the harmonic relationship of their constituent notes. There is also a solidity or groundedness in the sounds of three-note chords or triads. There is an archetypal basis to this fact, stemming from the systematic or patterned structure that underpins the triad, which has underscored music from Renaissance times right up to the modern musical forms of the twentieth century.

Waltz-time (3/4 time) music imbues a light and 'airy' quality that lends itself very well to dance, hence the popularity of the waltz since its origins. Even the colloquial use of the word 'waltz' to describe someone in their stride ("to move lightly, casually, with deceptive ease, etc.," according to the Concise Oxford Dictionary) suggests an intuitive understanding of the quality of three as embodying confidence and progression, while movement, balance, and coordination are also implied. *you left out The Mills Brothers!*

The Music of Four

Following on from chords in triadic form, four-part harmony then developed, with a richer quality achieved by 'doubling-up' one of the notes from the triad. With a second instrument or a human voice, the doubled note could be in unison, or in solo performance, a note one octave or two octaves apart would be used. Harmonies were assigned for four different voices: Soprano, Alto, Tenor and Bass. The theory of inversion also worked in four-note chords, with first, second and third inversions possible. The four 'voices', therefore, can sing vocal quartets, but quartets may also be instrumental, for example, string quartets and piano quartets, both of which have been very popular common forms since the eighteenth century.

The 'common' and predictable 4/4 time signature (simple quadruple) creates rhythms, which are restful and natural sounding, or solid and striding, according to the tempo. Examples of the former are Villa-Lobos guitar piece *Etude No. 5* (1929) in C major, with a 4/4 time signature and *andantino* (slightly faster than *andante* or 'walking pace'), and the first movements (*allegro*) of both 'Spring' and 'Autumn' from Vivaldi's *The Four Seasons* (1725). Examples of the latter (solid and striding rhythms) are the second movement (*largo*) of 'Winter' from *The Four Seasons*, and many Baroque pieces, such as Pachelbel's *Canon* (17th century), and the third movement (*adagio*) from Händel's *Sonata in A minor* (Op 1, #4) (18th century).

In the popular music idiom are many examples of 4/4 time. In fact, 4/4 time is not only pop music's most often used time signature, but is the most favored time signatures of all genres—hence the alternative term 'common'

We would have never made it through the 1920's, 30's and 40's without 4/4 time for dancing.

time. The harmonically strong Lennon-McCartney compositions *Girl* (1965) and *Michelle* (1965), being both pleasantly and moderately paced, as well as having simple undemanding melodies, enable an easy detection of common time in these songs. Wilfred Mellers (1976) in *Twilight of the Gods: The Beatles in Retrospect* describes *Girl's* melody of "gently arching quavers followed by rocking fourths and fifths" as "heart-easingly lovely," while the "regularly repeated quavers" (p. 61) of the vocalized 'dit-dit-dit-dit' in the 'middle eight' underscore the lyric, and yield an unmistakable, almost mechanical 'arithmetic' in 4/4 time.

Michelle is a more harmonically "sophisticated" song compared to *Girl* and Mellers speaks of "tritonal intrusions" in the melody, "swaying triplets" and "pentatonic innocence" (p. 63). More to the point, the structure of *Michelle*, as with *Girl*, 'recognizes' the 2nd and 4th beats per bar through its single melody in the first two bars on the 'down-beat' (first beat of the bar) and the third beat of the bar, and its insistent, mostly crotchet count in the remaining four bars of each verse line stress the 4/4 time most congently.

Thus, music in 4/4 time gives the impression of a centeredness based partly on its simple quadruple time, suggesting a 'completed' music where oppositionalism has found homeostasis. The result for the listener or performer is an experience, through feeling, that is precise and fully defining.

A flexibility is also engendered in music with a 4/4 time because it is availed of a readiness or 'predisposition' to accommodate unstructured or incompatible musical accompaniments. Other time signatures will 'permit' variation and virtuosity, but only 4/4 time has global appeal, as given by the preference for this time in so many genres, and so many cultures, suggesting an ease of use that well accommodates both simple folk music forms and more complex classical forms.

The Music of Five

In earlier times the pentatonic (five note) scale provided the basic notes of melody formation. This scale (akin to the Western octave, but not including the 5th and the 7th notes) was used in the Far East (for example, China and

Japan), throughout Africa, and even in the folk music forms of Scotland and Ireland. In the twentieth century, French composers Maurice Ravel and Claude Debussy used the pentatonic scale to effectively achieve an 'oriental' feel in such compositions as Ravel's 'Laideronette, impératrice des pagodes' from *Ma Mère l'oye* (1908), and in various passages throughout Debussy's *La Mer* (1905), and also in his 'Pagodes' from *Estampes* (1903). The preference for the pentatonic scale in the East may be attributed to the important, quintessential place the number five holds in eastern philosophy, but it would appear that an 'earth-bound' veneration for the number five also manifested among the common folk throughout Europe.

The 5/4 time signature is mercurial and makes only rare appearances in classical music. This time signature usually charms or surprises the listener—largely by its novelty effect. Music in 5/4 time is tenacious in its rhythm, and lack of familiarity can be disarming to the novice, who may find it difficult to give recognition to the 'extra' beat in each bar. This disorientation is probably due to the conditioning effect of duple and quadruple time signatures (especially 4/4) and triple time signatures (especially 3/4) that predominate Western music. American jazz composer Paul Desmond's *Take Five* (1959) is a modern jazz example of 5/4 time, although its simple bass line and chord patterns are rather repetitive, so that the 5/4 beat soon becomes recognizable and predictable.

Lennon-McCartney's *Good Morning Good Morning* (1967) is the only song in the entire Beatle repertoire that consistently uses 5/4 time, as opposed to the occasional bar or two of 5/4 in other songs, which make an appearance purely as a means of accommodating a complex melody in 4/4 or similar simple time. *Good Morning Good Morning* maintains a melody in 5/4 time for four bars in the first, third and fifth verses, and three bars in the second and fourth verses. The verses are further complicated by intermittent time changes of 7/4, 3/4 and 4/4. Lennon's 'skipping' vocal (melodically and dynamically speaking), in quavers and crotchets, disguises the 5/4 time very successfully, and the song could easily be passed over as a quirky but uncomplicated, 'on-the-beat' number in common time or similar, convincingly executed by the rhythmic accenting of each beat in the bar. But even a casual listener may detect something 'tricksterish' afoot with a little close attention. Recall Schimmel's (1993) comments, where she points out the "unusual, even rebellious" (p. 106) nature of the number five, and the fact that it was considered a "naughty," unruly number that stirred up "the well-ordered cosmos" (p. 107).

In classical music, the quintet (five performers, or composition for five performers) is usually two violins, two violas and a cello, as popularized by Mozart, Beethoven and Brahms. One oddity in music history is the *quinton*, a five-stringed violin used in eighteenth-century France, but rarely used today, although the idea has been maintained in popular music (for example, the five-stringed electric Bass guitar).

Although Brahms was challenged by the task of composing a five-bar theme in his *St Antoni Variations*, this complex motif may go undetected by the casual listener. Wagner uses a five bar phrase (17-21) three times in his Prelude to *Tristan and Isolde*, but each repetition gives a different dramatic effect according to the build up of emotional tension in the piece.

The presence of the number five in music is an oddity and a dichotomy to both listener and performer. The veneration for the number five in Eastern cultures has seen the number represented in eastern music as the pentatonic scale, which suggests an appreciation in the East for the number five's quintessential quality—a quality that has not been ignored in the West. There is, no doubt, a pleasant aspect to the five-note form in melodies which use the pentatonic scale, yet an 'unruly' aspect particular to number five seems ever-present and unrelenting, as for example, in the 5/4 time signature.

The Music of Six

The 6/8 time signature and other compound duple time signatures have two beats per bar, which give an alternating rhythm similar to 2/4 time, but each beat has a pulse of three, totaling six pulses in each bar. In 6/8 time, for example, there are two dotted-crotchet beats per bar, with a pulse of three quavers in duration. The beat is most readily detected in the music, while the pulse is usually 'felt'.

George Harrison's *I Me Mine* (1970), in 6/8 time, indicates a strong two beats per bar in the verses, but the chords themselves, although accenting the threefold pulse of each beat, do not disturb the moderately-paced, 'step-by-step' feel (in two) of the rhythm so established by the time signature. The 4/4 time change for the chorus (with a medium rock tempo) marks an obvious shift in time and tempo, and the four beats per bar quicken the pace until the return to 6/8 time, which restores the moderate (in two) tempo.

One interesting point concerning 6/8 time, and a main factor of music generally, is the issue of freedom of interpretation. In compositions that use 6/8 time it is possible to re-score them in 3/4 time. For example, *I Me Mine*, just described as a 6/8 piece, has also been interpreted as a 'bright waltz' in 3/4, which points to the fact that while interpretation of time signature may vary for the same composition, six beats per bar can have a waltz time feel, and may evoke similar responses in the listener. Overall, the triadic connection of six with three mentioned in "Six (The Hexad)" is also present in musical composition (after all, $2 \times 3 = 6$).

Prelude No. 5 (1940) by Villa-Lobos, possibly the most melodic and peaceful of his five preludes, also features two pulses per bar. Performed at a pleasant pace (*poco animato*) its 6/4 signature and melody, consisting mainly of crotchet notes, is easily counted until the *Meno* ('less quickly') section. The change to the third section, *Piu moso* ('faster'), has strong 'crotcheted' chords throughout, again for practical purposes giving the listener an idea of the two-pulse feel in each bar. In fact, throughout the piece, the pulse is so prominent that any waltz feel is negligible. The strong point of this prelude is its melody, although it may be a *post hoc* contrivance to suggest that the strong melody is due entirely to some 'magical' quality of 'sixness'. However, the melody line does demonstrate a dependence on a count of six in keeping with its time signature. Again, it is the pulse (the pairings of three), a common dynamic of sixfoldedness, that most characterizes the piece.

The sextet (six performers) usually consists of two violins, two violas, and two cellos, but in modern jazz, for example, any combination of instruments is possible. For example, percussion (drums), piano, bass and guitar, plus two brass or wind instruments (for example, saxophone and clarinet) is quite common.

In conclusion, a waltz-time feel can be accommodated to music scored in 6/8 time because of the two pulses of three in each bar (suggesting two bars of 3/4 time). Thus, the characteristics of number six are akin to those of number three, and therefore apply to the use of the number six in music as well.

The Music of Seven

Seven makes its appearance in the septet (a group of seven performers) as an instrumental composition with seven parts. Schimmel (1993) records that Renaissance composers, in order to venerate the mystical appeal of the number seven, used seven voices to honor the Virgin Mary, "or else allude to the 7 gifts of the Holy Spirit" (p. 135), and Bach features a "sevenfold repetition of the Credo in his B Minor Mass" (p. 25). As Schimmel also writes, the seven notes of the European scale (ending in the octave) and the seven keys are analogous to the periodicity that sevenfold systems portray.

Seven marks completion, but it is a transitional number (like nine) and this may explain the complexity, and hence, the rarity of musical forms with a seven-beat time signature. That is, as uneven numbers tend to move toward symmetry, in the form of even-numbered configurations, it is perhaps understandable that music in 5/4 and 7/4 has a certain hesitancy about it (the naïve listener constantly searches for, or expects that extra note to appear from somewhere to round out the 'oddness' of every 'uneven' bar). Thus are time signatures such as 5/4 and 7/4 complex. The unaccustomed ear seems to have an unconscious desire to impose symmetry, marked by a pressing insistence for a return to the less complex, comparatively safer 4/4, or even 3/4. Consequently, 5/4 and 7/4 can be difficult to 'think' or 'feel' (depending on one's approach to music). Each particular composition may depend on the feel it evokes by way of 'complete' five- or seven-beat rhythmic patterns, which the listener must take on board at the expense of convention.

The composition *Unsquare Dance* (1961) by Dave Brubeck is exemplary for its modern jazz rhythm, simplified to an almost primitive level, depending on hand-clapping to accent the second, fourth, sixth and seventh beats of each bar. This piece, like *Take Five*, is also repetitive, given the innovative and experimental nature of compositions in such obscure time signatures. The mathematical construction of 7 as 4 + 3 is easily employed in *Unsquare Dance*. By splitting the 7/4 time signature into recurring 4/4 + 3/4 pairs, the piece is mathematically accessible. Perhaps, unconsciously, this is precisely what the listener (and performer) does, as it seems this piece, and similar compositions in 'unsquare' time lend, themselves to reconstruction as 4/4 + 3/4 (or 3/4 + 4/4), or similar multiples.

A perfect example is *All You Need Is Love* (1967) by Lennon-McCartney. This song has been nominally scored in alternating bars of 4/4 and 3/4, but this 'simplification' is an obvious compromise for a piece that might be better scored as a 7/4 arrangement. As Mellers (1976) also notes: "one could think of it as being in 7/4, with an occasional extra beat" (p. 103). (The song, if scored in 7/4, would have an extra beat in the sixth bar of each verse, while the chorus is in 4/4.) Another example of a 'pop' tune in 7/4 time is Pink Floyd's *Money* (1973), which also seems to force an alternating 3/4 + 4/4 pattern. Philosophically and archetypally, the triad/tetrad relationship is dualistic in nature, showing a complementary resonance which seems to give compositions in 7/4 their primitive immediacy.

Like the 5/4 time signature, 7/4 is a rarity in music, and in both cases, this is probably due to the asymmetrical patterns these 'odd' time signatures produce. The listener can become accustomed to such asymmetry, but this usually depends on the melody and a consistent bass-line, chord structure and rhythm, which forces the time signature upon the listener—a time signature which 'refuses to be squared'.

The Music of Eight

Eight-beat time signatures do appear from time to time, but are generally rare. The quaver (eighth note) can provide the beat length in many time signatures

(2/8, 3/8, 4/8, 6/8, 9/8, 12/8, etc.), but 8/8, when used, is often marginalized in favor of the more common time of 4/4. The John Lennon composition *How* (1971) from his *Imagine* album (an album which marked a turning point in Lennon's musical style—a shift to a more mature and subdued approach in musical forms) reflects a mellowed approach in his song-writing, and features a nominal 8/8 time signature, though actually in 4/4 time. The song's persistent, quaver-note melody hints at the 8/8 time signature in the first place (which accommodates the six bars of 3/8 and two bars of 5/8, and leads to the four bars of 4/4 in the 'bridge'), but it is noteworthy that *How* is the only composition that Lennon ever wrote in 8/8 time among the hundreds of songs he composed until his early death in 1980.

The octet, a piece for eight voices or instruments, or an eight-instrument ensemble, is not as common as the duo, trio, or quartet, etc., and it would seem that the conspicuous absence of the number eight in any major capacity in music theory has gone largely unaddressed. Even the octave, as the last note in the scale, merely becomes a new tonic for the higher octave. From a practical point of view, this absence may be due to the fact that eightfold forms and structures can often submit to a more simplified fourfold pattern without much loss of 'meaning' to such forms or structures.

It is ironic that four makes the number eight redundant when circumstances allow for substitution. In fact, Schimmel (1993) notes that the number eight has long been considered an 'auspicious number' by the ancients, and as described in the chapter "Eight (The Ogdoad)," the number eight can be taken as a 'higher' form of the number four, since it shares so much of the phenomenology of the number four.

Archetypally and musically, the similarity in symbolism between the numbers four and eight is seen to be so, purely by the inconspicuous absence of eight, as if its location between the two transitional numbers, seven and nine, implied that eight was merely a bridge or transitional point itself between two active principles. Notwithstanding this absence of eight in music, the octave's major role is that of establishing the scale unit—double the frequency of any note and you have its octave.

The Music of Nine

The time signature of 9/8 follows the same cumulative pattern regarding beat, as already given in waltz-time and 6/8 time. That is, instead of one or two beats per bar, 9/8 has three beats per bar of three pulses each, totaling nine quavers per bar. The number nine is featured in other time signatures as well, for example, 9/12.

Villa-Lobos' *Etude No. 12* (1929) in A minor, performed with *animé* (spirit), is an exceptionally fast piece, but the rapid-firing triple pulses in each beat are still discernable, and the three-beat rhythm of each bar, with its tenacious hold on the listener, has an over-powering effect, especially with the shift in tempo to *piu mosso* (faster) in the middle before it gradually slows down (*rallentando*) and returns *a tempo*.

The Dave Brubeck jazz composition *Blue Rondo à la Turk* (1960), arranged in rondo form, and in 9/8 time, is also lively, but more consistent in pace, combining a Turkish rhythm with a blues feel. This rhythm is not played as three groups of three (1-2-3, 1-2-3, 1-2-3), but as three groups of two plus one group of three (1-2, 1-2, 1-2, 1-2-3). This breakdown is unusual and runs counter to one's intuition, given the expected re-structuring of a more amenable 'three groups of three'. Again, the demands of musical diversity and free expression undermine the rigidity of rulebound notions that only serve to hinder developments in music.

Like the 7th, minor 3rd, and major 3rd (in jazz and blues particularly), the 9th interval has also been adopted to broaden the expressive range of these music forms. Major, minor, augmented and diminished 9ths (from tonic to octave to the supertonic, totaling nine steps) have a peculiar dissonance that may be used effectively in a 'pure' form, using only the 2nd notes (the supertonics), or in chordal form with other notes to reduce the dissonance through harmony.

Like the octet, the nonet (a piece for nine voices or instruments, or a nine-instrument ensemble) is not as common as the duo, trio, or quartet, etc., (though it was the Miles Davis Nonet that introduced the Cool Jazz genre in the 1940s). Nevertheless, the qualities of number nine in music, like the number six, mirror those of the number three, when manifested as rhythmic arrangements, time signatures, or harmonic structures. The numbers six and nine are inter-connected with the number three primarily because they are multiples of three.

Summary

Music as a human construction developed from the fundamentals of ritual pattern making and other rhythmic forms, which relied on resonance and vibration (for example, drums, pipes and strings). From the Dark Ages to the Renaissance, and right up to the modern era, music continually evolved into a language which was capable of expressing natural processes in even more sophisticated ways, in almost every culture. Consonance and dissonance are shown to be subjective categories, while musical scales vary too from culture to culture.

All the numbers, one through nine, show their quantitative and qualitative effects in music, consistent with their characteristics as outlined in previous chapters. The numbers two, three, four, six and nine have shown rhythmic influences which are accessible and 'natural' sounding to the listener, while the number five and seven create a hesitancy in such time signatures as 5/4 and 7/4, which may be due as much to a lack of familiarity with these signatures as it is to a lack of symmetry in configurations of five and seven. However, it is probably more likely that the unfamiliarity is the direct result of avoidance because of the lack of symmetry. The tendency is to unconsciously break complex time signatures (for example, 7/4) into simpler, paired time signatures (for example, 4/4 + 3/4 = 7/4).

The number eight is a peculiar exception, not appearing too often in any music genre, yet remaining inconspicuous in its absence. Apart from the octave, eight falls short in its contribution to music theory: where eight could be used, four seems to suffice.

At every stage in the evolution of music, number has figured and prefigured in its development, contributing to compositional structure and performance (harmony, melody, time signature, tempo, rhythm, etc.), and defining and establishing music as it has come to be known with the immutability and reliability of its regulating and configurational properties.

Certainly, music has an arbitrary dimension largely dependent on cultural factors, and even individual preferences. As Jones (1983) has stated in *Physics as Metaphor*: "music cannot exist or be explained apart from a participating listener, or without reference to human experience (p. 155). But, without the ordering properties of number, music would never have been born, nor borne in the mind of the listener, no matter how dependent it is on "human choice and value" (p. 155). Without number only the chaos of noise would exist—or perhaps only silence.

This chapter shows that the author has an in-depth and wonderful understanding of music and musical examples.

Plate 21. UNIVERSUM [THE UNIVERSE]

The alchemical Unus Mundus (One World) is embodied in the synchronistic experience of the "medieval missionary [who] tells that he has found the point where heaven and Earth meet . . ." This dazzling image is known as the Flammarion Woodcut (unknown artist), from Camille Flammarion's L'atmosphère: Météorologie Populaire *(Paris, 1888), a meteorological work meant for the lay public. [SOURCE: Wikimedia Commons; Colorization: Hugo Heikenwaelder, Vienna, 1998] see more deeper, r. 199*

SYNCHRONICITY

The best definition is Jung's: meaningful coincidence

Something has meaning when it proves to be an organic part of an ordered whole.

Gerhard Adler

In this chapter, recurring ideas of number are seen to underlie the concept of synchronicity in such concepts as the *Unus Mundus*, the Law of Large Numbers, and more generally, the number archetype. The concept of synchronicity is so challenging to conventional thought—indeed, readers may find the ideas compelling to say the least—that a detailed exposition and discussion of the basic precepts of the theory of synchronicity are first undertaken in this chapter before launching into the specific relevance of synchronicity to number *per se*.

One of the chief aims of the scientific quest is to look for antecedent conditions of an event that may accurately explain the occurrence of that event in rational terms, which is to say, in causal terms. The scientific objective, then, is to trace events back to first causes. Ironically, virtually all religions attribute a divine origin or *Prima Causa* as first principle of the Creation, so the idea of causality has been around for a long time. Similarly the secular view of the layperson is that natural events must have causal origins. But it seems we might claim that any event could be classed as provisionally acausal if the ability to completely understand the nature of that event in causal terms cannot possibly reach the level where it might accommodate an explanation within a framework of descriptive language (or other discourse using, say, a mathematical model). Consequently, a seemingly adequate explanation ultimately may not, or cannot describe or even identify, all the pertinent

Caution, Reader: this gets pretty heady!

antecedents or contingencies of an event to a satisfactory degree, if at all, upon closer analysis. The first claim draws attention to the fact that causal models are relative structures, valid only in accordance with the current epistemological foundations upon which such models are built. The second suggests that by the natural limitations of human cognitive functions the description of many phenomena in causal terms may come to be seen as less informative than first thought.

In an ideal world, the more astute investigator, very much aware of these limitations, would not continue on the scientific quest as if, in relation to the first claim, understanding by the function of reason alone was sufficient for the task. In relation to the second claim, one would not expect the investigator to hold that absolute knowledge was attainable by that very function. However, such precautions also have their limitations, and the modern physicist or psychologist, for example, must get around these limitations by constructing pragmatic models that necessarily marginalize the incomprehensible. Enter synchronicity and paranormal phenomena (psi), which have long been considered acausal for the two reasons just given. They cannot be thoroughly described in causal terms, and as a corollary of this fact, they may possibly have factors associated with them that are barely knowable in human terms, if ever knowable at all. As a consequence of these facts, Jung dealt with the incomprehensibility of the acausal by first dealing with the causal.

Jung's Idea of Causality

One of Aristotle's four causes, the *efficient cause*—previously discussed in the chapter on the number four—is akin to the modern understanding of cause in the cause/effect dyad, where the cause is the agent or event that leads to the effect. One other of Aristotle's four causes, the *final cause*, concerns purpose, and is therefore teleological in nature. This latter cause undermines conventional thinking which has it that cause must precede effect, and this issue will be raised shortly. Generally speaking causal theory is a scientific and philosophical convention that holds that causes and effects may be related according to impressions gained by:

(i)   Temporal precedence: causes must come before effects.

(ii)   Temporal and spatial contiguity: causes and effects must occur together in time and space.

(iii) Constant conjunction: the effect(s), which follow a cause, must occur on a regular basis.

Jung agreed (1960, para. 836), as per (i) and (ii) above, that in order to establish causal links between a cause and an effect, the cause must precede the effect, and both must occur together. Grounded in the classical tradition of positivistic science, Jung also claimed "there must be a transmission of energy from the cause to the effect," since effect is always the result of some kind of energy flow (Aziz, 1990, p. 73. See also Jung, 1960, para. 840). When it is no longer possible to posit energy exchange as an intrinsic component of the phenomenon the event is considered acausal.

Jung (1960, para. 819) argued that on the strength of (iii) alone, it is clear that statistical truth underlies the causal world. Thus we must accept that no absolute case can be made for so-called causal events, in the sense of trying to explain cause-and-effect phenomena as events that are eternally and forever explainable causally. As a working hypothesis, therefore, causality must be supplemented by other world-views.

Causality, then, is congruent with a world that is taken as 'natural', (that is, obeying the classical laws of physics, for example) while acausality embodies the principle of discontinuity, or lack of connectedness ("inconstant connection," to use Jung's term). But, as mentioned, the causal world has been constructed from statistical truth, as a result of a 'scientific' outlook. Consequently, as rationally minded human beings we have become conditioned to a scientific world-view to the effect that causal events are the only events that make sense, while acausal events stultify our reason. Jung proposed the theory of synchronicity as a means of encompassing acausal events into an ordered framework that would offer a more complete picture of our phenomenological world.

Synchronicity

According to Jung, two or more events constitute synchronicity when a meaningful connection—a meaningful association—can be made between the events, but it is only synchronicity when meaningfulness is the connecting principle between the events with no causal connections (Jung, 1960, para. 849-850). Furthermore, synchronistic events are not merely coincidences resulting from chance (even though they generally appear as chance events) because they are also characterized by their meaningfulness (para. 967). Of course this meaningfulness, as a defining element of synchronicity, can only be acknowledged if a certain content in the psyche is made conscious at a time when a physical event of "equivalence" in the real world is also made conscious. Only then can we speak of synchronicity in practical terms (para. 858). Theoretically, and according to Jung, "a synchronistic event remains a synchronistic event whether or not its meaningfulness is recognized" (Aziz, 1990, p. 76).

For Jung, a synchronistic event usually involves an archetype (archetypes are nodal points or structural components of the collective unconscious that govern or influence our patterns of behavior). The archetype forms the substructure of the synchronicity, connecting at least two events (an exo-psychic one, and an endo-psychic one) with a common theme, and acting as a defining quality throughout the experience, thereby, intensifying the meaningfulness (Jung, 1960, para. 912). Synchronicity is not time-dependent in the causal sense where cause must precede effect — the physical event may occur *at the same time* as an experience in the psyche (an internal image), or even after this experience (para. 984). Nor is it dependent on spatial determinants (a phenomenon similar in nature to the quantum effect of nonlocality).

The relativization of space and time is a hallmark of synchronicity, as indeed it is of paranormal phenomena. That is, so-called normal phenomena supposedly follow the causal patterns outlined above, whereas synchronicity and psi characteristically infringe those causal precepts. Since space-time now exists as a unitary term in modern physics because the two are inseparably

[handwritten marginal note at top of page, partially legible]

united as a four-dimensional construct, Jung suggests it is reasonable to think of synchronicity and psi in terms of space-time relativity. Specifically, Jung (1960, para. 837) was certain that if space and time might be "psychically relative" as well, then "the moving body [as in PK (psychokinesis) phenomena] must possess, or be subject to, a corresponding relativity." Likewise, since ESP (extra-sensory perception) and synchronicity cannot be explained in terms of energy transmission, the simultaneity of synchronistic events (i.e., synchronistic events "falling together in time") comes about because "synchronicity [is] a psychically conditioned relativity of space and time" (para. 840). — *An excellent capsulization of the topic!* *[handwritten]*

Meaningfulness

The issue of meaningfulness needs some clarification. In its simplest form, meaningfulness (in a Jungian sense) is present at the feeling level (although a degree of intellectual satisfaction can be present), and since meaning is interpretative, it may also be highly subjective (Jung, 1971, para. 723*ff*). But, this subjective component is seen as necessary, and in fact, does not detract from the objective reality of the feeling (Aziz, 1990, p. 65). Jung defines feeling as the conscious function of evaluation that results in the "acceptance or rejection ('like' or 'dislike')" of a content in consciousness (1971, para. 724).

Feeling may give rise to associated factors, such as simple and complex emotional responses, which include the affective components of belief and disbelief (the cognitive components of belief and disbelief may also be affected). But more importantly, the likelihood of healing or change in outlook may result (especially if a certain shiftless form of single-mindedness is present). Any or all of these factors may be present to varying degrees of emotional intensity, according to the numinosity of the experience (Jung, 1960, para 982; Jung, 1971, para. 681). Ultimately the result is a transformation of personality in some way, which Jung saw as the embodiment of the individuation process, "having for its goal the development of the individual personality" (Jung, 1971, para. 757).

Examples of Synchronicity and Coincidence

At this point it may be necessary to illustrate the concept of synchronicity, and Jung gives an example in his essay *Synchronicity* (1960, para. 912, 915). In 1759, while in Gothenburg, Swedish religious leader and scientist Emmanuel Swedenborg had a vision of a house on fire hundreds of miles away in Stockholm. He gave the Gothenburg city authorities an account of this fire, including such details as the owner of the house, and the time the fire was put out. Jung writes:

> When…the vision arose in Swedenborg's mind of a fire in Stockholm, there was a real fire raging there at the same time, without there being any demonstrable or even thinkable connection between the two (para. 912).

Jung makes a point of this "fire burning in him [Swedenborg] too" as being the prime determinant of the synchronistic event: two events, one physical, one psychic, and this was born out in Swedenborg's biography, whereby his psychological state gives indication of the likelihood of an 'inner fire'. That is, Swedenborg's inner fire is of particular psychological (meaningful) significance, and is not simply a typical psi phenomenon, although Jung believed that ESP and PK share the same phenomenology as synchronicity (para. 840, 863, 977-979).

Another example is the phenomenon of clock stopping at the time of the clock-owner's death. It has also been reported that an individual (a family member, friend, or caregiver), who has unilateral or mutual emotional ties with someone (i.e., a loved-one), may be 'contacted' or 'visited' by the loved-one at the time of the loved-one's death. This is another form of synchronicity, and is similar to precognitive dreams and visions, which involve foreknowledge of events.

Then why can't all this be scientific, too? It's inductive, isn't it?

The Law of Large Numbers

One ostensible explanation of synchronicity (and, in fact, psi phenomena) depends on an appeal to the Law of Large Numbers which, as defined by John

Allen Paulos in *Beyond Numeracy* (1991), is effected when the "difference between the probability of some event and the relative frequency with which it occurs necessarily approaches zero" (p. 39). For example, Paulos notes (rather stoically) that coincidences of people's premonitory dreams of natural disasters with the actual real life disasters are "unimpressive" and to be expected, "[g]iven the half billion hours of dreaming each night in this country [United States]—2 hours a night for 250 million people—we should expect as much."

Statistically, a vast number of topics, themes and scenarios in people's dreams (and visions, no doubt) would be covered in the time available—especially with so many people with different backgrounds, different problems and real life issues on their minds. Any match with real world events is inevitable and of no consequence—neither paranormal effect, "inconstant connection," nor synchronicity, then, need be postulated to explain these anomalous 'matches'. This reasoning might ostensibly explain Swedenborg's vision.

The Law of Large Numbers implies that now more than ever, with over 6 billion people on the planet, there are more *meaningless* coincidences than ever before. The Law embodies the categorical assumption that synchronicity and certain kinds of psi (for example, precognitive dreams), no matter how outstanding or remarkable, or on the other hand, no matter how likely they may be (if the Law holds true), must, on parsimonious grounds, be taken as *meaningless* coincidences, according to the laws of probability.

By such a statistical law one can say that if enough trials are run, if enough samples are taken, if an experiment is repeated often enough, the result one wants is not only probable, but also highly likely. By this reasoning, one is free to believe that a first trial (or experiment or observation) may yield a result that should be considered a *mere coincidence*—especially if the result challenges our causal world-view, or in fact, even if it is believable and well within normal experience. Repeated experimentation (replication) is supposed to determine whether or not these coincidences are to be taken as new facts about the world.

Such facts, then, as Jung would claim, are actually statistical truths, from which the human world comes to be structured *meaningfully* (since the truths are believable). Prior to becoming statistical truths, these new facts would be congruent with low *a priori* probabilities. From a different perspective, Swedenborg's vision, as a clairvoyant event, would be given a low *a priori* probability, since there are no records of similar visions concerning the fire. But as Peter Delin writes in 'Skepticism and Credulity' (2002):

> One might have thought that to the scientist, striving to obtain an objective view of the universe, a piece of evidence for a proposition would have a status independent of his previous opinions, but this is not so.... [H]e attaches a certain probability to the phenomenon or theory, and demands stronger or weaker evidence in accordance with this *a priori* probability. (p. 32)

A less conservative scientific approach would mean accepting the fact that there is no reason to assume that (say) a psi phenomenon is a mere coincidence. To do otherwise would mean making an unwarranted assumption prior to any form of measurement. Further investigation may reveal the phenomenon to be causally explicable, or on the other hand, it might be placed in the more established categories of ESP or PK.

Problems with the Law

The Unique Case: There are a couple of other problems with the Law of Large Numbers. As just stated it seems that the meaningful coincidence (the coincidence of a personal nature) is absorbed into the sphere of meaningless coincidences and treated indiscriminately from all other coincidences, which may well be meaningless. The uniquely personal precognition, for example, is not unique in a statistical sense because its qualitative, i.e., meaningful elements are not, nor cannot be considered by the Law—it is merely 'allowed' to occur because the Law of Large Numbers 'admits' the probability of its occurrence. As rare or as unlikely as it may appear, it is not a statistical anomaly. The problem with the Law is that it explains too much in the single

PRECLUDED INFLUENCES → LAW →

word 'probability', but at the same time, misses the point because it precludes the possibility of other explanations, such as certain forms of correspondence between the components of the so-called coincidence.

Put another way, while there may be a great many people dreaming or having visions about neutral (i.e., non-personally relevant) events (such as earthquakes, tornadoes, or even fires in Stockholm), which can be 'explained' by the Law, the power of the Law is greatly reduced when these precognitive dreams have contents which are personal or familial. Dreaming about the death of a loved-one, for example, which then occurs in real life at the same time as the dream, is a phenomenon that cannot be justly considered within the probabilistic framework of the Law. The reason for this limitation comes from the fact that such a dream or vision has a meaningfulness of a nature that makes it unique when compared to only similar dreams by others who do not know and did not dream about that particular loved-one's fate.

Upon reflection, then, it is still possible that Swedenborg's vision was a paranormal phenomenon. The continued accrual of details associated with the fire, as reported by Swedenborg, reduces the probability of the vision being a chance occurrence (against the Law, it becomes more and more improbable that other people could have produced similar reports like Swedenborg's in all its detail). The more particular and detailed the event, the less likely can precognition or clairvoyance of an event be explained by the Law.

The Retrieval Cue: Hines (1998) also appeals to the Law to justify the same argument that "if an event is given enough opportunities to occur, sooner or later it will occur" (p. 51). Further, the "*retrieval cue*" mechanism plays a part. When an event in the real world does match a 'forgotten' dream, it is immediately recalled (p. 51). Hines believes such dreams are "reliably prophetic" only because they have been "selectively" remembered by real life cues and thereby "come true" (p. 51). Dreams that are irrelevant to real life events are suitably never remembered.

But Hines ignores the dreams that are not forgotten, and do not depend on cues, and in fact, usually hold an overpowering (because relevant) emotional component for the dreamer. The 'reality' of the dream and the reality of the event merge and give the dream a quality of 'truthfulness' in its own right—it is not simply a coincidence. Furthermore, often it is the case that the dreamer has these dreams *at the time* of the real life event and *not before* the event. Either way, the claim of synchronicity is warranted.

The *Unus Mundus*

By appealing to the concept of the alchemical *unus mundus* ('one world') Jung was able to unify (at least conceptually) psyche and matter (world events) where causal connections are not necessary (although causality must be included in the *unus mundus*). This concept links existence at every stratum into one unified total system where an interrelatedness exists between the strata in a way which is not seen as planned or coordinated at some transcendent or supraordinate level.

Such a concept compares with the postulates of sub-atomic particle physics. Samuels, Shorter and Plaut state in *A Critical Dictionary of Jungian Analysis* (1992):

> In both [synchronicity and atomic physics] we observe rapid interaction and interchange of the entities involved; and in both there are patterns and probabilities to be found...[T]he non-Einsteinian notion of 'action-at-a-distance', in which two distinct sub-atomic particles behave harmoniously, as though each 'knew' what the other is doing, may be compared to the theory of archetypes. (p. 157)

Any meaningful connection made between inner and outer events may not necessarily be attributed to projection, coincidence, chance or accident—it goes deeper than this. There is, according to the *unus mundus* concept, a 'secret mutual connivance' between inner and outer events (this issue is taken up in the chapter "The Reasonable Mind"). The psyche is creating the event (an 'act of creation in time') purely by being the observer of the event. But even this statement is inaccurate, because, again, cause-and-effect is suggested. The archetypal substratum is suggestive of a causal orderedness, whereas in fact inner and outer processes are *contingent* with each other (the archetype is psychoid in nature and conceivable as a substratum, fundamental to life itself, giving life its particular meaningful quality). This concept is illustrated in Figure 63.

Figure 63. *In the unus mundus (framed), our world of inner and outer events is unified into a singular but multi-dimensional experience. Archetypes (as components of the 'psychoid substrate') are contingent with 'acts of creation in time', and they give that experience its specific quality. If the same archetype is activated in two subjects distanced from each other (i.e., outside the 'normal' sensory means of contact), then synchronicity, S (signified by the intersection of the dotted concentric circles), is possible between one or both subjects, and S would qualify as a paranormal experience otherwise known as ESP. (Note that the dotted concentric circles, signifying the activated archetype, do not imply a field.)*

The archetype is activated at a particular moment according to intra-psychic necessity. At the time, it just happens—in the example given in Figure 63—that both persons experience the same archetype, which might translate as an ESP experience. The *unus mundus* 'contains' the human subject, who also 'contains' the archetypes, which are like nodal points with an 'action potential'. The archetype directs one's experience, according to the nature of the archetype, towards encounters (events) that are thereby 'constructed' ('created') by the psyche. The archetype, then, is as Jung (1960) asserts:

> the introspectively recognisable form of *a priori* psychic orderedness. If an external synchronistic process now associates itself within it, it falls into the same basic pattern—in other words, it too is "ordered." (para. 965)

The *unus mundus* is synchronistic in nature, where space and time are relativised. This is not to say that time and space do not exist, for that would undermine the possibility of an experience.

In Figure 63, mention was made of the fact that the archetype does not manifest as a field. In *A Glossary of Terms Used in Parapsychology* (2003), Michael Thalbourne describes and defines William Roll's 'psi-field' as:

> analogous to an electromagnetic or gravitational field...in which it is postulated that physical events associated with physical objects produce changes in the psi fields surrounding those objects...and that these 'psi traces' are communicated via intermediary psi fields to the psi field of a percipient. (p. 94)

The effect of the object's 'psi-traces' on the percipient's own psi-field constitutes an ESP experience by way of the field's physical influence (or 'intersection') with the percipient's brain. The ubiquity of the archetype appears to have correspondences with Roll's psi-field. The only problem with Roll's hypothesis is that it is a causal explanation that involves energy exchange—the field's *physical* effect on the brain is being offered to explain ESP phenomena, so that it stands in contra-distinction to the nature of the archetype in synchronicity theory. Jung's hypothesis of synchronicity insists on the acausal factor. The "inconstant connection, through contingence, equivalence, or 'meaning' " (Jung, 1960, para. 963) with physical and psychic events is the only means of acceptably accounting for the variables that constitute the synchronistic phenomenon.

In fact, in parapsychology today, postulating 'energic' causal hypotheses that might explain psi phenomena is a somewhat anachronistic activity, and some parapsychologists are now constructing hypotheses using the nonlocality concept based on the findings of quantum physics. Experimental evidence of nonlocality already exists, and many physicists including David Bohm, like Sir James Jeans, entertain the likelihood that the old (historical) cause-and-effect paradigm is definitely inadequate in explaining all phenomena.

'Historical' causal thinking makes it difficult to accept the basic tenets of synchronicity theory, especially as it applies to the relativization of space and time, so that some confusion has arisen over the notion of clock-time simultaneity. Aziz makes an important point concerning the implication of the word 'synchronicity'. Jung (1960) has suggested the existence of a "psychic relativity of space and time" (para. 840), which invokes the idea of an "irrepresentable space-time continuum" (para. 948). But in necessarily dealing with the categories of space and time as 'fixed' concepts, which come about "in the course of…mental development" (para. 840), and are the reference points of all experiences in consciousness, he has not been entirely clear in his clarification of the relativization of time and space as a continuum. Therefore, Aziz explains:

> In this continuum the time and space restrictions as we know them are nonexistent and accordingly there is no "before" or "after".… The synchronicity principle, then, as its etymology indicates, does relate to "a kind of simultaneity" [writes Jung, 1960], for in the space-time continuum everything exists en bloc. (p. 71)

This is precisely what Jung (1960) suggests in a roundabout way, even though it takes him a while to get to the point—the idea of everything existing 'en bloc' constitutes the *unus mundus*. The fact that a physical component of a synchronistic event may occur (say) in the future, only to be confirmed after the event (a case of precognition), is neither here nor there as far as the spacetime continuum is concerned. That is, although it would be classed as a paranormal event, it is, relativistically speaking, quite 'normal' in the spacetime continuum. The *unus mundus* concept addresses this fundamental point, and again, the archetypes of the collective unconscious, as crucial components contingent with the human experience of matter, psyche, and the spacetime continuum, stand as the contents and constituents of the orderedness of mind in the universe.

Synchronicity and the Archetype of Number

This long and eventful passage through the complexities of synchronicity theory serves the purpose of leading to a deeper understanding of the archetypal form of number as it relates to synchronistic events. The above-mentioned order and pattern in the cosmos corresponds with the principle of the number archetype, and Jung considers the properties of the natural numbers to be contributing factors in synchronistic phenomena. An acausal orderedness is assigned to natural numbers by the fact of their *a priori* 'just-so' (axiomatic) qualities. Jung (1960) states:

> Since the remotest times, men [*sic*] have used numbers to establish meaningful coincidences, that is, coincidences that can be interpreted.... Number, therefore, is in one sense an unpredictable entity.... It is the predestined instrument for creating order, or for apprehending an already existing, but still unknown, regular arrangement or "orderedness." (para. 870)

Jung notes the numinosity and mystery of both synchronicity and number, and the bearing they have on our lives. Natural numbers occur with great frequency in our lives, more commonly in patterned (geometric) or sequential form. Such forms, in their expressions and representations, set up the conditions for order and meaning. So long as number presents in this way, often as spontaneous products of the unconscious, the numinous and symbolic aspects of number will be deemed as having more than that which is consciously applied to them.

Jung states that numbers were pre-existent to consciousness, so that they occasionally condition consciousness, rather than does consciousness condition the form taken by number. The number archetype may also show an interconnectedness with other archetypes, so that representations of numbers in consciousness are meaningful in terms other than numerical. This other-than-numerical meaning comes about because, from the point of view that numbers are archetypes and archetypes have affects on each other, archetypal patterns may be meaningfully 'read off' numbers as they appear in mantic processes, in the same way that dark clouds may signify rain, or a disease may be read off from its signs and symptoms. However, only the probability of successful readings can be assumed, in the same way that a successful diagnosis and subsequent prognosis are probabilistically determined. Mantic arts, therefore, rely on number as the means by which information is attained by divinatory methods (these issues are taken up in subsequent chapters).

The methods of the mantic arts put order to the 'irrational' (or apparently chaotic) state of the universe. An ordered world is one in which we feel most suited, and putting order to the world is an innate human process, given that archetypal structures are innate in the psyche, thus forming the nodal points around which experiences constellate, so that building a mind, and a world patterned by that mind, is not only possible and preferable, but is inevitable. The universe, having its structures in place before humans walked the earth, shows a symmetry, pattern and order, which are reflected in how we perceive that universe. Having evolved in such a universe, its very structure *meaningfully* predetermines who we are and how we experience the world.

Summary

Jung's essay on synchronicity was, in part, an attempt at putting synchronicity within the grasp of the researcher by first placing this anomalous phenomenon within a theoretical framework. But synchronicity poses a very real problem for psychologists, philosophers and physicists because its basic premise conflicts with the perceived (or received) model of the world as we ordinarily experience it. By the theory, we are given to consider meaning from a perspective that not only sees the integration of experiences of the physical world *into* our thoughts and feelings, but also sees many events in the physical world as concomitant with those thoughts and feelings in ways explicable only by the ordering principle of the archetype.

Statistical analysis of data in the quantitative sciences is crucial in testing theories, and is the paragon of research tools in experimentation. However, certain forms of statistical treatment, such as applying the Law of Large Numbers to explain anomalies, does not always give a qualitative account of data. That is not their purpose. Thus, the particular quality of a unique case may remain undetected as a result of an exclusively quantitative approach.

Our existence in the universe reflects a relationship that is contingent in, and with nature, and this relationship can be expressed in the alchemical construct of the *unus mundus*. Therefore, conceptually, the number archetype can function synchronistically, thus providing a 'mechanism' underlying mantic systems, such as numerology, astrology, and *I Ching*. These three systems are discussed next.

Look, let's simplify this:
Causal can be explained
and understood in inductive
rational (18th Cent) terms.
Acausal cannot be. It is
more deductive from all
possible influences which
must be accounted for
and not precluded before
a "synchronicity" ———

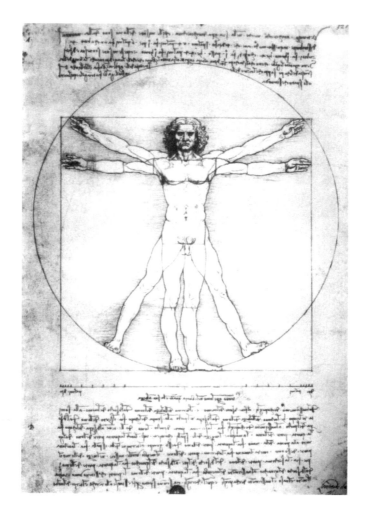

Plate 22. THE VITRUVIAN MAN

Leonardo da Vinci's Vitruvian Man *(1492), was designed under the fundamental belief that numbers underpin all creation and all things observable—even the morphology and behavior of the species* Homo sapiens. *The ancients believed that people were of a certain type and behaved a certain way because the power of specific numbers caused them to behave that way [SOURCE: National Aeronautics and Space Administration, USA].*

NUMEROLOGY

To seek to see in everything something no one
has yet seen and no one has yet thought of.

Georg Christoph Lichtenberg

In the chapter "A Brief History of Number" mention was made of various types of numbers dating back to Pythagorean times, with the inference that qualities, not just quantities, were applicable to number. Each of the natural numbers was assigned to various personalities of the Greek and Roman pantheons (other cultures made the same associations with their gods). Thus the single-digit numbers embodied the same characteristics as the gods. The gods, being socially constructed representations of archetypes (where numbers are archetypes too), are personified human predispositions and unconscious processes, and these predispositions and processes can further be related to the numbers associated with the gods. In *Numbers Will Tell* (1973), Moore and Setley give the god-like meanings of the single (fadic) digits (*see* Table 24). Note that associations between gods and numbers are also included.

Since archetypes can govern particular behaviors, in that they determine the form of an instinct leading to that behavior, numbers too might be considered to have influence on human behavior. This chapter considers the proposition that numbers can have influence on our lives, and how it might be possible to predict that influence. *The problem here is one of determinism.*

The Gospel of Numbers According to John King

John King (1996) objects to the types of number meanings listed in Table 24, and considers them to be derivative of astrological descriptions. But it can be seen that they compare quite favorably with the traditional descriptions of the gods who were identified with the numbers 1 to 10. King proposes a set of meanings, which are "ancient and well-documented numerological attributes of the first numbers" (p. 192; *see* Table 25).

Table 24. *The Fadic Numbers, the Associated Greek and Roman Gods, and the Number Meanings.*

#	GOD	MEANING
1	Apollo: Beneficent Power	"1 represents all that is creative. It is a beneficial number and governs success, happiness and prosperity."
2	Eros/Cupid: Relationship	"2 represents change, restlessness and unsettled conditions. It is the number of music and public activities. A friendship number."
3	Kronos/Saturn: Time and Old Age	"3 represents ambition and authority. It governs religion, law, money and publishing."
4	Zeus/Jupiter: Joy and Music	"4 represents music, science, justice and rebellion."
5	Hermes/Mercury: Travel and the Intellect	"5 represents travel, nervousness, and literary matters. It governs communication and gambling."
6	Aphrodite/Venus: Love	"6 is a personality number and the number of magnetism. It represents love, sex, all the arts, and lecturers."
7	Athena/Minerva: Wisdom	"7 represents occultism, astrology, numerology, and palmistry. This number governs entertainment and the amusement field."
8	Demeter/Ceres: Earth	"8 represents business, land and real estate… and anything pertaining to the earth. It is a number of worry and melancholy."
9	Hephæstus/Vulcan: Fire	"9 represents force and energy. It is the number of fire, injuries, and accidents. 9 governs… metals, writers and the medical profession."

I find these tables frightening....

Table 25. *Numbers and Their Meanings.*

#	MEANING
1	authority, leadership, independence, material wealth, seclusion, and isolation
2	femininity, sexual attractiveness, fertility, secrecy, sensitivity, tact, tolerance, and stillness
3	harmony, fruition, pregnancy and childbirth, family, equilibrium, enlightenment, and resurrection
4	discipline, stability, practical skill, domesticity, and community service
5	creativity, intuition, radicalism, innovation and spiritual energy
6	harmony, marriage, devotion, orderliness, fidelity, emotional warmth and seaworthiness
7	physical or military strength, self-discipline, sexual attractiveness, global perspective, majesty, spirituality, skill in meditation, and spiritual leadership
8	good fortune, justice, regeneration, motherhood, sense of proportion and equity
9	change, transformation, skill in magic, sexual energy and healing
10	perfection, completion, perseverance, and closure

Most of these meanings are supported by the findings detailed in the previous chapters, although there are many anomalies:

1. "material wealth" in #1 belongs in #5
2. "stillness" in #2 belongs in #3
3. "harmony" appears twice (#3 and #6), but belongs in #6 only
4. "sexual attractiveness" appears twice (#2 and #7), but belongs in #2 only (#7 being 'virginal')
5. "creativity" in #5 belongs in #2
6. it is unclear why "seaworthiness" belongs with #6

7. "motherhood" in #8 belongs in #3 (#7 being 'virginal')
8. it is not clear how "skill in magic, sexual energy and healing" belong with #9

These anomalies may be due to the fact that King has taken these meanings from a number of different cultural sources. As mentioned previously, it is unreasonable to expect cultures that differ historically and geographically to show complete agreement on symbolic issues (by their symbolic nature alone, numbers are paradoxical and constantly defy description). Starting with the symbol, number representations are derived by the heuristic methods available to a given culture, and these vary according to the geographical, historical, and social environment of that culture. But it is the number archetype which serves as the starting point in the meanings of numbers, which are shown to be as close to an absolute framework as can be expected, as is mirrored in the consistent natures and attributes of the gods—even from culture to culture (*see* Table 24).

Numerical qualities characterize the gods, suggesting not just an interconnectedness of archetypes through a mirroring of qualities in gods and numbers, but also a reducibility of gods to numbers. Thereby the ancients considered numbers sacred, and this sacredness is maintained in any number system that favors qualitative factors over quantitative factors.

It is not suggested that quantities lack importance when compared to the qualities of numbers, but it is maintained that qualities are determined from different criteria, which may appear to marginalize the rational common sense ground given by numbers from their quantitative aspects. With number symbolism we are required to recognize that number representations are indicative of qualities that underlie those representations. While assigning godlike attributes to numbers might seem an anachronism in the current era, the archetypal aspects of numbers generate values and meanings that can and do have influences in consciousness. Numerology supposedly has its basis in this fact, where value and meaning are 'assigned' to number on the basis of the influence of the number archetype.

*see Runic stones
and I-ching.
(advanced Algebra)*

Numerology—The Basics

Numerology is the study of the occult meaning of numbers, but it is also a form of divination. In Pythagoras' time numerology flourished and became a complex philosophical system that was inevitably linked to the fundamental belief that numbers underpinned all creation and all things observable—even human behavior. If the harmony of the spheres had universal significance, it made sense to apply this ordering principle to human behavior. It was believed that people were of a certain type and behaved a certain way because the power of specific numbers caused them to behave that way.

King (1990) writes that numerology serves five main purposes: (1) interpretation; (2) diagnosis; (3) analysis; (4) prediction, and (5) invocation, charms, and spells. Interpretive methods give information about character and personality. Diagnosis and analysis look at number patterns and number recurrences that might emerge in a person's numbers. Prediction is aimed at giving forecasts or recommendations based on number outcomes. Invocations, charms and spells are practical applications of the numbers themselves as symbols to be held in consciousness, so that the 'metaphysical' and 'metatemporal' aspects of numbers can come to the fore, bringing about the changes or effects that correspond to those numbers.

So, the single integers (the fadic numbers) and their multiples, and even prime numbers, all had magical or mystical significance which in psychological terms means that some kind of archetypal (previously sacred, godlike) quality in a number was discernable in an individual by the very fact of the resonance or 'vibration' of that number in that individual.

The number of a person could be determined in various ways. The usual way of determining a person's number, still in use today, is to reduce the birthdate (day, month, and year) to a single digit, known as the *ruling number* or *birthpath*. Reducing a number means to keep adding the digits together in a number if it is larger that 10 until a single digit is reached. Sometimes 11, 22 and 33, etc.—the so-called 'master' numbers—are not reduced to 2, 4, and 6, respectively, because they have special meanings in their double-digit form.

See Dana Cooper and Sharon Hutton.

By way of example, for a person born 25th December, 1945 (25.12.1945, or in the USA, 12.25.1945) the ruling number is:

$$2 + 5 + 1 + 2 + 1 + 9 + 4 + 5 = 29 \Rightarrow 2 + 9 = \underline{11} \Rightarrow 1 + 1 = \underline{2}$$

The person would then read a description of his or her type by consulting the reading for #2 (and also the master number #11), which might also give advice on suitable vocations, or recommend appropriate partnerships based on their type.

Some numerologists use the *birth number* (the day of the month reduced to a single digit, therefore excluding the month and year). Thomas Muldoon in *Numerology and You* (1988) feels that the month and year on their own do not warrant reduction because the information gained is not sufficiently personal.

Another popular method in numerology is the substitution of the letters of a name with the numbers that stand for the letters in that name according to one or both of two ancient systems used in the West. The first method makes use of the Pythagorean alphabet (*see* fig. 64):

Figure 64. *The Pythagorean alphabet.*

1	2	3	4	5	6	7	8	9
A	B	C	D	E	F	G	H	I
J	K	L	M	N	O	P	Q	R
S	T	U	V	W	X	Y	Z	

The second method makes use of the Chaldean alphabet (*see* fig. 65):

Figure 65. *The Chaldean alphabet. Letters were not ascribed to the #9 because the number nine was sacred in ancient Babylon.*

1	2	3	4	5	6	7	8
A	B	C	D	E	U	O	F
I	K	G	M	H	V	Z	P
J	R	L	T	N	W		
Q		S		X			
Y							

Using either one (or both) of these methods yields the *destiny number* or *expression number*. A name like Albert Einstein converts to #9 in the following way using the Pythagorean alphabet (see fig. 66).

Figure 66. *The name Albert Einstein converted to a number.*

$$A + L + B + E + R + T + E + I + N + S + T + E + I + N$$
$$1 + 3 + 2 + 5 + 9 + 2 + 5 + 9 + 5 + 1 + 2 + 5 + 9 + 5 = \underline{63} \Rightarrow 6 + 3 = \underline{9}$$

Although Albert Einstein is a #9, the Chaldean alphabet has him as a #10 (or #1). Some numerologists do not reduce the #10 to #1, because they feel that the #10 has special significance. Although #10 carries the same symbolism as #1, the character traits of the person will be more pronounced because they are magnified tenfold.

It is usual that a different number will result depending on the system because the letter values are not always the same from system to system. Numerologists advise individuals to use the alphabet that yields a destiny number that 'feels right' for the client according to the reading for that number, or according to the numerologist's personal experience.

Problems with Numerology

There are many other methods of number construction and interpretation in numerology, but those just described are the most often used. However, there are two major flaws in these methods.

First, there is no absolute sense in which the ruling number (birthpath) can hold any relevance to a person's specific moment of birth. In the West, the time period in years in which we count dates back to the nominal birth date of Jesus Christ—the *beginning* of the year 1 AD (i.e., zero on the timeline), but now reckoned to be 4 AD. Technically, four years should be subtracted from a person's birth year if Christ's birth year is to be taken as a major historical (absolute?) reference point. In other words, although the year gives a time of birth, it is arbitrarily assigned according to the culture, and has no fixed or absolute reference to anything in time or space regardless of the culture. In Japan, for example, even though the western calendar is used, the year is also counted from the beginning of the reign of the current Emperor. (Note also the many different calendars in use throughout the Middle and Far East, and even Mexico and South America.)

Also, the calendar in use in the West (and in most parts of the East) is the Gregorian calendar, which replaced the Julian calendar in 1582 AD because its year was eleven minutes and ten seconds too long. Europe eventually accepted the Gregorian calendar, but some countries took longer than others to make the change. For example, in England it was not until the year 1752 that eleven days were omitted from that year—the year the Gregorian calendar was adopted. While the length of the year may now be more accurate, these missing days indicate the arbitrary nature of time keeping (should the real birthdate of those people born prior to the adoption of the Gregorian calendar be re-calculated?). The number of months in a year may also vary according to the culture. The Hebrews, for example, have a thirteenth month which is used cyclically (see the chapter "Seven (The Heptad)").

Second, as mentioned, the name a person has been given can be converted to a number by at least one of two methods. The numerologist's advice of choosing the destiny number that feels right (according to one's intuition no doubt) is rather haphazard if one's intuition is not reliable, or one's ego gets in the way. Another problem concerns the form of the person's name. Some numerologists insist on using the full name given in the birth certificate, but a person might prefer to shorten their given (or christian) name(s), or may not like using certain names recorded on their birth certificate. Again, numerologists claim that one form of the name or the other is preferred according to the method used, or purpose served by the name. The destiny number, for example, requires that *all* the letters of *all* the names given at birth be used.

In addressing these issues (though most numerologists do not discuss them) numerologists claim that there are correspondences at work in these methods. Once a person accepts a method, that person becomes attuned to that method, and this philosophy also applies to the numerologist when he or she chooses one particular number system over another, or even invents one. King, for example, has his own numerological system. He numbers the letters of the alphabet according to the Celtic alphabet and other sources, which include modified Kabbalistic letter values (see *gematria* in the chapter "The Symbolism of Number"). Although King's system is internally consistent, his methodology is arbitrarily constructed. For example, he discusses the difficulty in deciding whether or not to count the silent K in the surname KNIGHT. If sound is an important consideration, the K is redundant, but King counts it in because the name dates back to medieval times when the K was sounded in the word *Knyghtes* (meaning 'knight'). The problem is that some numerologists would include the K without hesitation, while others might decide not to include it at all.

King's understanding of number is a traditional (religious, even magical) one, and he makes no attempt to align his ideas with psychological (archetypal) processes, even though he does relate the gods of various cultures to the fadic numbers. Nor does he rationalize the inconsistencies between the various methods of deriving a person's numbers—except to claim that his system is more in keeping with the ancient Greek tradition, the *Kabbalah*, and 'medieval hermeneutic occult' philosophy.

In fact, most numerologists would not rationalize numerology because to do so means it would be contingent upon numerologists to take steps towards applying the scientific method to numerological methods and practices. In other words, while the methods of numerology may be reliable, they are not yet proven valid in scientific terms. Even though numerology takes a qualitative look at number meanings and correspondences, actually involving a specious use of archetypal symbolism, this approach does not help validate the methods of arriving at these meanings and correspondences. The birth-date, for example, is shown to be dependent on the calendar being used. To pre-empt the next chapter, astrology too depends on the birth-date and time, as well as the geographical location of birth, but these details correspond to real terrestrial and celestial events. The birth location, time, and date of birth 'fix' the position of the planets, signs, and houses in a natal chart, but in numerology, dates are taken as having qualities in their own right.

The method of reduction, too, assumes that (say) the numbers 246, and 12 (i.e., 2 + 4 + 6), and 3 (i.e., 1 + 2), all have the same essential meaning. Some numerologists give individual treatment to the 'hundreds', and the 'tens', etc., but this process only stretches the range of possible interpretations, which can result in a nebulous confusion of contradictory statements due to excess information. After all, too much information can be as bad as too little. In the above example (#246), a numerologist might first give a client the individual meanings of 2 (x 100), 4 (x 10), and 6, followed by 12 (by reduction), and finally 3 (by reduction). Thus, from a three-digit number, at least three distinctly different readings are possible, all of which have to be woven into a tapestry of meaning that makes sense to the individual.

Furthermore, from a traditional viewpoint, multiple digit numbers can be interpreted from within certain contexts (see Table 26). One has to be certain that the context is appropriate for the number under consideration. For example, if a person is reading the *Pentateuch* in Hebrew (or the Old Testament), and an apparently mystical reference to the three-digit number in our example (#246) appears in the text, is that number to be taken as referring to 'intellectual' or 'terrestrial' issues? Numerology, however, is grounded upon some important archetypal facts, and these are discussed next.

Table 26. *Number Ranges and Their Classifications.*

NUMBER RANGE	NUMEROLOGY	GEMATRIA
1-9	Instinctual	Divine
10-99	Emotional	Celestial
100-999	Intellectual	Terrestrial
1000-9999	Intuitive	Future
10,000 +	Celestial	n/a

The Number Archetype as a Mechanism of Change

Although the methodology of numerology can be faulted, numbers do have qualities when those numbers are represented as manifestations in consciousness, and the number archetype plays a key role in these representations. For the numerological principle to make sense, then—that numbers have meanings and influences that affect the individual, so that the individual can be described by numbers—one must consider the symbolic aspect of the number, and not be so taken with the methods by which one's numbers are derived. For example, if change, in the form of a move toward qualities associated with a particular number, is sought in one's life, King (1990) states that this is achievable by "consciously, favoring, using, displaying, noticing or otherwise emphasizing the number associated with the attribute one wishes to promote" (p. 193). Of course, this kind of change can be effected without numbers, and would likely as not, be the result of determination, will-power, discipline and possibly a measure of the placebo-effect.

King may agree in part that such psychological mechanisms of change may be involved in an individual's progress, but he would more likely suggest that it is the number resonating in the psyche that has the major influence in bringing about change, and this is an important point. The number is more than a substitute for words. The number one may mean 'leadership', but it also means 'isolation', and the number seven may mean 'military strength' but it also means 'spirituality'—these words must therefore be seen as linguistic or cultural approximations to the symbolism of the numbers. To take the symbol as the mechanism for change makes sense psychologically because it connects with unconscious knowledge so far unexpressed. The symbol even draws on experiences going back to the dawn of time because the number archetype has a deeper and longer history in the evolution of the psyche than has any culture.

Meditation on a batch of related words, concepts and ideas would have limited reward psychologically because they are restricted to the short history of the language being used, whereas numbers run deeper, even to the past of our pre-linguistic ancestors. King (1990) hints at the raw empiricism of number when he says:

> the power of number is very pure, very abstract. A number is at once a very simple thing, something a small child could recognize in many instances, yet, at the same time, it represents a very extremely profound and complex concept. The simpler and clearer we can keep whatever liturgical or ritual devices we use to approach the mystery of number, the greater the likelihood that we will achieve success. (p. 193)

The 'liturgical or ritual devices' refer to our cultural products (deities, dance, prayer, and other practices), at the basis of which there is likely to be a very strong association with number.

While the hearts of most numerologists may be in the right place, and their arguments suggest a reliance on core meanings of number from an archetypal perspective, numerological methodologies are still arbitrary and therefore, largely not valid insofar as the numbers are constructed on *relative* (i.e., time periods and names) not *absolute* frameworks. If an individual wants an interpretation or prognostication of their life situation based on their 'numbers', they might best be served by astrology or the *I Ching*, which are systematically and methodologically more consistent.

Summary

Numerology dates back to ancient times when highly intuitive individuals recognized correspondences between numbers and the behaviors and events surrounding people's lives. The numerological philosophy underlying the universe—the idea that number gives structure and order to all things—was the central dogma of the Pythagoreans. A person's name or date of birth, the month they were born, etc., could all be used as a starting point in interpreting the circumstances of a person's past, present, and future life. However, any method used to perform such a task is based on an arbitrary calendar or alphabetical system, as well as other subjective methodologies. Nevertheless, the meanings of the numbers are seen to embody principles already assigned to the numbers, based on mythological, natural (physical/environmental), and psychological assertions, which have loose-fitting archetypal overtones.

Numbers do have deeper 'resonances' in the psyche than do the words that have come to be associated with those numbers. Numbers are archetypal, whereas words and ideas always involve cultural factors embodied in language and must be learned. Numbers are immutable, whereas cultural products change.

The more generalized divinatory systems of astrology and the *I Ching*, which use numbers indirectly to derive meaning, are underscored by the same archetypal pattern as that which underlies numerology. These two systems are reviewed next.

This is why the Church discourages this method. If accuracy is questionable, doesn't that take at least second place in the favored place of free will and faith?

Plate 23. THE TWELVE SIGNS OF THE ZODIAC

Zodiac array in a sixth-century synagogue at Beit Alpha, Israel. Numbers figure prominently in astrology, but the structural basis of astrology and its methodology owes more to number than just a mathematical (astronomical) pattern structure. A qualitative (interpretive) aspect in the astrological method is intrinsically determined by quantitative (numerical) patterns in the cosmos, so that numbers also figure meaningfully in the methods of astrology [SOURCE: National Aeronautics and Space Administration, USA].

ASTROLOGY

Understand that thou thyself art another world in little, and
host within thee the sun and the moon, and also the stars.

Origen

not had for the Catholic
— matter of Theologians "who also
believed in reincarnation!

Astrology has served as an inspiration for humanity for thousands of years, up to and including the modern era. In the early twentieth century, the composer Gustav Holst confided to a friend: "As a rule I only study things that suggest music to me.... Recently the character of each planet suggested lots to me" (1914, cited in Kennedy, 1974). So saying, his highly acclaimed "The Planets" suite of seven movements (one for each planet) of 1916 is a testament to the power of human creativity when inspired by age-old archetypal concepts—in this case, the planets.

While the planets and other astrological phenomena may inspire (say) the artist or composer, it has long been a contentious issue that the planets, and the signs, etc., are more than a source of inspiration, but actually have some kind of 'cosmic' influence as well—particularly because the reliability of astrology is still in question. In *Jung and Astrology* (1992), Hyde claims:

> If Saturn Returns had regularly produced a crisis for twenty-nine year
> old individuals, or if transits worked with clockwork precision, then
> astrology would certainly not be so marginal. (pp. 172-173)

Hyde correctly recognizes that an infallible astrology "would carry more status [than it currently does]...and assume real market value" (p. 173), but in recent decades astrology has found itself in a position where it is not necessarily better or worse off in terms of status and market value than any

see Richard Tarnus'
"Psyche and Cosmos"

of the accepted disciplines of our highly regarded institutions. Peer-reviewed journals such as *Correlation* are devoted exclusively to astrological studies and scientific findings not only produce some remarkable concordances with traditional claims, but also raise keen debate amongst skeptics who argue that the findings are probably artifacts of one form or another. Social criticism of science, too, and the many catastrophes in medicine (for example) have come into focus more and more. Meanwhile homeopathic medicine has grown in popularity, along with a host of other alternative approaches to the treatment of human suffering, thus demonstrating a degree of disillusionment in the populace with allopathic medicine.

However, the old quest for scientific certainty and truth about the world and the human condition is shown to be very much driven by fallible human beings, who are often as much to blame for failure as the disciplines themselves. The reliability of a certain truth, therefore, depends not only on the exactitude of the discipline, the science, or the art, but on the practitioner or interpreter as well. And further, even if the truths of (say) counseling or psychology are reliable, the individual is still the final arbiter in deciding the direction of his or her life. Such a precaution is used just as much by astrologers when their advice fails. However, diviners, when reminding the individual of his or her choices and freewill, are usually accused of falling back on this disclaimer as a means of 'getting off the hook' should 'prediction' fail.

This state of affairs, for both the sciences and astrology, must be as it is, because a recipe book for life (if it could be written), that could guarantee truth and certainty, would have a dubious value in any society, not because its authenticity would be questioned, but more so because no imperfect being could possibly live up to even its most basic tenets. Laws, it has been said, are made to be broken. Be that as it may, human imperfection does not stop the books from being written because any guidance is better than none at all.

While astrology is about guidance, no self-respecting astrologer would ever consider astrology to be about certainty or truth. What good astrologers *will* offer the client is an interpretation of 'cosmic' patterns, or advice on how to make the most of his or her potential, or remind him or her of how deeply entrenched a behavior can be, or give a description of tendencies in his or her character and personality.

Again, these offerings do not sound any different from those proffered by the more respected social sciences of psychology, psychiatry, sociology, etc. The only major difference is the methods by which astrology constructs its interpretation, or advice, or personality type, or character description of the client. On the one hand, astrology has arrived at its methods empirically over many thousands of years. Uncounted numbers of observations have formed the foundations of its methodology. Lyall Watson elaborates this point in *Supernature* (1973):

> an awareness of cosmic forces predisposed man [*sic*] to certain ideas and patterns, and,…, despite the fact that each contributing astrologer could see only his [*sic*] little bit of the structure, the final synthesis took on a natural and relevant form. (p. 73)

On the other hand, the scientific methodologies at the basis of the modern social sciences, at the very most, are only centuries old, insofar as they do not draw from antiquity. In either case, both cosmologies have, thus far, relied on empirical data for 'proof' of efficacy, but where real advances have been made, both have also relied on the intelligence, the intuition, and the interpretive skills of their practitioners.

While the various personality tests and typologies have been arrived at through the painstaking rigors of psychometric analyses, the ancient art of astrology is built on experience, thereby establishing a tradition that is claimed to have honed the art down to an exact science (or pseudo-science). Ordinarily, this comparison between astrological and psychological methodologies might suggest the possibility of a complementarity between the two, but since the two general domains, science and pseudo-science, are diametrically opposed for ideological and cosmological reasons, many practitioners on both sides of the fence might be offended that a comparison and relationship could be made or implied using an empiricist argument.

In fact, pseudo-science, although a scientific term, is often used as a pejorative. More correctly, astrology is a proto-science, and like the social sciences it has its procedures, methods, ways of dealing with its results, and approach to its subject. With so much in common, it is unlikely, however, that the similarities between these two major worldviews will ever be acknowledged, since the prejudice appears to have an emotional basis rather than a common-sense one. Even so, the main point being made here is that the sciences and the proto-sciences have many factors in common.

With all these assumptions in mind, a broader (less limited) explication of the numerical structure underlying astrology may proceed with less skepticism than might ordinarily be warranted when broaching such a controversial subject as astrology.

The Beginning and Basic Structure of Astrology in the West

In 560 BC the Greek mathematician and astronomer Anaximander named the twelve signs of the western zodiac. The 'scales', and the eleven 'animated' beings grouped around a circle (hence the word zodiac, derived from two Greek words meaning 'animal circle') form the basic structure of astrology. The word zodiac can also mean 'wheel of life', and it is often more appropriate to consider the zodiac from a cyclical perspective, as a life cycle. But it is number that drives this cycle or wheel, as will be seen when the 'laws' and 'aspects' used in astrology are discussed below.

The fundamental principle of astrology is that the personality of an individual is governed by the positions of the planets in the signs and the transits of these planets (movement of close planets in front of more distant planets). From a numerical point of view, there are three major number-related factors underlying the structure and function of astrology, which John Anthony West, in *The Case for Astrology* (1991), calls the Law of Two, the Law of Three, and the Law of Four. Along with these major factors comes another number-related factor, the aspects, which are the specific angles between planets known as 'conjuction', 'opposition', 'trine', 'square', 'quincunx', and 'sextile'. There are other aspects, but these have only a weak influence in the chart.

The Law of Two

The Law of Two involves duality or polarity. The twelve signs are alternatively assigned a positive ('male', active) or negative ('female', passive) value. Thus: Aries (+), Taurus (–), Gemini (+), Cancer (–), Leo (+), Virgo (–), Libra (+), Scorpio (–), Sagittarius (+), Capricorn (–), Aquarius (+), and Pisces (–). The positive signs tend to be extraverted or outgoing, while the negative signs tend to be introverted or introspective.

The few studies in this area have produced inconclusive results, and astrology as a means of determining the Jungian attitude types (extraversion and introversion) is not yet considered reliable or valid by orthodox science. For example, Dean and Kelly (2003) report that extraversion cannot be predicted from star-signs, but this result depended on self-reporting, and given that extraversion can be a form of defense mechanism adopted by depressive types, according to Anthony Storr (1973), there is the likelihood that many typically introverted star-sign types are typing themselves as extraverts because they want to believe they are extraverts. They therefore complete self-reports (and even act) as if they were born-extraverts, going against their natural predisposition to introversion. This kind of behavior usually results in exhaustion, anxiety, and other psychological problems. No conclusions about astrology can be reached from experiments that follow such limited methodologies.

The Law of Three

The Law of Three refers to the three *modes* or *quadriplicities*—Cardinal, Fixed and Mutable. They are called quadriplicities because there are four signs in each quadriplicity. Each quadriplicity has a specific quality. Cardinal signs have an *active* quality, Fixed signs have a *cautious* quality, and Mutable signs have an *adaptable* quality (*see* Table 27).

By the nature of 'squared' relations in astrology (see the square aspect below) different signs that share the same quadriplicity (for example, Virgo and Pisces) tend to be antagonistic or badly aspected to each other because they are separated by 90°.

Table 27. *The Signs of the Zodiac, the Quadriplicities (modes), and the Triplicities (elements).*

	FIRE (+)	EARTH (-)	AIR (+)	WATER (-)
CARDINAL	Aries	Capricorn	Libra	Cancer
FIXED	Leo	Taurus	Aquarius	Scorpio
MUTABLE	Sagittarius	Virgo	Gemini	Pisces

The Law of Four

The Law of Four refers to the *triplicities*—Fire, Earth, Air, and Water—which are also known as the *elements*. The triplicities are referred to as such because there are three signs to each element (*see* Table 27).

Sheila Geddes, in *The Art of Astrology* (1980), writes that the Fire type tends to be "enthusiastic, energetic and positive" (p. 25), the Earth type tends to be "static, practical and negative" (p. 26), the Air type tends to be "intellectual, communicative and positive" (p. 26), and the Water type tends to be "emotional, impressionable and negative" (p. 26). Different signs in the same triplicity have a trine aspect, and since the trine is considered a good aspect, they usually harmonize in relationships.

The Aspects

The Conjunction: The two planets are 0° (± 8°) apart. They are in the same sign, same triplicity, and same quadriplicity. This threefold commonality means the characteristics of the sign, triplicity, and quadriplicity, powerfully reinforce each other, which can be favorable or unfavourable. The conjunction has a strong effect in the chart.

The Opposition: The two planets are 180° (± 8°) apart (maximally polarized). As with number-two symbolism, the opposition is either a difficult aspect (because of the imbalance of forces) or, as Geddes (1980) claims, a favorable aspect if the "native learns to use it well" (p. 55). Usually the only thing two planets in opposition have in common is the fact that they are both in a positive sign or a negative sign. This commonality is favorable. The opposition has a strong effect in the chart.

The Trine: The two planets are 120° (± 6°) apart. They are in the same triplicity (for example, both planets are in a fire sign or a water sign). This commonality allows a favorable aspect, so that the trine is considered good. The trine has a strong effect in the chart.

The Square: The two planets are 90° (± 6°) apart. These planets are not in harmony because they are in the same quadriplicity (either Fire/Water, Earth/Fire, Earth/Air, or Air/Water). The square has a strong effect in the chart.

The Quincunx: The two planets are 150° (± 2°) apart. They have no commonality (signs, modes, and elements are all incompatible), so the aspect is an unfavorable one. The quincunx has a weak effect in the chart.

The Sextile: The two planets are 60° (± 4°) apart. The aspect is harmonious because the planets will both be in positive or negative signs. They will also be in compatible elements (either Fire/Air or Earth/Water). The sextile has a moderate effect in the chart.

The Science of the Aspects

There appears to be some empirical evidence that the aspects can create harmony or disharmony (discordance), thereby bringing about favorable or unfavorable events. In the 1950s, the prominent astrologer and philosopher John Addey undertook a statistical analysis of nonagenarians and polio victims. He found a qualitative difference between two classes of aspects—the 'applying' aspect, which involves a fast planet or the Sun closing in on a slower planet, and the 'separating' aspect, where the two spheres are moving apart from each other. West (1991) writes that applying aspects "breed tension, excitement, action," while the separating aspect "signifies a release, an extension, a dilation, passivity" (p. 322).

West (1991) reports that Addey found a "significant preponderance of separating aspects in the nonagenarian's charts" (p. 322), but the polio victims were found to have applying aspects "significantly more frequently than separating aspects" (p. 323). It is a medical fact that polio victims are usually bright, nervous and active, while "dull, plodding types rarely contract polio" (p. 323). Nonagenarians, on the other hand, tend to be just the type to live long lives. They tend to conserve energy and look after their physical resources. The applying and separating aspects sensibly describe these two types.

Addey conducted further studies, including a 'wave analysis' on the data taken from his subjects' charts. He found that distinct patterns (unmistakable wave forms) emerged if data were plotted on a 360° time-line covering a one-year period, whereas control group data yielded only chance results (that is, no wave forms). He also tested clergymen, doctors, and even redheads, and found particular waveforms in the group data for each type of subject. Different waveforms appeared for different groups, but the important fact that Addey discovered is that the birth chart, showing the aspects of the 'spheres', is also a record of the 'harmonics' that exist between the spheres.

Addey's results have been questioned by Geoffrey Dean in a 1997 *Correlation* article titled 'John Addey's Dream'. Dean's article amounts to a very sophisticated, statistically based criticism of Addey's methods, but Dean does not present any replication studies by other researchers to show that Addey's findings for polio victims and nonagenarians might be statistical flukes— he only presents some theoretical arguments and statistical modeling that demonstrates how important sample size and other criteria are in statistical analysis. Addey's work may yet provide the scientific basis for psychologist Michel Gauquelin's discovery that eminent professionals have the traditional planet ruling their profession in the first sector (the 'rise') or fourth sector (the 'superior culmination') of their birth chart significantly more often than is expected by chance alone. Mars was prominent in these sectors for eminent doctors, members of the military, and sports men and women, the Moon was prominent for politicians and writers, Jupiter was prominent for actors, and Saturn was prominent for scientists.

In *The Truth About Astrology* (1983), Gauquelin analyzed the charts of tens of thousands of eminent professionals and found significant appearances of the relevant planets in the first and fourth sectors without fail in every study undertaken since the 1950s. After studying Gauquelin's vast data file, Addey found some very significant results when he analyzed the 3rd and 4th harmonics (the trine and square aspects, respectively). As West (1991) notes:

> Mars and Saturn, the 'strict' planets, manifest powerfully in the fourth harmonic in the samples of scientists and soldiers, and four is the number of 'material' (the four elements), of concretization. The third harmonic becomes prominent in groups of writers and artists. Three is traditionally the number of 'relationship', the synthesizing faculty, that which reconciles opposites. (p. 326)

The square and the trine are two of the most important aspects in astrology because they have the strongest influence on the native. At the basis of this finding is the number symbolism usually associated with the numbers three and four.

Numbers in Astrology

Of great importance are the effects that numbers have in the astrological chart in the form of harmonics (aspects), and the implications that these effects have on terrestrial events. Most of the fadic numbers are represented in astrology:

#1. The number one can only figure meaningfully in the zodiac in the sense that the zodiac, as a cyclical system, represents the totality or wholeness of the psyche (on an individual level) and humanity in a more general sense.

#2. Number-two symbolism is present in the aspect of the opposition, which is typified by a twofold or dualistic effect in the chart. The opposition can be favorable or unfavorable. Signs are positive or negative, demonstrating a dualistic categorization of the signs.

#3. The trine is a 'good' aspect, and symbolically, is in keeping with the 'relational' factor associated with the number three. (Signs and planets in trine are in the same triplicity.)

#4. 'Irreconcilable oppositionalism' has been noted in fourfold models, and this factor is confirmed by the astrological finding of an absence of harmony in planets or signs in square aspect. (Signs and planets in square are in the same quadruplicity.)

#5. The quintessence was shown to embody 'capricious' and 'controversial' characteristics, and the quincunx, as it happens, is not harmonious.

#6. In number symbolism, number three and number six have similar phenomonologies, and it is not surprising that the trine and the sextile are both harmonious. Traditionally, the number six is a symbol of harmony and balance, and the sextile aspect supports this tradition.

#7. It is to be noted that the three remaining fadic numbers (i.e., seven, eight, and nine) do not feature in astrology. Number seven does not produce a harmonic of $360°$ ($360 \div 7 = 51.428\ldots$). Recall the difficulty in producing the heptagon graphically, as mentioned in the chapter "Seven (The Heptad)."

#8. Understandably, the number eight, as in music, has little or no presence in astrology, since eight would be a variation of the square aspect. Geddes mentions the semi-square (half a square or $45°$), which might be taken as a subtle presence of the number eight. Like the square, it is also unfavorable, but is weak in force.

#9. Finally, common sense would have it that number nine (a multiple of three) would be harmonically incorporated into the trine. Number nine, as a transitional number (like number seven), may be absent in astrological aspects because its influence would be too weak, although it would undoubtedly be favorable, like the trine and the sextile.

Altogether astrology largely shows a dependence on the natural number system. Number not only gives structure to the astrological chart, but also is the only means by which meaningful interpretations can be constructed from raw empirical data. The natural numbers provide a structural link between celestial and terrestrial events.

Summary

Astrology is a form of divination that is claimed to have the capacity to discern the personality of the native. The Laws of Two, Three, and Four, and the aspects, embody the principles of number symbolism, all of which, to varying extents, have been supported by the empirical findings of John Addey and Michel Gauquelin. Their experimental work and research into the mechanisms of astrology (particularly the planets and aspects) support the traditional claims concerning astrology, that the planets have influences on terrestrial events, and that the natal chart is a celestial, number-based schematic of the personality.

Numbers figure prominently in astrology, but the structural basis of astrology and its methodology owes more to number than just a mathematical (astronomical) pattern structure. A qualitative (interpretive) aspect in the astrological method is *intrinsically determined* by quantitative (numerical) patterns in the cosmos, so that numbers also figure meaningfully in the methods of astrology. A revised version of the age-old 'harmony of the spheres' philosophy may prove valid in our age, and the influence of the spheres on personality and human affairs may not be superstition after all.

Plate 24. CREATING
THE *I CHING*

*This artwork, unearthed in the
Xinjiang region, China, depicts King
Fu Hsi (right), the originator of the I
Ching, and Nuwa (left; a mythological
character best known for creating
and reproducing people after a great
calamity) [SOURCE: Wikimedia
Commons].*

Numerology, Tarot and
astrology have never
held any fascination for
or to me — as a psychic,
I always thought that
their complication were
gateways to more vagueness.

I CHING

The method of the I Ching does indeed take into account
the hidden individual quality in things and men.

C. G. Jung

The *I Ching* is an ancient Chinese system of divination, consisting of a book of 64 hexagrams (six-line symbols) and their corresponding readings. The user generates a hexagram reading, which depicts a scenario (with commentary) that ostensibly describes the past, present, and even future life situation of the user. The *I Ching* was first introduced into the English-speaking world in 1899 through James Legge's book *I Ching* (1971), which was a translation of the original Chinese text. The 'emblematic representations' (the hexagrams, or six-line diagrams) were a mystery to Legge, and his skepticism, and the fact that he did not use the *I Ching* personally, is evident throughout the text. Richard Wilhelm's book *I Ching or the Book of Changes* (1989) and Ritsema and Sabbadini's book *The Original I Ching Oracle* (2005) are two of the most in-depth works to date on this enigmatic divinatory system. This chapter looks at the method underlying the *I Ching* process, with a special consideration of how numbers are used in that process.

The Origins of the *I Ching*

Legend has it that King Fu Hsi (2953-2838 BC) laid down the basics of the *I Ching* system. King Wên, the founder of the Chou dynasty (1150-249 BC), wrote most of the original text, and his son Chu Kung, the Duke of Chou expanded the text further. Buddhist and Taoist philosophies are evident in the *I Ching*, as is the influence of Confucius, who authored the commentaries that supplement the readings.

The major principle of the *I Ching*, which instills it with a meaningful structure, is the binary or yin/yang philosophy, and it is this philosophy that activates that meaningful structure, in the sense that change is inevitable and comes about as a result of the resonance between the two polar opposites of yin and yang. Capra (1988) describes this resonance as the dynamic interplay of the 'archetypal' opposites of yin and yang.

The yin represents the principles of Earth, passivity, the 'feminine', the negative, and darkness, while the yang represents the principles of Heaven, activity, the 'masculine', the positive, and light. The two actually depend on each other because they hold the universe in balance. Therein lies the principle of twoness or duality. The two elements of the yin/yang binary system are represented as 'broken' and 'unbroken' lines in the *I Ching* (*see* fig. 67).

Figure 67. *The yin and yang lines.*

Yin   Yang

By various combinations of yin and yang (yin/yin, yin/yang, yang/yin, and yang/yang) the four duograms are formed (*see* fig. 68). The duograms represent a four-step continuum, moving from old yin to old yang—a gradual shift from one polar opposite to the other.

Figure 68. *The Four Duograms.*

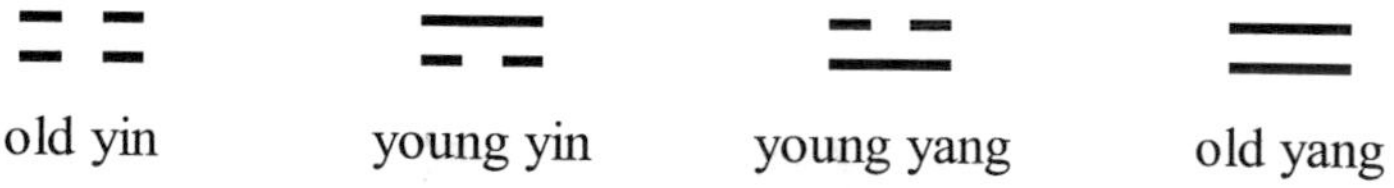

old yin   young yin   young yang   old yang

By the addition of a yin or a yang line to each of the duograms, eight trigrams (the *pa kua*) are formed (*see* fig. 69).

Figure 69. *The Eight Trigrams (pa kua).*

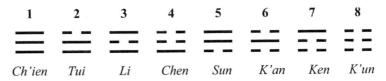

1	2	3	4	5	6	7	8
Ch'ien	Tui	Li	Chen	Sun	K'an	Ken	K'un

The trigrams also represent a continuum, but in eight steps, from Heaven through to Earth. The individual trigrams are magnified in meaning above and beyond the simple degrees of yin and yang, or the duograms. For example, Heaven (☰) symbolizes creativity, masculinity, activity, and the Father (*see* Table 14 for the meanings of the other trigrams).

Finally, pairing the trigrams produces the 64 hexagrams. For example, the combination of two trigrams, *K'un* plus *Ch'ien*, gives the hexagram called *T'ai* (*see* fig. 70).

Figure 70. *Constructing Hexagram #11: 'Earth above Heaven' (T'ai).*

In most cases the hexagrams have new names corresponding to their unique qualities. The hexagrams (the paired trigrams) also range as a continuum from the most yang (Hexagram 1: 'Heaven above Heaven') to the most yin (Hexagram 64: 'Earth above Earth') (*see* fig. 71).

Figure 71. *Hexagram 1: Heaven above Heaven (Chi'en)*
and Hexagram 64: Earth above Earth (K'un).

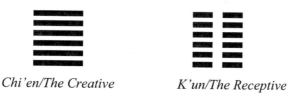

Chi'en/The Creative   *K'un/The Receptive*

Using the *I Ching*

To consult the 'oracle' of the *I Ching*, one must generate a hexagram, which involves first, posing a meaningful (sensible) question to the *I Ching*, followed by the repeated casting of 64 yarrow sticks to generate all six lines of the hexagram. The modern method involves throwing three coins six times. Each throw of the coins produces one of the six yin or yang lines, so that, throw by throw, the hexagram is built from the bottom up. The coins may show three-of-a-kind on some occasions, which means the yin or yang line is a 'changing' line that changes into its opposite—either yin to yang, or yang to yin. In other words, a second hexagram is produced based on the first hexagram.

The 64 hexagrams each have their own unique reading, as does each changing line, and it is the readings that form the main text of the *I Ching*. One reads the first hexagram reading in the context of past and present events. The changing line readings pre-empt the reading for the second hexagram, which is a forecast or prognostication of the scenario discussed in the first reading.

Investigating the *I Ching*

Edward M. Covello (1977) found that the yin/yang substructure underlying the hexagrams was meaningfully operative in the hexagram symbols and their corresponding readings. That is, the derivation of the hexagram symbols was not arbitrary, but was arrived at rationally and systematically over many centuries. Covello stated that:

> One of the more fascinating aspects of the *I Ching* is that it can be viewed as a mathematically ordered cosmology. Its surprisingly systematic structure renders many of its assertions amenable to controlled investigation. (p. 115)

So saying, Covello investigated the various symbolic systems in the *I Ching* for their meaningfulness. Covello found, by analyzing the line structures making up the hexagrams, and classifying the words used in the text, that 'concreteness' (associated with 'earthy, pictorial, and regressive') was characteristic of the 'Yin principle', and 'abstractedness' (associated with 'heavenly' and 'potency') was characteristic of the 'Yang principle'. Within the abstract-concrete dimension exists a continuum or spectrum of meanings as determined by the number of yin or yang lines in the hexagrams. It is important to recognize that yin and yang are not either good or bad, as Von Franz (1980b) makes clear:

> The Chinese were detached and philosophical enough to say that even if it is bad for me it might be good as a whole. From the beginning they had a wiser or more objective view of what we call good and bad, and saw it more as something in the ensemble of existence. (p. 47)

In the late 1940s, in Jung's *Foreword* to Wilhelm's book *I Ching or the Book of Changes* (1989), Jung claimed that:

> the method of the *I Ching* does indeed take into account the hidden individual quality in things and men [*sic*], and in one's own unconscious as well. (p. *xxviii*)

This claim was partly prompted by Jung's use of the *I Ching*, but he was also responding from an ancient Chinese philosophical way of thinking where "natural laws are merely statistical truths and must necessarily allow for exceptions" (p. *xxii*). Jung, therefore, saw the processes of the *I Ching* as one such exception to 'statistical truth', in the sense that the random element (chance) was essential to the functioning of the *I Ching*.

How to Find Meaning in the *I Ching* Text

Von Franz (1974) believes the hexagrams "signify the sixty-four possible aspects of the *unus mundus*" (p. 105). Our 'psychophysical nature' is represented by the hexagrams, and by following their numerical structure, one can recognize the ordered way in which the images or scenarios of the hexagrams are presented. Arithmetical procedure is the mechanism in part that leads to the meanings of the hexagrams (in the form of hexagram readings), but true meaning only resonates and emerges in consciousness on the basis of one's personal experience, as well as one's thoughts and feelings about the readings. Consciousness is the final arbiter—either one sees meaning or one does not.

This is not to say that the meaning is not there in some absolute sense. Often the answer is right under our nose, so to speak, but we fail to see it. In point of fact, where no perceivable meaning can be gained from the reading, one must reconsider one's question or motives at the outset. Von Franz (1980a) feels that the *I Ching* should be used only in "very serious situations and not as a drawingroom game" (p. 53). A 'burning' question, or a state where one is "at an impasse and in a state of emotional tension" (p. 53) is more conducive to the *I Ching* process because archetypes (the "nuclear dynamisms of the psyche," p. 53) are more likely to be constellated in these states. One can then 'expect' a more rewarding and meaningful outcome because the archetype has a conditioning effect on certain 'psychological probabilities'. As Jung (1963) says: "The *I Ching* endeavors to organize the play of the archetypes…into a certain pattern, so that a 'reading' becomes possible" (para. 401). In this sense, Jung implies a *meaningful* reading.

Insofar as meaning is determined in the reading, it is as though an inner voice (the unconscious) is reflected in the reading, but the meaningfulness of this voice is aligned with the physical process of generating the hexagram (the process is both physical and psychological). Von Franz (1974) makes sense of this idea from a Jungian synchronistic perspective that incorporates the *unus mundus* concept. All events (physical and psychological) are meaningfully related to each other, and are united in the *unus mundus*:

Although the nonperceptual potential continuum or *unus mundus* appears to exist outside time, certain dynamic manifestations of it break through into our ordinary temporal sphere in the form of synchronistic occurrences. To understand the nature of these manifestations is the aim of the *I Ching*. Its function clearly presupposes a certain "probability" in the existence of synchronistic events. (p. 11)

Synchronicity and the *I Ching*

Following Jung, von Franz brings the synchronicity concept into the *I Ching* process. According to synchronicity theory, a general principle of 'acausal orderedness' underlies these 'synchronistic occurrences'. Such an orderedness is present in matter (for example, radioactive decay), and in the psyche (as in the uniform associations we make with natural integer concepts).

Synchronicity would be only a momentary peek at this orderedness, but it depends on the subject's recognition of this '*tertium comparationis*' (that third thing—the meaning—which emerges from the comparison of two causally unrelated occurrences). Most importantly, the synchronistic event falls within a probability field governed by this acausal orderedness. The individual, at any given time, is a player in that field of probability (the *unus mundus*), in the sense that the psyche is itself an aspect of that field, and the specific quality of that field, as determined by that time moment, makes prediction possible, according to the degree to which the archetype is activated.

Archetypes—predispositions in the psyche that can determine cognitive and behavioral outcomes, and even external events—form partial constituents of the *unus mundus*, since archetypal themes act as nodal points around which synchronistic events tend to constellate. Such themes are observed in the analysand in the therapeutic situation, or in mystical experiences. Peat (personal communication, January 15, 2007) amplifies these points by mentioning that "the patterns made by the yarrow stalks are an image within our temporal world of something within the Eternal so that what we see is a seed or the potential within the present moment. That to me is a powerful parallel to a psychological explanation. It also gives a sense of divination as holding the potential for something to unfold."

Numbers, as archetypes, are ultimately the most practical and reliable foundation for any system of divination, since numbers determine structure, pattern, and orderedness. Numbers thus form the essence of the *I Ching*, extending beyond spatial and temporal considerations to the *unus mundus*.

From the perspective of number, the use of the *I Ching* implies an attempt (at the very least) to harness or access that underlying principle of order in the *unus mundus* that might give a momentary peek (as an act of creation in time) into the orderedness of the *unus mundus*.

Summary

The *I Ching* is an ancient Chinese form of divination based on the principle of duality, the yin and the yang. From a simple yin/yang polarity is derived four duograms, followed by eight trigrams, and finally the 64 hexagrams. The hexagram symbols are meaningfully derived, and meanings underscore the readings and interpretations associated with each hexagram. The *I Ching*, by dint of the yin/yang resonance, embodies change, and its fundamental philosophy is that wisdom can be obtained through the acceptance of change, and that in the flux of events is the possibility of knowing that in the present are the seeds for solutions in the future.

Prediction is not only possible, but also probable because the ordering principle of the number archetype (as the natural number series) is taken into account in the establishment of the meanings of the hexagrams. The synchronistic relationship between psyche and matter, at a qualitative time moment, underpins the generation of the hexagram so that meaningful statements are *stochastically* associated with that time moment.

The *I Ching* uses number to put order to life themes, and arranges these themes in a systematic and meaningful matrix. Systems of divination that use number to determine meaningful outcomes rely on the pattern or sequencing effect of number, in the same way that mathematical laws and formulae use number to make predictions about physical systems. The Titius-Bode Law, discussed next, exemplifies this use of number as a means of making predictions.

Plate 25. Johann Daniel
Titius (1729-1796)

[SOURCE: Wikimedia Commons]

Plate 26. Johann Elert
Bode (1747-1826)

[SOURCE: Wikimedia Commons]

THE TITIUS-BODE LAW

Everything is dual in nature, three in principle,
and fourfold in manifestation.

Plato

In 1766, the German astronomer Johann Daniel Titius developed a series of numbers that later became known as the Titius-Bode Law or Bode's Law. This Law lists the relative mean distances of the planets of our solar system to the Sun. Titius started with the series:

0, 3, 6, 12, 24, 48, 96, 192, 384, 768.

He then added 4 to each of these terms:

4, 7, 10, 16, 28, 52, 100, 196, 388, 772.

This series is given by the formula $r_n = 4 + (3 \times 2^n)$, where:

(i) r_n = the radius of the planet n's orbit. That is, the mean distance from the Sun in Astronomical Units (AU) × 10, where Earth's mean distance = 1 AU.

(ii) $n = -\infty$ for Mercury and 0, 1, 2, 3, 4, 5, 6, 7, 8, for successive planets, Venus, Earth, Mars, (Ceres), Jupiter, Saturn, Uranus, Neptune, and Pluto.

(This formula is included only for purposes of comparison. The modifications made in later years by other astronomers rectified the formula's inaccuracies, making it possible to not only calculate the planets' mean distances from the Sun, but also the distances of satellites from their planets.)

A New Law of the Solar System Applied

The above series provided very accurate approximations of the actual relative distances from the Sun to the planets known at the time (*see* Table 28). It was Johann Elert Bode who today gets the credit for this discovery, even though he did not publish until 1772, six years after Titius developed the series. As impressive as the Law was at the time, it was still treated as not much more than a numerological oddity and skeptics felt sure it would prove to be inaccurate with the possible later discovery of planets beyond Saturn. Furthermore, the number 28 in the series did not indicate a planet at all (the fifth place in the series was later attributed to the asteroid belt, and planetoid Ceres in particular, which had an observed distance of 27.7).

Table 28. *The Planets and Comparisons between Observed Distances and Expected Distances according to the Titius-Bode Law.*

PLANET	*n*	OBSERVED DISTANCE	EXPECTED DISTANCE BY THE 'LAW'
Mercury	$-\infty$	3.9	4
Venus	0	7.2	7
Earth	1	10.0	10
Mars	2	15.2	16
(Ceres)	(3)	(27.7)	(28)
Jupiter	4	52.0	52
Saturn	5	95.5	100
Uranus	6	192.0	196
Neptune	7	300.9	388
Pluto	8	397.0	772

Nine years later in 1781, William Herschel discovered a planet (Uranus) and attention was turned again to the Titius-Bode Law, because the observed distance, 192, corresponded fairly accurately with the Titius-Bode Law calculation of 196. Then, in 1800, the major planetoid just mentioned was discovered and named Ceres by Italian astronomer Giuseppe Piazzi.

At that time it looked as though the Law might prove to be a fruitful starting point in the search for planets beyond Uranus, even if no mathematical, astronomical or physical reason could explain the Law's apparent accuracy. As it happened, astronomers noted that the orbit of Uranus was irregular, which they attributed to an eighth planet. The position of this planet (Neptune) was calculated independently by John Couch Adams and Urbain Le Verrier in 1846 (both astronomers used the Law in their search for Neptune). Johann Galle actually confirmed its existence only weeks later, but its relative distance was 301, and not 388, as suggested by the Law for an eighth planet.

With the discovery of Pluto by Clyde Tombaugh in 1930, relative distance of 397 (not 772, according to the Law), it became apparent that skeptics were right to refute, on scientific grounds, the alleged accuracy and validity of this series of numbers that was generated by such a simple formula. It seemed after all that the universe was far too complex to have its secrets so easily exposed. This assumption seemed reasonable—Titius's series proved to be inadequate at predicting the relative distance of planets beyond Uranus.

The Seven Stages of the Law

In the centuries since Bode published the Law, modifications were made to rectify the above-mentioned problems, as well as other astronomical inconsistencies, which arose when trying to apply the Law in its pure (original) form to the satellite systems of the outer planets. Table 29 details these changes to the Law in the form $r_n = a + b \times c^n$, while the following seven stages give a brief history of the Law up to the beginning of the twentieth century:

Stage 1: The original Law, as developed by Titius and Bode, was successful for calculating the orbits for the planets only (including Ceres, but not including Neptune and Pluto). Later, attention turned toward the satellite systems.

Stages 2, 3 and 4: Wurm, in 1787, felt that a related law existed for the satellites of the outer planets (Jupiter and Saturn), but in the form $r_n = a + b \times 2^n$, where $n = -\infty, 0, 1, 2, \ldots$, with variations for Jupiter and Saturn in 'a' and 'b'.

Stage 5: Gilbert altered 'c' of the Law, seeing no reason why that number should be the natural number two. (In the cases of both Wurm and Gilbert, the units of distance were the radii of the parent planets.)

Stage 6: Challis further applied Gilbert's equation to Uranus, and he also felt that the Law's 'inaccurate' results were due, as Michael Nieto states in *The Titius-Bode Law of Planetary Distances* (1972): "to the masses and mutual actions of the member bodies" (p. 25).

Stage 7: Charlier, using the same formula, changed 'a', 'b' and 'c' again for Saturn's satellite system, but this formula also accommodated Saturn's rings with the orbits from $n = -\infty$ to -1.

Unfortunately, in all seven stages, none of the modifications were accurate compared with observed results (in some cases being out by a few percent), and this is particularly disappointing, given the fact that in these modifications, as Nieto points out, there is "a fair amount of arbitrariness in their parameterisation" (p. 28). It is this arbitrariness which casts a dim light on mathematical certainty. Overall it maintains the Aristotelian viewpoint that mathematics gives a close-fitting description of the universe, but does not reveal any fundamental, mathematical 'truth' about its phenomenology. As Nieto states:

> If there is truth in the Law, the original form should be thought more likely to be a *good first guess, but certainly not necessarily the best guess* to which to refer theories! (p. 29)

Table 29. *The Titius-Bode Law in the Form* $r_n = a + b \times c^n$

STAGE	INVESTIGATOR	a	b	c	TO DETERMINE THE ORBITS OF:
1	Titius-Bode, 1766/1772	4.00	3.00	2.00	Mercury, Venus, Earth, Mars, Ceres, Jupiter, Saturn
2	Wurm, 1787	0.39	.29	2.00	Mercury, Venus, Earth, Mars, Ceres, Jupiter, Saturn, Uranus
3	Wurm, 1787	3.00	3.00	2.00	Jupiter's satellites
4	Wurm, 1787	4.50	1.60	2.00	Saturn's satellites
5	Gilbert, 1802	3.08	.87	2.08	Saturn's satellites (in units of Saturn's radius)
6	Challis, 1828	3.08	.87	2.08	Satellites of Jupiter, Saturn, Uranus (in units of planets' radii)
7	Charlier, c. 1900	1.50	1.60	1.50	Saturn's satellites

Nieto means that if the Titius-Bode Law still fails to align with the observed measures of planetary distance, even after adjusting the form $r_n = 4 + (3 \times 2^n)$ to the form $r_n = a + b \times c^n$, where a, b and c are not necessarily natural numbers, then a completely new formulation should be sought. But, Nieto may be wrong. It must be noted that it may be the literal-mindedness of those using the formula that gives rise to its failure, when in fact there may be nothing wrong with the formula. Perhaps, the formula only describes 'perfect' systems (the Platonist would be satisfied with this assumption). Of course, this assumption is neither here nor there for the pragmatic researcher who is merely intent on adjusting the Law to make it work at all times—or at least for our solar system. It may have been assumed that the inaccuracies were due to unaccounted variables, but instead of searching for these variables, astronomers only tried to fine-tune the Law.

While it is true that many theories or ideas do not hold weight in the light of further discoveries, it is also true that nature does show a specific mode of expression through number, and this fact must not be ignored. Thus, in any field where numbers can be applied, the task for the researcher should be to discover the relationship between the object under investigation and the numerical pattern phenomenal to that object, while still accounting for missing variables or extenuating circumstances that might undermine that relationship. In the case of the Law, those earlier astronomers were not entirely up to the task. They tried adjusting and re-adjusting the Law to make it fit the real world, but did not think about such causes in the solar system that might have undermined the Law. This was a mistake, as will be seen in the next section.

Why the Law Failed

Returning to the Law and its inaccuracies, it is of interest to note some startling facts concerning these outermost planets:

1. Pluto, and Neptune's larger moons Triton and Nereid all show peculiar orbits. Pluto rotates in the opposite direction to that of most of the other planets. Triton has a retrograde orbit (it orbits backwards), and Nereid's orbit is the most eccentric of any satellite or planet in our solar system.

2. Pluto at perihelion (closest distance to the Sun) is actually closer to the Sun than Neptune.

3. The plane of Pluto's orbit is tilted more so than any other planet in our solar system.

Taking these three anomalies into consideration, it has been suggested that a catastrophe occurred in our solar system's remote past, which might account for the failure of the Law when applied to Neptune and Pluto. Pluto (and possibly its moon Charon discovered in 1978) may once have been satellites of Neptune. Robert Harrington and Mark Littman in *Nemesis* (1988) proposed as much. Pluto and Charon may have been one single moon of Neptune, which fragmented and, as two new planetoids, were thrown out to their current positions. Pluto is certainly closer to the size of Triton and Nereid, and it is remarkably smaller than the four gas 'Giants' (in fact only 0.2% the mass of the Earth). Triton and Nereid may have both been captured by Neptune (which actually has eight moons in total, although six of these are very small).

It has been postulated that satellites of other outer planets were also captured as a result of the same, or another, catastrophe. Even as early as 1979, Isaac Asimov (*Asimov on Astronomy*) suggested that Jupiter's outer satellites, and Saturn's satellites Phoebe (which has a retrograde orbit) and possibly Janus were all captured. According to Asimov, the nature of this catastrophe may have involved the asteroid belt, which is believed to have been a planet. Due to immense tidal forces on this hypothesized planet, situated, as it would have been between the Sun on one side and Jupiter on the other, it was ripped apart at some time during the early stages of the formation of our solar system.

If this theory is correct, then the Titius-Bode Law is not incomplete, but is fit only in describing 'perfect' solar systems. It is possible that before the catastrophe, Neptune had an orbit closer to that of Pluto's (397), which would certainly accommodate the Law reasonably well (a discrepancy of only 2.3%, given the actual distance of Neptune at 388).

Pluto, on the other hand, would be far too close to the Sun for good reason—it should not have an independent orbit. In fact, as recently as 2004, Michael Brown, of the California Institute of Technology in Pasadena in California, stated that Pluto does not deserve to be called a planet since astronomers have found many round objects beyond Neptune—several of them being quite large. It would even be possible for a planet to exist well beyond Pluto appropriate to 772 in the series laid down by the Law.

As it happens, Pluto and Charon do not completely account for the peculiarities in the orbits of Uranus and Neptune, and so a tenth planet has been postulated. This postulate has been around since the mid-1800s. These orbital peculiarities were based on prior estimates of the masses of Uranus and Neptune, but more accurate data for the masses of the outer planets gained from the Pioneer 10 and 11 and Voyager 1 and 2 missions have raised doubts about this postulate. However, the conclusion that there is no tenth planet is based on the assumptions that the probe data are accurate, and that the statistical criteria of what constitute 'normal' orbits for these outermost planets are valid. According to Daniel Whitmire and John J. Matese, in an article titled 'Periodic Comet Showers and Planet X' (1985), the tenth planet would have a great elliptical orbit and would pass through the Oort comet cloud. In 1987, Whitmire and Matese estimated the orbital plane of Planet X to be about 45°. Surprisingly, Planet X's distance from the Sun is estimated to be somewhere between 800 to 1400 normalized units (80-140 AU × 10), the maximum of which would be out by only 10% of the figure 1540 (154 AU, where n = 9) predicted by the Law.

In 2003, Michael Brown, Chad Trujillo (Gemini Observatory, Hawaii) and David Rabinowitz (Yale) discovered a tenth planet—designated 2003-UB313 (temporarily nicknamed Xena). In a 2005 Caltech media release it was stated that Xena is 97 times the Earth-Sun distance, which makes it 970 AU and within the estimated range posited by Whitmire and Matese. It is theorized to have originally been in the orbit of Neptune before it was flung out into space, thus accounting for its unusual 44° inclination (out by a mere 1° of Whitmire and Matese's original estimate!). Possibly being the tenth planet, it is—unfortunately for the Law—out by a staggering 63%, given that 1540 AU is where Xena is hypothesised to be.

It might appear that modern astronomy has usurped the Law once and for all. In defense of the Law, however, if we can accept that catastrophe explains Xena's unusual orbit, then catastrophe, as already argued, is likely to explain why Xena is where it is rather than somewhere else (say, at 1540 AU)! And we must remember that Xena (and perhaps Pluto) are proxy planets—not put there by natural process like the inner planets, but are likely to have been moons of the gas giant Neptune.

If these discoveries and all this speculation were not confusing enough, on August 24, 2006, the International Astronomical Union issued for the first time a formal definition for the term *planet*: "a celestial body that is in orbit around the Sun, has sufficient mass for its self-gravity to overcome rigid body forces so that it assumes a hydrostatic equilibrium (nearly round) shape, and has cleared the neighbourhood around its orbit." There are now a number of minor or so-called *dwarf planets* because these have *not* cleared the neighbourhood around their solar orbits. Among them 2003-UB313, Ceres, and Pluto—in fact, if Pluto is not downgraded, as many as 14 other objects will have to be included as proper planets, and that appears to be too many. So, now there are only eight proper planets: Mercury, Venus, Earth, Mars, Jupiter, Saturn, Uranus and Neptune.

It is yet to be decided which other bodies will be termed *dwarf planets* besides the three just mentioned, but we might also wonder if there will ever be any more *proper planets* whose physical parameters will comply with the formal definition. On the one hand, the definition may make it difficult to apply the Titius-Bode Law with the same degree of confidence as has been the case in the past, although that confidence has waned over the decades as we have seen. On the other hand, it has never been a better time to use the Law to make predictions because the Law has in fact not been shown to fail after all—there is now good reason to start a renewed search for proper planets beyond Neptune. Only future discoveries are going to solve the riddle of our solar system in the context of the Titius-Bode Law.

The Law as a Cosmic Truth?

Notwithstanding the possibility of catastrophes, which may account for the Law's inaccuracies, the Titius-Bode Law may also have universal significance and validity based on the universal laws that may apply to the formation of all solar systems. This postulation is based on the fact that a nebular period (the time when a solar system forms according to the dynamics of rotating gases, gas pressure, and gravitational forces) must exist as a crucial developmental stage for *all* solar systems. The Law would have *a priori* mathematical reality, nascent in this formative stage for any solar system. Note that electromagnetic theories and gravitational theories have also been postulated to explain the formation of solar systems, all with major problems in themselves, but as it happens, they do not convincingly support the Titius-Bode Law either. (These theories are too complex to detail here. The interested reader should consult Nieto's book, especially chapters 12-14.)

The series developed by Titius has a Platonist (Idealistic) aesthetic about it and might well have arisen by pure intuition. Why, after zero, is the first number in the series three? Why is each term (excluding zero and three) twice the previous term? Why then, did Titius add four to each of these terms? All this in accordance with the formula $r_n = 4 + (3 \times 2^n)$. Can we expect a formula to account for massive collisions or near misses that may or may not have occurred any number of times during the formation of our solar system? Each number in the series only approximates a mean distance, which itself is an average of two distances (perihelion and aphelion) due to orbital eccentricities. Can a series of numbers generated so easily be expected to account for the eccentricities of each planet? No two planets in our solar system even have the same eccentricity.

In the Titius-Bode Law it is possible to intuit the presence of number as an ordering principle in and of nature, although in a modest form—Bode himself was convinced that there was a physical reason for the Law's accuracy. From a Pythagorean perspective, the appearance of the numbers two, three and four in the Titius-Bode Law may have metaphysical and symbolic significance. It must be stated that while numbers form the foundations of modern science, this fact is also true of numerology, astrology and other occult 'sciences' and mantic systems for which the rational sciences are showing increasing support. With particular reference to the Law, the number two calls to mind Heraclitus' observation of the regulative function of opposites and the universal principal of balance sought through 'gravitational' principles. The number three refers to the physical experience of three dimensions (i.e., space). The Pythagoreans saw the principle of threeness as pertaining to astronomy and, in fact, they considered number three as having 'authority' in the dynamics of the cosmos. The number four makes its appearance as an 'additive' principle referring to the necessary inclusion of 'stability and flexibility' in the equation—crucial dynamic elements in the mediation of cosmic orderedness. (In the chapter "Dirac's Creation Equation" we see again that the number four, magnified tenfold, has cosmic applications.)

This type of number usage illustrates the qualitative thinking involved in symbolic discourse. While these numerical (or numerological) ideas seem valid aesthetically, it would be difficult, or even impossible, to make such a Pythagorean or symbolic discourse acceptable to the traditionally trained, scientifically minded person, since a major requirement of the discourse would be that it fit into the scientific paradigm. While it is perfectly acceptable to posit lawful (mathematical) models, which 'explain' nebular, electromagnetic, and gravitational phenomenologies, it is another remove altogether to expect that some kind of lawful 'quality' should be admitted into a domain that has thus far been kept exclusively quantifiable. The laws used in physics, for example, propagate acceptance mainly because they work. Yet these laws are only statistical truths, which describe statistical reality in a universe based on 'statistical causality', to use Pauli's term. They are no more binding or absolute than laws derived any other way (that is, *pseudo*-scientifically) such as the Titius-Bode Law. To be fair, scientists will use any method that gets results, as the history of the Law has shown. Whichever paradigm is adhered to, the believer will always 'know' that there is something more to the universe beyond the ordinary grasp of the traditional scientist, but the skeptic, it seems, will not be convinced until every one is convinced.

The Mathematician's Approach to Law-Making

When a law such as the Titius-Bode Law becomes unreliable, the skeptic is quick to disparage former claims to its legitimacy, while its successes are claimed as mere coincidence. Rarely, if ever, do they take the same attitude to failed laws derived by the scientific method—they simply accept that it is a matter of 'going back to the drawing board' and getting it right.

In 1913, Mary Blagg developed a formulation which was dramatically more complex than the form $r_n = a + b \times c^n$, but this formula was extremely accurate for calculating *all* the planetary distances to the Sun, and the satellite distances of the planets Jupiter, Saturn and Uranus as well. In the 1940s, D. E. Richardson developed a similar formulation, equally complex, but equally successful. Both formulations, although different, use "a geometric progression in 1.73 (*not* 2) multiplied by a periodic function of the planet number" (p. 3). (Chapter 7 of Nieto's book gives these formulae, too complex to be explained here.)

In regard to the formulae of Blagg and Richardson it is apparent that, while they are both unquestionably accurate, it also becomes apparent that mathematicians, like all scientists, can produce more than one formulation to describe the behavior of a phenomenon in the universe, but for that reason alone, do not in themselves provide any clues as to the mathematical underpinnings of that phenomenon. In fact, the vast 'playground' of mathematics allows for anything but unique formulations. For example, P. E. Chase, in the nineteenth century, proposed his own planetary distance Law, $r_n = \pi/32(1 + n \cdot \pi)$, where n = 1, 2, 3, 5, 9, 17, 33, 65, 97, and so on. Although quite accurate in describing planetary distances, this is another case where mathematical 'versatility' is demonstrated in the 'playground' of mathematics, because these accurate results were derived from a series which is *ad hoc* in the numbers n, derived purely to yield the correct results. Hardly good science, yet those of an Aristotelian mind-set would applaud it because it works. If one, and only one, formulation was invented (or discovered) that worked all the time, we might be in a position to accept that Plato was right. However, Plato will always have the benefit of the doubt because mathematical applications (whether they work or not) serve the real world, not the world of ideals.

Mathematicians, physicists, and scientists in general, would like their theories to be compelling, aesthetic and simple (admittedly subjective categories), but this is not always possible. In 'Quantum Mechanics and the Aether' (1954), Paul Dirac (mathematician and physicist) claimed:

> With all the violent changes to which modern physical theory is subjected, there is just one rock to which one can always hold fast—the assumption that the fundamental laws of nature correspond to a

beautiful mathematical theory. This means a theory based on simple mathematical concepts that fit together in an elegant way so that one has pleasure working with it. (p. 142)

West (1991) holds this same tenet: "it would appear that even scientifically, it is more 'logical' to accept a theory that is aesthetically satisfying than one that is not" (p. 225). Mathematicians Roger Penrose, Bertrand Russell, and G. H. Hardy all maintain the same view that mathematics not only possesses truth but supreme beauty, such that "Beauty in mathematics is an end in itself and a means to that end" (Penrose). Likewise Herman Weyl's aesthetic sense, which dominated his thinking on all subjects, prompted his tongue-in-cheek comment: "My work always tried to unite the true with the beautiful; but when I had to choose one or the other, I usually chose the beautiful." It must follow that if the scientists who work with these theories cannot see the elegance or beauty of a theory or formulation, it may be very likely that there are some very dissatisfied scientists out there.

The Titius-Bode Law gave astronomers not only a useful formula, which will surely influence astronomers in the future, but also presented mathematics as an art form. By using natural numbers only (2, 3 and 4) the Law *was* compelling, aesthetic and simple. When it failed, the Law was modified, or reformulated, or its familiar form was rejected out of necessity, so that a new formulation became the tool that was successful purely because it explained our solar system in mathematical terms—not because it might be considered axiomatic or profoundly true of the universe, and certainly not for aesthetic reasons. Thus it is that Platonic Idealism strongly conflicts with physical reality, since physical reality always falls short of the ideal.

Summary

Somewhat ideally, it seems that reliable and immutable laws can be developed that will explain certain aspects of the universe, but will also be simple and elegant. This ideal is a Platonist one, fit only for a perfect universe. The fact is the universe is a complex interplay of chance occurrences, immense forces and cataclysms that do not permit the formulation of immutable laws. The Titius-Bode Law, in its original form, was seemingly axiomatic and certainly elegant. At first it proved accurate in measuring the orbital distances of our planets, but it began to fail. Thereby the Law went through many modifications and reformulations, but while still serving a practical purpose, it lost its simple and elegant aesthetic.

Mathematicians and physicists remain optimistic that their formulae and theories, whether they need modification or not, might hold some kind of aesthetic, so that a deep satisfaction and belief in the efficacy of the sciences will be held as well, in spite of the reality of an unpredictable universe. It is the new field of chaos theory that is now shedding light on our unpredictable universe, and we are beginning to learn that even in chaos there is cosmos, and that in each *is* the other.

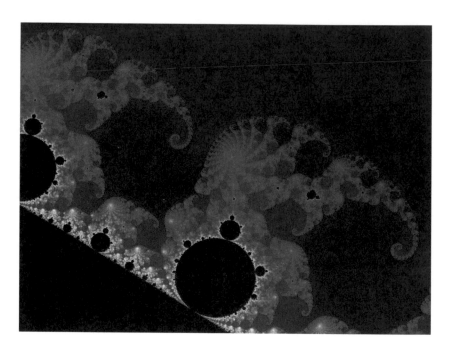

Plate 27. ORDER FROM CHAOS

The beauty and order; form and color, that can emerge from chaos is exemplified in this portion of a Mandelbrot set. Benoit Mandelbrot added a new dimension to the field of chaos theory when he introduced the fractals—the "geometries of nature" [SOURCE: Wikimedia Commons].

"The only way you can recognize chaos and not be threatened by it is to see it as another form of order in the making."

— J.R.

THE CHAOS OF NUMBER

Chaos is an order of infinite complexity.

F. David Peat

"Maybe it is Chaos
that is the food
for order, so that more
chaos can move us forward."
_R_

The mind is an order-seeking organism. All cultural products are evidence
of the human capacity to put order to the 'chaotic' universe in which
we find ourselves. Our cities, our civilization, our technology, our economy,
and so on, are all relatively successful attempts at maximizing resources and
minimizing waste, but there are chaotic systems which seem to defy our
attempt at creating a cosmos (Greek: *cosmos* = 'order, world'). Chaos theory
emerged in the midst of this failure and uncertainty as a gallant effort on
the part of mathematicians, physicists, and even meteorologists towards
determining the patterns, symmetry and non-randomness that might exist
in these chaotic systems.

As the chapter "Two (The Dyad)" makes clear, antithetical relationships
exist between pairs of opposites, and this condition is no less true of the dyad
of order and chaos. In *The Philosopher's Stone* (1991), F. David Peat describes
the dualistic friction that exists between order and chaos:

> Order and chaos are viewed as opposing forces. Order is seen in a
> positive light. It is associated with harmony, law, control, regularity,
> discipline, determinism, form, rule, rhythm, and structure, whereas
> chaos is disorder, misrule, contingency, randomness, chance, and lack
> of harmony. (p. 161)

Chaos theory gives mathematicians, meteorologists, geologists, computer
programmers, and economists, etc., a new way of tackling the age old problem

of the unpredictability of fluid dynamics, weather patterns, earthquakes, the stock market, and so on.

Historically, the more intuitive type (shaman priests, witch-doctors, sooth-sayers, seers, astrologers, and prophets) resorted to systems of divination in order to deal with the irrational (or at least the unknown), and people depended on these individuals to come up with answers that might empower them to act appropriately, or at least provide a palliative that might assuage the anxiety that doubt and uncertainty invariably instilled in them. If and when systems of divination failed or fell short of the demands made upon them (and these systems seemed, and may still be, applicable within limited areas of life and world events—for example, personality, behavior, appropriate action, and probable outcomes) people generally resigned themselves to fate, or higher powers.

In the modern world, the physicist, the mathematician, and scientists in general are now expected to relinquish all doubt. Religion and divination are the resort of the relatively few who still believe in such things. But the demands on the scientist are often impossible to meet—not only complex systems, but even simple systems can often be difficult to describe and predict. For example, the unpredictable nature of our solar system, described in the previous chapter, made a mockery of the Titius-Bode Law. Our disciplines are constantly at work refining and modifying, and even abandoning laws and formulae that fail to predict unforeseen events, and chaos theory emerged as part of this ongoing process.

Understanding Chaos

In the 1960s, the meteorologist and mathematician Edward Lorenz designed a computer program that would calculate changes in rising hot air. He found that even very small variances in the initial data would produce major variations in the outcomes. A new term arose—*the butterfly effect*—that described this type of dynamic. Theoretically, chaotic and unpredictable events of spectacular magnitude in one part of the world could be the result of (say) a mere flap of a butterfly's wings in another part of the world.

The unpredictability of such outcomes is entirely dependent on the small variations that contribute to the overall pattern, and the same applies to weather patterns and even the stock market. As a result of this work, Lorenz produced the first graphic representation of a chaotic system—the Lorenz attractor—a spiral-like curve that does not intersect or repeat a path previously taken (*see* fig. 72). Minute deviations in the system prevent a path from being repeated. Hence, the Lorenz attractor describes a chaotic system.

Figure 72. *A Lorenz attractor.*

In a special sense, the Lorenz attractor resembles the sigmoid shape of the number eight, the lemniscate: ∞. Both represent, or at least symbolize, potentially infinite circularity or movement, symmetry, alternation, and even repetition and regeneration. In another sense, the bimodal brain is represented by the symmetry of the Lorenz attractor, where the indeterminate nature of human behavior may depend on cognitive functions that involve continuous 'switching' from one hemisphere to the other, in an unpredictable manner. In psychology, the onset of psychoticism, schizoid tendencies, depression, and even normal decision-making processes, may all be described by the Lorenz attractor, without it necessarily providing any degree of insight that would result in the generation of models that might predict these changes. These are all new avenues of possible research that may revolutionize psychology and the neurosciences.

The Lorenz attractor is also known by a more general term—the *strange* attractor—because its geometry is so irregular. Even by the 1970s, with the confirmation of chaos theory in areas such as geography (earthquakes, flooding), astronomy (asteroid movement, celestial orbits), and ecology (population fluctuations in people and insects), outcomes were still unpredictable, until the nature of the strange attractor revealed a hidden order previously undetected.

Fractal Geometry

Benoit Mandelbrot added a new dimension to the field of chaos theory with the introduction of the *fractal* (Latin: *fractus* = 'broken'). Fractal geometry concerns the geometry of objects that topographically remain the same even when they are broken into smaller and smaller sections. This kind of geometry is typical of chaotic systems. Pappas makes an important point about fractals in *The Magic of Mathematics* (1994):

> These geometric objects endlessly repeat themselves on an ever shrinking scale.... Fractals have come to be labeled the *geometry of nature* and with the use of present day computers, fractal geometry is used to describe aspects of nature (clouds, ginger root, coast lines) that in the past would not have been described using Euclidean geometric methods. (p. 43)

While polygons in two-dimensional space, and the pyramid, cube, and sphere, and so on, in three-dimensional space are well understood, and formulae exist to determine the measures of these objects, the geometry apparent in coastlines, trees, cloud shapes, etc., seem too variable and irregular to be measured in Euclidean terms. But fractal geometry is a move in the direction of putting order to these chaotic objects because they allow a certain degree of measurement.

Ultimately a paradox arises in the measurement of (say) a coastline, and it is none other than Zeno's paradox discussed previously in the chapter "Infinity." This paradox arises because infinite regression is suggested in the procedure used to measure a coastline. The appearance of a coastline is only as accurate as the map portraying the coastline is detailed. F. David Peat points out that the circumference of the whole coastline of (say) the British Isles will be shorter than the aggregate of individual, more detailed large scale sections of the total coastline because the imperfections of the coastline—the rough cliff edges and inlets, and so on—are only visible in close up (*see* fig. 73).

Figure 73. *Measuring a section of coastline A_1B_1 is a formidable task, since accuracy of the circumference depends on detail. Zooming in on (a) shows the section A_2B_2 to be quite irregular, as shown in (b), and therefore longer than is suggested in (a). Complications arise as increased detail is revealed with even more irregularity in A_3B_3 and A_4B_4. There is no end to the problem and a final measurement becomes impossible [Based on F. David Peat's (1991) Figure 7.1 on page 165 of* The Philosopher's Stone. *New York: Bantam]*

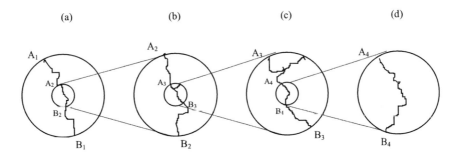

(a)   (b)   (c)   (d)

As indicted in the above example, one can keep taking closer, more detailed sections of coastline, and measure rocks, pebbles, and ultimately even grains of sand, but as Peat claims:

> the result becomes longer and longer—without limit. In fact, the true circumference of the British coast is the same as that of North and South America combined! It is infinite. Thanks to the infinite detail of natural forms, the circumference of the British Isles is infinitely long. (1991, p. 165)

However, from examples such as coastline measurement, mathematicians were able to develop models that reproduced these complex natural shapes. Mandelbrot believed that fractal forms (curves and surfaces) were in fact more natural than the representations of nature produced by the old mathematics and geometry. That reality becomes clear when one realizes that fractional dimensions apply to almost everything in nature, from the coastline of a country to the slope of a mountain, or even the shape of a fern frond.

Mandelbrot employed the use of a 'generator', or algorithm (a calculation involving a repeated number of steps), which allowed the iteration of a procedure to be performed on a 'seed' that might be a regular polygon or even a straight line (*see* fig. 74).

The branching patterns of trees (*see* fig. 75), the vascular system, and even the manner in which metals may fracture can all be described by numbers, since they are the constituents of the algorithm, but Peat (1991) makes an important point, using the tree as an example:

> A fractal tree goes some way to explaining the complex branching of a tree…. [B]y modifying the simple rule by which a fractal is generated, it is possible to generate different generic shapes for oak, poplar, and evergreen. But a real living tree is like a book: It is the manifestation of forces and decisions that were made within its lifetime. From the first seedling to the gnarled and cracked trunk of an ancient oak, the tree speaks to us of its life, the variations in the seasons it has experienced…. A tree is a unique individual. (p. 172)

Individuality is determined by more than mere mathematical formulae, no matter how complex these formulae may be, and nature is not as simple in its design as fractal geometry suggests. Mathematical models are always representations of nature, and even though we gain insights into how nature may function from these models, the "organic subtlety of nature" (Peat, 1991, p. 173) cannot enter into fractal form, since the number of variables that determine the uniqueness of a process or system are myriad.

Figure 74. *The generator or algorithm 'instructs' a given line (step 0) to erupt into a peak (step 1), which itself consists of lines that will also erupt into peaks (step 2). The result (step 3) is a complex figure known as the Koch curve. It has a growth pattern reminiscent of forms in nature.*

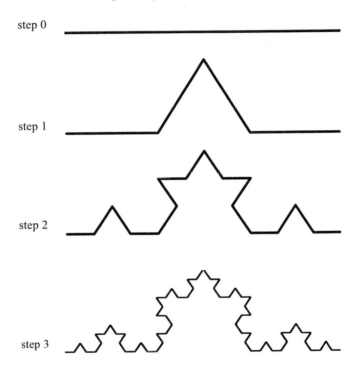

step 0

step 1

step 2

step 3

However, this fact does not mean that large numbers of variables cannot be accounted for and coded into an algorithm. But, as it stands, even the most complex fractal model cannot come close to reality, because it is bereft of natural complexity. For example, the Mandelbrot set and similar fractal landscapes, which produce limitless horizons of artificially generated panoramas that perpetually iterate themselves, look convincingly real only in the sense that, more than anything else, they generate depth and extension in space, even though the content (sea, land, flora, etc.) might be acceptably real. Algorithms are basically deterministic, and nature does not submit to deterministic models exclusively.

Figure 75. *A simple tree can be generated by iterated splitting of its branches.*

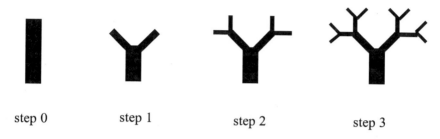

step 0   step 1   step 2   step 3

Chaos in the Algorithm

From the statement made by Hermann Weyl, that number has an 'abysmal' quality, we might even assume the possibility that the numbers used in the algorithm introduce that selfsame abysmal quality into the fractal. If so, it is unlikely that the effects of this abysmal quality could be identified until a certain degree of complexity in the fractal has been reached, because number is at its most irrational when it is interactive within complex systems. For example, while the artificial intelligence of computers replicate simple cognitive functions of the human brain, the vastly more complex brain produces emergent behaviors and functions that have come about as a result of continuous evolutionary modification. Eventually, computer systems may generate these emergent properties, but only as a concomitant of their increased complexity.

Not just one, but many algorithms will be necessary to even begin approximating an artificial intelligence that reaches the order of the human brain. And each algorithm must be capable of interaction with other algorithms. Just as in nature, a kind of interactionism exists in natural processes (for example, plant growth, crystal formation, or even decay and putrefaction) where any number of variables can influence a process, or have influence within a process, randomly (and, therefore, in unpredictable ways), and any number of times.

The hidden variability of number is there in nature as the very essence of nature's processes, just as number is there in the algorithm. For the mathematician working in the area of chaos theory and fractal geometry such facts are the stock in trade of scientific endeavor, so that they only mean 'business as usual'. The mathematician will argue that science is an accumulative discipline, and there is a tacit understanding that new systems are often improvements on old ones. Theoretically, there should be no reason why algorithms could not be written in order to 'replicate' the processes of photosynthesis, genetic coding, and even the whole panoply of environmental forces that exist in nature.

Algorithms, however, unlike natural processes, are not organic, multifactorial, or random in function. As Peat (1991) notes, they are "mechanical, unitary, and deterministic" (p. 176). Nevertheless, having recognized the irrational in its pure form (chaos) we have come closer to dealing with nature on its own terms, which is far from the ordered and systematic world view we have rigorously endorsed in the past to the exclusion of all else.

Summary

Chaos theory, strange attractors, fractals, and so on, have expanded our viewpoint and understanding of nature and its 'natural' processes by allowing the mathematician to construct more complex models of the world than those previously used. These models mimic many phenomena we see in nature. Some degree of order has been established in a previously chaotic area of our everyday experience, though reliable prediction of stock-market fluctuations, weather patterns, and other indeterminate systems are still beyond the grasp of chaos theory.

At the heart of chaos theory are both the rational *and* irrational components of number. In constructing algorithms, mathematicians use numbers as if they understood them completely, but they are not aware of the irrational component of number, and therefore, cannot allow for this irrationality as an influence in itself on outcomes. Only the quantitative value of number is recognized—the posited quantity. In the next two chapters the irrational aspect of number is discussed, how it stands behind the ways and means by which we construct the universe, and how an understanding of the psyche must be part and parcel of that construction.

Plate 28. SACRED GROVE

Photograph by George Edward Anderson (c. 1907). The Sacred Grove is the location where Joseph Smith, Jr., founder of the Church of Latter Day Saints, said he had his first vision in 1820. Landmarks that bear psychological and symbolic significance are ultimately hailed as sacred sites because transformational events are alleged to have taken place there [SOURCE: Wikimedia Commons].

THE ELEVEN GATES OF THE 11:11

Our mind still has its darkest Africa.

Aldous Huxley

Aldous Huxley, in *Heaven and Hell* (1994), wrote: "Like the earth of a hundred years ago, our mind still has its darkest Africa, its unmapped Borneos and Amazonian basins" (p. 83). It is understandable how the psyche, with its labyrinthine complexity, might come to be envisioned as an unknown region of an unexplored world, and the projection of this psychic fact (the unknown structure of the psyche) onto that world (i.e., concretization of the psychic fact) is also understandable. Edinger (1986a) describes the projection of a symbol from the archetypal psyche onto "concrete, external reality" as the "concretistic fallacy" (p. 149). Superstition, hallucination, fantastical beliefs, and so on, are all the result of the concretistic fallacy. Even the alchemist made the concretistic fallacy when he misconstrued psychic reality for physical reality. The same fallacy is made when "ultimate security" is sought in "physical well-being or literal, rigid truth" (p. 149). Projection, it seems, goes on all the time, and it is a causal factor underlying many social movements such as the one discussed next.

The Gates Start Opening

In *Golden Age* (1997)—"the magazine for personal transformation"—in an article entitled 'An Update on the 11:11', the visionary and prophet Solara writes rather esoterically of the eleven gates of the 11:11 as being "critical points in the Zone of Overlap in which different aspects of the Greater Reality are energetically anchored on the physical planet" (p. 66). In numerology, the number 11 is one of the Master Numbers. Eleven is the number of the idealist, the psychic, the religionist, and even the diplomat. As it happens, it is also the number of disorganization, so that number 11 might symbolize and reflect some kind of disorder or disruption in an individual's life or psyche if he or she becomes highly conscious of this number on a day-to-day basis, or as an inner experience.

Solara speaks of the potential for all people to make a "quantum leap from duality to Oneness" (p. 55) at certain times at certain places on our planet, and he refers to these events as great moments in human evolution. We identify these times and places by the cues which come from the double Master Numbers 11:11, which are "encoded into our cellular memory banks" (p. 55). Such a time occurred on January 1, 1992, when the first of eleven gates was opened. 'Master Cylinders' (groups of transformed individuals) were needed to anchor the energy of this event—one was the 'Omega Point' at the site of the Great Pyramids in Egypt, and the second was the 'Alpha Point' in Queenstown, New Zealand.

A second gate opened on June 5, 1993 in Ecuador, and a third opened on May 17, 1997 in Slovenija. Hundreds of thousands of individuals participated in these openings, each of whom has allegedly become 'Earth-Star Beings' through transformation processes often led by Solara. The creation of 'Islands of Light' on Earth (the pattern for a 'New World') is the goal of this worldwide movement. At this moment the 'Doorway of the 11:11' is opened and will remain so until December 31, 2011. Solara claims that millions of people the world over are becoming aware of the 11:11 when they see it, for example, on their digital clocks and elsewhere in the environment.

Projecting the Archetype of Unity

It is clear from these events how individuals can become deeply affected by the appearance of an image in consciousness—an image that seems strangely familiar, hence the fascination. Absolute truth is assigned to such an experience. A typical synchronicity emerges. The unconscious is attuned to the resonance of the symbol and intuitively 'detects' 11:11 when it makes its appearance. The image is projected into the environment, and it is seen everywhere—digital clocks, car registration plates, street signs, etc. The 4 × 1 configuration (i.e., 11:11) resonates with such archetypal power that it becomes too overwhelming to deal with in a personal way. Like-minded people the world over must be drawn into the event, and locations are 'discovered' globally so that the enormous energies of these collective psyches can be canalized. This phenomenon is an example of the Self mapped onto the world as described in the chapter "Five (The Pentad)."

Oneness symbolism (Unity, freedom from dissociation) can have a fourfold aspect so that the experience of unity is perceived, but not necessarily comprehended as a construction of sub-units indicating the fragmented whole. The sub-units may take the psychological form of the four functions that Jung describes. Thinking, Feeling, Sensation, and Intuition. Geographically, the four units might be represented as compass points on the landscape, or substantial physical landmarks that bear psychological and symbolic significance, as is demonstrated by the world-roving practices of the '11:11' people. Architectural space, such as the typical room of four walls, may be sought for its stabilizing influence, just as quaternity structures may also be sought or spontaneously produced endopsychically as internalized images. These and other representations of the number-four archetype are wholeness oriented.

Edinger (1986a) warns of the danger of "succumbing to the concretistic fallacy whenever we are tempted to apply a symbolic image to external physical facts for the purpose of manipulating those facts in our own interest" (p. 149). Solara is aware of the fact that numbers embody particular meanings which come from, as he calls it, 'cellular memory banks' (i.e., archetypal layers of the psyche), and speaks of waking up from the "cycle of duality and separation" (p. 55), signifying a drive, or desire for wholeness. But Solara's movement manifests as a Crusade, as if the personal experience could be made the experience of millions. Only the spiritually weak and emotionally hungry are ever drawn into such movements, and all too often the search for absolute truth 'out there' can only lead to dissatisfaction as a result of an optimism not matched by real personal sacrifice and honesty with oneself. The 1990s provided many examples of such movements, in the form of cults and sects. In this example, the number archetype has shown itself to be a force with which to be reckoned. Ultimately, then, the heavy burden of responsibility that comes with the experience of the archetype rests entirely with the individual. In cult-like movements, an attempt to ameliorate this responsibility is undertaken by an appeal to like-minded others.

While identification with the group may have the advantage of a community spirit, and safety in numbers, and might even help instill self-esteem and confidence (of a form), it is more often found that the objectives of the group manifest as a striving for the unity of the group over that of the individual. The individual—the one not divided—for its own psychological health can never afford to be swallowed up by the group. Usually it is just such a mind-set manifesting politically, for example, as an ideological cause that results in totalitarian regimes that reduce the individual to the lowest common denominator. Fostering a keen sense of one's self is a movement in itself away from the herd mentality.

Summary

There is nothing ordinarily wrong with expressing one's belief through a community *per se*, insofar as it serves as the mechanism by which archetypal energies can be mediated in consciousness. But when one forgets the inner reality and magically projects its images onto physical reality, the concretistic fallacy creates a disturbing illusion.

At first the projection protects the individual from overwhelming archetypal energies irrupting from the unconscious, but ultimately the individual must either face the threat of being swallowed up by the group, or recognize the inner processes, which started the whole deception in the first place. The challenge then is to integrate these images by recognizing their symbolic validity, as opposed to identifying with them (taking them literally) or projecting them into the environment as (say) magical places where transformations may take place. Movements are reminders of how rapturous are the archetypes when they manifest in consciousness. The number archetype is no exception.

Plate 29. CREATION OF LIGHT

The engraving Creation of Light *(1865) by Gustave Doré depicts a literal representation of Genesis 1:1 ("Let there be light"). In the beginning, God created the heavens and the earth, but modern physics offers numerous alternatives to that myth. Paul Dirac postulated a universe that did not come into existence 20 billion years ago, but has always existed, and is essentially static [SOURCE: Wikimedia Commons].*

PAUL DIRAC'S CREATION
EQUATION

The universe is not only stranger than we imagine,
it is stranger than we can imagine.

Sir James Jeans

The Cambridge theoretical physicist Paul Dirac is possibly best known for postulating the existence of antimatter in 1928. His anti-electron (the positron), later discovered by Carl Anderson in 1932, has the same mass as an electron, but its electrical charge is opposite (i.e., positive) to that of the electron. Dirac also postulated that when particles and anti-particles collided they would annihilate each other, leaving energy but no mass. In fact, the idea of matter meeting antimatter, with its devastating consequences (so popular as a science fiction motif), has been authenticated many times over in experiments using particle accelerators. Dirac went on to co-found a revolutionary form of physics—quantum mechanics—that has become fundamental in every aspect of our scientific and technological world today, particularly in the fields of electronics, biology and chemistry. But Dirac is less known for his so-called 'creation equation'. This chapter will look at Dirac's controversial ideas about the formation of our Earth, the universe and its future.

From the Relative to the Absolute

From observations of sub-atomic particles and their properties, Dirac developed the idea that matter could be created from energy, providing there were sufficient amounts of energy at the start. But antimatter would also be created at the same time. Appealing to Einstein's famous equation $E = mc^2$ (where c^2 is the square of the speed of light), any theorist could determine just how much energy (E) would be needed to create a desired amount of mass (m), and *vice versa*. These ideas are now well accepted in physics, but Dirac proposed a more controversial theory concerning the origins of the universe, which generated some disapproval amongst other theorists because it did not rely on the dualistic Big Bang/Big Crunch theory so popular with most physicists.

Dirac postulated a universe that did not come into existence 20 billion years ago, but has always existed, and is essentially static. Dirac claimed that gravitational forces are weakening between masses (stars, planets, etc.), while these masses themselves are increasing in size by the addition of new matter (mass is constantly being created from energy, for example, in the fusion reactions of stars). Distances between these masses are also increasing.

There seems to be a major contradiction in Dirac's theory in the light of Einsteinian physics, where gravity and mass are supposedly constant and cannot change within a system. Furthermore, by Einstein's theory, if mass was to increase, then so should gravity, but Dirac's theory states otherwise. Dirac countered these anomalies by asserting that the increase in mass and distance, and the decrease in gravity, are illusions, which come about because the matter in the universe is actually diminishing in mass and size, while the distances between masses only seem to be increasing at a faster and faster rate. Dirac had created a paradox of universal proportions because there seemed to be no way to reconcile these conflicting ideas.

Dirac's solution was simple. The illusions come about by changes at the atomic level only. The number of atoms is increasing in stars, while the stars' already existing atoms are shrinking, and the increase in new atoms just keeps up with the consumption of the fissionable mass. The star's gravitational effects on another mass, such as a planet, and the distance between the two do not alter.

By Dirac's reckoning this constant increase in the number of atoms means our Sun will burn for another 8 billion years. But this extra time can only be gained if new matter is created where matter already exists proportional to that mass. Dirac calls this process *multiplicative creation*. The impossible alternative, *additive creation*, where new matter appears randomly throughout the universe, would mean the Sun would have burned itself out 2 billion years ago. By Dirac's theory, this quick burn out would have occurred because the decrease in the Sun's gravity would increase its fusion rate faster than the rate of creation of new matter in the Sun.

With matter in (say) the Earth decreasing in size (including scientific instruments that measure distance and time) we get a false impression of increased distance between the Earth and (say) the Sun, and increases in the length of time it takes for light to reach the Earth from the Sun. In the same way, the 'red shift', measured in galaxies moving away from us, is an illusion created out of the fact that stars in these galaxies produced longer ('red' saturated) wavelengths of light billions of years ago, which we are only seeing now given the phenomenal distances the light has to travel. All those billions of years ago the universe was younger and atomic processes in 'low-mass' stars took place at a 'faster' rate, in 'seconds' that were longer than 'modern' seconds.

Matter, then, changes all those dimensions and magnitudes that we might have assumed were fixed and absolute. As mass 'increases', we perceive increases in distance, decreases in gravity between celestial bodies, and unchanging seconds. All of which are illusions—even the increase in mass is an illusion—mass actually remains constant, just like the speed of light. Only the number of atoms changes. As John Gliedman states in 'God's Numbers: Have We Found the Equation of Creation?' (1981):

> instead of adding new mass to physical objects, mass remains constant in a Universe, for with every passing year the "purchasing power" of matter declines: measuring sticks mark off shorter metres, clocks tick off shrunken seconds and atoms lose mass. Truly Dirac has produced a cosmological theory for our time. (p. 100)

Dirac's theory originates in some interesting numerical facts concerning atomic particles, nuclear and electrical forces, and gravity, which all involve magnitudes of 10^{40}. There are five main facts, as reported by Gliedman:

1. The size of the universe is 10^{40} times larger than the size of the electron.

2. The age of the universe is about 10^{40} times greater than the *chronon* (the smallest measure of time known in science), which is 1×10^{-24} seconds.

3. The electric force of attraction between the hydrogen atom and its central proton is 1×10^{40} times greater than the gravitational attraction between them.

4. The size of an elementary particle divided by the shortest length possible is 10^{40}

5. The total number of photons in the universe divided by the total number of particles in atomic nuclei is 10^{40}

Dirac showed that coincidence or chance was unlikely in the derivation of these figures, since any of these ratios could have had any value other than 10^{40} with much greater probability, but they did not. The ratio of 10^{40} for Dirac was instrumental in determining a theory of the universe that ties all these factors into one coherent whole. Changes in one ratio mean changes to the others, since they are all inter-connected. Dirac believed that this inter-connectedness constituted a relationship that is eternal in nature and reciprocal, whereby the ratios, if they change, must mean the parts also change.

Dirac figured that when the universe doubled in age, the electric/force gravity ratio would double also to 2×10^{40} to maintain the significant 10^{40} ratio. Experimentation disproved this conjecture, so Dirac came to the next inevitable conclusion that gravity within bodies must weaken as the universe ages.

Dirac's theory helps explain the drop in sea levels over the past 500 million years—an expanding Earth's surface would mean the ocean's basins would accommodate more water draining from the continents. Continental drift rates by conventional theories do not explain the huge distances between the continents. The Earth's crust would have to be expanding as well, since movement of the plates, being so slow, could not account for these large continental distances, given the age of the Earth.

Dirac's ideas seem to have stood the test of time. Stavros T. Tassos and David J. Ford, in their article 'An Integrated Alternative Conceptual Framework to Heat Engine Earth, Plate Tectonics, and Elastic Rebound' (2005), in the *Journal of Scientific Exploration*, have devised a theory that is very similar to Dirac's conception of an Earth that is increasing in size. They argue that the plate theory is incorrect, and they have produced impressive evidence that Fe^{2-} (later changing to FeO_2) is being produced at the Earth's core and is being thrust upward to increase the Earth's mass. They state:

> Physical evidence indicates that a thermally driven Earth, plate tectonics, and elastic rebound theory violate fundamental physical principles, and that Earth is a quantified solid body, the size of which possibly increases with time. Earth's core is considered as a low-temperature, high-energy/high-frequency, high-tension material, wherein new elements form, constituting the Excess Mass, which is then added atom-by-atom to the overlying mantle.... Iron ascends [towards the surface] in the form of reduced high pressure Fe^{2-}, to a depth of about 700 km. At shallower depths it then releases 4-5 electrons whilst oxidizing and decompressing at reducing confining pressures. Some of the released excess mass electrons travel as free electrons, and thereby cause microcracks to form...; these microcracks enlarge as their concentration increases and their cumulative internal electron pressure builds up; via this self-repulsive electron pressure a great mass of rock is uplifted over time. (p. 43)

With continued research into these quantifiable changes in the Earth's mass, it is possible that we may get closer to confirming Dirac's claims that have remained on the fringes of current scientific interest.

Testing the Archetype—Estimation and Interpretation

Dirac endeavored to logically schematize the universe through numerical principles, much like a Pythagorean or Platonist. He made the physical universe fit in with his numerically derived, or better, mathematically derived schema, without bending the Einsteinian rules, nor compromising any major axioms in physics, yet he still managed to offer some solutions to problems which have puzzled geologists, earth scientists, and physicists for some time.

Testing of Dirac's predictions regarding distance changes, while simultaneously eliminating the major problems with the Big Bang Theory, by undermining its theoretical basis altogether, would remain inconclusive, however, since there would always be other ways of interpreting these changes. But, from a 'numerological' perspective, we might ask if there is any significance to the constant appearance of 10^{40}, or specifically, the number 40, in Dirac's 'creation equation', other than its aesthetic appeal.

Before that, we must consider Dirac's use of estimates in his theory. How can Dirac have faith in his 10^{40} when the total number of photons in the universe (see [v] above) would have to be an estimate? This type of scholarship seems similar to that of the pyramidologists who see mathematical mysteries and other secret knowledge encrypted in the dimensions of the Cheops pyramid. For example, the distance from the Earth to the Sun, estimates of π, the density of the Earth, and even estimates of the speed of light have all been 'discovered' in the pyramid's dimensions, but the calculations, when scrutinized, are also based on approximate measurements. One of a number of ways of calculating π, for example, is by multiplying the lengths of the North and South walls of the Queen's Chamber by 10, and dividing this figure by the measure of the Great Niche in the East wall. The estimate of π comes out at 3.14159, but apart from the arbitrary arithmetic involved in this calculation, this estimate does not come very close to the estimate of π as used by the Egyptians of the time. They used $4(8/9)^2 = 3.1605$, which is less accurate than the pyramid-derived estimate. Why would the Egyptians have used a less accurate estimate? It is likely that the pyramidologists looked for answers by constructing them from facts that they generated themselves because these facts fit their theories.

However, the fact that Dirac used estimates may be irrelevant. NASA's successful space missions, which used estimates in the computer programs that calculated the trajectories of their spacecraft, were shown later to involve error rates of only fractions of inches, even over distances of many millions of miles.

By committing himself to his 'numerical' or 'numerological' idea, Dirac constructed a possible future 'truth'—a cosmology—that may be of value in answering questions that current cosmologies fail to answer. Paradigm shifts have occurred throughout the centuries in science and other disciplines when theories reached a dead end (as they continue to do), and even though Dirac's incomplete system may need further work, its current status already offers some 'better' alternatives to Big Bang/Big Crunch theories, with their major problems. While Big Bang theorists argue their case from mathematical proofs, we cannot deny that Dirac does the same thing. Furthermore, the axioms of mathematics, as shown by Gödel in the 1930s, are not even falsifiable as such. Dirac's 'creation equation' is similar to mathematical axioms, whereby, although its absolute validity may be questioned, it is nevertheless relativistically valid in terms of its practical and theoretical value.

In support of Dirac's theory, Rupert Sheldrake in *Seven Experiments That Could Change The World* (1994) discusses how the fundamental physical constants (for example, the universal gravitational constant, G; the velocity of light, c; and Planck's constant, h) could actually be changing in value. For example, estimates for c from 1928-1948 were down by 20 kilometers/second compared to the 1927 estimate, but rose again to the current value of $299,792.458 \pm .0012$ km/second (by definition). Also, G has fluctuated by .07% since 1970 between the values of 6.6699 and 6.6745 (the unit is 10^{-11} $m^3 \, kg^{-1} \, s^{-2}$). The currently accepted value is $6.672 \pm .003$. These constants are supposed to be unchanging, therefore "reflect[ing] an underlying constancy of nature" (p. 164). Sheldrake (1994) gives two main theories explaining these fluctuations of the fundamental constants:

1. "they are truly constant, and all variations in the empirical data are due to errors of one kind or another" (p. 187). The conventional view has it that experimental methods and precision improve with time so that the estimates of the true values of the constants become more and more accurate.

2. "one or more of the constants may vary in some smooth and regular manner with the age of the universe, or over astronomical distances" (pp. 187-88). This view supports Dirac's theory regarding gravity.

Sheldrake poses a third possibility which is the idea that constants may fluctuate, within limits, around average values which themselves remain fairly constant," and the classical idea of "changeless laws and constants" (p. 188) is simply not tenable anymore. Perfect order is an illusion and "most of the natural world is inherently chaotic (p. 188). (In part, this view is also supportive of Dirac's theory, where perfect order is an illusion, but Dirac does not go so far as to suggest that chaos rules supreme, or that laws and constants are fluctuating around an average value.)

An analysis of Dirac's theory would be incomplete if the symbolic aspects latent in the theory were not considered. Schimmel (1993) calls the number forty the number of completion. It bears similarities with the number four, as described in a previous chapter, but the magnitude of the number ten multiplies the number four to the level of *celestial* things, according to the rules of *gematria*.

The biblical references of the Flood (which lasted forty days and forty nights), Moses' forty years in the desert, and the forty years spent in the wilderness by the Israelites, as well as Christ's forty days and forty nights also spent in the wilderness, suggest long and enduring periods of trial and ordeal. There does not seem to be any relevance to anything cosmic or celestial in these time periods. Perhaps they are symbolic references to psychological processes only.

But Stonehenge, with its forty large stone pillars "arranged in a sacred circle with a diameter of 40 steps" (Schimmel, 1993, p. 245), was used to measure and calculate *astronomical* events, so that the celestial reference may still hold. Perhaps the ancients had an intuitive understanding of the cosmological relevance of number in the order of the cosmos. Since the number four relates quantitatively and qualitatively to the structure of the psyche, it follows that the way we experience the universe may be attuned to the actual and real structure of the universe, due to a numerical orderedness common to both (there would be a very real inter-connectedness of the psyche with the universal order). The number forty seems even more appropriate than the number four in this case, since it refers directly to the cosmos.

The number forty appears throughout many cultures and in many religions, and in many cases is applied to time periods (days, months, years, cycles, and eons), yet at the same time may refer to bleak, barren, and virtually uninhabitable voids. Both the most immense dimensions of our universe (the sense of the vastness of outer space even as grasped by the layperson, as compared with the ancient view of the vastness of space as characterized by the wilderness), and the greatest measures of time (the age of the universe compared with the 'seven days' of creation—'a day is as a thousand years'), force us to rescale the biblical proportions of space and time.

Since quantification is inappropriate in cases where infinite dimensions are evoked or implied, the most appropriate course of action here may be to focus on the things that appear to 'make sense' under impossible circumstances. Such action may require an appreciation of aesthetic and relational judgments, which oust the practical considerations of measurement. In a relativistic age, magnitudes and dimensions lose their absolute value anyway, so that we must 'rethink' our concept of the universe in order to give account of properties that currently defy understanding.

Thus we can see that ancient and modern ideas parallel each other. Though today it is easier to imagine a 'truer' scale of the universe because astronomical measurement has made this possible, for the ancients, the wilderness *was* the infinity of space, as far as conscious experience was concerned, and duration in time (40 time units) was intricately enmeshed with the vastness of that wilderness. Not only do we discover a biblical, unified concept of spacetime that pre-dates the same Einsteinian relativistic concept, but it also seems that spacetime is intrinsically isomorphic with the numerical representation of the totality of the psyche. Thereby, psyche, time, and space appear to mirror each other in their phenomenologies.

The number forty seems to be one of those numbers which resonates in the psyche with an appropriateness that befits the 'complete' or 'total' idea of a cosmic system of universal magnitude, where the psyche and the universe, the infinitesimal and the infinite, the bounded and the unbounded are all united, like spacetime. If theories like Dirac's Creation Equation prove to have validity (because it may prove to have greater explanatory power than current models) we will come to see ourselves as changing in ways previously unimagined, by way of the acceptance of numerical (numerological) ideas that do not seem applicable in the quantitative sciences. This is because the number forty evokes the categories of space and time beyond a mundane interpretation, so that conceptual 'realities' of a cosmic order are made possible.

The Symbol at Work

Dirac's theory shows an obvious focus on number from a perspective that seems to be more than just magnitudinal. Psychologically, there is the possibility that the number archetype became activated in Dirac's psyche yielding an intuitive awareness of the number forty (in the form of 10^{40}) as the means by which he (given the nature of his work) was able to make the 'right' numerical associations with infinitesimal (sub-atomic) and infinite (cosmic) numerical representations. Through the symbol (10^{40}), the archetype also worked emotionally, keeping Dirac on the 'right' track, because an imaginal, aesthetic approach was evoked in him, as opposed to a purely linear, rational approach which would have made it impossible for him to make some of the claims raised in his theory.

Dirac's rational judgment came into play when he deliberated upon his statements and put them into an Einsteinian perspective (which called for a modification of his ideas), thus maintaining the accessibility of his theory to scientific scrutiny. At the same time, Dirac did not question his aesthetic judgment because the number archetype, having preserved a deep conviction in him that he was onto something big because of its paradoxical truth, also fascinated and compelled him to arrive at his conclusions through intuitive anticipation rather than lackluster and unimposing routine (which always introduces the added risk of achieving very little).

While Dirac's theory is still not a mainstream theoretical standpoint for cosmologists and astrophysicists, it remains, like the Titius-Bode Law, an imaginative and fruitful piece of creative *and* scientific work that speaks to the power of the number archetype to evoke in the human mind some of our most fascinating and rewarding ideas.

Summary

Much of our scientific knowledge has been established outside the conventions of the scientific method—Dirac's theory of the nature and dynamics of the universe is no exception. Social criticism of science has indicated the variety of 'techniques', such as intuition, lucky guesses, hunches, and *ad hoc* hypotheses, etc., so often and necessarily employed by the scientist to help in the construction of new knowledge. Nevertheless, this knowledge *per se*, once accepted, furnishes us with a practical way of conceiving the universe, in the sense that some approximation to understanding that universe seems to have been achieved. Such a notion may be just as much an 'illusion' as the 'illusions' suggested in Dirac's universe. But, either way, they are illusions that become our realities.

Reliance upon the ideas of the cosmologist, which ostensibly explain the workings of our cosmos, sets the layperson the task of accepting ideas which at first might appear to be nothing but spurious theorizing, but ultimately, may become accepted as the new myth by which we live and mediate the world. In accordance with this view, the reasonably minded person will come to understand that making sense of the world often entails acceptance of things that do not make sense (at least not at first).

Plate 30. THE THINKER

Auguste Rodin's The Thinker *(1880; outside the Musée Rodin, Paris) is a depiction of the human being absorbed in deep thought. While insights may result, the reasonable mind accepts that reason is an orientation of consciousness that can be undermined by irrational factors [SOURCE: Picture taken by Deror Avi, 2005. Used with permission].*

THE REASONABLE MIND

*Nothing is more inimical to the progress of science
than the belief that we know what we do not yet
know. This is an error to which the inventors of
fanciful hypotheses are commonly subject.*

Georg Christoph Lichtenberg

The use of number generally takes place within the confines of mathematical axioms, socio-cultural determinants, and historical boundaries, with little realization of the full potential, or sometimes the inaccuracies in the theoretical and practical applications of number. New problems continually arise in the enterprises of humankind, which may draw attention to these potentialities and inaccuracies, but an increase in knowledge results when these potentialities are recognized, and the inaccuracies are rectified. Thereby human consciousness expands—a process that includes an increase in the perceived value, meaning, aesthetic quality, and apparent 'truth' in number.

Our limitations in space-time and consciousness restrict the immediate apprehension of that which will become knowledge (ideas ever-present, but undifferentiated), but the intuition of the existence of this knowledge causes us to project it into a supra-personal realm. Looking for a name, we call this source of knowledge 'the realm of pure thought', or 'the recesses of the human mind', or 'the Platonic realm of Ideas and Ideal Forms'. However, this source is not so much a place as it is a process—it is the dynamic, continual resonance of consciousness with the 'inner' and outer events of infinite nature (or the unconscious to put it in psychological terms). Used in this sense, the unconscious extends beyond a mind restricted in spacetime, to nature itself.

Of course the discursive factor inherent in the construct of the 'conscious-unconscious' dynamic is acknowledged. This psychological discourse is a way of talking about phenomena. Understandably, the terminology of that discourse is a construction. However, epistemological certainty is assured when an *isomorphism* of constructed discourses, on the one hand, and the phenomenal 'evidence' of our senses, on the other, becomes possible. But it is also understood that it is not a question of simply 'reading off' one thing for the other—this is clearly nonsense ('the map is not the territory'; a knowledge claim is not the *phenomenon* itself, just as the *phenomenon* is not the *noumenon*). Nor is epistemological certainty a matter, in any pragmatic sense, of getting to the 'truth'—this too is nonsense. The 'truth' (having decided what that 'truth' will be) is, after all, what we believe it to be, in spite of the consequences of that belief. Usually, practicality and expediency decide the consequences of belief, and the future of so-called epistemological certainty.

Number and Understanding

In our remote past, the gradual awareness of the ubiquitous presence of number and symmetry invariably led us to the simplest constructs of form and order. The capacity to perform such acts indicates the reality of a proclivity in the psyche for identifying order. But the sophistication of mathematical abstractions, for example, sprang from nature's original lead, constituted of internal (psychological) and external (environmental) factors in resonance. Nature as psyche/world leads the way to itself, which the limited ego complex interprets as knowledge about the psyche, or the world.

Ultimately, therefore, the development of mathematics, or more generally, the ability to understand and apply number, comes not from some kind of objective genius, but from a subjective interpretation of the sensory data and inner cognitive processes available to the mind, as determined by the limited function of consciousness. For some, there is no distinction here—the genius *is* expressed through a so-called 'limited function of consciousness'. The point, however, is that there is a need to recognize the distinction between relative claims and absolute claims. The way in which we utilize number has proved to be invaluable to us, but only ever is it a compromise between the limited and the unlimited, the relative and the absolute. Therefore, the way in which we apply our mental processes represents the current status only in the development of mind—a stage reached in an ongoing evolution of consciousness.

Not being aware of this perhaps limited but specific functioning of our minds and its unconscious connection with nature, cosmos and ultimately the universe, combined with our illusory sense of autonomy and separateness from the external world, it becomes reasonable to assume that our 'creations' (mathematics, number, symbolic abstractions, etc.) are human constructions originating entirely from the rational mind as a result of current knowledge, applied will, observation, and insight. However, Jung (1966b) reflects on the relativity of rational functioning:

> No matter how beautiful and perfect man [sic] may believe his reason to be, he can always be certain that it is only one of the possible mental functions, and covers only that one side of the phenomenal world which corresponds to it. But the irrational, that which is not agreeable to reason, rings it about on all sides. (para. 110)

Elsewhere, Jung (1971) amplifies this point:

> Human reason...is nothing other than the expression of man's [sic] adaptability to average occurrences, which have gradually become deposited in firmly established complexes of ideas that constitute our objective values. Thus the laws of reason are the laws that designate and govern the average, "correct," adapted attitude. (para. 786)

Given this restriction, our achievements in science are indeed monumental. The use of number, its application in mathematics, is remarkable (more for its reliability at prediction than anything else), especially in the world of invisible forces. This success it seems has created with it another entity: the illusion of mastery over nature, but there is no mastery because there is no understanding.

It is crucial to understand (if we can understand anything) that what we consider understood can only be what we decide is understood according to a certain degree of satisfaction. Often, it is not a case of understanding at all, but merely a case of becoming familiar with a thing. Like a young child that persistently asks "Why?," the more informed or inquisitive individual can always pose new questions because of his or her dissatisfaction with current explanations. Therefore, our knowledge and understanding of the world is in constant change, while true mastery implies omniscience and does not change.

To give examples, one might consider how it is possible to 'understand' what fire, magnetism, or gravity really are. Fire is "the active principal in combustion," says the Concise Oxford Dictionary, "in which substances combine chemically with oxygen from the air and usually give out bright light and heat." The light or heat apparently has something to do with the substance when it burns. Is that some of the energy (E) in the mass (m) to which Einstein refers in his equation $E = mc^2$? This is science at its most rational. One may be satisfied with either definition, or both, but *how* should we see one or the other as an *explanation* of fire, or ever be convinced that we could understand fire as it appears to be (that is, in its phenomenal form)?

The same problem arises when one grapples with the phenomenon of magnetism. Any child playing with two magnets learns that like poles repel and opposite poles attract. But, that invisible force, that undeniable physical effect acting at a distance is truly a marvel not at all 'explained' by common-place knowledge, or a simple formula, or a demonstration with iron-filings on a piece of paper.

As for gravity, how has Einstein's explanation come any nearer to explaining why such a force should exist? Frankly, science only ever fits lawful rules to phenomena—it may define and try to 'explain', but we can always dispute its claims to understanding. Clearly, reason forges ahead, but is not tempered along the way by empathy, feeling, or aesthetic appreciation. We remain enchanted, as always, by the empirical world.

We are beset by a phenomenal world that constantly challenges our understanding yet remains as illusive as ever. The sentiment has been stated many times, in many different ways, but effectively, if consciousness does not differentiate into other areas beyond a superficial appreciation or over-valuation of the rational function, we remain emotionally disadvantaged. For example, insecurity and fear, as long as their source remains unconscious, are always projected onto others. Invariably they wait in hibernation for the right trigger that, as history shows, always eventuates, unleashing all that we have to hand for the purposes of destruction. Where is our understanding in such cases? We are clearly not masters—not of nature, not even of ourselves. As long as we remember this we retain our humanness and this, in the final analysis, is of far greater importance.

The Secret Mutual Connivance

It is also important to consider another factor that offsets our reason and influences our interpretation of the world. Such a factor involves the activation of holistic modes of thought. Jung has termed this factor the 'secret mutual connivance' and it relates to unconscious processes in the human psyche. We observe matter and objective events, but immediately subjectify them with, and to, our unconscious processes. We each create our own reality—not *the* reality—and this is true of the individual in the fields of proto-science, philosophy and experimental science. Measurement, observation and experimentation are all tied up with psyche so that matter and events become the 'victims' of chance encounter with the psyche and are thereby defined. We cannot see the unconscious influences on our perceptions *and our environment* and this distorts any attempt at making objective statements.

It is important to note that this process does not simply involve the construction of interpretations or representations of reality, but also involves actual causal and acausal influences of the psyche on the environment. For example, Pauli (1994) states in his essay 'Matter':

> we do not assume any longer the *detached observer*...but an observer who by his [*sic*] indeterminable effects creates a new situation, theoretically described as a new state of the observed system. In this

way every observation is a singling out of a particular factual result, here and now, from the theoretical possibilities, thereby making obvious the discontinuous aspects of the physical phenomena. (p. 33)

Pauli adds, in regard to the arrangement of an experiment (say) by a physicist, that:

It rests with the free choice of the experimenter (or observer) to decide...which insights he will gain and which he will lose.... It does *not* rest with him, however, to gain only insights and not lose any. (Pauli, 1950, cited in Adler, 1989, p. 113)

Adler (1989) echoes Pauli's observation:

observer and experimenter form a total situation in which both variables influence each other to such an extent that any objective understanding of physical phenomena becomes impossible. (p. 112)

Jung (1959a) claims:

Between the conscious and the unconscious there is a kind of "uncertainty relationship" because the observer is inseparable from the observed, and always disturbs it by the act of observation. (para. 355)

Jung also states that:

a secret, mutual connivance exist[s] between the material and the psychic state.... This correspondence is simply *there* like any other agreeable or annoying accident, and it seems doubtful...whether it can be proved scientifically to be anything more than that. (Jung, 1960, para. 905)

It must also be inferred from these statements that both conscious *and* *unconscious* desires for a 'result' (or not) may have an influence in (say) the experimental sciences. Belief or disbelief (conscious or otherwise) in a hypothesis before it is tested may be enough to swing a result in the experimenter's favor. It is not surprising that so-called random surveys, which supply the raw data for studies (say) in psychology, not only often yield inconclusive results concerning a hypothesis, but also yield conflicting results when studies are replicated (assuming of course that the same procedures are followed, and no new confounding variables are introduced into the experiment).

While the scientific method may establish a statistical truth through repeated observation (so long as the results are always the same), the epistemological foundation of the scientific method is inadequate in the light of the secret mutual connivance. In a previous chapter ("Synchronicity") it was already argued that any kind of validity is always subjective, and can be based on meaningful rather than rational criteria. With the admission of the secret mutual connivance as a possible new variable previously not considered, it is now possible to hold the idea that a certain belief about the nature of the world, and the subsequent appearance of circumstances which recursively give rise to the idea that this belief created those circumstances, speak to one and the same phenomenon—a kind of Leibizian *"pre-established harmony"* (Jung, 1960, para. 937), but rather than being constructed on a supposedly absolute framework, these parallels are subjectively determined.

What is hardest to accept is the implication that perhaps all possible beliefs are 'true' and verifiable in reality because virtually every conceivable event that would validate this 'truth' could *probably* occur. (Although any number of specific events may not necessarily occur due to momentary conditions or circumstances prohibiting their occurrence at any given time, such events may still be possible under the appropriate conditions.) Such a possibility creates the paradox of multiple truths, even though many of these truths may be incompatible with each other. This paradox aligns with the paradoxical nature of consciousness as a 'world-creating' factor, in and of itself, that is responsible for acts of creation in time (an event is created based upon a certain belief; a state of the psyche).

In Buddhism it is said that with our thoughts we create the world, and in the words of C. G. Jung (1963):

> All the worlds that have ever existed before man [*sic*] were physically *there*. But they were a nameless happening, not a definite actuality, for there did not yet exist that minimal concentration of the psychic factor, which was also present, to speak the word that outweighed the whole of Creation: That is the world, and this is I! That was the first morning of the world...when...the ego, the son of the darkness, knowingly sundered subject and object, and thus precipitated the world and itself into definite existence.... [The] nature of the psyche itself...expresses [this psychological truth] either directly or clothed in transparent metaphors. This is understandable when we realise that a world-creating quality attaches to human consciousness as such. (para. 129)

The unconscious by its nature is the wellspring of consciousness. It is the source of all that is possible in all events born of human thought and action. As a totality, consciousness and the unconscious comprise the Self. As the Self, the world exists *in potentia*, but is made actual, by being made conscious by the ego. These complementarities—consciousness/unconscious, ego/Self, psyche/matter—speak to the broader issue of the paradoxical phenomenology of reality, as we must now see it. It is always the individual's ultimate decision as to what the world will be when he or she says with Jung: "That is the world..." (para. 129).

If the individual creates reality, if the truth is being sought and tested constantly, by whatever means available, only to yield self-fulfilling prophecies or unconsciously ascribed realities, what exactly is the nature or value of that truth at that given moment? From the perspective of the secret mutual connivance it appears that the truth is a creation in time—synchronistic time.

However, it is only accurate to say that this truth is the result of a time moment when the psyche/world state at that moment is understood as being contingent with that moment. Consequently, truth cannot be entirely adduced from anything concrete, since, for the most part, the psyche/world state is in constant flux, and rests somewhere between the absolute (the unchanging, the objective) and the relative (the ephemeral, the subjective).

Therefore, the nature and value of that truth is also in flux. It is the specific, personal value, or even the consensus of the group, that gives any relatively absolute framework to such transitory truths.

For one, or for many, it can be seen that consciousness of the reality we have created is itself justification alone for the truth of that reality. This reality (culture, history, principles, values, religion, etc.)—good or bad—reflects the subjectivity of our own experiments in consciousness. However, a truth that is shown to have archetypal significance reflects a different reality, a reality that shifts away from relative, ephemeral, and subjective factors towards more absolute, unchanging, and objective factors. This type of truth is based on the archetype (the only relatively absolute framework around which archetypal truths may constellate is the archetype itself). Any number of truths that make up a given reality will reflect both transitory and archetypal factors.

Number as a Principal Archetype of Order

Number has its place in the secret mutual connivance. As an archetypal reality in its own right it can be contingent with creative acts in time, so that causal and acausal orderedness are also contingent with the number archetype. Numbers as used in divinatory systems, for example, indicate such a contingency. Von Franz (1974) clarifies this point:

> The assumptions underlying these [divinatory] techniques are based on the idea that time does not form an "empty" frame for the events taking place within it, but rather represents a sequence of qualitative, inescapable conditions for the events possible at any given moment. This orderly sequence is isomorphic with the natural number series. Whether the latter objectively corresponds to characteristics of the physical world remains an open question. Most certainly its pattern is applicable to the phenomena of the collective unconscious, the ultimate foundation of all human cognition. (p. 302)

Synchronistic phenomena are conscious indications of the more-likely or more-probable events that describe typical human reactions or commonplace situations. Ordinarily, these potential reactions or situations lie dormant in the unconscious. To the degree that they correspond to particular archetypes, their possible occurrence, and even actuality, are drawn into consciousness by the archetype of number as an ordering principle, since the "concept of natural numbers rests on an archetypal foundation" (von Franz, 1974, p. 301).

Number is also important in its dual role of quantifying and qualifying matter and psyche. The number archetype avails the things of both the psyche and the world with two aspects (quantity and quality) when such things manifest in consciousness. Events and entities (natural or otherwise) may demonstrate sequential or periodic (numerical) phenomenologies, or they may demonstrate structured or patterned forms, all of which are quantifiable (numerable, and therefore, enumerative), and qualifiable (essential, and therefore, meaningful) in nature.

The former (the quantity) describes the natural numerical state or property of things naturally manifested or constructed, and these are empirically verifiable, while the latter (the quality) is the essence, the intrinsic meaning, of the thing contingent with the number archetype, which makes such manifestations perceivable, or constructions possible, as given lawfully by that archetype. The natural manifestations or representations of discovered and/or invented things occupy the world of matter, while the number archetype transcends that world, and occupies the world of the psyche (specifically, the collective unconscious).

The reasonable mind must now acknowledge two worlds: the first world—the world of matter—is the world of appearances that grows in consciousness, and is always there, but changes as the mind changes. This is the world within which the reasonable mind began and must claim as its own creation, since this world is ordered as the reasonable mind sees it to be ordered. The world's contents may be enumerated or attributed numerical significances by virtue of the world's 'orderedness'.

The second world—the world of psyche—includes the world of potentialities that lie dormant in the unconscious, and is always there, but does not necessarily change as the mind changes. This is the world within which the reasonable mind also began. It is a world constituted of archetypes (including the number archetype)—a world, which the reasonable mind believes is its own ontogenetic creation. But the numerical significances, which are attributed to both worlds, are only possible because their numbers were there as *a priori* 'realities' from the beginning.

Summary

Human reason, more than any other faculty of mind, has been responsible for great advances in knowledge, in such forms as the recognition and creation of symmetry and pattern, the sciences of mathematics and physics, and the use of number in general. However, reason by its very nature lacks the operative capability, by the judgments of reason alone, of constructing fully formed and complete insights into reality as it may be, as opposed to how it appears to be. Outside reason, the phenomenal world is as alien and unknown to us as it has always been.

Jung and others have shown that reason is a factor or orientation of consciousness that can be undermined by irrational factors. The psyche is one such irrational factor. Under the rubric of consciousness, the psyche literally creates the world as it experiences it, through beliefs and ideas held up as ultimate truths. The collective unconscious exerts an even greater influence through archetypal processes that form effectively universal truths that may even lean more towards an absolute, rather than a relative framework. These processes converge to form the secret mutual connivance.

Number provides the means by which probabilities of human action can be determined through (say) divinatory systems. The number archetype is a constituent of the archetypal field, so that the isomorphism of numbers with other archetypes allows the reading off of typically human reactions and situations.

The quantitative and qualitative aspects of numbers are also emphasized as providing a more complete picture of the involvement of number in our perception of the phenomenal world. With number, we count the world of objects, but must recognize too that number also gives these objects their meaning.

We can envision two worlds: the world of matter, and the world of psyche. Both, from their different perspectives, are as real as each other, even though each may be relativised by the other. The world of matter is a world of numerable and enumerative objects, while the world of psyche determines this to be so by asserting its *a priori* capacity to put order to the world in accordance with archetypal determinants.

CONCLUSION

*Fool: The reason why the seven stars are no
more than seven is a pretty reason.
Lear: Because they are not eight.
Fool: Yes indeed. Thou wouldst make a good fool.*

(*King Lear* Act 1: Scene 5)
William Shakespeare

Can the appreciation of number fall so easily within the grasp of one such as Shakespeare's fool? Should we endeavor to become good fools? We must recall that the fool in *King Lear* was of course no fool, and it was not the fool, but King Lear who had the psychological problems, even though he had an answer for the fool. Does the appearance of number in nature require a purely aesthetic intelligence in order to understand and appreciate its beauty—intelligence in the form of an ability to draw distinctions between numbers; an ability to recognize the inherent qualities that number brings to forms in nature? It would appear that an aesthetic outlook is a good starting point on the road to comprehending number in its myriad forms for it seems so readily available to anyone willing to develop this aesthetic sensibility.

The fool's view is as such: When there are seven stars we need only think on seven, and therein lies the aesthetic—the 'pretty reason' being that seven is a quantity and a quality incomparable with eight—and beyond the 'pretty reason' it seems there is nothing further to consider. That is, if we do not think beyond the experience of the visual impression. Were we to accept only the perception (for all its limitations) our experience of number would be like that of any non-human species, or even like our pre-linguistic ancestors, but at least we would not be in the position of wondering why seven stars were not eight.

However, we do not have the 'advantage' of our pre-conscious ancestors. We must recognize the fact that our cognitive abilities go beyond perceptions to apperceptions expressed in language. Since words are the structural units of that expression, we may find ourselves searching for the meanings of the units (the words) in the expressions that constitute the kinds of reasons that are set up to explain (say) the 'seven stars'. Like an obsessive philologist, the search for the number-meaning might surface if we stir up the linguistic depths. But all we will find are older words with cultural ties that link us back to nature— ties that are more concrete and less abstract, than our modern words. There is, therefore, a state of mind behind a fool's simple viewpoint that may at first be overlooked. It is the twofold state of acceptance and satisfaction of the way things appear, and the fool has these qualities.

We are ultimately asked to accept that our limited language can tell us something about a phenomenon, which stands as a verbal similacrum of that phenomenon. The snowflake, for example, has six sides, and *only* six sides, and that is simply the way it is. The statement is made, and it supposedly approximates a kind of knowing. There are reasons we can give to 'explain' the snowflake's appearance: facts concerning the structural capacities and properties of the H_2O molecule at low temperatures, and so on, but these are *only* reasons, although they do appear to refer to the deeper reality of the snowflake. They appear to explain the phenomenon, but the H_2O molecule too, like the snowflake, is as it is for reasons also expressible in number. One, therefore, cannot get past the fact that, like the fool, we have to accept that numbers have qualities.

More numbers, more knowledge, and inevitably, more questions emerge because meaningful structures and configurations are continually determined from numerical facts, and these facts give us much to consider. This book has been about those numerical configurations (patterns, sequences, etc.) and the considerations that resulted from those configurations.

Where do we find ourselves at the end of this book? Do we find ourselves back where we were at the beginning, like the fool, where number was considered an empirical experience, so that perhaps nothing can be said or done that will make it clearer than that? But, unlike the fool, will we wonder how it is all supposed to make sense? Hopefully not. Eventually, we must reach some kind of acceptance, and the major goal of this book was to get to that point by filling in the socio-cultural, historical, religious and scientific voids in our knowledge and experience that seem to need filling, so as to yield acceptance of the fact that not only does each number have its own unique properties, but that these properties might clearly indicate a greater 'archetypal' depth to number than previously supposed. And, if an appreciation of the subtleties and the nuances of number has emerged, then with that appreciation has come an awareness of the beauty, and therefore, the truth about number, since one cannot help but agree with Keats that truth and beauty are one.

If those voids are slowly filled, then we may come to that second and final state, which is one of satisfaction. And the offer of satisfaction always comes with a guarantee—if you are not satisfied you can continue your search for the truth, you can read another book. With belief there is no binding contract that cannot be broken.

Have we learned to count all over again? At the end of all our traveling, do we arrive where we began and know number for the first time? These are only more questions, adding to those just asked, and it seems that enough questions have been asked already. At this point, it is perhaps wiser to advise humbly, as did Shakespeare's fool, "when a wise man gives thee better counsel, give me mine again. I would have none but knaves follow it since a fool gives it" (Shakespeare, 1980, pp. 81-82).

It's brilliant authors like this who can never join or go to churches and probably never go to Temple, and are so caught up in the psychological "analysis of the analysis" they can't even pray or sit long enough to meditate.

This is very judgemental on my part, but I wonder if I could be on to something.

But "spirituality" was not the purpose in his writing what is otherwise a marvelous and insightful book.

Very often intellectuals have a way of talking themselves out of religion, spirituality and the meditative or contemplative, let alone faith or prayer experiences

REFERENCES

Adler, G. (1989). *Dynamics of the Self*. London: Coventure.

Appel, K., & Haken, W. (1977). Every planar map is four colorable. Part I. Discharging, *Illinois Journal of Mathematics*, 21, 429-490.

Appel, K., Haken, W. & Koch, J. (1977). Every planar map is four colorable. Part II. Reducibility. *Illinois Journal of Mathematics*, 21, 491-567.

Appignanesi, R. & Garrett, C. (1995). *Postmodernism for Beginners*. Cambridge: Icon Books.

Asimov, I. (1979). *Asimov on Astronomy*. New York: Bonanza Books.

Aziz, R. (1990). *C. G. Jung's Psychology of Religion and Synchronicity*. New York: University of New York Press.

Barrett, D. V. (1992). *Destiny and Your Dreams*. London: Treasure Press.

Barrow, J. B. (1993). *Pi in the Sky; Counting, thinking and being*. London: Penguin.

Berlin, B. & Kay, P. (1969). *Basic Color Terms*. Berkeley/Los Angeles: University of California Press.

Brown, J. A. C. (1971). *Freud and the Post-Freudians*. Hammondsworth, Middlesex: Penguin.

Butler, C. (1970). *Number Symbolism*. London: The Trinity Press.

Calder, N. (1977). *The Key to the Universe*. Harmondsworth: Penguin.

Campbell, K. (1986). *Body and Mind*. London: Notre Dame Press.

Capra, F. (1988). *The Tao of Physics*. London: Flamingo/Fontana.

Charlesworth, M. (1980). *Science, Non-Science and Pseudo-Science*. Burwood, Vic.: Deakin University Press.

Chetwynd, T. (1982). *Dictionary of Symbols*. London: The Aquarian Press.

Chinmoy, Sri. (1974). *Kundalini: The Mother-Power*. Jamaica, N.Y.: Agni Press.

Cirlot, J. E. (1962). *A Dictionary of Symbols*. New York: Routledge and Keegan Paul.

Covello, E. M. (1977). Symbolization of conscious states in the *I Ching*: A quantitative study. *Journal of Altered States of Consciousness*, 3, 111-129.

Crofton, I. (Ed.). (1986). *Concise Dictionary of Music*. Great Britain: Wm. Collins Sons & Co.

Crossley, J. N. (1987). *The Emergence of Number*. New York/Singapore: World Scientific.

Crossley, J. N. (2007). *Growing Ideas of Number*. Camberwell, Victoria: Acer Press.

Dean, G. (1997). John Addey's Dream: Planetary harmonics and the character trait hypothesis. *Correlation, 16*(2), 10-37.

Dean, G., & Kelly, I. W. (2003). Is astrology relevant to consciousness and psi? In J. Alcock, J. Burns, & A. Freeman (Eds.). *Psi Wars: Getting to Grips with the Paranormal* (pp. 175-198). Exeter, UK: Imprint Academic.

Delin, P. (2002). Scepticism and credulity. *Australian Journal of Parapsychology, 2,* 28-36.

De Rola, S. K. (1973). *Alchemy: The Secret Art*. London: Thames and Hudson.

Dirac, P. (1954). Quantum mechanics and the aether. *Scientific Monthly, 58,* 142.

Drioli, L. (Ed.). (1997). *Golden Age, 35,* 55, 66.

Edinger, E. F. (1984). *The Creation of Consciousness*. Toronto: Inner City.

_____ (1986a). *Ego and Archetype*. New York: Penguin.

_____ (1986b). *The Bible and the Psyche*. Toronto: Inner City.

_____ (1995). *The Mysterium Lectures: A Journey through C. G. Jung's Mysterium Coniunctionis*. Toronto: Inner City.

_____ (1996). *The Aion Lectures*. Toronto: Inner City.

Ellis, B. E. (1991). *American Psycho*. London: Macmillan-Picador.

First, M. B. (Ed.). (1994). *Diagnostic and Statistical Manual of Mental Disorders*. (4th. ed.). Washington, D.C.: American Psychiatric Association.

Flegg, G. (1983). *Numbers: Their History and Meaning*. London: André Deutsch.

Flynn, J. (1987). Massive IQ gains in 14 nations: What IQ tests really measure. *Psychological Bulletin, 101,* 171-191.

Foucault, M. (1977). *Discipline and Punish: The Birth of the Prison*. London: Allen Lane.

Galin, D. (1977). The two modes of consciousness and the two halves of the brain. In R.E. Ornstein. *Symposium on Consciousness*. Harmondsworth: Penguin.

Gauquelin, M. (1983). *The Truth About Astrology*. Oxford: Basil Blackwell.

Geddes, S. (1981). *The Art of Astrology*. Wellingborough: Aquarian.

Gliedman, J. (1981). God's numbers. *OMEGA Science Digest*, Sept./Oct., 98-100.

Goldbrunner, J. (1966). *Individuation*. Freiburg: University of Notre Dame Press.

Halley, H. (1972). *Bible Handbook*. Grand Rapids, Michigan: Zondervan.

Harrington, R. & Littman, M. (1988). *Nemesis*. New York: Weidenfeld & Nicholson.

Heline, C. (1991). *Sacred Science of Numbers*. Marinna del Ray, CA: DeVorss and Co.

Henderson, J. (1984). *Cultural Attitudes and Psychological Perspectives*. Toronto: Inner City.

Herrnstein, R. J. & Murray, C. (1994). *The Bell Curve: Intelligence and Class Structure in American Life*. New York: Free Press.

Hillman, J. (1979). *The Dream and the Underworld*. New York: Harper and Row.

Hillman, J. & Roscher, W. H. (1979). *Pan and the Nightmare*. University of Dallas, Irving, Texas: Spring Publications.

Hines, T. (1988). *Pseudoscience and the Paranormal: A Critical Examination of the Evidence*. Buffalo, NY: Prometheus.

Holmyard, E. J. (1957). *Alchemy*. Harmondsworth, Middlesex: Penguin.

Huxley, A. (1994). *Heaven and Hell*. London: Flamingo.

Hyde, M. (1992). *Jung and Astrology*. London: Aquarius Press/Harper Collins.

Ifrah, G. (2000). *The Universal History of Numbers: From Prehistory to the Invention of the Computer*. Harrisonburg, NY: John Wiley & Sons.

Jacobi, J. (1974). *Complex/Archetype/Symbol in the Psychology of C.G. Jung*. New York: Princeton University Press.

Jones, R. (1983). *Physics as Metaphor*. London: Abacus/Sphere Books.

Jung, C. G. (1958). *Psychology and Religion: West and East*. Princeton: Princeton University Press.

_____ (1959a). *Aion: Researches into the Phenomenology of the Self*. Princeton: Princeton University Press.

_____ (1959b). *The Archetypes and the Collective Unconscious*. Princeton: Princeton University Press.

_____ (1960). *The Structure and Dynamics of the Psyche*. Princeton: Princeton University Press.

_____ (1963). *Mysterium Coniunctionis*. Princeton: Princeton University Press.

_____ (Ed.). (1964). *Man and his Symbols*. New York: Doubleday/Anchor.

_____ (1966a). *The Practice of Psychotherapy* (2nd edn.). Princeton: Princeton University Press.

_____ (1966b). *Two Essays on Analytical Psychology* (2nd edn.). Princeton: Princeton University Press.

_____ (1968a). *Alchemical Studies*. New York: Princeton: Princeton University Press.

_____ (1968b). *Psychology and Alchemy* (2nd edn.). New York: Princeton: Princeton University Press.

_____ (1970). *Civilisation in Transition* (2nd edn.). Princeton: Princeton University Press.

_____ (1971). *Psychological Types*. Princeton: Princeton University Press.

_____ (1977). *C. G. Jung Speaking*. Princeton: Princeton University Press.

_____ (1976). *The Symbolic Life*. Princeton: Princeton University Press.

_____ (1987). *Dictionary of Analytical Psychology*. London: Ark.

_____ (1989). Foreword to *The I Ching or Book of Changes*. In R. Wilhelm. *The I Ching or Book of Changes* (pp. xxi-xxxix). C.F. Baynes (trans.). Princeton: Princeton University Press.

Kant, I. (1990). *Critique of Pure Reason*. J. M. D. Meiklejohn (trans.). Buffalo, NY: Prometheus.

Kennedy, M. (1974). *Notes*. In Holst: The Planets Op. 32. Hartwell, Victoria: World Record Club.

King, J. (1996). *The Modern Numerology: A Practical Guide to the Meaning and Influence of Numbers*. London: Blandford.

Kline, M. (1985). *Mathematics and the Search for Knowledge*. New York: Oxford University Press.

Lamy, L. (1981). *Egyptian Mysteries*. Lancashire: Thames and Hudson.

Legge, J. (1971). *I Ching*. New York: New American Library.

Lines, M. E. (1986). *A Number for Your Thoughts*. Bristol: Adam Hilger.

Luft, J. (1971). The Johari Window and self-disclosure. In G. Egan. *Encounter Groups: Basic Readings*. Belmont, CA: Brooks/Cole.

Martin, S. L. & Connor, A. K. (1968). *Basic Physics 1*. Sydney, NSW: Whitcombe and Tombs.

Mathers, S. C. (1986). *The Kabbalah Unveiled*. York Beach, Maine: Samuel Weiser.

McLeish, J. (1992). *Number: From Ancient Civilisation to the Computer*. London: Flamingo/Harper Collins.

Mellers, W. (1976). *Twilight of the Gods: The Beatles in Retrospect*. London: Faber & Faber.

Michell, J. (1988). *The Dimensions of Paradise: The Proportions and Symbolic Numbers of Ancient Cosmology*. London: Thames and Hudson.

Miller, G. (1956). The magical number seven, plus or minus two: Some limits on our capacity for processing information. *Psychological Review, 63*, 81-97.

_____ (1970). *Psychology: The Science of Mental Life*. Harmondsworth: Penguin.

Moore, G. & Setley, R. E. (1973). *Numbers Will Tell*. London: Arthur Barker.

Muldoon, T. (1988). *Numerology and You*. Brookvale, NSW: Simon & Schuster.

Myers, I. E. (1962). *The Myers-Briggs Type Indicator Manual*. Princeton: Educational Testing Service.

Neher, A. (1996). Jung's theory of archetypes: A critique. *Journal of Humanistic Psychology*, 36, 61-91.

Neisser, U. (Ed.). (1998). *The Rising Curve: Long-Term Gains in IQ and Related Measures*. Washington DC: American Psychological Association.

Neumann, E. (1973). *The Origins and History of Consciousness*. Princeton: Princeton University Press.

Nieto, M. M. (1972). *The Titius-Bode Law of Planetary Distances*. New York: Pergamon Press.

Ouspensky, P. D. (1964). *Tertium Organum*. New York: Borzoi.

Pappas, T. (1994). *More Joy of Mathematics*. San Carlos, CA.: Wide World Publishing/ Tetra.

Pappas, T. (1994). *The Magic of Mathematics*. San Carlos, CA.: Wide World Publishing/Tetra.

Pauli, W. (1994). *Writings on Physics and Philosophy*. New York: Springer-Verlag.

Paulos, J. A. (1991). *Beyond Numeracy*. London: Viking/Penguin Books.

Peat, F. D. (1991). *The Philosopher's Stone: Chaos, Synchronicity, and the Hidden Order of the World*. New York: Bantam.

Poincaré, H. (1952). *Science and Method*. New York: Dover.

Poncé, C. (1973). *Kabbalah: An Introduction and Illumination for the World Today*. San Francisco: Straight Arrow.

Reich, W. (1949). *Character Analysis*. New York: Noonday.

Ritsema, R., & Sabbadini, S. A. (2005). *The Original I Ching Oracle*. London: Watkins.

Roth, R. F. (2004). *The Return of the World Soul: Wolfgang Pauli, Carl Jung and the Challenge of the Unified Psychophysical Reality* [Electronic version]. Retrieved August 9, 2006, from: http://www.psychovision.ch/synw/jungneoplatonismaristotlep1.htm.

Sagan, C. (1978). *The Dragons of Eden*. New York: Ballantine.

Saggino, A. & Kline, P. (1996). The location of the Myers-Briggs Type Indicator in personality factor space. *Journal of Personality and Individual Differences*, 21, 591-597.

Samuels, A. (1986). *Jung and the Post-Jungians*. London: Routledge & Keegan Paul.

Samuels, A., Shorter, B. & Plaut, F. (1992). *A Critical Dictionary of Jungian Analysis.* London: Routledge and Keegan Paul.

Schimmel, A. (1993). *The Mystery of Numbers.* New York: Oxford University Press.

Schwaller de Lubicz, R. A. (1986). *A Study of Numbers.* Rochester, Vermont: Inner Traditions International.

Shakespeare, W. (1980). *King Lear.* Harmondsworth, Middelesex: Penguin.

Sheldrake, R. (1994). *Seven Experiments that Could Change the World.* London: Fourth Estate.

Sperry, R. W. (1976). An emergent theory of consciousness. In M. H. Marks & F. E. Gordon. *Theories in Contemporary Psychology.* New York: MacMillan.

Stevens, A. (1982). *Archetype: A Natural History of the Self.* London: Routledge & Keegan Paul.

Stewart, I. & Golubitsky, M. (1992). *Fearful Symmetry: Is God a Geometer?.* London: Penguin.

Storr, A. (1973). *Jung.* London: Fontana.

Sutherland, S. (1992). *Irrationality: The Enemy Within.* Harmondsworth: Penguin.

Tansley, D. V. (1980). *Radionics and the Subtle Anatomy of Man.* Saffron Walden, Essex: Health Science Press.

Tassos, St., & Ford, D. J. (2005). An integrated alternative conceptual framework to heat engine earth, plate tectonics, and elastic rebound. *Journal Scientific of Exploration, 19,* .

Terry, J. H. (1958). *Latin Reader.* London: Longmans, Green and Co.

Thalbourne, M. (2003). *A Glossary of Terms used in Parapsychology.* Charlottesville, VA: Puente.

Tillich, P. (1964). The importance of new being for christian theology. In J. Campbell (Ed.). *Man and Transformation Eranos, vol. 5.* New York: Pantheon.

von Franz, M.-L. (1974). *Number and Time.* Evanston, Ill.: Northwestern University Press.

———— (1978). *Time: Rhythm and Repose.* Lancashire: Thames and Hudson.

———— (1979). *Alchemical Active Imagination.* Dallas: Spring Publications.

———— (1980a). *Alchemy: An Introduction to the Symbolism and the Psychology.* Toronto: Inner City.

———— (1980b). *On Divination and Synchronicity.* Toronto: Inner City.

———— (1997). *Projection and Recollection in Jungian Psychology: Reflections of the Soul.* London: Open Court.

Warm, H. (2004) *Die Signatur der Sphären* [*The Signature of the Spheres*]. Hamburg: Keplerstern Verlag.

Watson, L. (1973). *Supernature: A Natural History of the Supernatural.* London: Coronet.

Weisskopf, V. (1966). *Knowledge and Wonder* (2nd Ed.). Cambridge, MA: MIT Press.

Werblowsky, R. J. Zwi (1986). Jewish Mysticism. In Elie Kedourie (Ed.). *The Jewish World: Revelation, Prophecy, and History.* London: Thames and Hudson.

West, J. A. (1991). *The Case for Astrology.* London: Penguin/Arkana.

Westcott, W. W. (1974). *Numbers: Their Occult Power and Mystic Virtues.* London: Theosophical Publishing House.

Weyl, H. (1949). *Philosophy of Mathematics and Natural Science.* Princeton: Princeton University Press.

Whitmire, D. P. & Matese, J. J. (1985) Periodic Comet Showers and Planet X. *Nature, 313,* 36-38.

Whyte, L. L. (1977). *Accent on Form: An Anticipation of the Science of Tomorrow.* Westport, CT: Greenwood Press.

Wigner, E. (1960). The unreasonable effectiveness of mathematics. *Communications in Pure and Applied Mathematics, 13,* 1-140.

Wilhelm, R. (1989). *I Ching or the Book of Changes.* London: Penguin/Arkana.

Wilkerson, T. E. (1976). *Kant's Critique of Pure Reason: A Commentary for Students.* Oxford: Clarendon.

Wilmer, H. (1987). *Practical Jung.* Wilmette, Illinois: Chiron.

Wilson, S. (1957). *The Man in the Grey Flannel Suit.* London: The Reprint Society.

INDEX

Pari Publishing is an independent publishing company, based in a medieval Italian village. Our books appeal to a broad readership and focus on innovative ideas and approaches from new and established authors who are experts in their fields. We publish books in the areas of science, society, psychology, and the arts.

Our books are available at all good bookstores or online at **www.paripublishing.com**

If you would like to add your name to our email list to receive information about our forthcoming titles and our online newsletter please contact us at **newsletter@paripublishing.com**

Visit us at **www.paripublishing.com**

Pari Publishing Sas
Via Tozzi, 7
58040 Pari (GR)
Italy

Email: info@paripublishing.com